Did you know that the United States Capitol dome is 287 feet tall and contains almost 9 million pounds of iron?

HARCOURT
SOCIAL Studies
States and Regions

Harcourt
SCHOOL PUBLISHERS

www.harcourtschool.com

HARCOURT SOCIAL Studies

States and Regions

Series Authors

Dr. Michael J. Berson
Professor
Social Science Education
University of South Florida
Tampa, Florida

Dr. Tyrone C. Howard
Associate Professor
UCLA Graduate School of Education &
    Information Studies
University of California at Los Angeles
Los Angeles, California

Dr. Cinthia Salinas
Assistant Professor
Department of Curriculum and
    Instruction
College of Education
The University of Texas at Austin
Austin, Texas

Series Consultants

Dr. Marsha Alibrandi
Assistant Professor of Social Studies
Curriculum and Instruction
    Department
North Carolina State University
Raleigh, North Carolina

Dr. Patricia G. Avery
Professor
College of Education and Human
    Development
University of Minnesota
Minneapolis/St. Paul, Minnesota

Dr. Linda Bennett
Associate Professor
College of Education
University of Missouri–Columbia
Columbia, Missouri

Dr. Walter C. Fleming
Department Head and Professor
Native American Studies
Montana State University
Bozeman, Montana

Dr. S. G. Grant
Associate Professor
University at Buffalo
Buffalo, New York

C.C. Herbison
Lecturer
African and African-American Studies
University of Kansas
Lawrence, Kansas

Dr. Eric Johnson
Assistant Professor
Director, Urban Education Program
School of Education
Drake University
Des Moines, Iowa

Dr. Bruce E. Larson
Professor
Social Studies Education
Secondary Education
Woodring College of Education
Western Washington University
Bellingham, Washington

Dr. Merry M. Merryfield
Professor
Social Studies and Global Education
College of Education
The Ohio State University
Columbus, Ohio

Dr. Peter Rees
Associate Professor
Department of Geography
University of Delaware
Wilmington, Delaware

Dr. Phillip J. VanFossen
James F. Ackerman Professor of
    Social Studies Education
Associate Director, Purdue Center for
    Economic Education
Purdue University
West Lafayette, Indiana

Dr. Myra Zarnowski
Professor
Elementary and Early Childhood
    Education
Queens College
The City University of New York
Flushing, New York

Content Reviewers

Dr. Davarian L. Baldwin
Assistant Professor
History Department
Boston College
Chestnut Hill, Massachusetts

Dr. Steven Conn
Associate Professor
Department of History
The Ohio State University
Columbus, Ohio

Dr. Patricia Espiritu Halagao
Assistant Professor
College of Education
Department of Curriculum Studies
University of Hawai`i at Manoa
Honolulu, Hawai`i

Dr. Chris Mayda
Associate Professor of Geography
Department of Geography and Geology
Eastern Michigan University
Ypsilanti, Michigan

Dr. Judith Meyer
Associate Professor
Geography, Geology, and Planning
Missouri State University
Springfield, Missouri

Dr. William B. Stanley
Dean
School of Education
Monmouth University
West Long Branch, New Jersey

Dr. Fay A. Yarbrough
Assistant Professor
Department of History
University of Kentucky
Lexington, Kentucky

Classroom Reviewers and Contributors

Deborah Batchelor
Field Consultant
Maryland Coucil on Economic
   Education
Towson University
Towson, Maryland

Melissa Bearden
Teacher
Otter Creek Elementary School
Little Rock, Arkansas

Kathy Bisol
Teacher
Bradford Elementary School
Bradford, Massachusetts

Dr. Maria E. Franquiz
Associate Professor
The Division of Bicultural-Bilingual
   Studies
The University of Texas at San Antonio
San Antonio, Texas

Dr. John George
Chairperson
Education Department
Hood College
Frederick, Maryland

Judy Jones
Curriculum Generalist/Renewal
   Specialist
St. Louis Public School District
St. Louis, Missouri

Bridgette Shook
Teacher
Pierre Creative Arts
Flint, Michigan

Joy Wright
Teacher
Oaklandvale Elementary School
Saugus, Massachusetts

Jean Wuensch
Supervisor of Curriculum and
   Instruction
Montclair Public Schools
Montclair, New Jersey

Harcourt
SCHOOL PUBLISHERS

Maps
researched and prepared by

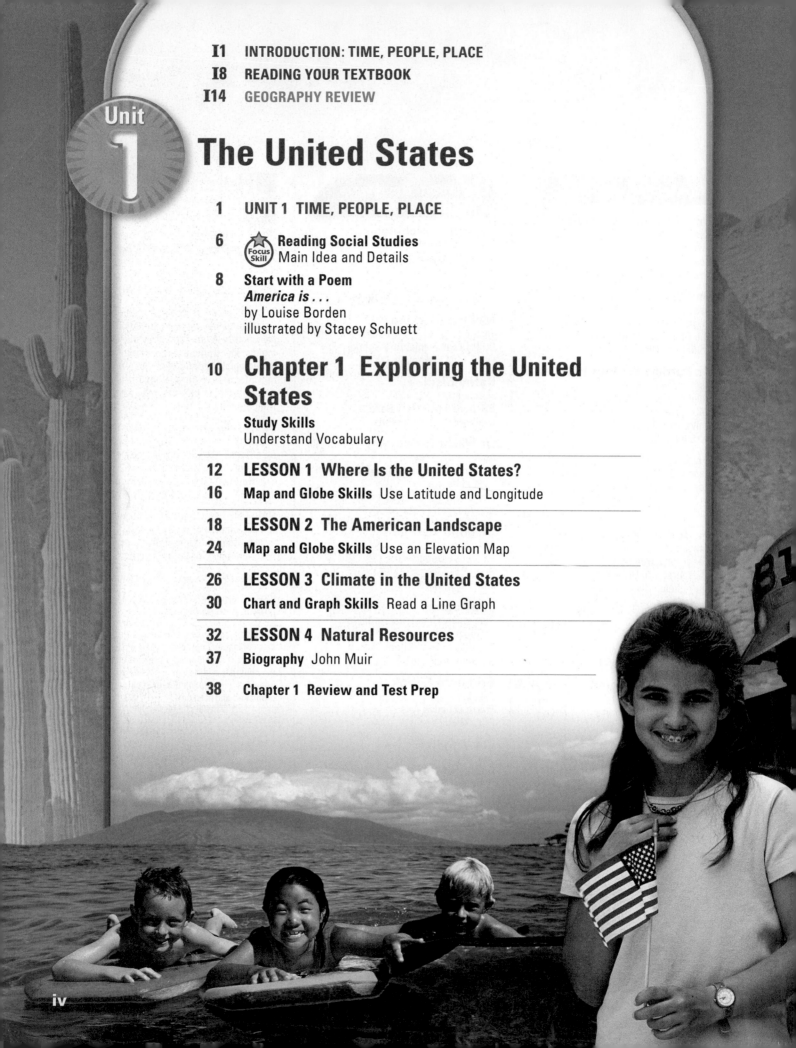

Unit 1

The United States

iv

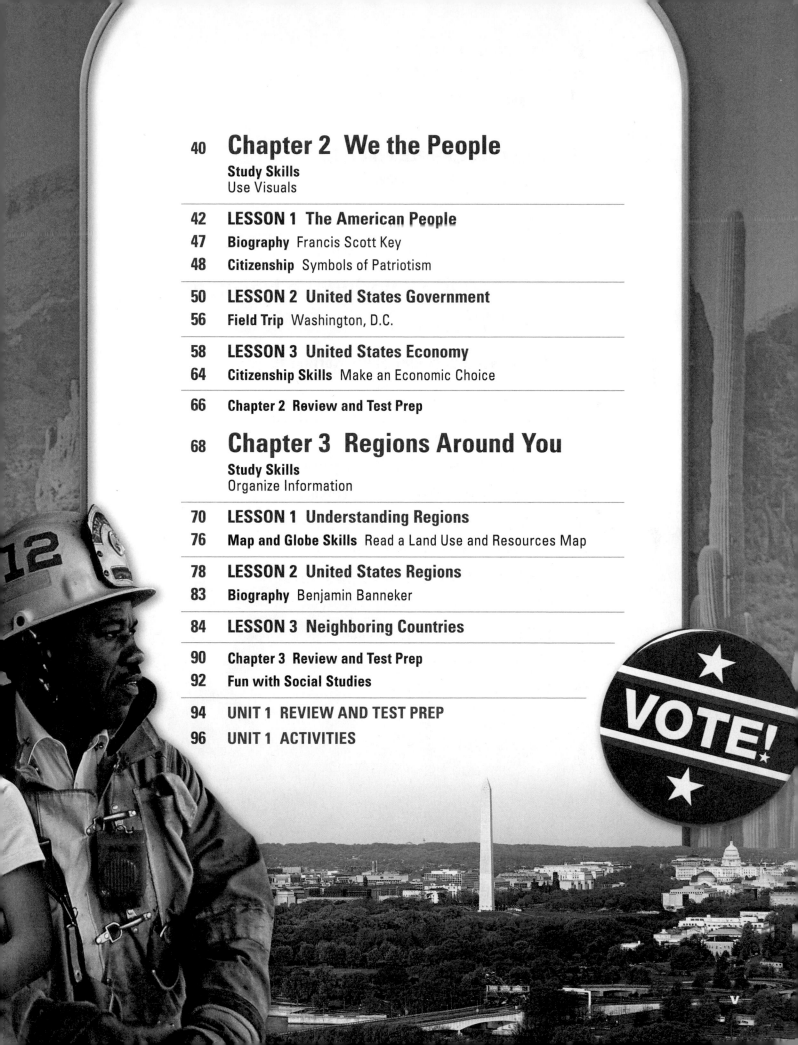

VOTE!

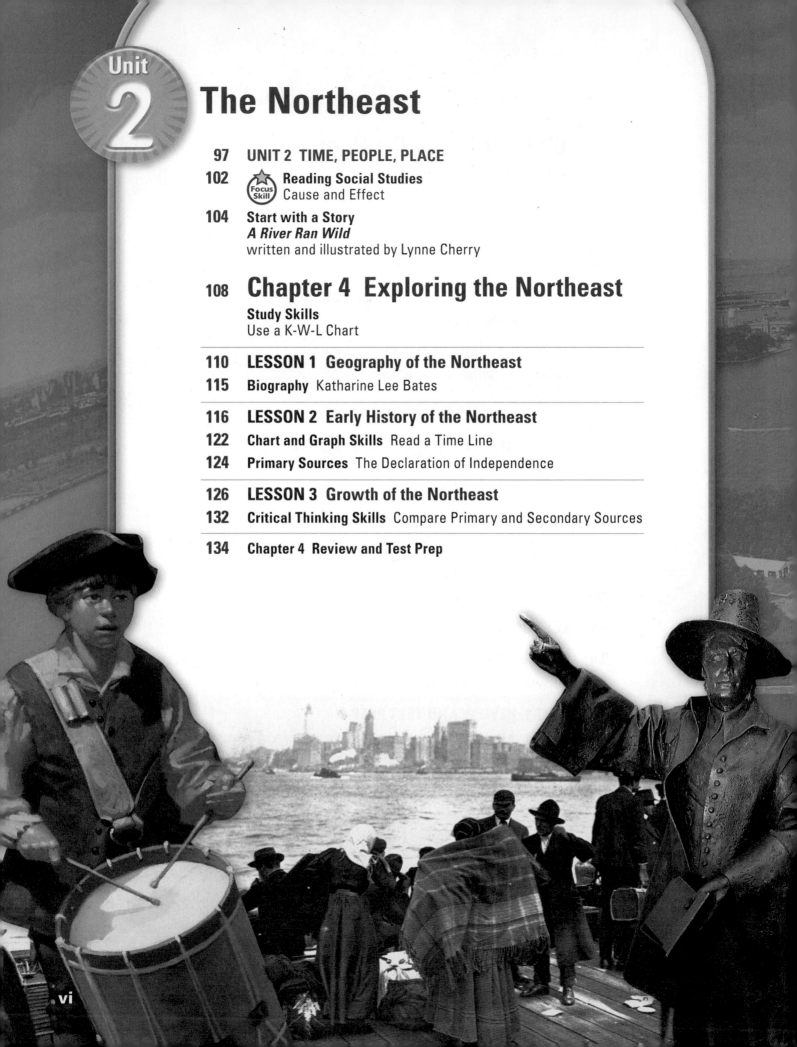

Unit 2

The Northeast

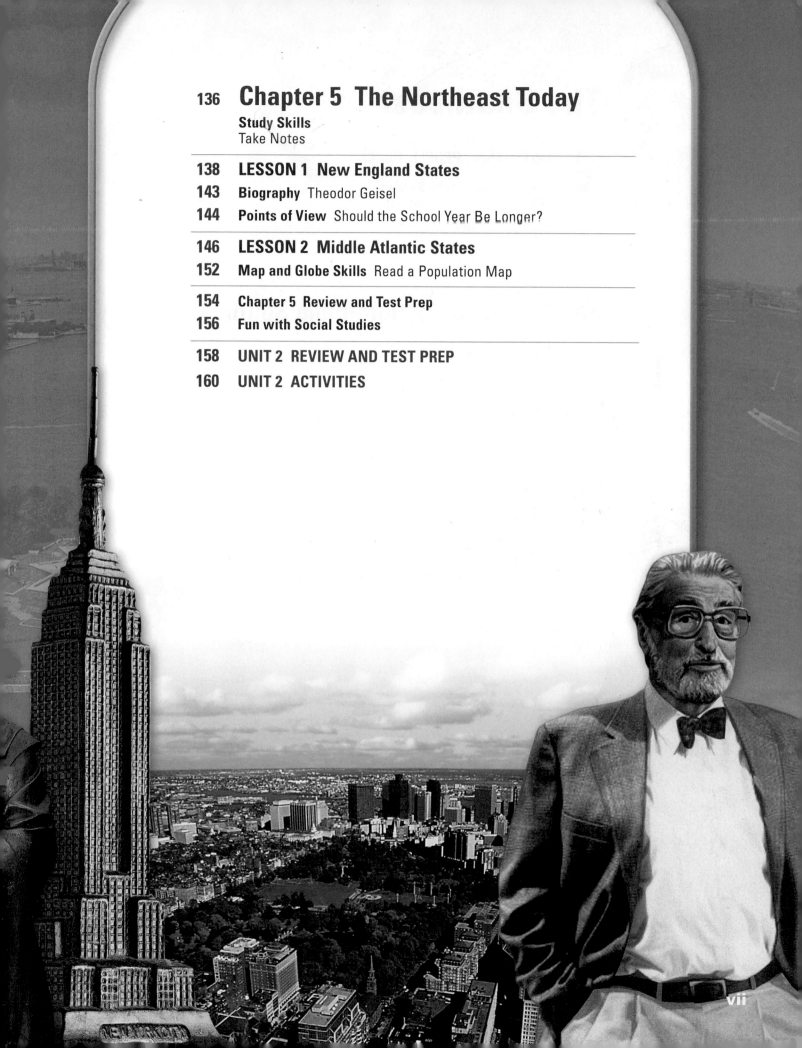

Unit 3

The Southeast

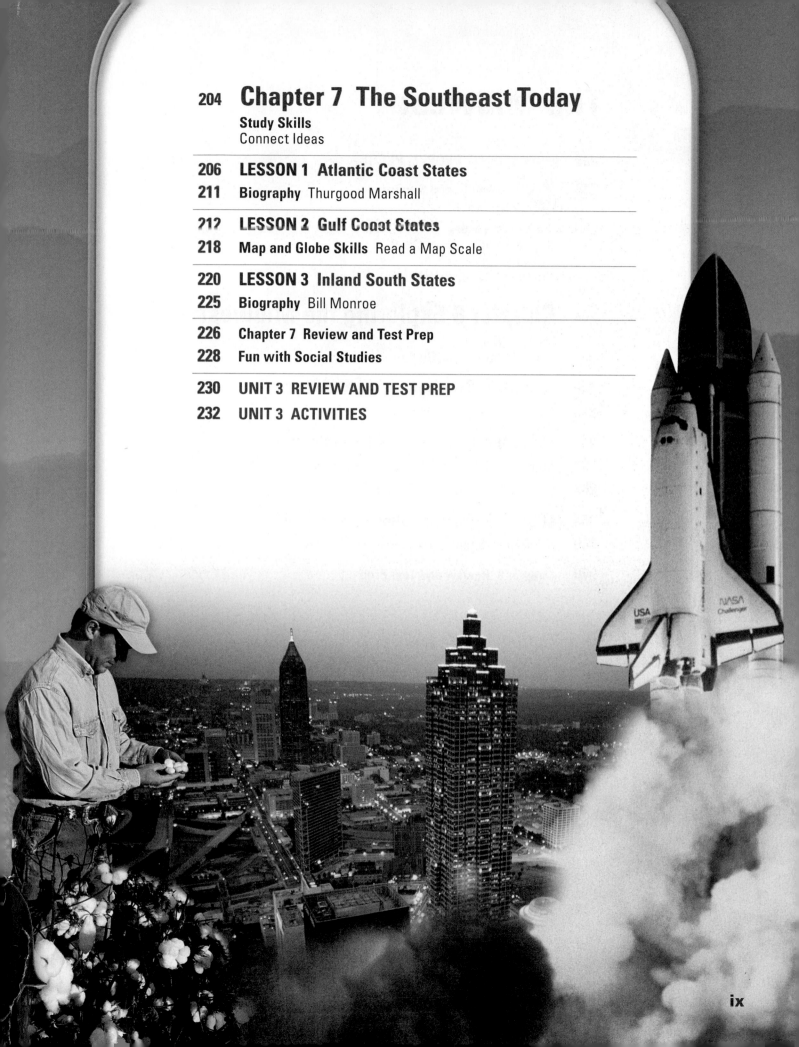

Unit 4

The Midwest

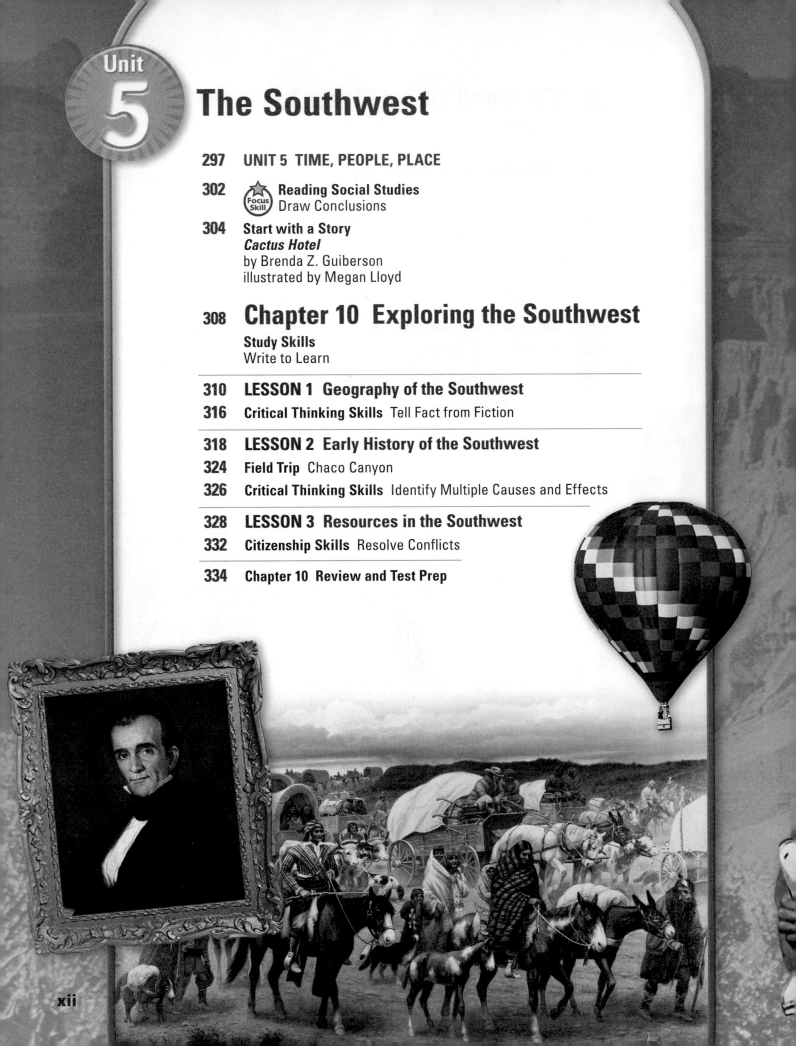

Unit 5

The Southwest

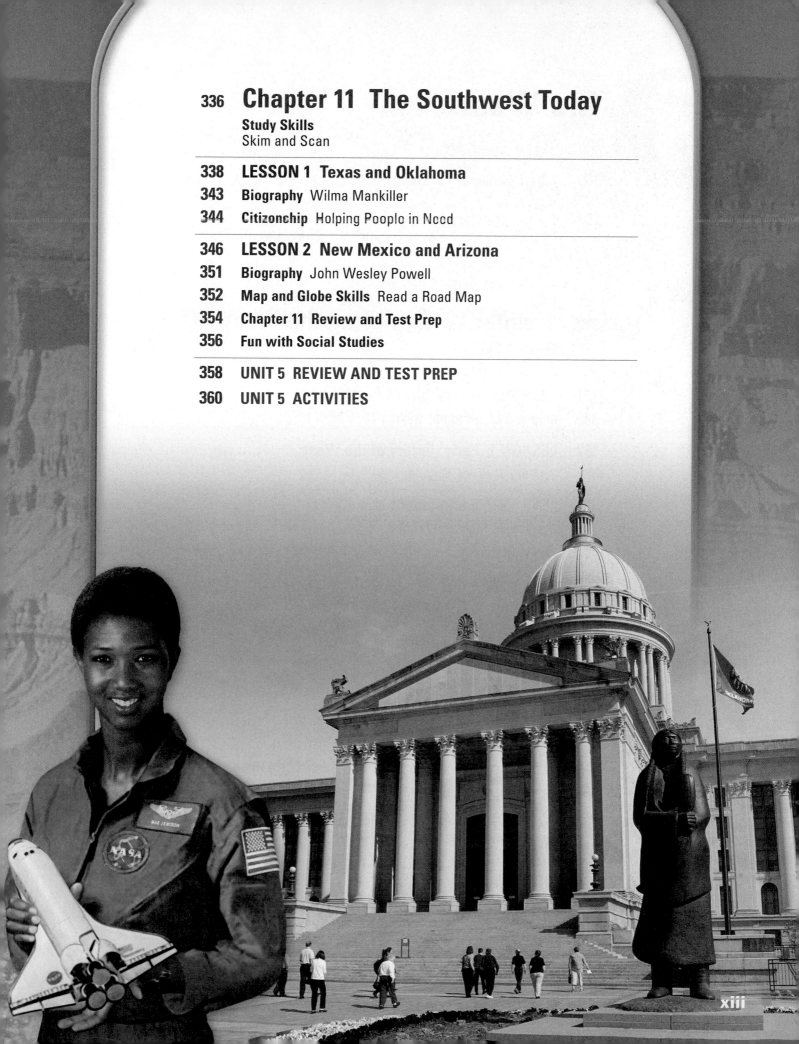

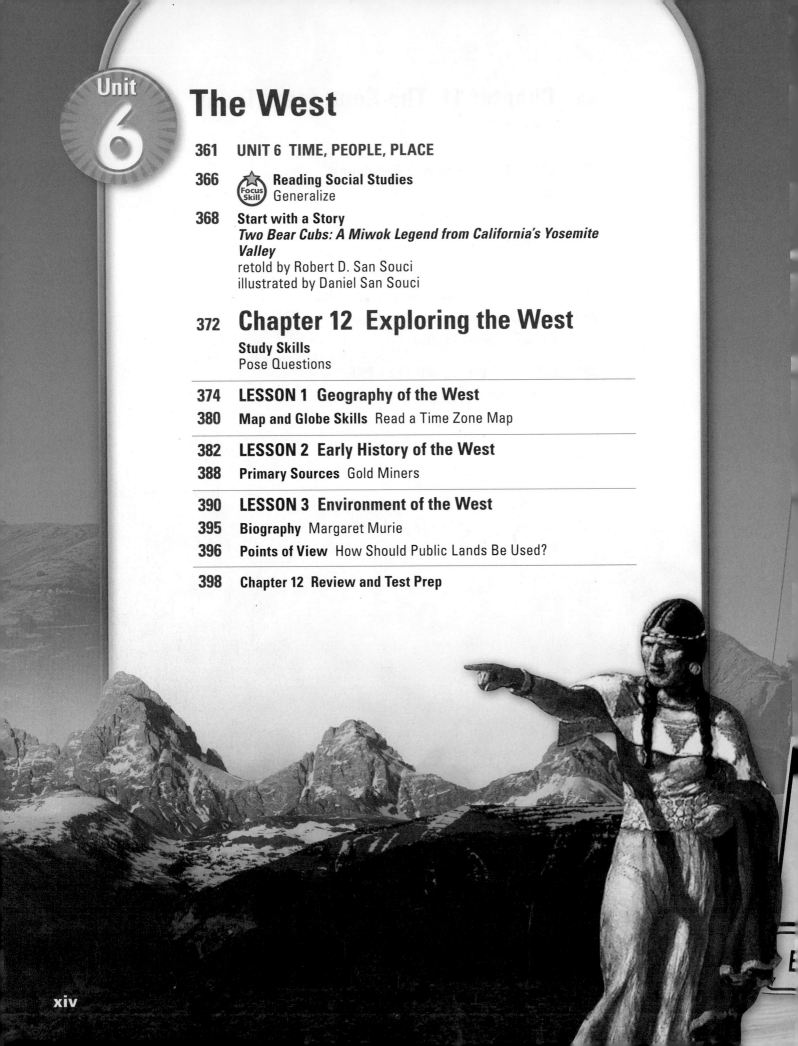

Unit 6

The West

SCENIC BYWAY
Wyoming
BEARTOOTH

Features

Illustrations

The Story Well Told

"America is a tune. It must be sung together."

Gerald Stanley Lee, minister and writer (1862–1944)

Have you ever wondered what makes up the United States of America? You know that it is made up of 50 states, but do you know what those states are like? This year, you will find out.

You will study the geography of the United States. Geography is the study of the Earth's surface and the ways people use it. You will also learn about history, economics, government, and culture. You will learn how areas change over **time**. You will find out how **people** change the places they live and are changed by these places. Throughout your study, you will also discover the importance of **place**.

States and Regions

As you read this book, you will learn to think as a geographer, or a person who studies geography. Learning about geography involves not only the present but also the past. Studying history helps you see how the present is connected to the past. It also helps you see how some places change over time and how other places stay the same.

As you learn to recognize these connections, you will begin to think the way a historian thinks. A historian is a person who studies the past.

Historians **research**, or carefully study, the time in which events in different places happened. They look for clues in the objects and papers that people left behind.

They read journal entries, letters, newspaper stories, and other writings by people. They also look at photographs, films, and artwork.

By carefully studying such **evidence**, or proof, historians are better able to understand what the world was like at the time. It helps them **interpret**, or explain, the past.

Historians look at how events in a place are connected to one another. One way they do this is by using time lines. A time line shows the **chronology**, or time order, in which events happened. A time line can also show how one event may have led to another.

Geographers look closely at people who live in places around the world. After all, places would not be what they are today without people. People locate places, build them, change them, and make them grow.

Because of this, it is important to study not only people of the present but also people of the past. Geographers need to know about the people who founded a place. They also need to know about any newcomers who caused the place to grow or change. In addition, they need to know about the people who make a place what it is today.

When studying people in a place, it is important to think about points of view. A person's **point of view** is how that person sees things. A point of view is shaped by a person's background and experience. It

can depend on whether a person is old or young, male or female, or rich or poor. People with different points of view may see the same event or the same place in very different ways.

People from the past can often serve as models for how to act when troubling events take place. People today can identify key **character traits**—such as trustworthiness, responsibility, fairness, compassion, respect, and patriotism—that people from the past showed. They look at how these character traits help make people into good leaders today, just as they did in the past.

It makes sense that geographers spend much of their time studying places. Places are fascinating. Every place on Earth has features that set it apart from all other places. Often those features affected where events happened in the past, and they may affect where they will happen in the future.

To better understand the features of a place, geographers often study maps. Maps show a place's location. But they can show much more. They can tell a lot about the people who lived there long ago. For example, they can show the routes people followed, where they settled, and how they used the land.

Maps can also tell about people who live in different places today. They can show which people live where, how many people live in each place, and how people in a place earn their living.

Maps, like other evidence, help geographers write a clearer story of the past, present, and future. They are just one valuable tool geographers use to show how time, people, and place are connected.

GREAT SMOKY MOUNTAINS NATIONAL PARK

AN INTERNATIONAL BIOSPHERE RESERVE

Reading Your Textbook

GETTING STARTED

Unit Title •

The Southeast

Unit 3

• Your textbook is divided into six units. Each unit has a title that tells what the unit is about.

The Big Idea

Growth and Change
The Southeast is experiencing changes that give it one of the fastest-growing populations of any region in the United States today.

What to Know
✓ What is the geography of the Southeast?

✓ What important events took place in the Southeast during our nation's early history?

✓ How do ports in the Southeast affect the region and the United States?

✓ What is the Southeast like today?

• The Big Idea tells you the key idea you should understand by the end of the unit.

• These questions help you focus on the Big Idea.

LOOKING AT TIME, PEOPLE, AND PLACE

• TIME pages tell you when some important events in the unit took place.

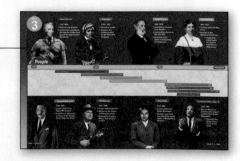

PEOPLE pages introduce • you to some of the men and women you will read about in the unit.

• PLACE pages show you where some of the events in the unit took place.

READING SOCIAL STUDIES

The Reading Social Studies Focus Skill will help you better understand the events you read about and make connections among them.

This statement explains why this Focus Skill is important.

The Focus Skill is modeled for you, and you will be asked to practice it.

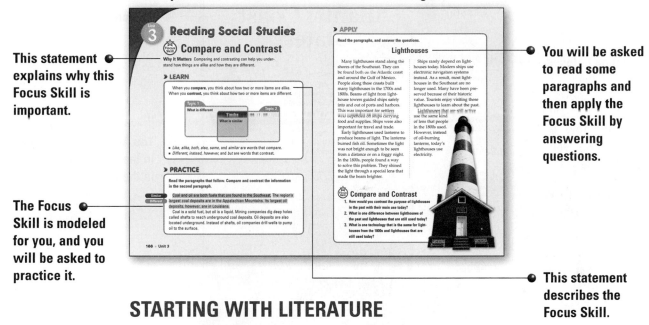

You will be asked to read some paragraphs and then apply the Focus Skill by answering questions.

This statement describes the Focus Skill.

STARTING WITH LITERATURE

Each unit begins with a song, poem, journal, story, or another special reading selection.

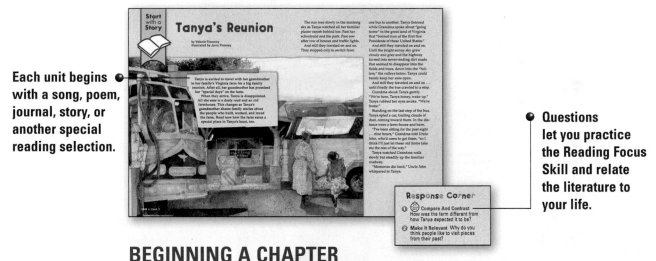

Questions let you practice the Reading Focus Skill and relate the literature to your life.

BEGINNING A CHAPTER

Each unit is divided into chapters, and each chapter is divided into lessons.

This Study Skill provides you with a strategy that you can use to remember and organize what you read.

Chapter title and number

READING A LESSON

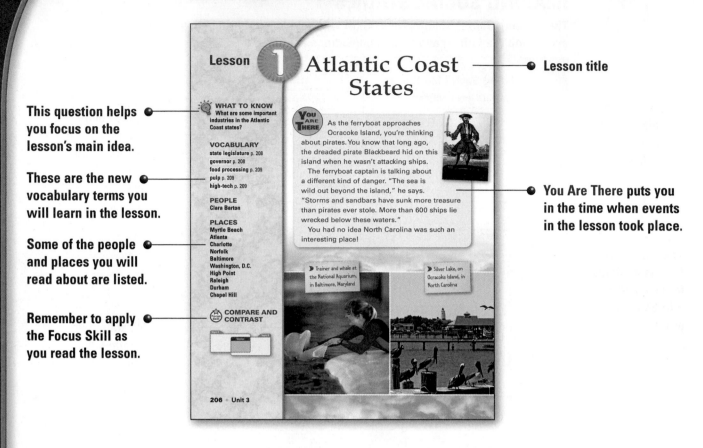

This question helps you focus on the lesson's main idea.

These are the new vocabulary terms you will learn in the lesson.

Some of the people and places you will read about are listed.

Remember to apply the Focus Skill as you read the lesson.

Lesson title

You Are There puts you in the time when events in the lesson took place.

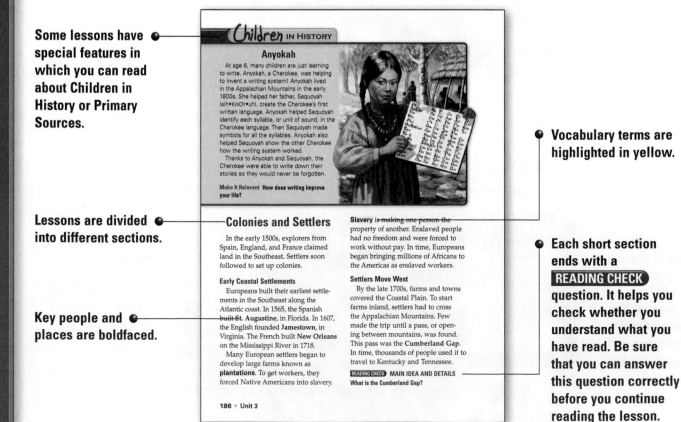

Some lessons have special features in which you can read about Children in History or Primary Sources.

Lessons are divided into different sections.

Key people and places are boldfaced.

Vocabulary terms are highlighted in yellow.

Each short section ends with a **READING CHECK** question. It helps you check whether you understand what you have read. Be sure that you can answer this question correctly before you continue reading the lesson.

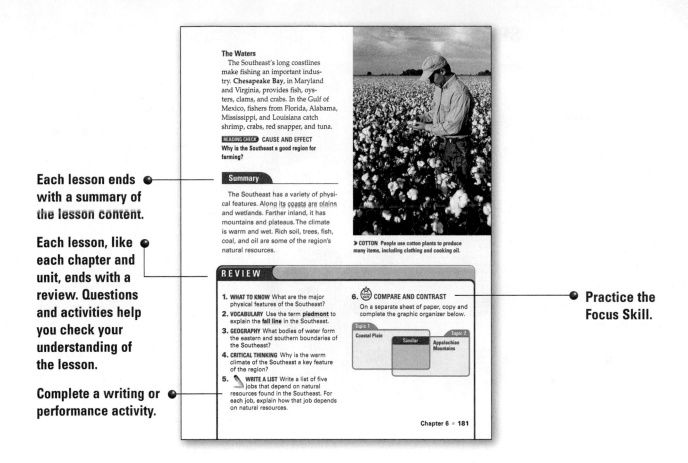

Each lesson ends with a summary of the lesson content.

Each lesson, like each chapter and unit, ends with a review. Questions and activities help you check your understanding of the lesson.

Complete a writing or performance activity.

The Waters

The Southeast's long coastlines make fishing an important industry. **Chesapeake Bay**, in Maryland and Virginia, provides fish, oysters, clams, and crabs. In the Gulf of Mexico, fishers from Florida, Alabama, Mississippi, and Louisiana catch shrimp, crabs, red snapper, and tuna.

READING CHECK CAUSE AND EFFECT
Why is the Southeast a good region for farming?

Summary

The Southeast has a variety of physical features. Along its coasts are plains and wetlands. Farther inland, it has mountains and plateaus. The climate is warm and wet. Rich soil, trees, fish, coal, and oil are some of the region's natural resources.

▶ COTTON People use cotton plants to produce many items, including clothing and cooking oil.

REVIEW

1. **WHAT TO KNOW** What are the major physical features of the Southeast?

2. **VOCABULARY** Use the term **piedmont** to explain the **fall line** in the Southeast.

3. **GEOGRAPHY** What bodies of water form the eastern and southern boundaries of the Southeast?

4. **CRITICAL THINKING** Why is the warm climate of the Southeast a key feature of the region?

5. **WRITE A LIST** Write a list of five jobs that depend on natural resources found in the Southeast. For each job, explain how that job depends on natural resources.

6. **COMPARE AND CONTRAST**
On a separate sheet of paper, copy and complete the graphic organizer below.

| Topic 1 Coastal Plain | Similar | Topic 2 Appalachian Mountains |

Practice the Focus Skill.

Chapter 6 ▪ 181

LEARNING SOCIAL STUDIES SKILLS

Your textbook has lessons that help you build your Citizenship Skills, Map and Globe Skills, Chart and Graph Skills, and Critical Thinking Skills.

This statement tells you why it is important to learn this skill.

You will be able to practice and apply the skill.

SPECIAL FEATURES

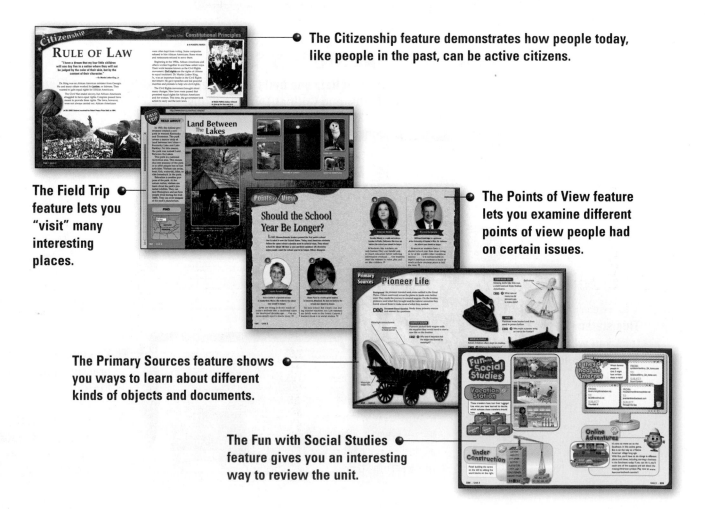

Biographies give in-depth background about some of the people who lived at the time.

Each biography focuses on a trait that the person showed.

A time line shows when the person was born and died and some key events in his or her life.

The Citizenship feature demonstrates how people today, like people in the past, can be active citizens.

The Field Trip feature lets you "visit" many interesting places.

The Points of View feature lets you examine different points of view people had on certain issues.

The Primary Sources feature shows you ways to learn about different kinds of objects and documents.

The Fun with Social Studies feature gives you an interesting way to review the unit.

FOR YOUR REFERENCE

At the back of your textbook, you will find different reference tools. You can use these tools to look up words. You can also find information about people, places, and other topics.

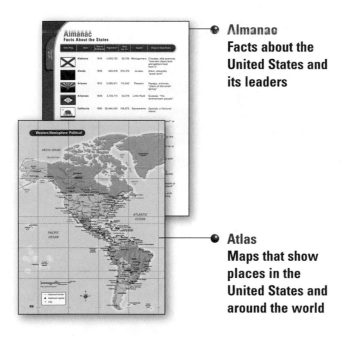

Almanac
Facts about the United States and its leaders

Atlas
Maps that show places in the United States and around the world

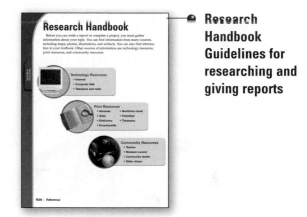

Research Handbook
Guidelines for researching and giving reports

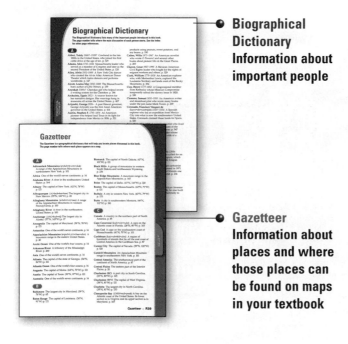

Biographical Dictionary
Information about important people

Gazetteer
Information about places and where those places can be found on maps in your textbook

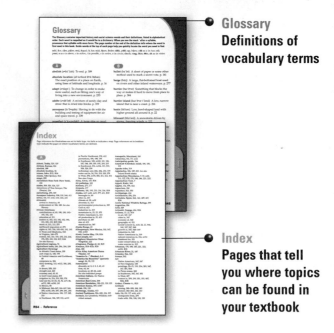

Glossary
Definitions of vocabulary terms

Index
Pages that tell you where topics can be found in your textbook

The Five Themes of Geography

Learning about places is an important part of history and geography. Geography is the study of Earth's surface and the way people use it. When geographers study Earth and its geography, they often think about five main themes, or topics. Keeping these themes in mind as you read will help you think like a geographer.

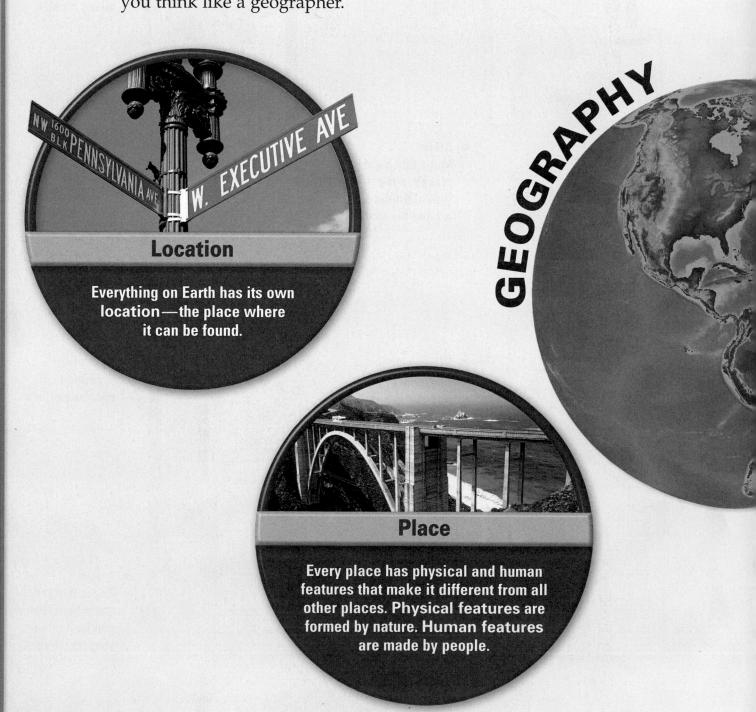

GEOGRAPHY

Location
Everything on Earth has its own location—the place where it can be found.

Place
Every place has physical and human features that make it different from all other places. Physical features are formed by nature. Human features are made by people.

Human-Environment Interactions

People and their surroundings interact, or affect each other. People's activities may change the environment. The environment may affect people. Sometimes people must change how they live to fit into their surroundings.

Movement

People, goods, and ideas move every day. They move in your state, our country, and around the world.

THEMES

Regions

Areas of Earth with main features that make them different from other areas are called regions. A region can be described by its physical features or its human features.

Looking at Earth

A distant view from space shows Earth's round shape. You probably have a globe in your classroom. Like Earth, a globe has the shape of a sphere, or ball. It is a model of Earth. It shows Earth's major bodies of water and its continents. **Continents** are the largest land masses. Earth's seven continents, from the largest to the smallest, are Asia, Africa, North America, South America, Antarctica, Europe, and Australia.

Because of its shape, you can see only one-half of Earth at a time when you look at a globe. Halfway between the North Pole and the South Pole on a globe is a line called the **equator**.

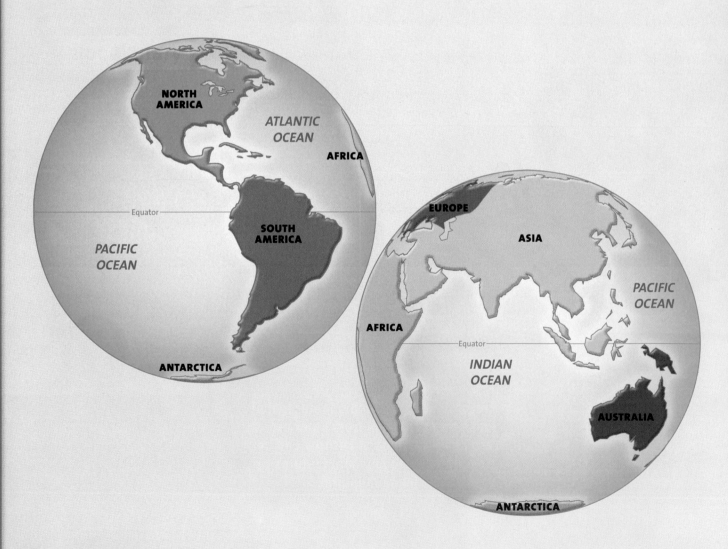

The equator divides Earth into two equal halves, or **hemi-spheres**. The Northern Hemisphere is north of the equator, and the Southern Hemisphere is south of it. Another line on the globe is called the **prime meridian**. It is often used to divide Earth into the Western Hemisphere and the Eastern Hemisphere.

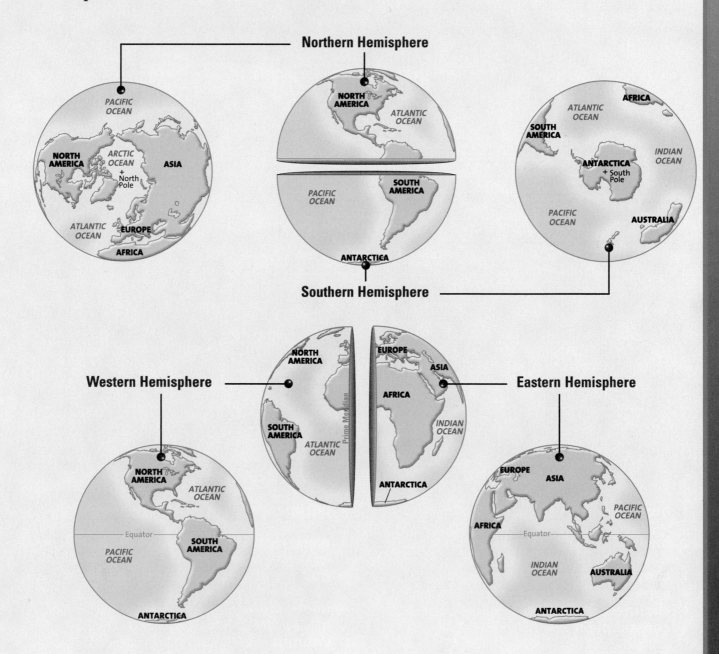

GEOGRAPHY REVIEW

Geography Terms

1. **basin** bowl-shaped area of land surrounded by higher land
2. **bay** an inlet of the sea or some other body of water, usually smaller than a gulf
3. **canyon** deep, narrow valley with steep sides
4. **cape** point of land that extends into water
5. **channel** deepest part of a body of water
6. **coastal plain** area of flat land along a sea or ocean
7. **delta** triangle-shaped area of land at the mouth of a river

8. **fall line** area along which rivers form waterfalls or rapids as the rivers drop to lower land
9. **glacier** large ice mass that moves slowly down a mountain or across land
10. **gulf** part of a sea or ocean extending into the land, usually larger than a bay
11. **inlet** any area of water extending into the land from a larger body of water
12. **isthmus** narrow strip of land connecting two larger areas of land
13. **marsh** lowland with moist soil and tall grasses

14 **mesa** flat-topped mountain with steep sides
15 **mountain pass** gap between mountains
16 **mountain range** chain of mountains
17 **mouth of river** place where a river empties into another body of water
18 **peninsula** land that is almost completely surrounded by water
19 **plain** area of flat or gently rolling land
20 **plateau** area of high, mostly flat land
21 **savanna** area of grassland and scattered trees

22 **sea level** the level of the surface of an ocean or a sea
23 **source of river** place where a river begins
24 **strait** narrow channel of water connecting two larger bodies of water
25 **swamp** area of low, wet land with trees
26 **tributary** stream or river that flows into a larger stream or river
27 **volcano** opening in Earth, often raised, through which lava, rock, ashes, and gases are forced out

Reading Maps

Maps give important information about the world around you. A map is a drawing that shows all or part of Earth on a flat surface. To help you read maps, mapmakers add certain features to their maps. These features often include a title, a map key, a compass rose, a locator, and a map scale.

Mapmakers sometimes need to show certain places on a map in greater detail. Sometimes they must also show places that are located beyond the area shown on a map.

A **map title** tells the subject of the map. It may also identify the kind of map.
- A **political map** shows cities, states, and countries.
- A **physical map** shows kinds of land and bodies of water.
- A **historical map** shows parts of the world as they were in the past.

A **map key**, or **legend**, explains the symbols used on a map. Symbols may be colors, patterns, lines, or other special marks.

An **inset map** is a smaller map within a larger one.

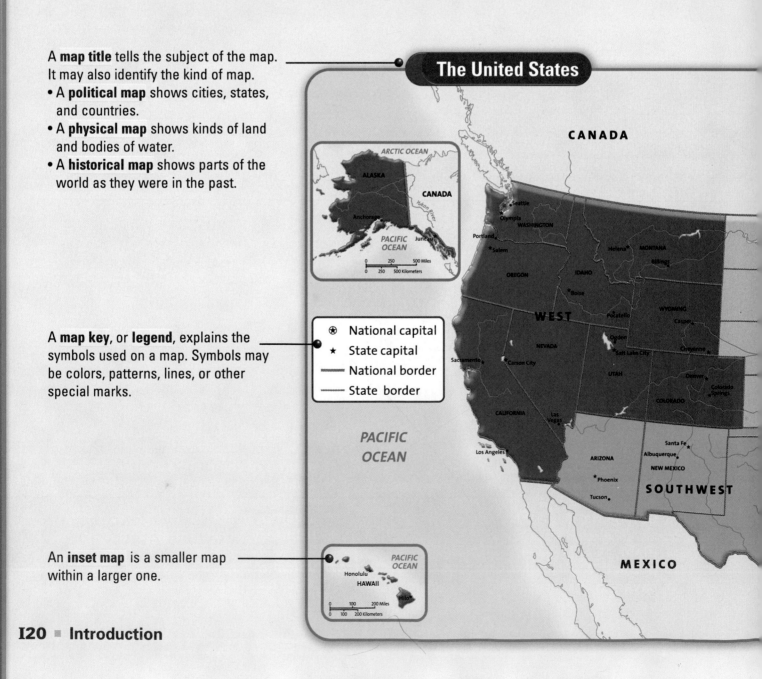

The United States

⊛ National capital
★ State capital
── National border
── State border

Find Alaska and Hawaii on the map of the United States on pages R8–R9. The map there shows the location of those two states in relation to the location of the rest of the country.

Now find Alaska and Hawaii on the map below. To show this much detail for these states and the rest of the country, the map would have to be much larger. Instead, Alaska and Hawaii are each shown in a separate inset map, or a small map within a larger map.

A **locator** is a small map or globe that shows where the place on the main map is located within a larger area.

A **map scale**, or **distance scale**, compares a distance on the map to a distance in the real world. It helps you find the real distance between places on a map.

A **compass rose**, or direction marker, shows directions.
- The **cardinal directions** are north, south, east, and west.
- The **intermediate directions**, or directions between the cardinal directions, are northeast, northwest, southeast, and southwest.

Finding Locations

To help people find places on maps, mapmakers some-times add lines that cross each other. These lines form a pattern of squares called a **grid system**.

Look at the map of the United States below. Around the grid are letters and numbers. The columns, which run up and down, have numbers. The rows, which run from left to right, have letters.

Each square on the map can be identified by its letter and number. For example, the top row of squares on the map includes square A-1, square A-2, square A-3, and so on.

United States

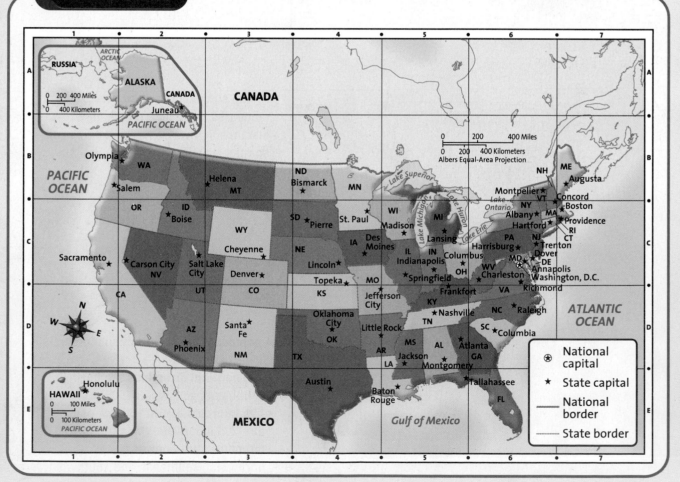

The United States

Unit 1

The Big Idea

Geography
The United States has diversity in its landscapes and its people.

What to Know

- What are the physical features of the United States?
- How did the United States become a nation of many cultures?
- How do the government and economy of the United States work?
- What are the major regions of the United States?

Unit 1

Time

The United States

• **1500s** Explorers and settlers begin to arrive in North America, p. 44

• **1600s** European settlers and African workers arrive in large numbers, p. 44

1500   **1600**   **1700**

At the Same Time

1500 Benin is the most powerful kingdom in western Africa

1605 India is united under the Mogul Empire

The United States

1787 As a new nation, the United States writes its Constitution, p. 51

1920 More Americans live in cities than on farms, p. 45

Present Almost 300 million people live in the United States, p. 45

1800

1900

Present

1795 China reaches its greatest size under the Qing rulers

1918 World War I ends in Europe

Present More than 6 billion people live on Earth

Native Americans

People

Native Americans

- The first people to live in the Americas had many different ways of life and spoke many different languages
- They used natural resources around them for food, clothing, and shelter

First Wave

- Early 1600s to about 1750, people from England and other European countries settled the Atlantic coast; people from Spain settled the Southwest and Florida
- Enslaved Africans arrived

Second Wave

- From 1820 to 1870, more than 7 million people arrived
- Many people from Germany and Ireland settled the Northeast and Midwest
- Many people from China arrived in California

First Wave

Second Wave

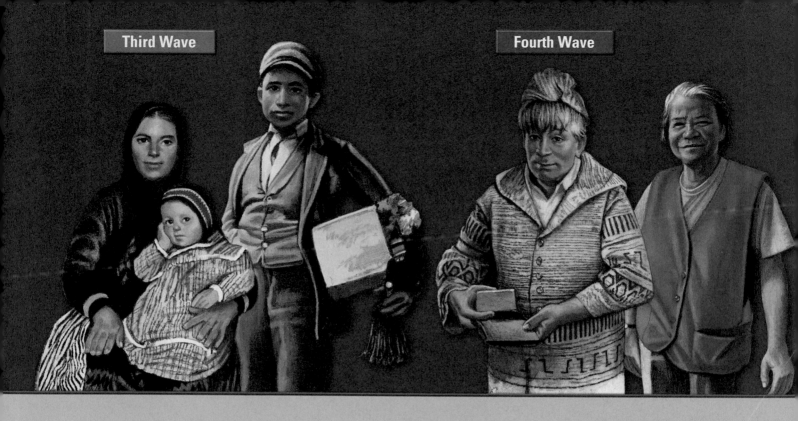

Third Wave

- From 1881 to 1920, about 23 million people arrived in the United States
- Many were from Austria, Italy, Hungary, and Russia
- People from Japan entered Hawaii and California

Fourth Wave

- Beginning about 1965, arrivals from Asia and the Caribbean increased
- Many came from China, Vietnam, the Philippines, the Dominican Republic, Cuba, and Jamaica

Americans Today

- There are about 300 million Americans
- Nearly one out of every ten Americans is foreign born
- Today, the United States is a nation of diverse cultures

Americans Today

Place

The United States of America

CANADA

RUSSIA

ARCTIC OCEAN

ALASKA   CANADA

Bering
Sea   Juneau ★

0   150   300 Miles
0 150 300 Kilometers

PACIFIC OCEAN

Olympia ★ WASHINGTON

Salem ★

CASCADE RANGE

OREGON

Helena ★ MONTANA

IDAHO

★ Boise

ROCKY

WYOMING

NORTH
DAKOTA

Bismarck ★

SOUTH
DAKOTA

Pierre ★

NEBRASKA

Cheyenne ★   INTERIOR

PACIFIC
OCEAN

COAST RANGES

SIERRA NEVADA

Sacramento ★

GREAT
BASIN

Carson City ★

NEVADA

Salt
Lake
City

UTAH

MOUNTAINS

Denver ★   PLAINS

COLORADO   KANSAS

CALIFORNIA

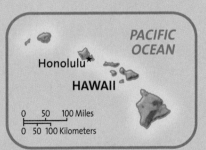

PACIFIC
OCEAN

Honolulu ★

HAWAII

0   50   100 Miles
0 50 100 Kilometers

ARIZONA

★ Phoenix

Santa Fe

NEW MEXICO   TEXAS

MEXICO

⊛ National capital
★ State capital
— National border
— State border
◻ Northeast
◻ Southeast
◻ Midwest
◻ Southwest
◻ West

Great Basin

0   200   400 Miles
0   200   400 Kilometers
Albers Equal-Area Projection

Mississippi River

Appalachian Mountains

CANADA

MINNESOTA

WISCONSIN
★ St. Paul

Lake Michigan

MICHIGAN
Lansing ★

Lake Erie

MAINE
Augusta ★

NEW HAMPSHIRE
VERMONT

Montpelier ★

Lake Ontario

NEW YORK
Albany ★

Concord ★
Boston ★

MASSACHUSETTS
Providence ★
Hartford ★

RHODE ISLAND
CONNECTICUT

IOWA
★ Des Moines

Lincoln ★

ILLINOIS
Springfield ★

INDIANA
Indianapolis ★

OHIO
Columbus ★

PENNSYLVANIA

Trenton ★
Harrisburg ★

NEW JERSEY
DELAWARE

Dover ★

Topeka ★

WEST VIRGINIA
Charleston ★

Annapolis ★
Washington, D.C.

MARYLAND

Jefferson City ★

MISSOURI

Frankfort ★
KENTUCKY

VIRGINIA
★ Richmond

OKLAHOMA

ARKANSAS

Nashville ★
TENNESSEE

Raleigh ★
NORTH CAROLINA

APPALACHIAN MOUNTAINS

★ Oklahoma City

Little Rock ★

ALABAMA

SOUTH CAROLINA
Columbia ★

COASTAL PLAINS

ATLANTIC OCEAN

MISSISSIPPI

GEORGIA
★ Atlanta

Montgomery ★

Jackson ★

Baton Rouge ★

Tallahassee ★

Austin ★

LOUISIANA

FLORIDA

BAHAMAS

Gulf of Mexico

Coastal Plain

Rocky Mountains

N
W   E
S

Reading Social Studies

⭐ Focus Skill Main Idea and Details

Why It Matters Finding the main idea and details can help you understand what you read.

❱ LEARN

The **main idea** is what a paragraph or a passage is mostly about. The **details** give more information about the main idea.

Main Idea
The most important idea

⬆

Details		
Facts about the main idea	Facts about the main idea	Facts about the main idea

- Usually, each paragraph in a passage has a main idea and details. The whole passage also has a main idea and details.
- The main idea is often, but not always, the first sentence. The other sentences give the details.

❱ PRACTICE

Read the paragraphs that follow. Identify the main idea and details in the second paragraph.

Main Idea
Details

Rivers affect the land around them. When rivers flood, they overflow their banks. This makes the soil richer. Sometimes rivers change their course over time. They cut new channels into the land.

People often settle in river valleys. The weather in river valleys is mild. The rich soil is good for farming. Rivers can also help people move crops to markets.

Read the paragraphs, and answer the questions.

Hiking in the Appalachians

People from all over the United States hike in the Appalachian Mountains. More than half of the nation's population lives within a day's drive of some part of the mountain range. Roads lead to many hiking trails along its length, from Canada to Alabama. Hikers can find many online maps and guides to help them get ready for visiting the Appalachians.

Many people hike in the Appalachians to see a wide variety of plants and animals. Hikers can see some of more than 6,000 different kinds of plants. They may spot deer, black bears, raccoons, hawks, and other wildlife.

Hikers of all skill levels walk the trails of the Appalachians. Most of the trails are not very steep. Hikers do not need special climbing equipment—just good hiking shoes.

Even a beginning hiker can have a great time in the Appalachians.

People hike in the Appalachians in all seasons. In summer, the weather is warm. If a hiker gets hot, creeks provide a place to cool off. Temperatures can be cool in spring and fall. In winter, parts of the Appalachians get snow, especially at higher elevations. Only those with experience should hike these snow-covered trails.

One trail—the Appalachian Trail—is more than 2,000 miles long. It stretches from Maine to Georgia. Beginning hikers may walk only a mile or two. Experienced hikers may hike the entire Appalachian Trail in one summer!

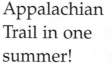

 Focus Skill

Main Idea and Details

1. What is the main idea of the first paragraph?
2. Which sentence tells the main idea of the second paragraph?
3. What details explain that hikers in the Appalachians are at many different skill levels?

America is...

written by Louise Borden
illustrated by Stacey Schuett

Not long ago, school children in England asked American author Louise Borden, "What is it like to live in America?" This poem is Borden's answer. Read now how Borden celebrates the people of the United States, their land, and their ideas.

America is. . .

America is our country.
It is the place we call home.

We are the nation
whose name means freedom

to people all over the world.

America is . . .

fifty states
from the Atlantic coast
to the Pacific Ocean
and beyond.
The United States
of America. . . .

America is . . .

the swamps and bayous
of the Deep South.

And ponds that glimmer
from east to west.

And lakes so huge and deep,
they seem as big as an ocean.

And rushing streams,
and creeks,
and brooks.

And rivers that are long and wide,
that bring our states together
as one vast land
from the Hudson
to the Ohio
to the Mississippi
to the Columbia . . .
this is America.

And America is . . .

the prairie:

tall grass,
and wind,
and stars.
Listen.
This is America.

America is . . .

the stone walls
of New England,
the forests of the Northwest,
the osprey
and oysters

of the Chesapeake Bay,
and Minnesota winters
10 degrees below zero
and sometimes colder.

The West and its ranches
are part of this nation too.

With ten-gallon hats
and boots and spurs.
With herds of cattle
and lassos in cowboys' hands.

Rodeo!
Yippee-yei-yay!

This is America.

America is . . .

rugged mountains
with caps of snow

and deserts
that are hot and dry—
110 degrees in the shade. . . .

It is a nation
where fifty states meet,
where we are all one.

Response Corner

1. **Focus Skill** Main Idea and Details
   What is America?

2. **Make It Relevant** Do you think
   the author is describing places
   she has visited? Why or why not?

STUDY SKILLS

UNDERSTAND VOCABULARY

Using a dictionary can help you learn new words that you find as you read. It can also help you learn new meanings of a word you already know.

- **A dictionary shows all the meanings of a word and tells the origin of the word.**

- **You can use a chart to list and organize unfamiliar words that you look up in a dictionary.**

spring (spring´) [from Middle English *springe*] *n.* **1.** A source or supply of water coming from the ground. **2.** The season between winter and summer. **3.** An elastic object or device that returns to its original shape after being crushed or changed. **4.** The act of leaping up or forward.

Word	Syllables	Origin	Definition
spring	SPRING	Middle English	A source or supply of water coming from the ground

PREVIEW VOCABULARY

landform p. 18   **tributary** p. 21   **precipitation** p. 27

Crater Lake National Park, in Oregon

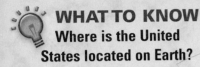
Where Is the United States?

VOCABULARY

hemisphere p. 13

equator p. 13

prime meridian p. 13

continent p. 13

relative location p. 14

border p. 14

gulf p. 15

PLACES

United States
North America
Canada
Mexico
Pacific Ocean
Atlantic Ocean
Gulf of Mexico

MAIN IDEA AND DETAILS

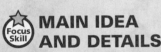

YOU ARE THERE

Your homework is very interesting tonight. You will write an e-mail you might send to a student in China. In your e-mail, you write, *I live in the United States.*

"The student in China might not know where the United States is," your mother says. She smiles and points to a globe of the world across the room. "Try looking at the globe. It will help you describe where the United States is on Earth."

ALASKA

THE UNITED STATES

HAWAII

Global Address

There are many ways to describe a place's location. One way is to give its global address, or where it is on Earth.

Which Hemispheres?

To give the global address of the United States, you can say in which **hemispheres**, or halves of Earth, it lies. Geographers use two imaginary lines to divide Earth into hemispheres. One line, called the **equator**, circles Earth halfway between the North Pole and the South Pole.

Every place north of the equator is in the Northern Hemisphere. Every place south of the equator is in the Southern Hemisphere. Because the United States lies north of the equator, it is in the Northern Hemisphere.

Another imaginary line, called the **prime meridian**, divides Earth into the Western and Eastern Hemispheres. Because the United States lies west of the prime meridian, it is in the Western Hemisphere.

Which Continent?

You can also use continents to describe the global address of the United States. The seven **continents** are the largest land areas on Earth. The United States is part of the continent of **North America**.

READING CHECK ⚡**MAIN IDEA AND DETAILS**
Which hemispheres are part of the global address of the United States?

ILLUSTRATION Which continent lies south of North America?

CANADA

NORTH AMERICA

ATLANTIC OCEAN

PACIFIC OCEAN

MEXICO

SOUTH AMERICA

Relative Location

Another way to describe a place's location is to give its relative location. The **relative location** of a place is where it is in relation to other places on Earth.

Between Two Countries

You can use other countries to describe relative location. Most of the United States lies south of **Canada** and north of **Mexico.** In fact, our nation shares its northern border with Canada and much of its southern border with Mexico. A **border** is a line that shows the end of a place.

Between Two Oceans

You can also use bodies of water to describe relative location. Water covers most of Earth's surface. Most of that water is in the oceans. The United States lies between two of the world's oceans. The **Pacific Ocean** forms the country's western border. The **Atlantic Ocean** is its eastern border.

Your State's Relative Location

There are ways to describe in more detail where you live. You could name your state and describe its relative location. Most Americans live in one of the 48 states that lie between Canada and Mexico.

MAP SKILL **REGIONS** The seven continents, from the largest to the smallest, are Asia, Africa, North America, South America, Antarctica, Europe, and Australia. Which oceans border North America?

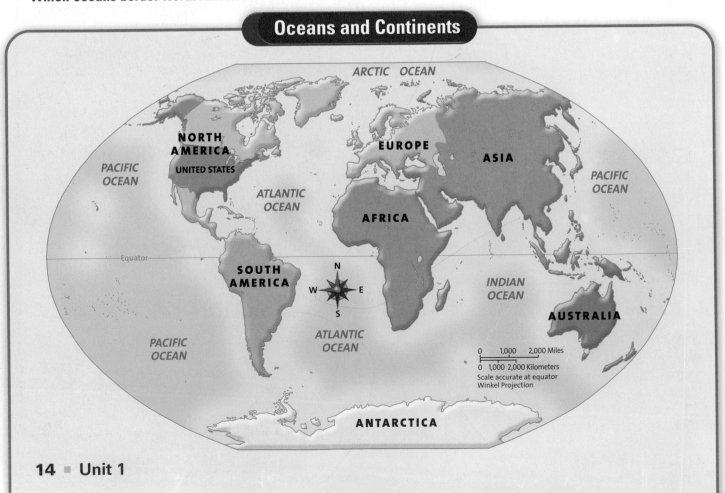

Oceans and Continents

▶ **FOUR CORNERS** The borders of four states—Arizona, Colorado, New Mexico, and Utah—meet at an area called the Four Corners.

Perhaps you live near the **Gulf of Mexico.** A **gulf** is a part of an ocean or a sea that reaches into the land. The Gulf of Mexico is part of the Atlantic Ocean. It forms part of the southern border of the United States.

READING CHECK ☼**MAIN IDEA AND DETAILS**
How do you describe a place's relative location?

Summary

The United States is located on the continent of North America in the Northern and Western Hemispheres. The Atlantic Ocean, the Pacific Ocean, the Gulf of Mexico, Canada, and Mexico form its borders.

REVIEW

1. **WHAT TO KNOW** Where is the United States located on Earth?

2. **VOCABULARY** Use the terms **equator** and **prime meridian** to explain **hemisphere**.

3. **GEOGRAPHY** What countries and oceans border the United States?

4. **CRITICAL THINKING** Why do you think identifying location is the first step in studying a place's geography?

5. **WRITE A LETTER** Write a letter that you might send to a student in another country. In your letter, describe where you live.

6. (Focus Skill) **MAIN IDEA AND DETAILS**

   On a separate sheet of paper, copy and complete the graphic organizer below.

   Main Idea
   You can use bodies of water to describe the relative location of the United States.

   Details

Use Latitude and Longitude

Why It Matters By stating latitude and longitude, you can describe the **absolute location**, or exact location, of a place.

❱ LEARN

Lines of latitude and longitude cross to form a grid over a map or globe. To describe a place's absolute location, you name the line of latitude and line of longitude closest to it.

Lines of latitude run east and west. The equator is a line of latitude. Find the equator on Map A. It is marked 0°, or zero degrees. All other lines of latitude are measured in degrees north or south from the equator.

Lines of longitude run north and south. The prime meridian is a line of longitude. Find the prime meridian on Map A. Like the equator, it is marked 0°. All other lines of longitude are measured in degrees east or west from the prime meridian.

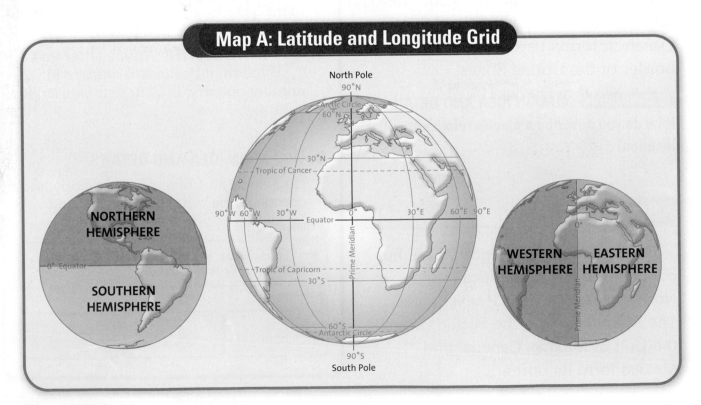

Map A: Latitude and Longitude Grid

Map B: United States Latitude and Longitude

> PRACTICE

Use Map B to answer these questions.

❶ Between which two lines of latitude does most of the United States lie?

❷ Which city is located near 40°N, 105°W?

> APPLY

Make It Relevant Use latitude and longitude to describe your community's location.

Map and Globe Skills

The American Landscape

WHAT TO KNOW
What are the major landforms in the United States?

VOCABULARY
landform p. 18

sea level p. 19

plateau p. 20

source p. 21

tributary p. 21

mouth p. 21

basin p. 22

canyon p. 22

PLACES
Coastal Plain

Appalachian Mountains

Interior Plains

Great Lakes

Mississippi River

Rocky Mountains

Intermountain Region

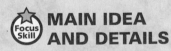 MAIN IDEA AND DETAILS

YOU ARE THERE You're about to take a trip across the United States with your family. You read a travel guide to learn what you might see. You will see many different landforms. **Landforms** are features such as mountains, hills, valleys, and plains that make up Earth's surface.

The United States covers a huge area. In fact, it is the fourth-largest country in the world. It is so big, that you can see just about every kind of landform here. You can also see many rivers, lakes, and other bodies of water.

In the East

Your trip starts on a sandy beach along the Atlantic Ocean. The land here is flat and low. In fact, you are standing at sea level. Land that is at **sea level** is level with the surface of the ocean.

The Coastal Plain

The flat lands stretching along the Atlantic Ocean make up what is called the **Coastal Plain**. A coastal plain is an area of low land that lies along the coast of an ocean.

In Massachusetts, the Coastal Plain is a narrow strip of land only 10 miles wide. Farther south, the plain gets much wider. By the time you reach the Gulf of Mexico, the Coastal Plain is hundreds of miles wide.

The Appalachian Mountains

As you move west from the Coastal Plain, the land rises higher and higher. Finally, you reach the highest lands in the eastern United States—the **Appalachian** (a•puh•LAY•chee•uhn) **Mountains.** This chain of mountains stretches more than 1,500 miles from Alabama into Canada.

The Appalachians are the oldest mountains in North America. They were once very tall. Over time, rain and wind have worn down their peaks. Now the mountains appear rounded, and no peak is higher than 7,000 feet.

READING CHECK ⦿**MAIN IDEA AND DETAILS**
What two major landforms cover most of the eastern United States?

> **A VARIETY OF LANDFORMS** The United States has thick forests, rocky deserts, grassy plains, tall mountains, sandy beaches, and many other landforms.

United States: Land and Water

Legend:
- Mountains
- Plateaus
- Hills
- Plains

RUSSIA
ARCTIC OCEAN
Brooks Range
ALASKA
Alaska Range
CANADA
PACIFIC OCEAN
0 200 400 Miles
0 400 Kilometers

CANADA

0 200 400 Miles
0 200 400 Kilometers
Albers Equal-Area Projection

Coast Ranges
Cascade Range
Columbia Plateau
Columbia River
ROCKY MOUNTAINS
Snake River
Black Hills
Missouri River
GREAT PLAINS
Lake Superior
Mississippi River
Lake Michigan
Lake Huron
Lake Ontario
Lake Erie
St. Lawrence River
Hudson R.
Connecticut R.

Coast Ranges
Sierra Nevada
Central Valley
GREAT BASIN
Great Salt Lake
Colorado Plateau
Colorado River
Gila River
INTERIOR PLAINS
Platte River
Arkansas River
Ozark Plateau
Red River
Illinois R.
River
CENTRAL PLAINS
Wabash River
Ohio River
James R.
APPALACHIAN MOUNTAINS
PIEDMONT
Tennessee River
Savannah R.
COASTAL PLAIN
ATLANTIC OCEAN

PACIFIC OCEAN
Pecos River
Brazos River
Sabine R.
Mississippi River
Alabama R.
COASTAL PLAIN

HAWAII
PACIFIC OCEAN
0 100 Miles
0 100 Kilometers

Rio Grande
COASTAL PLAIN
MEXICO
Gulf of Mexico

N W E S

MAP SKILL **PLACE** Four major landforms are mountains, plateaus, hills, and plains. What kind of landform covers most of the middle part of the United States?

In the Middle

After you cross the Appalachian Mountains, you reach a huge area of low, grassy lands. You are now on the **Interior Plains.** These plains reach north from Mexico, through the middle of the United States, and into Canada.

The Central Plains

The eastern part of the Interior Plains is known as the Central Plains. Here you see wide rivers, grassy hills, and forests. In the northern part of the Central Plains are the **Great Lakes.** These five connected lakes—Superior, Michigan, Huron, Erie, and Ontario— form the largest group of freshwater lakes in the world.

The Great Plains

Most of the land on the Interior Plains is flat, but there are some hills. On the Ozark Plateau (pla•TOH), you see low mountains covered by forests. A **plateau** is a high, flat area of land. Farther west, the land becomes flatter and higher. You are now on the Great Plains, the western part of the Interior Plains. Here you see few rivers or lakes and hardly any trees. Grasslands stretch across the land for miles. The Great Plains is home to mountains such as the Black Hills of South Dakota and Wyoming.

A Mighty River

Hundreds of rivers flow through the United States. The mighty **Mississippi River** is one of the longest rivers in North America. It runs through the middle of the Interior Plains.

Like all rivers, the Mississippi starts at a high place and flows to lower land. Its source is a small lake in Minnesota. The **source** of a river is the place where it begins. From the lake, the Mississippi flows south for 2,340 miles.

Along its route, the Mississippi is joined by many tributaries. A **tributary** is a river or stream that flows into a larger river. Together, a river and its tributaries make up a river system. Some major tributaries of the Mississippi River system include the Ohio, Missouri, and Arkansas Rivers.

The Mississippi River system drains rain and melted snow away from the surrounding lands. It then carries this water all the way to the river's mouth at the Gulf of Mexico. The **mouth** of a

MISSISSIPPI RIVER

SOURCE

Missouri River

Ohio River

TRIBUTARY

Red River

Arkansas River

Tennessee Ri

Gulf of Mexico

MOUTH

 MAP SKILL **LOCATION** Which tributaries join the Mississippi from the east?

river is the place where it empties into a larger body of water.

READING CHECK **SUMMARIZE**
What is a river system?

In the West

Traveling west from the Interior Plains, you see many different landforms. There are tall mountains, deep valleys, green forests, vast deserts, and miles of rocky coastline.

The Rocky Mountains

The first mountains you see in the West are the **Rocky Mountains.** These mountains are also called the Rockies. They form North America's longest mountain range, or group of connected mountains. The Rockies stretch more than 3,000 miles from Mexico all the way to Alaska.

The Rockies are young mountains. They are steep, rugged, and tall. Wind and water have not yet worn down their peaks. More than 40 peaks in Colorado are higher than 14,000 feet.

West of the Rockies

West of the Rockies, you see that the land gets lower. You are now in the **Intermountain Region,** or the land between mountain ranges.

The Great Basin covers the middle part of the Intermountain Region. A **basin** is low, bowl-shaped land with higher ground around it. The Great Basin has some of the driest and lowest lands in North America.

The Great Basin lies between the Columbia Plateau in the north and the Colorado Plateau in the south. Much of the land on both plateaus is carved into canyons. A **canyon** is a deep, narrow valley with steep sides.

Pacific Mountains and Valleys

More mountains lie west of the Intermountain Region. The Sierra Nevada (see•AIR•ah ne•VAH•dah), Cascade Range, and Coast Ranges

▶ **THE GRAND CANYON** is one of the deepest and largest canyons in the world. It stretches about 280 miles across the Colorado Plateau in Arizona.

run through California, Oregon, and Washington. The Coast Ranges give the western coast of the United States a rocky, rugged look. In Alaska, the Alaska Range has the highest peak in North America, Mount McKinley.

Broad valleys spread between many of the Pacific Mountains. These valleys have rich soil that is good for growing crops.

READING CHECK ⬤MAIN IDEA AND DETAILS
What landforms cover the western United States?

Summary

The United States has many different landforms. Some parts of the country have tall mountains. Other parts have flat plains and plateaus or deep valleys and canyons. The United States also has long coastlines and many large rivers and lakes.

▶ **OLYMPIC NATIONAL PARK** The Olympic Mountains in Washington are home to many trees, ferns, mosses, and other plants.

REVIEW

1. **WHAT TO KNOW** What are the major landforms in the United States?

2. **VOCABULARY** What is the difference between a river's **source** and its **mouth**?

3. **HISTORY** What are the oldest mountains in North America?

4. **CRITICAL THINKING** Which landforms do you think are best for farming? Why?

5. 🖌 **MAKE POSTCARDS** On an index card, make a postcard that shows a landscape found in the United States. On the back of the card, describe what the picture shows.

6. (Focus Skill) **MAIN IDEA AND DETAILS**
   On a separate sheet of paper, copy and complete the graphic organizer below.

   Main Idea
   Many mountain ranges run through the western United States.

   Details

Use an Elevation Map

Why It Matters Elevation (eh•luh•VAY•shuhn) is the height of the land above sea level. An elevation map can tell you how high or how low different areas of the country are.

❯ LEARN

The map on page 25 uses colors to show a range of elevations. Each color stands for an area's highest and lowest elevations, as well as all the elevations in between.

The map also uses shading to show **relief**, or differences in elevation. Dark shading shows steep rises and drops in elevation. Light shading shows gentle rises and drops.

❯ PRACTICE

Use the map on page 25 to answer these questions.

❶ What is the elevation of Santa Fe, New Mexico? Is the land there higher or lower than the land near Boston, Massachusetts? How do you know?

❷ What is the elevation of Kansas City, Missouri?

❸ How does elevation change along the Mississippi River from its source to its mouth?

❯ APPLY

Imagine that you are planning a trip from Washington, D.C., to San Francisco, California. Place a ruler across the map to connect the two cities. Write the elevation of each city, and tell how the elevation will change as you travel.

Elevations of the United States

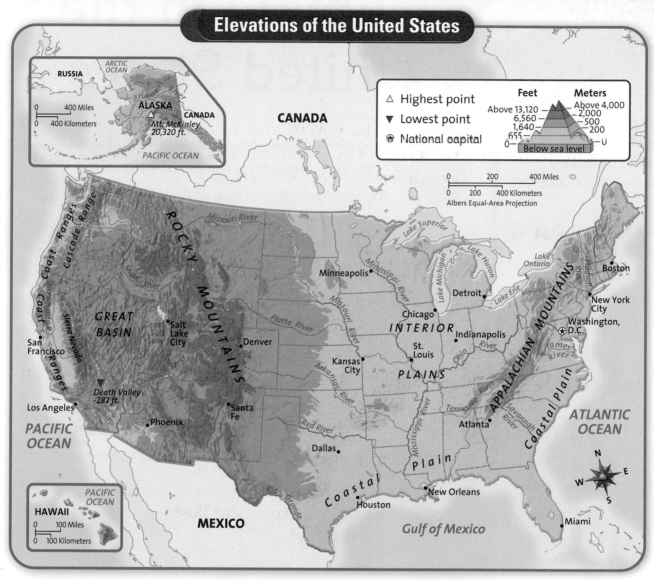

	Feet	Meters
△ Highest point	Above 13,120	Above 4,000
▼ Lowest point	6,560	2,000
	1,640	500
⊛ National capital	655	200
	Below sea level	0

RUSSIA
ARCTIC OCEAN
ALASKA
CANADA
Mt. McKinley
20,320 ft.
PACIFIC OCEAN
0 400 Miles
0 400 Kilometers

CANADA

0 200 400 Miles
0 200 400 Kilometers
Albers Equal-Area Projection

Coast Ranges
Cascade Range
Columbia R.
Snake River
Missouri River
Lake Superior
Lake Michigan
Lake Huron
Lake Ontario
Lake Erie
Hudson River
Boston
Minneapolis
Detroit
New York City
Chicago
Washington, D.C.
INTERIOR
Indianapolis
APPALACHIAN MOUNTAINS
GREAT BASIN
Great Salt Lake
Salt Lake City
ROCKY MOUNTAINS
Platte River
St. Louis
Denver
Mississippi River
Missouri River
James River
San Francisco
Sierra Nevada
Coast Ranges
PLAINS
Kansas City
Ohio River
Arkansas River
Coastal Plain
ATLANTIC OCEAN
Death Valley -282 ft.
Colorado River
Tennessee River
Savannah River
Los Angeles
Santa Fe
Atlanta
PACIFIC OCEAN
Phoenix
Red River
Mississippi River
Dallas
Coastal
Plain
Rio Grande
New Orleans
Houston
Miami
MEXICO
Gulf of Mexico
N E S W

HAWAII
PACIFIC OCEAN
0 100 Miles
0 100 Kilometers

▶ **MOUNT MCKINLEY, in Alaska, is the tallest mountain in North America. It has an elevation of 20,320 feet. Some people call the peak by its Native American name, *Denali* (duh•NAH•lee), which means "The Great One" or "The High One."**

Map and Globe Skills

Lesson 3

Climate in the United States

WHAT TO KNOW
Why are there big differences in climate across the United States?

VOCABULARY
temperature p. 27
precipitation p. 27
climate p. 27
humidity p. 28

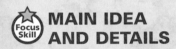

MAIN IDEA AND DETAILS

Main Idea

Details

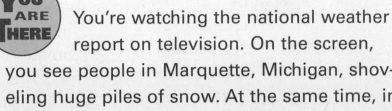

YOU ARE THERE

You're watching the national weather report on television. On the screen, you see people in Marquette, Michigan, shoveling huge piles of snow. At the same time, in Miami, Florida, children are playing on a sunny beach. A rainstorm floods the streets of Seattle, Washington. Meanwhile, the mayor of Las Vegas, Nevada, complains that the city's dry spell continues.

You wonder, "How can the weather be so different on the same day in the same country?"

The Big Picture

How would you describe today's weather where you live? You could talk about the **temperature**, or how hot or cold the air is. You could also talk about the amount of **precipitation** (prih•sih•puh•TAY•shuhn), or water that falls to Earth's surface as rain, sleet, or snow. You might mention how windy it is. The temperature, the wind, and the precipitation in a place on any given day make up the weather.

What Is Climate?

How would you describe the climate where you live? **Climate** is the kind of weather a place has over a long time. You might have a very cold winter one year, however, the climate there is usually warm and dry. To describe climate, you have to look for patterns in the weather over many years.

Effects of Weather and Climate

In a large country such as the United States, types of weather and climates vary from place to place. Still, no matter where you live, weather and climate play an important role in daily life. They affect what clothes people wear and where they choose to live. They can also affect how people earn a living and what they do for fun.

READING CHECK ⚙ **MAIN IDEA AND DETAILS**
What are the main factors that make up weather?

❱ **WEATHER has a great effect on people's daily lives. How did the weather in your community today affect you?**

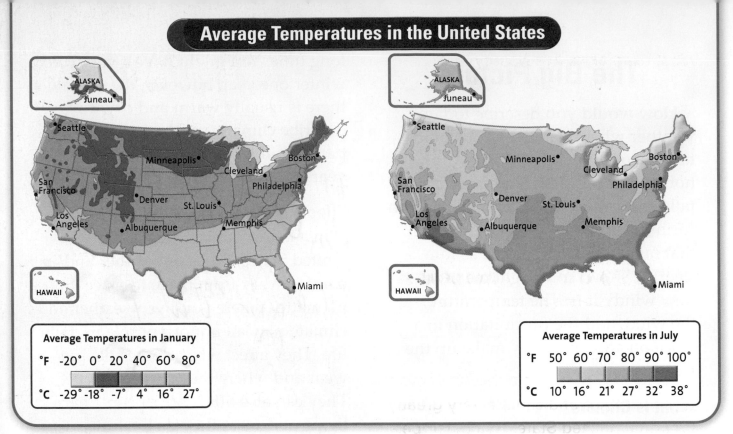

Average Temperatures in the United States

Average Temperatures in January

°F -20° 0° 20° 40° 60° 80°

°C -29° -18° -7° 4° 16° 27°

Average Temperatures in July

°F 50° 60° 70° 80° 90° 100°

°C 10° 16° 21° 27° 32° 38°

MAP SKILL **PLACE** These maps show the average January and July temperatures in the United States. Which city is colder in January—Minneapolis or Philadelphia? Which city is warmer in July—Cleveland or Denver?

A Variety of Climates

Different parts of the United States have very different climates. There are many reasons for the differences.

How Far from the Equator?

Places in the United States are located at different distances from the equator. Those distances affect climate. The sun's warming rays hit the equator directly all year round. As a result, the closer a place is to the equator, the warmer it usually is.

This explains why Hawaii has a much warmer climate than Alaska. Hawaii is the state closest to the equator, while Alaska is the state farthest from the equator.

What Is the Elevation?

Elevation also affects climate. In general, temperatures become cooler as you go higher above sea level. For this reason, although Hawaii's climate is mostly warm, its high mountain areas are cold.

How Far from the Ocean?

Oceans affect climate, too. They warm the land near the coast in winter and cool it in summer.

Oceans also add moisture, or **humidity** (hyoo•MIH•duh•tee), to the air. Humid, or moist, places usually get more rain than drier places. Because Hawaii is surrounded by the Pacific Ocean, it gets more rain than any other state.

What Landforms Are Nearby?

The landforms that are near a place also affect its climate. For example, the mountain ranges in the western United States act like walls. They block moist Pacific air from reaching land on their eastern side. As a result, eastern Oregon gets much less rain than western Oregon.

READING CHECK **⭐MAIN IDEA AND DETAILS**
How do oceans affect climate?

Summary

The weather and climate vary greatly across the United States. Wind, temperature, and precipitation affect weather. Distance from the equator, from sea level, and from the ocean influence a place's climate. Nearby landforms affect the climate of a place, too.

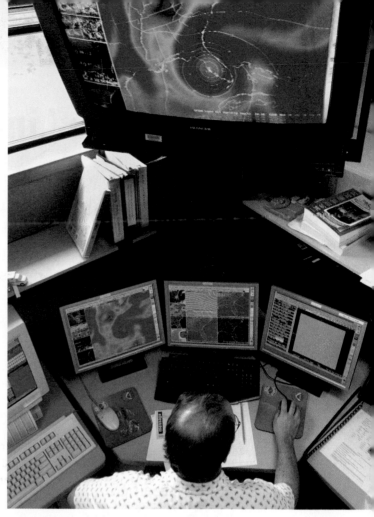

❯ **METEOROLOGY** Scientists use computers to study weather and climate.

REVIEW

1. **WHAT TO KNOW** Why are there big differences in climate across the United States?

2. **VOCABULARY** How are **humidity** and **precipitation** related?

3. **GEOGRAPHY** What is the difference between weather and climate?

4. **CRITICAL THINKING** How does the climate where you live affect your life?

5. **GIVE A WEATHER REPORT** Think about a day when you liked the weather. Write a one-minute report describing that day's weather. Then present the report to your classmates.

6. **(Focus Skill) MAIN IDEA AND DETAILS**

On a separate sheet of paper, copy and complete the graphic organizer below.

Main Idea

Weather and climate play an important role in people's lives.

Details

Read a Line Graph

Why It Matters People use numbers to measure the weather. Scientists look for patterns in those numbers over a long period of time to describe climate. A **line graph** can make it easier to find these patterns because it shows changes over time.

❯ LEARN

Follow these steps to read a line graph.

Step 1 Read the graph's title and labels. They tell you what information the graph gives.

Step 2 Use the dots and numbers on the graph to find specific data.

Step 3 Study the way the line on the graph slants. It tells you, in general, how the data changed over time.

❯ **DEATH VALLEY** During summer, Death Valley, in California, is one of the hottest places in the United States.

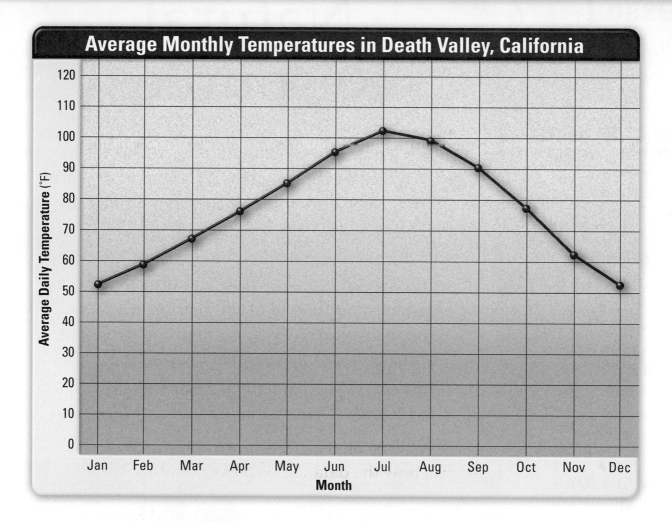

Average Monthly Temperatures in Death Valley, California

Average Daily Temperature (°F) / Month

▶ PRACTICE

Use the line graph to answer these questions.

1 Which is the hottest month in Death Valley? How can you tell from this graph?

2 How does the temperature of Death Valley change over the period of one year?

▶ APPLY

Record and graph the daily high temperatures in your community each day for a week. Then use your graph to write a paragraph describing the week's weather.

Chart and Graph Skills

Lesson

Natural Resources

WHAT TO KNOW
What are some important natural resources in the United States?

VOCABULARY

natural resource p. 32
renewable p. 33
groundwater p. 34
industry p. 34
mineral p. 35
nonrenewable p. 35
environment p. 36
conservation p. 36

MAIN IDEA AND DETAILS

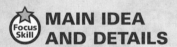

YOU ARE THERE You wake to the loud buzz of your alarm clock. You're still sleepy, but you head to the kitchen for breakfast. You pour a bowl of your favorite cereal and a big glass of juice. Then you brush your teeth, wash and dress, grab your backpack, and rush to catch the bus to school.

Just an ordinary morning, right? Maybe, but none of it would be possible without natural resources. What is a **natural resource**? It's something found in nature that people can use, such as water, soil, and trees.

Land Resources

The United States has many important natural resources. People depend on them to grow food, raise animals, and build homes.

Soil

Much of our nation has fertile soil, especially in its river valleys and on its plains. This rich soil helps farmers grow large amounts of food. Every year, farmers in the United States grow wheat, corn, fruits, soybeans, and other crops.

Ranchers in the United States also depend on soil. They need grasses and crops to feed their cattle and other livestock.

Trees

Trees grow well in many parts of our nation. In fact, forests cover nearly one-third of the land in the United States. People use trees to make homes and many wood products, such as furniture. Pencils and the paper in this book are made from trees, too.

Renewable Resources

Trees are an example of a resource that is **renewable**. People can plant new trees to replace the ones they use. However, trees need many years to grow. For this reason, people in the United States work together to use forest resources wisely.

READING CHECK Ŏ**MAIN IDEA AND DETAILS**
Why are natural resources important?

▶ **CORN FARMING** People started growing corn in North America more than 3,000 years ago. Today, corn is our nation's largest crop.

▶ **FISHING** American fishers catch about 10 billion pounds of fish and shellfish each year.

Water Resources

Water is perhaps our most important natural resource. People cannot survive more than a few days without it. People get fresh water from several sources and use it in many ways.

Getting Fresh Water

Lakes, rivers, streams, and groundwater supply almost all the fresh water people use. **Groundwater** is the water that sinks beneath Earth's surface when it rains or snows.

In some places, people dig deep wells to get groundwater. In others, people pump water from rivers or human-made lakes. They may dig ditches and lay pipes across the land to bring water into dry areas.

Using Water

People use water in many ways. They drink it and use it to wash and to cook. People also use water for boating and other activities for fun.

Industries use a lot of water, too. An **industry** is all the businesses that make one kind of product or provide one kind of service. For example, farmers need water to grow crops, and fishers catch fish in the water.

In some parts of the United States, water is used as a source of power. The energy from moving water can be used to produce electricity. That electricity lights homes and offices and runs machines in factories.

READING CHECK 👁 **MAIN IDEA AND DETAILS**
What are the major sources of fresh water?

Minerals and Fuels

Some natural resources are not as easy to see as water, trees, or soil. They are buried deep under the ground.

Minerals

Minerals (MIN•uh•ruhlz) are natural substances found in rocks. Copper, gold, silver, and other metals are minerals. They are used to make wire, coins, pots, and jewelry. Iron, marble, and limestone are used to construct buildings. Sand and gravel are used to build roads.

Fuels

Other underground resources are fuels. A fuel is a natural resource that is used to make heat or energy. The United States has large amounts of oil, natural gas, and coal. People use oil and natural gas to cook food, heat buildings, and run machines. They use oil and coal at power plants to produce electricity. Other industries use oil to make gasoline, plastics, paint, tires, and many other products.

Nonrenewable Resources

Minerals and fuels are examples of resources that are **nonrenewable**. They cannot be replaced. Once nonrenewable resources are used up, they are gone forever. Even renewable resources can become scarce, or limited, if overused. For this reason, Americans try to use natural resources wisely.

READING CHECK Ö**MAIN IDEA AND DETAILS**
How do people use fuels?

GRAPH An oil pump brings oil to the surface from underground. Which state is the top oil-producing state?

Top Oil-Producing States

Barrels of Oil per Year (in millions)

States: Texas, Alaska, California, Louisiana, New Mexico, Oklahoma, Wyoming

State

People and Resources

When people use natural resources, they change their **environment**. They change the surroundings in which people, plants, and animals live.

Using Resources Wisely

Over time, people have realized that all resources are limited. People today understand the importance of conservation (kahn•ser•VAY•shuhn). **Conservation** is the protecting of natural resources and using them wisely.

Using fewer natural resources is one way to conserve them. People can save oil by driving less. Many Americans also recycle, or reuse, products. Recycling paper, for example, conserves trees.

READING CHECK ⓞ **MAIN IDEA AND DETAILS**
Why is conservation important?

▶ **RECYCLING** People use recycled plastic bottles to make rugs, clothing, and playground equipment.

Summary

The United States is rich in natural resources. People depend on these resources to survive and live well. For this reason, Americans try to protect natural resources and use them wisely.

REVIEW

1. **WHAT TO KNOW** What are some important natural resources in the United States?

2. **VOCABULARY** Explain how a **renewable** resource differs from a **nonrenewable** resource.

3. **GEOGRAPHY** How do people use minerals?

4. **CRITICAL THINKING** How do people change their environment when they use natural resources?

5. **WRITE A LIST** List three activities that you did this morning before school. Explain how each activity on your list used natural resources.

6. **MAIN IDEA AND DETAILS**
On a separate sheet of paper, copy and complete the graphic organizer below.

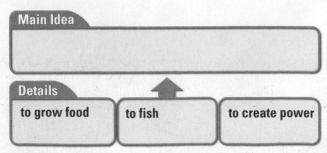

Main Idea

Details

| to grow food | to fish | to create power |

John Muir

Biography

Trustworthiness
Respect
Responsibility
Fairness
Caring
Patriotism

"I have done the best I could to show forth the beauty, grandeur, and all-embracing usefulness of our wild mountain forest reservations and parks."

John Muir (MYUR) wrote these words more than 100 years ago in his book *Our National Parks.* At that time, conservation was a new idea. Many people thought our nation's resources would last forever. Muir knew better. He dedicated his life to protecting the environment.

Muir traveled around much of the United States. The wild beauty of the country inspired him. Muir began writing articles and books urging people to protect and enjoy wilderness areas.

With a friend, Muir founded one of the nation's first environmental groups. He also persuaded the government to set up national parks. These parks included Yosemite National Park and Sequoia National Park in California. For these reasons, many people today call John Muir the Father of Our National Park System.

Why Character Counts

How did John Muir's actions show that he respected the environment?

Time

1838		1914
Born		Died

1892 Muir helps found the nation's first environmental group

1901 Muir publishes *Our National Parks*

GO ONLINE

For more resources, go to
www.harcourtschool.com/ss1

Visual Summary

The United States has a variety of landforms and bodies of water.

Summarize the Chapter

Focus Skill **Main Idea and Details** Complete this graphic organizer to show that you understand the important ideas and details about the geography of the United States.

Main Idea

The United States is diverse in its geography, climate, and natural resources.

Details

Vocabulary

Identify the term from the word bank that correctly matches each definition.

1. anything in nature that people can use, such as water, soil, and trees

2. all the businesses that make one kind of product or provide one kind of service

3. water that falls to Earth's surface in the form of rain, sleet, or snow

4. an imaginary line that divides Earth into the Northern and Southern Hemispheres

5. the height of the land above sea level

6. the surroundings in which people, plants, and animals live

7. features, such as mountains, hills, and valleys, that are on Earth's surface

8. the place where a river starts

Word Bank

equator p. 13	**precipitation** p. 27
landforms p. 18	**natural resource** p. 32
source p. 21	**industry** p. 34
elevation p. 24	**environment** p. 36

Scientists study the different climates in the United States.

The United States has many important natural resources.

 Facts and Main Ideas

Answer these questions.

9. In which hemispheres is the United States located?

10. What three features do people use to describe weather and climate?

11. Name one renewable resource and one nonrenewable resource.

Write the letter of the best choice.

12. Which of these statements best describes the relative location of the United States?
    A It is south of Mexico.
    B It is west of the Atlantic Ocean.
    C It is north of Canada.
    D It is east of the Gulf of Mexico.

13. Which landform stretches between the Appalachian Mountains and the Rocky Mountains?
    A Coastal Plain
    B Colorado Plateau
    C Interior Plains
    D Intermountain Region

14. Which of the following does not affect the climate of a place?
    A distance from the equator
    B distance from the forest
    C distance from sea level
    D distance from the ocean

 Critical Thinking

15. How do you think climate and landforms affect the activities people do for fun?

16. Why do you think most large cities in the United States are located along rivers?

Skills

Use Latitude and Longitude

17. Examine the map of the United States on page 17. Which city is located closest to 40°N, 105°W?

Read a Line Graph

18. Study the line graph on page 31. Which month is usually hotter in Death Valley—March or October?

Write an Informative Report
Write a report that describes the climate, landforms, and bodies of water in the place where you live. Include facts and details that tell what makes your area different from other areas.

Write a Summary Write a summary that describes two of the natural resources of the United States, the ways people use them, and the ways people change their environment when they use them.

STUDY SKILLS

USE VISUALS

Visuals can help you better understand and remember what you read.

- Photographs, illustrations, diagrams, charts, and maps are different kinds of visuals. Many visuals have titles, captions, or labels that help readers understand what is shown.

- Often, the information in visuals is also in the text, but the visuals show the information in a different way. Visuals may also show new information.

Checklist for Visuals

✓	What kind of visual is shown? a photograph
	What does the visual show?
	What does the visual tell you about the topic?
	How does the visual help you understand what you are reading?

PREVIEW VOCABULARY

patriotism p. 43

population p. 45

government p. 50

We the People

The United States Capitol, in Washington, D.C.

Lesson

Time

1500   1750   Present

Early 1500s
The first Europeans
settle in the Americas

1820
Millions of people begin to
arrive in the United States

1920
Most Americans
live in cities

WHAT TO KNOW
Why do Americans have different ways of life, and what unites them?

VOCABULARY
culture p. 43
patriotism p. 43
immigrate p. 44
population p. 45
rural p. 45
urban p. 45
suburb p. 45

MAIN IDEA AND DETAILS

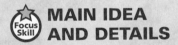

Main Idea

Details

The American People

YOU ARE THERE You and your family have watched other Fourth of July parades, but this one will be special. You have come to Washington, D.C., the nation's capital, to celebrate Independence Day. As you look around at the thousands of spectators lining Constitution Avenue, you see people of different backgrounds and ways of life. Like you, they are waving American flags. Like you, they are proud to be Americans!

▶ **AMERICANS** These children may have many different backgrounds, but they are all Americans.

▶ **MOUNT RUSHMORE NATIONAL MONUMENT** This monument honors George Washington, Thomas Jefferson, Theodore Roosevelt, and Abraham Lincoln.

The American Nation

The United States is a nation of great diversity, or many differences. Americans come from many different **cultures**, or ways of life. Yet many things unite us.

What We Share

As Americans, we are proud of our nation. We share our **patriotism**, or love of country. We celebrate holidays that mark important events in our history. For example, the Fourth of July honors the beginning of our nation.

Monuments all over the United States help Americans remember the people and events that have shaped our nation. The Washington Monument in Washington, D.C., for example, honors George Washington, the nation's first President.

Out of Many, One

The United States has a motto, or saying, that describes the American people—*E Pluribus Unum*. These Latin words mean "Out of Many, One." People of different cultures and from many countries have come to this country. Together, we have become something new—Americans.

READING CHECK Ŏ**MAIN IDEA AND DETAILS**
What are two things that Americans share?

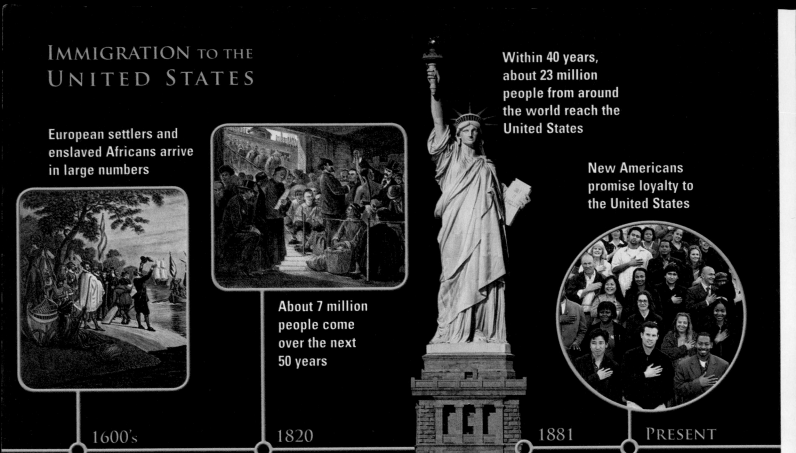

IMMIGRATION TO THE UNITED STATES

European settlers and enslaved Africans arrive in large numbers

About 7 million people come over the next 50 years

Within 40 years, about 23 million people from around the world reach the United States

New Americans promise loyalty to the United States

1600's   1820   1881   PRESENT

Who Are Americans?

We Americans have many different backgrounds and cultures. The reason is that we have come from places all over the world.

The First Americans

No one knows for sure how or when the first people came to the Americas. There are many different ideas. One idea is that long ago, hunters traveled to North America from Asia. Over thousands of years, more and more people followed.

After early people reached North America, they kept moving to the east and to the south. Over time, the groups now called Native Americans, or American Indians, settled across North America and South America.

Later Arrivals

Native Americans were the only people in the Americas until the late 1400s. Then explorers from Europe began to arrive—followed by settlers. Also, at this time, people from Africa were forced to come to the Americas and to work without pay.

After the United States became a country, a large number of people immigrated here. To **immigrate** is to come to a country to make a new life. These people, or immigrants, came to the United States from all over the world. So many people came that in the 1850s, Herman Melville wrote, "We are not a nation, so much as a world."

READING CHECK ☉MAIN IDEA AND DETAILS
Who were the first people to live in what is now the United States?

Where Americans Live

As waves of immigrants continued to arrive, the population of the United States grew. **Population** is the total number of people who live in a place.

Almost 300 million people now live in the United States. We all live in one country, but the kinds of places where we live have changed over time.

From Farms to Cities

Until the late 1800s, most Americans lived in **rural** areas, or in the country-side. Many families lived and worked on farms. By 1920, more Americans lived in **urban** areas, or cities, than on farms. These cities grew as businesses created more jobs.

From Cities to Suburbs

As cities grew, some people chose to move to **suburbs**—towns or small cities near a large city. In the 1950s, many families moved from large cities to the suburbs. One of the first suburban areas in the United States was Levittown, New York.

Today, more than four-fifths of Americans live in cities or in suburbs. Like Levittown, suburban areas today are usually more spread out than cities. Instead of living in tall apartment buildings, most people in suburban areas live in houses with yards.

Many suburban people go to the city for work or entertainment. City people often travel to the suburbs to shop at malls.

Children IN HISTORY

Gene Schermerhorn

Imagine New York City with dirt roads, horse-drawn carts, and barns filled with cows and pigs. That is what Twenty-third Street was like when six-year-old Gene Schermerhorn moved there in 1848. Young Gene had fun trying to lasso pigs. He also liked to swim in Beekman's Pond.

The city soon changed. Overhead wires brought electricity to Gene's neighborhood. Barns gave way to tall apartment buildings. Streets were paved, and Beekman's Pond was filled in so a new street could be built.

Gene's family moved away. When he was 45 years old, Gene visited his old city block. He could hardly believe the changes!

Make It Relevant What changes have taken place in your neighborhood?

Moving to Warmer Climates

Just 50 years ago, most Americans lived in the northeastern and in the central parts of the United States. In recent years, many Americans have moved south and west. Many have moved there to enjoy the warmer climates of states such as Florida and Arizona. Today, three-fifths of Americans live in the southern and western parts of the country.

READING CHECK ✪**MAIN IDEA AND DETAILS**
In which parts of the country do most Americans live?

Summary

Immigration has made the United States one of the most diverse nations in the world. Today, Americans have different ways of life and live in different kinds of places. Yet patriotism unites us.

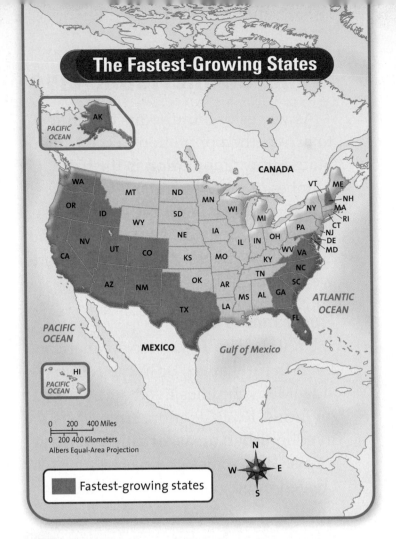

The Fastest-Growing States

■ Fastest-growing states

MAP SKILL **REGIONS** Which of the fastest-growing states border the Gulf of Mexico?

REVIEW

1. **WHAT TO KNOW** Why do Americans have different ways of life, and what unites them?

2. **VOCABULARY** Write a sentence explaining how a **suburb** is related to an **urban** area.

3. **HISTORY** When did many families in the United States begin to move from large cities to the suburbs?

4. **CRITICAL THINKING** Why do you think new cultures formed when people moved to the United States?

5. ✎ **WRITE A MOTTO** Write a motto for your school. Make sure it tells something important about your school and its students.

6. (Focus Skill) **MAIN IDEA AND DETAILS**

On a separate sheet of paper, copy and complete the graphic organizer below.

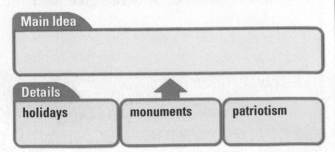

Main Idea

Details
holidays   monuments   patriotism

Francis Scott Key

Biography

Trustworthiness
Respect
Responsibility
Fairness
Caring
Patriotism

"I saw the flag of my country waving over a city—the strength and pride of my native State...."

Francis Scott Key was born in Maryland in 1779. In 1814, British soldiers attacked the United States. At first, Key was opposed to the war. However, Key's love of country quickly inspired him to join the fight and serve as a general's aide.

The British captured Key's friend Dr. William Beanes. They held him prisoner on a ship in Baltimore Harbor. Key went to the ship to get Beanes released. The British agreed to release him. Even so, they held Keys and Beanes on the ship until after the British attack on Fort McHenry, which guarded the harbor.

The attack lasted for 25 hours. All the while, Key kept his eyes on the fort's flag. As long as it flew, Americans still held the fort. During the night, silence fell.

At dawn, Key saw that the American flag still flew over Fort McHenry. The British then freed Key and Beanes. On their boat trip home, Key wrote the poem that became known as "The Star-Spangled Banner."

Why Character Counts

In what ways did Key display patriotism?

Time

1779 — Born
1843 — Died

1800 Key becomes a lawyer

1814 Key writes a poem after watching the attack on Fort McHenry

GO ONLINE
For more resources, go to
www.harcourtschool.com/ss1

Symbols of Patriotism

"Hats off!
Along the street there comes
A blare of bugles, a ruffle of drums,
A flash of color beneath the sky:
Hats off!
The flag is passing by!"

—from "The Flag Goes By" by Henry Holcomb Bennett

OUR FLAG

These poetic words describe a symbol of patriotism for the United States—the American flag. Symbols stand for important ideas or beliefs. Some symbols can be seen and touched, such as flags and statues. Other symbols cannot always be seen or touched, but they certainly affect our feelings. They include songs, poems, and mottoes. The American flag is one of our country's best-known symbols of patriotism. It has been a symbol since the creation of the first official American flag in 1777.

▶ PLEDGE OF ALLEGIANCE Many people show patriotism by reciting the Pledge of Allegiance to the flag (above left).

▶ **THE LIBERTY BELL** (left) hangs in Philadelphia, Pennsylvania, today.

Americans also have other symbols that express their patriotism. Each symbol has a special meaning. Each one reminds us about ideas or beliefs that are part of patriotism. The Liberty Bell was rung on July 8, 1776, to celebrate the first public reading of the Declaration of Independence. The bell is a reminder of the freedom for which Americans have been and are willing to fight. The Statue of Liberty in New York Harbor is another symbol. It reminds people that the United States offers freedom and opportunities to people all over the world.

Make It Relevant How do you think symbols of patriotism help unite Americans?

▶ **THE BALD EAGLE** (above) was made the national bird of the United States in 1782. The Statue of Liberty (below) holds a lighted torch that represents liberty.

United States Government

WHAT TO KNOW
How is the United States government organized?

VOCABULARY
government p. 50
constitution p. 51
democracy p. 51
republic p. 51
legislative branch p. 52
executive branch p. 52
judicial branch p. 53
checks and balances p. 53
majority rule p. 54

PEOPLE
Benjamin Franklin
George Washington

PLACES
Philadelphia

MAIN IDEA AND DETAILS
Focus Skill

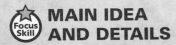

YOU ARE THERE The year is 1787. American leaders are gathering in **Philadelphia.** Their job is to make a government for the United States. A **government** is a system of leaders and laws for making decisions for a community, state, or nation.

You watch as **Benjamin Franklin** enters the Pennsylvania State House. "That is Benjamin Franklin," your mother whispers. "He will help **George Washington** and the others make a strong, fair government."

A Plan of Government

In 1787, the United States was a new country. It needed a strong government to make and carry out laws.

The Constitution

George Washington, Benjamin Franklin, and 53 other leaders worked for four months. Finally, they agreed on a **constitution**, or plan of government. The Constitution explains how our nation's democracy works. In a **democracy**, people can elect leaders to govern them. This makes the United States a **republic**, a government that gets its power from the people. In fact, the Constitution begins

66 We the people . . . 99

The Duties of Government

The Constitution says that it is the "supreme law of the land." In other words, the Constitution contains our nation's highest laws. Everyone must obey those laws, including leaders.

The Constitution explains what the United States government should do. It says that the government should treat all Americans fairly and protect their freedom. It gives the government the right to have an army, to declare war, and to make peace. It also allows the government to make paper money and coins. The Constitution explains how the government takes care of issues that affect all Americans.

READING CHECK ⚙ **MAIN IDEA AND DETAILS**
What form of government does the United States have?

❯ **OUR NATION'S FOUNDERS** worked together to create the United States Constitution.

The Three Branches

Our Constitution also describes how the national, or federal, government is organized. It lists three branches, or parts, of the government and tells what each one does.

The Legislative Branch

The **legislative branch** makes the laws. The main body in the legislative branch is Congress. It is made up of two parts, the Senate and the House of Representatives, or the House.

Voters in each state elect two senators to represent them in the Senate. The number of representatives each state has in the House depends on its population. States with large populations have the most representatives.

The Executive Branch

The **executive branch** carries out the laws that Congress makes. The leader of the executive branch is the President of the United States. Voters elect a President every four years.

Upon taking office, the President promises to preserve, protect, and defend the Constitution of the United States. This oath is a reminder that the Constitution is the highest law of our country. Even the President must obey what the Constitution says.

The President has one of the most important and difficult jobs in the world. The President deals with other countries. The President is also the leader of the United States military.

The Presidential Seal

Background This important symbol of our federal government is stamped on all official documents that the President signs.

The 50 stars stand for the 50 states.

The bald eagle is our national bird. The eagle holds an olive branch—a symbol of peace.

Our nation's motto, *E Pluribus Unum*, means "Out of Many, One."

The bald eagle holds arrows to show that the nation will defend itself.

DBQ Document-Based Question Why do you think the eagle holds both an olive branch and arrows?

Branches of the Federal Government

LEGISLATIVE BRANCH	EXECUTIVE BRANCH	JUDICIAL BRANCH
Writes laws that are used by the entire nation	Enforces, or carries out, national laws	Makes sure that laws follow the Constitution

CHART Which branch of the federal government writes laws that are used by the entire nation?

The Judicial Branch

The **judicial branch** is made up of the Supreme Court and certain other courts. These courts have the job of making sure that laws agree with the Constitution. They also see that laws are carried out fairly.

The Supreme Court is the nation's highest court. Its nine judges, called justices, are chosen by the President and approved by Congress. Once appointed, justices may serve for life.

Checks and Balances

The writers of the Constitution wanted to make sure that one branch of the government did not become too powerful. To do this, they created a system of **checks and balances**. It provides ways for each branch to limit, or check, the power of the other branches.

READING CHECK ⚙️**MAIN IDEA AND DETAILS**
Why do you think the federal government has three branches?

➤ WASHINGTON, D.C.

The Role of Citizens

The Constitution is about both the government and the people. It lists rights and freedoms that Americans have and describes the duties of American citizens.

Rights and Freedoms

Under the Constitution, decisions are made by **majority rule**. Each citizen who is at least 18 years old gets one vote. The person or idea that gets the most votes wins. The right to choose leaders and make decisions by majority rule is an important right of American citizens.

The Bill of Rights is a part of the Constitution that lists many rights and freedoms that Americans have. These include freedom of speech, freedom of the press, and freedom of religion.

The Bill of Rights also gives Americans the right to petition the government to change a law. A petition is a signed request. Citizens may sign petitions to ask for a new law or to change an old one.

The Bill of Rights also provides protection for Americans who are accused of crimes. An accused person has a right to a trial by jury. A group of citizens, called a jury, decides if the person is innocent or not.

➤ **VOTING is both a right and a responsibility of citizenship.**

⚡ FAST FACT

In the 2004 presidential election, nearly two-thirds of all United States citizens age 18 and over voted.

Duties of Citizens

Americans have duties that balance their rights. The right to choose leaders is balanced by the duty to vote in elections. The right to a trial by jury is balanced by the duty to serve on a jury when called.

The government trains and pays soldiers to protect the country in times of war. It also helps people rebuild after floods and other natural disasters. In return, citizens have the duty to pay the costs of running the government.

The Constitution gives the government the right to collect taxes to pay these costs. Most people pay an income tax, which is a part of the money they earn at their jobs.

READING CHECK Ŏ**MAIN IDEA AND DETAILS**
What are two rights and two duties that Americans have?

❯ **SOLDIERS** Members of the National Guard pass out water to those in need.

Summary

The Constitution tells how the United States government is organized. It describes the duties of the legislative, executive, and judicial branches. It also describes the rights of citizens.

REVIEW

1. **WHAT TO KNOW** How is the United States government organized?

2. **VOCABULARY** Write a sentence explaining what a **democracy** is.

3. **CIVICS AND GOVERNMENT** Which branch of the government decides if laws agree with the Constitution?

4. **CRITICAL THINKING** How does the Constitution help unite Americans?

5. ✎ **WRITE A PETITION** Think of a law that you think should be changed or a new law that should be passed. Make a petition for classmates to sign. Be sure to explain why the law should be changed or passed.

6. (Focus Skill) **MAIN IDEA AND DETAILS**
On a separate sheet of paper, copy and complete the graphic organizer below.

Main Idea

The United States government has three branches.

Details

FIELD TRIP

READ ABOUT

In 1790, government leaders agreed that the United States needed a capital city. They decided that it should not be part of any state. Maryland and Virginia each gave some land for a national capital. George Washington picked the exact spot where the city was built, along the Potomac River.

Government leaders decided to name the capital city Washington, D.C. The first part of the capital's name—Washington— honors George Washington, our nation's first president. The second part of the name— D.C.—stands for District of Columbia. This part honors Christopher Columbus.

FIND

MARYLAND

Washington, D.C.

VIRGINIA

WASHINGTON, D.C.

THE NATIONAL MALL (right) in Washington, D.C., is a park surrounded by national museums, monuments, and important government buildings. The Washington Monument (above) stands near the center of the mall.

THE WHITE HOUSE

VIETNAM VETERANS MEMORIAL

NATIONAL ARCHIVES

SMITHSONIAN MUSEUM

LINCOLN MEMORIAL

A VIRTUAL TOUR

GO **ONLINE**
For more resources, go to
www.harcourtschool.com/ss1

Lesson 3 United States Economy

WHAT TO KNOW
How does the United States economy work?

VOCABULARY

economy p. 58
free market p. 59
factors of production p. 59
profit p. 60
supply p. 60
demand p. 60
manufacturing p. 61
service industry p. 61

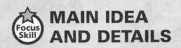

MAIN IDEA AND DETAILS

> **YOU ARE THERE**
Every Saturday you and your uncle shop for fresh foods at the farmers' market.

"How's business, Mrs. Eastman?" your uncle asks as he pays for a jar of honey.

"Great!" she replies. "The economy is booming."

"What's an economy?" you ask your uncle.

"Well," he answers, "the **economy** is all the producing, selling, and buying that people do. It's all the ways people use resources to meet their needs."

> **SHOPPING** This worker and customer at a farmers' market are both part of our nation's economy.

▶ **BUILDING** Construction companies need workers, materials, and equipment to build houses.

A Free Market Economy

In the United States, the economic activities of people have little government control. This kind of economy is called a **free market** economy. It is also called a free enterprise economy. Here, people can make, sell, and buy almost anything they want to. They can start almost any kind of business.

The government does set some limits. For example, businesses are not allowed to sell certain dangerous products. Also, businesses must offer a safe workplace, and they must limit the pollution they cause.

Factors of Production

In a free market economy, people—not the government—own or manage the resources that businesses need. As you have learned, one kind of resource is natural resources. They include land, water, minerals, and fuels. Another kind of resource is capital resources, such as money, buildings, and equipment. The third kind of resource is human resources, or workers. These three kinds of resources are called the **factors of production**.

READING CHECK ◉ **MAIN IDEA AND DETAILS**
In a free market economy, who makes most of the decisions about a business?

How Business Works

Think of all the businesses that you know about. Some businesses, like the company that made your shoes, are large. Others, like a neighborhood pet-sitting business, may be small. As different as businesses are, they all have a few basic things in common.

Making a Profit

The goal of most businesses is to make a profit. **Profit** is the money that a business has left after it pays all its bills. If you owned a business, how would you try to make a profit? You would probably keep your costs as low as possible. You would try to choose the best price for your product and sell as much of it as you could.

Supply and Demand

In deciding how much you could charge, you would consider supply and demand. **Supply** is the amount of a product or service that is available. **Demand** is the amount of a product or service that people want and are willing to pay for.

Imagine that you sell honey at a farmers' market. If you only have a little honey (weak supply), and many people want to buy it (strong demand), you might charge $7 a jar. If many farmers are selling honey (strong supply), and few people want to buy it (weak demand), you might lower your price to $5.

READING CHECK ☼**MAIN IDEA AND DETAILS**
What is the goal of most businesses?

Economic Activities

Agriculture

Service

A Diverse Economy

The United States is a large country with a varied geography and a diverse population. As a result, the United States also has a diverse economy.

Growing and Producing Items

In the past, agriculture, or farming, was the main economic activity in our country. Today, agriculture is still important, but it is a smaller part of the economy.

As cities grew, manufacturing became a larger part of the economy. **Manufacturing** is the making of products. Most manufacturing is done in large factories. The United States is a leading producer, or manufacturer, of cars, steel, and many other products.

Service Industries

Today, service industries make up the largest part of our economy. A **service industry** is a business in which people are paid to do things for other people. For example, a service worker might repair a customer's car or help someone open a bank account.

About four out of every five workers in the United States now have jobs in service industries. They include nurses, doctors, store clerks, lawyers, caregivers, and plumbers. People who work for the government, such as public school teachers and police officers, have service jobs, too.

READING CHECK ☕**MAIN IDEA AND DETAILS**
What are three main industries in the economy of the United States?

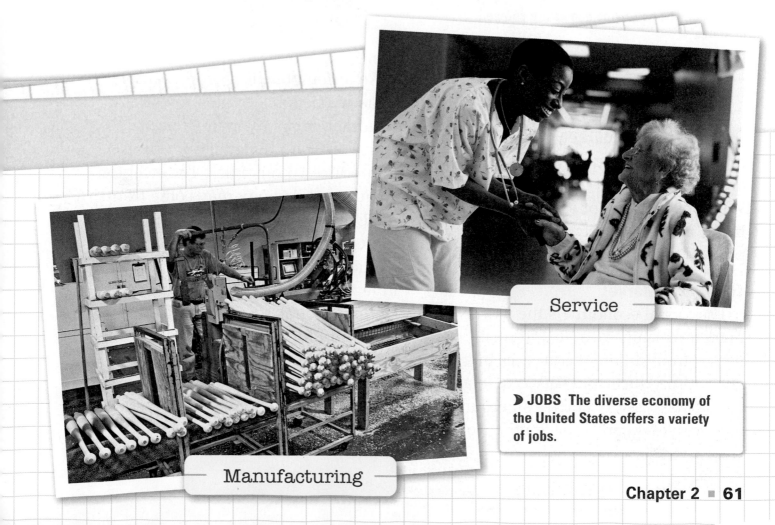

Service

Manufacturing

▶ **JOBS** The diverse economy of the United States offers a variety of jobs.

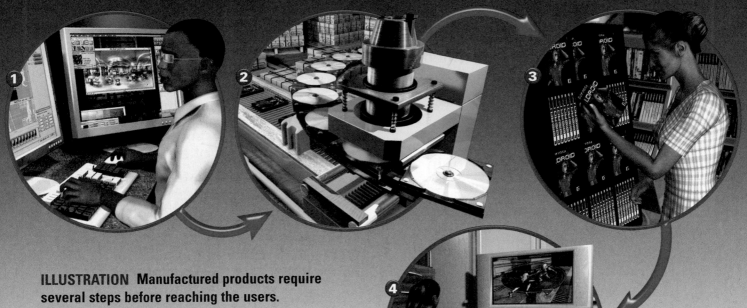

ILLUSTRATION Manufactured products require several steps before reaching the users.
1. Designers use computers to form pictures and sound.
2. Materials are assembled.
3. The games are shipped to stores around the world.
4. Users enjoy the games at home.

What happens before the games are shipped to stores?

A Global Economy

At a farmers' market, all the sellers and buyers are usually from one local area. They are part of a local economy. When people buy or sell products made in other countries, they become part of the global economy.

The World Market

The global economy is the world market in which people and businesses from different countries buy and sell products and services. In a global economy, countries all around the world depend on each other for goods and services.

An automobile is a good example of how the global economy works. Automobile manufacturers need many different materials and parts to produce automobiles. The steel for an automobile body may come from the United States or China. The glass for its windows may be produced in Mexico. The CD player may be made in Japan. Leather for the seats may be shipped from Argentina. The factory that assembles all these materials and parts may be in the United States or another country. Although the factory may be in the United States, it may be owned by a company in another country.

Global Workers, Global Buyers

Workers are also part of the global economy. For example, a company in the United States may hire workers in India to write software for its computers. A company in China may hire Americans to translate product instructions into English.

People even travel to different parts of the world to buy services. For example, many people from other countries come to the United States to go to college.

The global economy provides more opportunities for American businesses and buyers. American products and services can find new customers in other countries. The products and services of other countries offer more choices to American buyers.

READING CHECK ⏺ **MAIN IDEA AND DETAILS**
How are workers a part of the global economy?

▶ **GLOBAL MONEY** Most countries print their own money.

Summary

The United States has a free market economy. Agriculture, manufacturing, and service industries are the main parts of this economy. American businesses and citizens are also part of the global economy.

REVIEW

1. **WHAT TO KNOW** How does the United States economy work?

2. **VOCABULARY** Give examples of **manufacturing** and **service industries**.

3. **ECONOMICS** How is the United States economy different now than it was in the past?

4. **CRITICAL THINKING** What is one way in which you take part in the global economy?

5. ✏️ **WRITE A BUSINESS PLAN** Write a paragraph about a business you would like to start. Tell what you will sell and why people will want it.

6. ⭐(Focus Skill) **MAIN IDEA AND DETAILS**
   On a separate sheet of paper, copy and complete the graphic organizer below.

   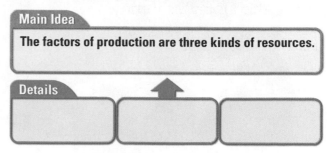

   Main Idea
   The factors of production are three kinds of resources.

   Details

Make an Economic Choice

Why It Matters When you make decisions about what to buy, you are making economic choices.

❯ LEARN

Sometimes you want to buy two items but only have enough money for one. If you give up one thing to buy another, you make a **trade-off**. What you do not buy becomes the **opportunity cost**. Follow these steps to make good economic choices.

Step 1 List three items that you would like to buy and how much each one costs.

Step 2 Decide how much money you have, how much you want to spend, and how much you want to save.

Step 3 Decide what you can buy with the money. Think about the trade-offs and opportunity costs.

Step 4 Make an economic choice. Then think about whether your decision was the best choice.

❯ **ECONOMIC CHOICES** People make choices when they use banks (left) or buy goods (below).

❯ PRACTICE

Imagine that your class is going on a field trip to a park. There, you want to rent a bike for $13. You also want to buy a T-shirt that costs $11. You have $15 to spend. Use these steps to make your economic choice.

1 What are your choices, and how much does each one cost?

2 How much money do you want to spend?

3 What is the trade-off and the opportunity cost of each economic choice? Which item do you want more?

4 Make and explain your choice.

❯ APPLY

Think of two products or services that you would like to buy. Suppose that you have enough money to buy one item, but not both. Explain to a partner the trade-off and opportunity cost of your choice.

❯ **DAILY DECISIONS** Even a visit to a park can include economic choices.

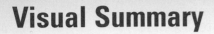
Visual Summary

Early 1500s
Europeans settle in
North America

Summarize the Chapter

Main Idea and Details Complete this graphic organizer to show that you understand the important ideas and details about the people, government, and economy of the United States.

Main Idea

The United States is a diverse nation.

Details

 Vocabulary

Write a sentence or two to explain how the terms in each pair are related.

1. **immigrate** (p. 44), **population** (p. 45)

2. **urban** (p. 45), **rural** (p. 45)

3. **government** (p. 50), **constitution** (p. 51)

4. **democracy** (p. 51), **majority rule** (p. 54)

5. **economy** (p. 58), **free market** (p. 59)

6. **supply** (p. 60), **demand** (p. 60)

 Time Line

Use the chapter summary time line above to answer these questions.

7. In the early 1500's, who began to settle in North America?

8. What important event happened in 1787, and why was it important?

9. What industry makes up the largest part of today's economy?

1787
United States leaders write the Constitution

Today
Service industries make up the largest part of the economy

TEST PREP Facts and Main Ideas

Answer these questions.

10. Why is the United States considered ". . . not so much a nation as a world"?

11. How is life in a suburb different from life in a city?

12. Why does the government collect taxes?

13. What kinds of activities make up an economy?

Write the letter of the best choice.

14. What are you describing when you talk about a group's language, religion, arts, foods, or clothing?
    A culture
    B demands
    C mottoes
    D patriotism

15. What is the main job of the legislative branch of the government?
    A to make laws
    B to carry out laws
    C to enforce laws
    D to interpret laws

16. Which of the following is an example of a manufacturing business?
    A coal mine
    B dairy farm
    C shoe factory
    D bookstore

TEST PREP Critical Thinking

17. How do you think immigration has affected life in the United States?

18. Why does a democracy depend on active citizens?

19. How has the economy of the United States changed over time?

TEST PREP Skills

Make an Economic Choice

20. Think about an economic choice you or someone you know has made recently. What were the trade-offs involved? What were the opportunity costs?

writing

Write a Report Write a short report about how the population of the United States has changed since it became a country. Be sure to include a description of how the places where most Americans live have changed over time.

Write a Summary Think about the rights and duties of citizens of the United States. Then write a summary that tells how those rights and duties are related.

STUDY SKILLS

ORGANIZE INFORMATION

A graphic organizer can help you make sense of the facts you read.

- Tables, charts, and webs are graphic organizers that can show main ideas and other important information.

- A graphic organizer can help you classify and categorize information. It can also help you understand the relationship between the topic of the chapter and the topic of each lesson.

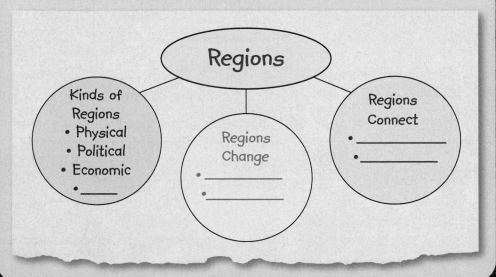

Regions

Kinds of Regions
- Physical
- Political
- Economic
- _____

Regions Change
- _____
- _____

Regions Connect
- _____
- _____

PREVIEW VOCABULARY

region p. 71

technology p. 74

county p. 80

Regions Around You

Yosemite National Park, in California

Lesson 1

Understanding Regions

💡 **WHAT TO KNOW**
Why do people divide places into regions?

VOCABULARY

region p. 71
interdependence p. 71
natural vegetation p. 72
ethnic group p. 73
modify p. 74
technology p. 74
communication p. 74

⭐ **Focus Skill**

MAIN IDEA AND DETAILS

Main Idea

Details

YOU ARE THERE You and your family are driving across the United States, from the Atlantic Ocean to the Pacific. Day by day, the view from the window changes. You drive through forests, grasslands, and deserts. You stop in big cities and small towns. You try new foods, like catfish in Mississippi and chilies in New Mexico. No two places are exactly alike. Yet every place has some things in common with the places around it.

❯ **VISITING REGIONS** This scrapbook shows only a few of the many regions you could pass through during a trip across the United States.

Summer Roadtrip

What Are Regions?

Think of all the different landforms, climates, countries, people, and industries that are part of our world. It would be difficult to describe them all at the same time.

For this reason, people divide the world into regions. A **region** is an area with at least one feature that makes it different from other areas.

A Variety of Regions

Each place in the United States is part of many kinds of regions. The place where you live may be part of an urban region, a coastal region, and a Spanish-speaking region. Instead, it may be part of a rural region, a desert region, and a mining region.

A region may be large or small. The continent of North America is a region. The neighborhood where you live is a region, too. Understanding regions makes it easier to understand the world. We can talk about how the places are alike and different.

Regions Depend on One Another

Regions differ, but they still depend on one another. Animals in a desert region may depend on rivers that flow out of a mountain region. People in urban regions depend on farming regions for food. These are examples of **interdependence**—people and places depending on one another for resources, products, and services.

READING CHECK Ö**MAIN IDEA AND DETAILS**
What is one example of a region?

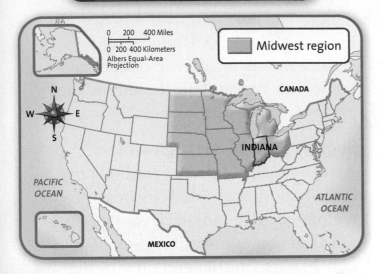

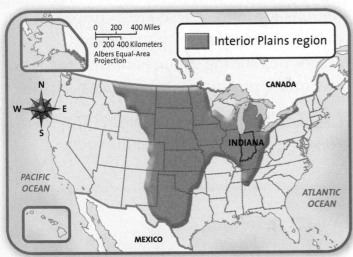

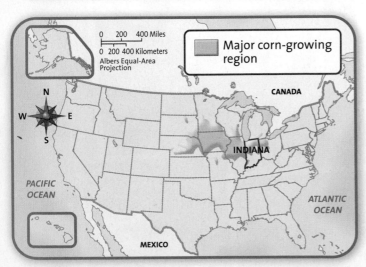

REGIONS This map shows that a place can be part of more than one region at the same time. What are three regions that the state of Indiana is part of?

Kinds of Regions

People create many kinds of regions. However, regions can be sorted into four main types.

Political Regions

A political region is a place where people share a government. Every state, city, and town is a political region. The United States is also a political region.

Creating political regions helps people live and govern in an organized way. All the people who live in a city follow the same local laws and have the same city leaders. They also know exactly where their city begins and ends. A city's boundaries, or borders, are set by law.

Physical Regions

Physical regions are based on natural features. These features include landforms, rivers, climates, or the kinds of wildlife that live in an area. Physical regions also may be based on natural vegetation. **Natural vegetation** is the plant life that grows in an area.

Physical regions are based on nature, but people still define them. A forest ranger, for example, might divide the United States into regions. These regions might be based on the kinds of trees that grow in different places.

Unlike political regions, physical regions do not have exact borders. For example, the change from one landform region or climate region to another happens gradually.

> CHINATOWN, a neighborhood in San Francisco, California, is an example of a cultural region.

Economic Regions

Economic regions are based on the way people in an area use resources to meet their needs. For example, many people in Texas, Louisiana, and Oklahoma earn a living by drilling for oil. Others earn a living by making products from oil. For this reason, these three states could be grouped together as one economic region—an oil-producing region.

Most places belong to several different economic regions at the same time. Oklahoma is not only an oil-producing region. The state also has many farms, ranches, factories, and service industries.

Cultural Regions

A cultural region is an area in which the people share certain ways of life. A cultural region may be defined by religion, by language, or by the main ethnic group that lives there. An **ethnic group** is made up of people from the same country or people with a shared way of life.

The United States has a variety of cultural regions. At the same time, the entire United States could be called a cultural region. The reason is that everyone who lives here shares certain American ways of life.

READING CHECK ⟳ MAIN IDEA AND DETAILS
What are the four main types of regions?

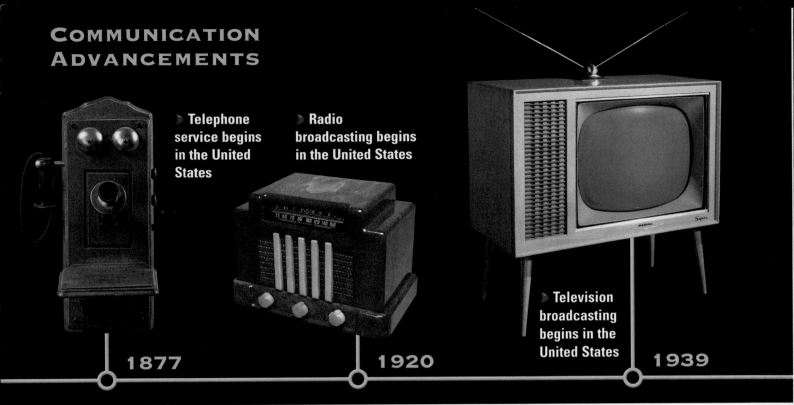

> Telephone service begins in the United States

> Radio broadcasting begins in the United States

> Television broadcasting begins in the United States

1877

1920

1939

Regions Change and Connect

All regions develop and change over time. Many changes are caused by natural events. Regions also change when people **modify**, or change, the environment to meet their needs.

People Change Regions

The United States started with 13 states. Today, it has 50 states. This example is just one of how people can change political regions.

As our nation grew, people also changed many physical regions. They blocked the flow of rivers to get more water and power. They cleared trees to make way for farms and towns.

Years later, some businesses built factories near the farm towns. Agricultural regions changed to manufacturing regions. In many places, immigrants then moved to the towns to work in the factories. As a result, the town's cultural regions changed and rural farm towns became urban regions.

People Connect Regions

People make connections between regions. Streets, highways, railroads, and airports link regions. They allow people to travel and trade ideas and goods between different places.

Technology helps connect regions, too. **Technology** is the way people use knowledge and tools to make or do something. It makes communication all over the world possible. **Communication** is the way people send and receive information.

Most people today use telephones, cellular phones, and fax machines to communicate. They also use computers to connect to the Internet and send electronic mail, or e-mail.

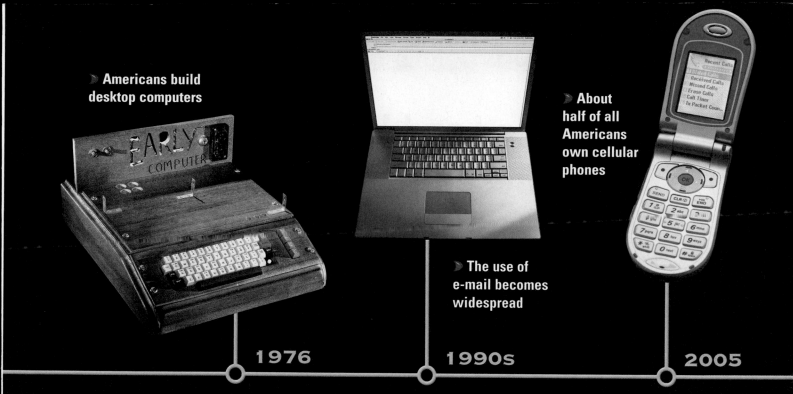

> Americans build desktop computers

1976

> The use of e-mail becomes widespread

1990s

> About half of all Americans own cellular phones

2005

Television and radio are forms of communication, too. They allow people to see and hear what is happening in different regions.

READING CHECK Ŏ**MAIN IDEA AND DETAILS**
How does transportation connect regions?

Summary

Dividing places into political, physical, cultural, and economic regions makes it easier to understand the world. People change and connect regions.

REVIEW

1. **WHAT TO KNOW** Why do people divide places into regions?

2. **VOCABULARY** Explain the meaning of the term **natural vegetation**.

3. **GEOGRAPHY** What are some forms of communication that connect regions today?

4. **CRITICAL THINKING** How are political regions different from other kinds of regions?

5. **DRAW A MAP** Draw a map of your classroom. Divide the room into regions based on what is done in each area. Then explain why you divided the room the way that you did.

6. **MAIN IDEA AND DETAILS**
(Focus Skill) On a separate sheet of paper, copy and complete the graphic organizer below.

Main Idea

Details

| Blocking rivers | Clearing trees | Building cities |

Read a Land Use and Resources Map

Why It Matters People in every region of the United States depend on the land and its resources. The land provides people with food and water, places to live, fuels to use, clothes to wear, and many other products.

❯ LEARN

The map on page 77 is a land use and resources map of the United States.

Step 1 Use the colors on the map key to see how land is used in each place.

Step 2 Use the symbols to see where natural resources are.

Step 3 Notice that the map does not show every kind of land use and resource in the United States. It shows only some of the most important ones.

❯ **NATURAL RESOURCES** People use the land and waters of the United States to provide important resources. We cut lumber, catch fish, and grow crops.

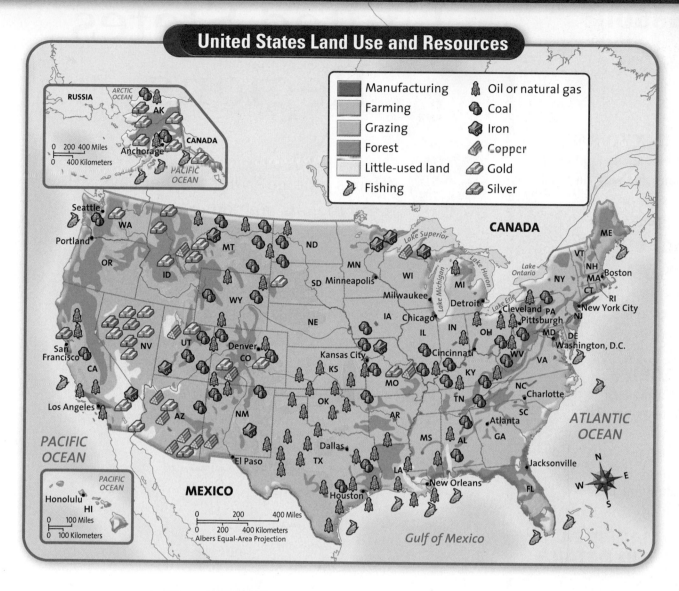

❯ PRACTICE

Use the map to answer these questions.

❶ How is most of the land used in Missouri?

❷ What resources do both Kentucky and Ohio have?

❯ APPLY

Make It Relevant Find a land use and resources map of your state. Write three questions about the map. Then exchange questions with a partner, and answer the questions you receive.

Map and Globe Skills

United States Regions

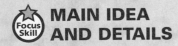

YOU ARE THERE

"Here's a riddle," your teacher says. "How many regions are you in right now?"

No one says a word.

"You're on the continent of North America," the teacher hints. "That's one region."

"Country—United States!" a classmate adds.

"State!" you say, adding your state's name.

"Right," the teacher says. "That's three so far."

"Is a city a region?" someone asks.

"It sure is," the teacher answers. "That makes four regions. Let's keep going!"

FAST FACT

When settlers founded Nashville in 1779, it was part of North Carolina. Tennessee did not become a state until 1796.

Regions of the United States

RUSSIA
ARCTIC OCEAN
0 200 400 Miles
0 400 Kilometers
ALASKA
CANADA
PACIFIC OCEAN

0 200 400 Miles
0 200 400 Kilometers
Albers Equal-Area Projection

CANADA

WASHINGTON
MONTANA
NORTH DAKOTA
MINNESOTA
Lake Superior
NEW HAMPSHIRE
VERMONT
MAINE

OREGON
IDAHO
SOUTH DAKOTA
WISCONSIN
MICHIGAN
Lake Huron
Lake Ontario
THE NORTHEAST
NEW YORK
MASSACHUSETTS
RHODE ISLAND
CONNECTICUT

WYOMING
THE WEST
NEBRASKA
THE MIDWEST
IOWA
Lake Michigan
Lake Erie
PENNSYLVANIA
NEW JERSEY
DELAWARE
Washington, D.C.
MARYLAND

NEVADA
UTAH
COLORADO
ILLINOIS
INDIANA
OHIO
WEST VIRGINIA
VIRGINIA

CALIFORNIA
KANSAS
MISSOURI
KENTUCKY
NORTH CAROLINA

PACIFIC OCEAN
ARIZONA
NEW MEXICO
OKLAHOMA
ARKANSAS
TENNESSEE
THE SOUTHEAST
SOUTH CAROLINA

THE SOUTHWEST
TEXAS
ALABAMA
MISSISSIPPI
GEORGIA
ATLANTIC OCEAN

LOUISIANA

PACIFIC OCEAN
HAWAII
0 100 Miles
0 100 Kilometers
MEXICO
Gulf of Mexico
FLORIDA

MAP SKILL **REGIONS** This map shows how this textbook divides the United States into five large regions. In which region of the United States is your state located?

Our Country's Regions

The United States is made up of 50 states. Each state is a political region with exact borders.

Five Regions

People often group states together into regions. This makes it easier to study parts of the United States.

This textbook groups all the states into five large regions—**the Northeast, the Southeast, the Midwest, the Southwest,** and **the West.** The states that make up each region are all located in the same part of the United States. They share similar physical features, economies, and ways of life.

The National Capital

Washington, D.C., our nation's capital, is called a federal district. It is not part of any state. The district's representatives in Congress have limited voting power. However, people in the district vote for the President and elect local leaders.

READING CHECK **MAIN IDEA AND DETAILS**
Into what five regions are all the 50 states grouped in this textbook?

Regions Within a State

Every state is a political region with its own government. Each state also is divided into smaller political regions.

Counties

Nearly every state is divided into political regions called **counties**. Some states have different names for this kind of region. Louisiana is divided into parishes. Alaskans divide their state into boroughs (BUHR•ohz).

The town or city that is the center of a county's government is called the **county seat**. County governments make their own laws. They also have their own courts and police to enforce those laws.

Cities

Cities are another kind of political region within states. For example, each state chooses a capital city to be the center of its government. In the same way, each city sets up its own **municipal** (myu•NIH•suh•puhl), or city, government.

In most cities, a mayor or a city manager leads the executive branch of city government. A city council forms the legislative branch. It makes the city's laws. Larger cities also have their own courts and judges to enforce city laws.

READING CHECK ⊙ **MAIN IDEA AND DETAILS**
What are two kinds of political regions within a state?

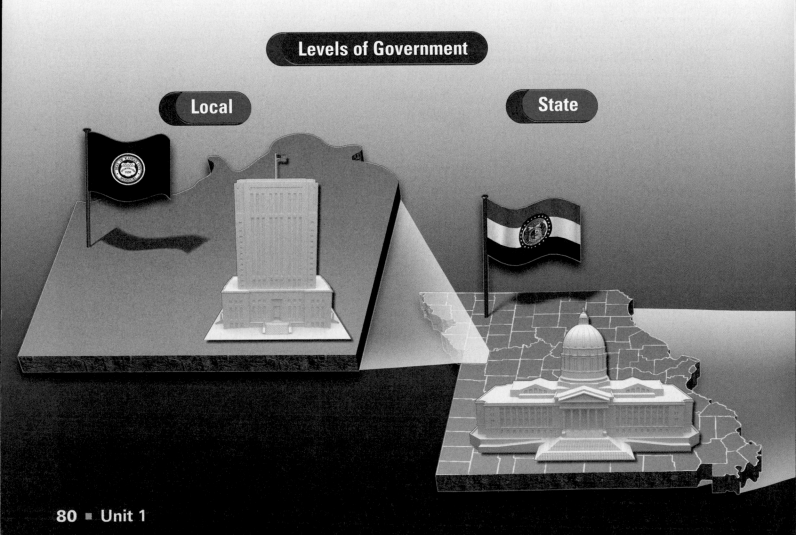

Levels of Government

Local   **State**

Government Services

The United States has three levels of government—federal, state, and local. Each level collects taxes to pay for services that it provides to people.

Federal Government Services

The federal government provides services, such as overseeing the postal service, for the entire country. It represents all Americans when dealing with other countries.

The federal government also makes **treaties**, or agreements between groups or countries. Some treaties are made to avoid or stop wars. Others are agreements about trading goods, services, or information.

State Government Services

State governments provide services for the people who live in their state. They take care of state roads and parks. They oversee public schools and state colleges and universities. They also help people in their state who do not have enough money to pay for food, shelter, health care, and other basic needs.

Local Government Services

Counties and cities provide services for the people in their communities. They build and repair local streets. They provide police and fire protection. They oversee libraries and public schools. In addition, counties are in charge of local elections.

Federal

ILLUSTRATION Local governments govern counties and cities. The state government in Missouri governs all of Missouri. The federal government in Washington, D.C., oversees the whole country.

Washington, D.C.

Special Districts

To organize all these services, people often divide counties and cities into even smaller regions called special districts. Many counties and cities are divided into voting districts, school districts, and police districts.

READING CHECK ⚙ **MAIN IDEA AND DETAILS**
What services do state governments provide?

Summary

The United States has many kinds of regions. States are grouped into large regions. They also are divided into smaller regions, such as counties and cities. States, counties, and cities all have governments that provide services to the people who live in them.

REVIEW

1. **WHAT TO KNOW** What kinds of political regions does the United States have?

2. **VOCABULARY** How are state capitals and **county seats** alike and different?

3. **GOVERNMENT** What are three political regions in which you live?

4. **CRITICAL THINKING** How do the names of the five regions used in this textbook describe their locations?

5. ✎ **MAKE A CHART** Make a three-column chart titled *Government Services.* Label the columns *Federal, State,* and *Local.* Then list the services that each level of government provides.

6. 🌟 **MAIN IDEA AND DETAILS**

On a separate sheet of paper, copy and complete the graphic organizer below.

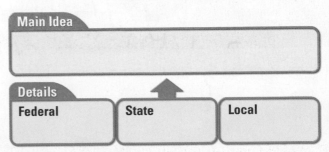

Main Idea

Details		
Federal	State	Local

Benjamin Banneker

Biography

Trustworthiness
Respect
Responsibility
Fairness
Caring
Patriotism

"*The color of the skin is in no way connected with the strength of the mind or intellectual powers.*"

Benjamin Banneker is remembered as a planner of Washington, D.C. Banneker lived at a time when African Americans had very few rights. Still, he became a respected scientist, inventor, and author.

Banneker spent most of his life on his family's farm near Baltimore, Maryland. He used borrowed books to teach himself mathematics and science. Banneker built clocks. He worked out new ways to predict the movements of the sun and moon. He also wrote almanacs that reported his work.

In 1791, the government chose Banneker to work with Pierre Charles L'Enfant (LAHN•Fahnt). Their job was to plan the nation's new capital, Washington, D.C. However, L'Enfant was fired. Banneker and Andrew Ellicott, L'Enfant's replacement, completed the city's plan. Today, our nation's capital stands as a monument to the planners' hard work.

Why Character Counts

Why do you think people respected Banneker in the past and continue to respect him today?

Time

1731		1806
Born		Died

1791 Banneker helps plan Washington, D.C.

1791–1802 Banneker publishes his almanac

GO ONLINE
For more resources, go to
www.harcourtschool.com/ss1

Neighboring Countries

WHAT TO KNOW
With what other regions does the United States share North America?

VOCABULARY
province p. 85

territory p. 85

commonwealth p. 87

tropics p. 88

rain forest p. 88

tundra p. 89

PLACES
Canada
Mexico
Central America
Caribbean
Puerto Rico
U.S. Virgin Islands
Greenland

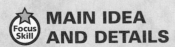
MAIN IDEA AND DETAILS

YOU ARE THERE Imagine soaring far above Earth in a space shuttle. You are hundreds of miles above North America. Still, the continent is easy to identify. The blue waters of the Atlantic, Pacific, and Arctic Oceans clearly define its shape.

You cannot see the borders between the countries in North America. Like most borders, they are imaginary lines. As viewed from space, no countries can be seen. All you see is one continent that all those countries share.

▶ **CANADIAN ROCKIES** The Rocky Mountains extend across borders in North America. The Rockies shown here run through Banff National Park in western Canada.

Canada

Canada is North America's largest political region. In fact, Canada is the second-largest country in the world.

Canada's Political Regions

Canadians divide their large nation into 13 smaller political regions. Ten of the regions are called provinces. A **province** is a political region similar to a state in the United States. The other three political regions are territories. A **territory** is an area owned and governed by a country.

Canada's Geography

Like the United States, Canada has a variety of landscapes. In fact, some landforms and waterways stretch across parts of both countries.

Mountains with forests stretch across the western part of Canada. In central Canada, farmland and ranch land cover the Interior Plains. The Great Lakes and the fertile St. Lawrence River valley lie in the eastern lowlands. Much of northern Canada is very cold and icy.

The Border We Share

Because northern Canada is so cold, most people live in the south. About two out of three Canadians live within 100 miles of the United States border. They have plenty of space to spread out. Canada and the United States share the world's longest unprotected border.

READING CHECK ☼**MAIN IDEA AND DETAILS**
Where in Canada do most people live?

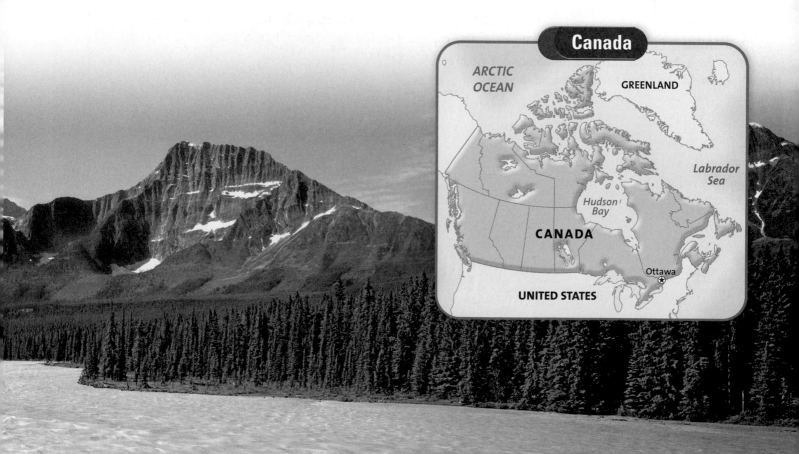

Canada

ARCTIC OCEAN

GREENLAND

Labrador Sea

Hudson Bay

CANADA

Ottawa

UNITED STATES

Mexico

Mexico's official name is *Estados Unidos Mexicanos*, meaning "United States of Mexico." As the name explains, Mexico is made up of states. Like the United States, Mexico also has one federal district that is not part of any state. This is where Mexico City, the capital of Mexico, is located.

Mexico's Geography

Mexico has a varied geography. As in our country, two large mountain ranges run through eastern and western Mexico. The Mexican Plateau stretches between the mountains. This is an area of rich farmland and big cities. Much of northern Mexico is desert. The south has a wetter climate, with grassy plains and forests.

> **MEXICO CITY** is surrounded by tall mountains. On most days, however, the mountains are not visible because of the smog that settles on the city.

Mexico's People and Economy

More than 100 million people live in Mexico. Most of them have Native American and Spanish backgrounds. Spanish is Mexico's official language.

Most Mexicans live in cities, such as Mexico City. Many also live along the Rio Grande. This river forms much of the border between Mexico and the United States. Important industries in Mexico include manufacturing, farming, ranching, mining, and oil production.

READING CHECK **COMPARE AND CONTRAST**
How are Mexico's political regions like those in the United States?

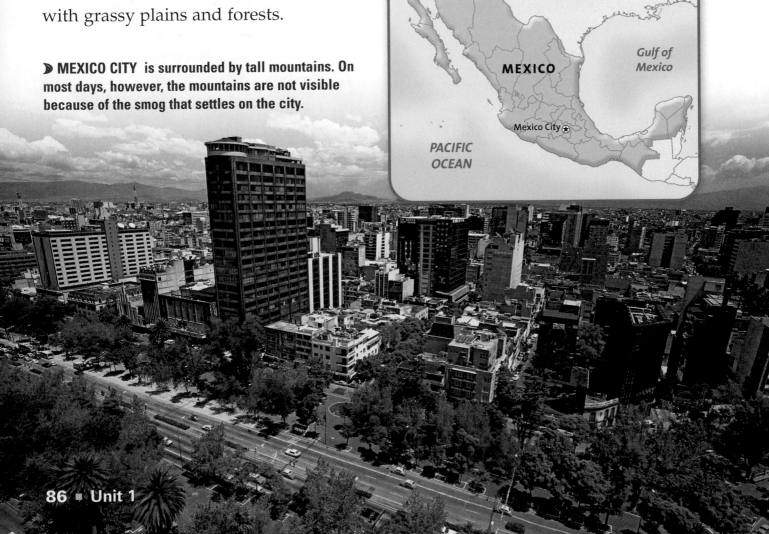

Mexico

UNITED STATES

Gulf of Mexico

MEXICO

Mexico City ⭐

PACIFIC OCEAN

▶ BEACHES People walk along one of the many beaches in the Caribbean region.

Central America and the Caribbean

ATLANTIC OCEAN

Caribbean Sea

Caribbean islands
Central America

Central America and the Caribbean

Central America is part of North America. So, too, are the islands of the Caribbean (kair•uh•BEE•uhn) Sea.

Central America

Central America is a region that is made up of a narrow strip of land that connects North and South America. This region is divided into seven countries. The Pacific Ocean forms Central America's western boundary. The Caribbean Sea, which is part of the Atlantic Ocean, shapes the region's eastern boundary.

The Caribbean

Hundreds of islands lie off the east coast of Central America in the Caribbean Sea. Together, these islands make up the **Caribbean** region.

Some of the islands, such as Cuba, are large. Others are so small and have so few resources that no one lives on them.

Several Caribbean islands are part of other countries. **Puerto Rico,** for example, is a commonwealth of the United States. Being a **commonwealth** means that it is a territory of the United States but that it governs itself. People who are citizens of Puerto Rico are also citizens of the United States.

The Virgin Islands of the United States, or the **U.S. Virgin Islands**, are also a territory of the United States. About 50 small islands make up this territory. People who live on the U.S. Virgin Islands are citizens of the United States as well.

Land and Climate

Central America and the Caribbean are both located in the **tropics**. This area around the equator has a warm climate all year. Because of the warmth and large amount of precipitation, rain forests cover much of the land in these two tropical regions. A **rain forest** is a wet area, usually warm, in which tall trees, vines, and other plants grow close together. Many people visit these regions to enjoy hiking in the forest.

Central America and the Caribbean have several mountains. In fact, many of the islands are the peaks of underwater mountains. Much of the land has fertile soil, too. It helps farmers grow coffee, sugarcane, and bananas and other tropical fruits. Both regions also rely on selling goods and services to the many visitors that come each year.

READING CHECK ⓘ **MAIN IDEA AND DETAILS**
What parts of the Caribbean region are also parts of the United States?

❯ **RAIN FORESTS** Visitors to Central America's rain forests can walk across "skybridges" (below). They might see birds such as this toucan (left) perched high in the treetops.

Greenland

The last region of North America is a huge island off the northeast coast of Canada. It is **Greenland**—the world's biggest island.

Because Greenland lies so far north, it has a very cold climate. Nearly all of it is a **tundra**—a flat, treeless plain that stays mostly frozen. Greenland is a territory of Denmark, a country in Europe. Still, very few Danish people live there. Most Greenlanders are native people called Inuit.

READING CHECK ♻**MAIN IDEA AND DETAILS**
Why does Greenland have such a cold climate?

Summary

Canada, Mexico, Central America, the Caribbean islands, and Greenland are the North American neighbors of the United States.

▶ **GREENLAND** Most Inuit earn a living fishing for shrimp, halibut, and other seafood.

REVIEW

1. **WHAT TO KNOW** With what regions does the United States share North America?

2. **VOCABULARY** Explain what it means to be a **commonwealth** of the United States.

3. **CIVICS AND GOVERNMENT** How do Canadians divide their nation?

4. **CRITICAL THINKING** How do the climates of Greenland and Central America make life in these regions different?

5. **MAKE A COLLAGE** Use magazines, newspapers, or your own artwork to make a collage that illustrates the diversity of North America's regions.

6. (Focus Skill) **MAIN IDEA AND DETAILS**

On a separate sheet of paper, copy and complete the graphic organizer below.

Main Idea

North America has a great variety of landforms and climates.

Details

People divide the world into regions.

Visual Summary

Summarize the Chapter

Main Idea and Details Complete this graphic organizer to show that you understand the important ideas and details about the regions of the United States.

Main Idea

Each place is a part of many kinds of regions.

Details

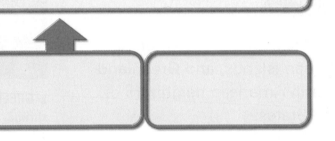

TEST PREP ✓ Vocabulary

Identify the term from the word bank that completes each sentence.

1. Computers and other kinds of _____ help connect regions.

2. A _____ is an area with at least one feature that sets it apart from other areas.

3. In many cities, the mayor is the head of the _____ government.

4. Puerto Rico is a _____ of the United States.

5. People in an _____ have the same heritage or have a shared way of life.

6. The _____ of regions means that they rely on one another for resources, products, and services.

7. Regions change when people _____ them.

Word Bank

region p. 71   **technology** p. 74

interdependence p. 71   **municipal** p. 80

ethnic group p. 73   **commonwealth** p. 87

modify p. 74

Technology helps connect regions.

The United States can be divided into five large regions.

 Facts and Main Ideas

Answer these questions.

8. What features are used to define a physical region?

9. What are three kinds of political regions in the United States?

10. What forms of communication connect regions in the United States?

Write the letter of the best choice.

11. Which kind of region has exact boundaries?
    A a cultural region
    B an economic region
    C a physical region
    D a political region

12. Which kind of government in the United States can make treaties with other countries?
    A county government
    B municipal government
    C federal government
    D state government

13. How do Mexicans divide their nation?
    A into states
    B into territories
    C into provinces
    D into commonwealths

 Critical Thinking

14. How do people modify the environment to meet their needs?

15. In what ways are the regions of North America interdependent?

16. How is Washington, D.C., different from other cities in the United States?

 Skills

Read a Land Use and Resources Map
Use the map on page 77 to answer these questions.

17. What is the main land use in Nevada?

18. What fuel resources are found in Oklahoma?

19. Where in Michigan is most manufacturing done?

writing

Write a Narrative Imagine traveling across the United States. Write a story describing your journey. Describe how the land and climate change as you travel from east to west across the country.

Write a Report Write a report about the four main kinds of regions. Explain what features are used to define each kind of region, and give an example of each region.

Fun with Social Studies

In the Rocky Mountains

The Eastern Hemisphere

A View of the Indian Ocean

Between Mexico and Canada

Down the Mighty Mississippi

From the Atlantic to the Pacific

Did You See That?

Some of these DVDs don't belong on these shelves. Which titles do not belong?

Tricky T-Shirts

Who should wear each T-shirt?

John Muir

Francis Scott Key

Benjamin Banneker

Free William

A Man, a Plan, a Capital

I ♥ Wilderness

Treasure Terms

Match the clues on the map to the vocabulary terms. The first letters of the correct terms will spell a word that Americans treasure.

gulf   rural

humidity   supply

technology

interdependence

In the countryside

A body of water that reaches into the land

Groups that depend on one another

Knowledge and tools people use

Moisture in the air

The amount of a product or service that is available

Online Adventures

GO ONLINE

GEOGRAPHY CHALLENGE

Northeast

Midwest

West

Southwest

Southeast

Geography Card

3

Start

An important American symbol is missing, and nobody knows where to find it! Get ready, because you and Eco will have to travel around the country to solve this online mystery. You need to solve puzzles to find out which symbol has been lost. Collect the eight clue cards to see who the suspects are and where the symbol might be hidden. Play now at **www.harcourtschool.com/ss1**

HARCOURT

ECO

Review and Test Prep

THE BIG IDEA

Geography The United States has diversity in its landscape and its people.

Reading Comprehension and Vocabulary

Exploring the United States

Most of the United States is located on the continent of North America. Of the country's 50 states, 48 are between Canada in the north, Mexico in the south, the Atlantic Ocean in the east, and the Pacific Ocean in the west.

To describe such a large country, people divide it into <u>regions</u>. Some regions, such as cities and states, are based on government. Each level of government collects taxes to pay for services.

Other regions are based on physical features. These include landforms, climates, rivers, and natural vegetation.

For example, the Interior Plains region is flat land in the middle of the United States.

Still other regions are based on <u>culture</u> or the economy. Immigrants from around the world have brought their ways of life to the United States. Our nation's natural resources, workers, and technology make the economy strong and diverse.

As people build communities, they often change regions. They also connect regions by using transportation and communication technology.

Read the summary above. Then answer the questions that follow.

1. What is the meaning of the word <u>region</u>?
   - **A** one of the seven largest areas of land on Earth
   - **B** an area where people live
   - **C** an area with at least one feature that sets it apart from other areas
   - **D** an area with exact borders

2. What is the main purpose of taxes?
   - **A** to protect peoples' rights
   - **B** to pay for government services
   - **C** to decide court cases
   - **D** to make a place easier to study and understand

3. What kind of landform covers most of the middle of the United States?
   - **A** hills
   - **B** mountains
   - **C** plains
   - **D** plateaus

4. What does <u>culture</u> mean?
   - **A** peoples' ways of life
   - **B** the number of people who live in a place
   - **C** how people use natural resources
   - **D** the ways people send and receive information

Facts and Main Ideas

Answer these questions.

5. Where is the United States located?

6. What kind of landform covers most of the area that lies west of the Intermountain Region?

7. Why is water our most important natural resource?

8. What is the main job of each branch of the federal government?

9. What is the Bill of Rights?

10. Why do people divide places into regions?

Write the letter of the best choice.

11. Which of these physical regions has some of the driest areas in North America?
    A the Coastal Plain
    B the Central Plains
    C the Great Basin
    D the Rocky Mountains

12. Why are trees a renewable resource?
    A People can use trees to make many products.
    B Different kinds of trees grow in different environments.
    C People can plant new trees to replace the trees they cut down.
    D Trees need soil and water to grow.

13. A manufacturing area is an example of what kind of region?
    A cultural
    B economic
    C physical
    D political

14. Which of these North American regions is north of the United States?
    A the Caribbean
    B Central America
    C Canada
    D Mexico

 ## Critical Thinking

15. In what ways is the region where you live interdependent with other regions in the United States and the world?

16. Why do rights come with responsibilties?

 ## Skills

Use Latitude and Longitude

Use the map below to answer the following questions.

17. Which city is located closest to 39°N, 82°W?

18. What is the absolute location of the capital of Ohio?

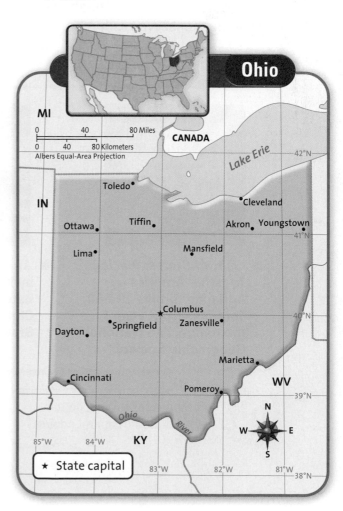

Activities

Show What You Know

Unit Writing Activity

Write a Persuasive Article Write a newspaper article explaining why you think conservation is important.

■ Explain how people use natural resources.

■ List ways that people can help conserve those resources.

■ Describe what might happen if people do not conserve resources.

Unit Project

Make an Atlas Make an atlas about the nation.

■ Gather information about the geography of the United States.

■ Illustrate the atlas with maps and drawings.

■ Include information about the people, the government, and the economy.

Read More

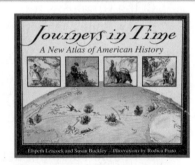

■ *Quilt of States: Piecing Together America* by Adrienne Yorinks and 50 librarians from across the nation. The National Geographic Society.

■ *America the Beautiful* by Katharine Lee Bates, illustrated by Chris Gall. Little, Brown.

■ *Journeys in Time: A New Atlas of American History* by Elspeth Leacock and Susan Buckley. Houghton Mifflin.

For more resources, go to
www.harcourtschool.com/ss1

The Northeast

The Big Idea

Cities and Growth

Many early settlements in the Northeast grew into some of the largest cities in the United States today.

What to Know

- ✓ What is the geography of the Northeast?
- ✓ What role did the Northeast have in the early history of the United States?
- ✓ What changes affected the growth of cities in the Northeast?
- ✓ What is the Northeast like today?

Unit 2

Time

The Northeast	• **1500s** Europeans begin to explore the Northeast, p. 118	• **1600s** English settlers establish eight colonies in the Northeast, p. 119	**1773** Britain has 13 colonies along the Atlantic coast, p. 119 •

1500   **1600**   **1700**

At the Same Time

 1542 West Spanish explorer Juan Rodríguez Cabrillo explores what is now the California coast

 1670 Southeast The city of Charles Town becomes the center of life in South Carolina

The Northeast

• **1776** Colonial leaders sign the Declaration of Independence, p. 120

• **1882** Thomas Edison opens the world's first electric power plant, p. 128

Present The Northeast is one of the most crowded regions of the United States, p. 130

1800

1900

Present

1764 Midwest St. Louis is founded by a French fur trader from New Orleans

1930s Huge oil deposits are discovered beneath the desert in Saudi Arabia

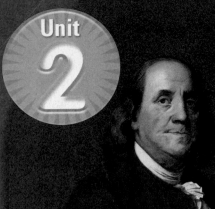

Unit 2

Benjamin Franklin

1706–1790

- Philadelphia leader and famous inventor
- Started the first city fire department and public library

Thomas Alva Edison

1847–1931

- New Jersey inventor with over 1,000 patents
- Invented the electric light bulb and the phonograph

People

1700

1706 • Benjamin Franklin   1790

1800

1847 •

Theodor Geisel

1904–1991

- Author known as Dr. Seuss
- Published *The Cat in the Hat* in 1957

Alvin Ailey

1931–1989

- Dancer and choreographer
- Founder of the Alvin Ailey American Dance Theater

Katharine Lee Bates

1859–1929
- Massachusetts teacher and poet
- Author of the poem "America the Beautiful"

Norman Rockwell

1894–1978
- Artist born in New York City
- Illustrated American ways of life
- Many of his paintings were used as covers for the magazine *Saturday Evening Post*

1900 | **PRESENT**

Thomas Alva Edison	1931
1859 • Katharine Lee Bates	1929
1894 • Norman Rockwell	1978
1904 • Theodor Geisel	1991
1931 • Alvin Ailey	1989
1944 • Rudolph Giuliani	
1953 • Nydia Velázquez	

Rudolph Giuliani

1944–present
- Served as New York City's mayor
- Led the city after the attacks on September 11, 2001

Nydia Velázquez

1953–present
- Born in Puerto Rico
- Became the first Puerto Rican woman elected to the United States House of Representatives

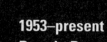

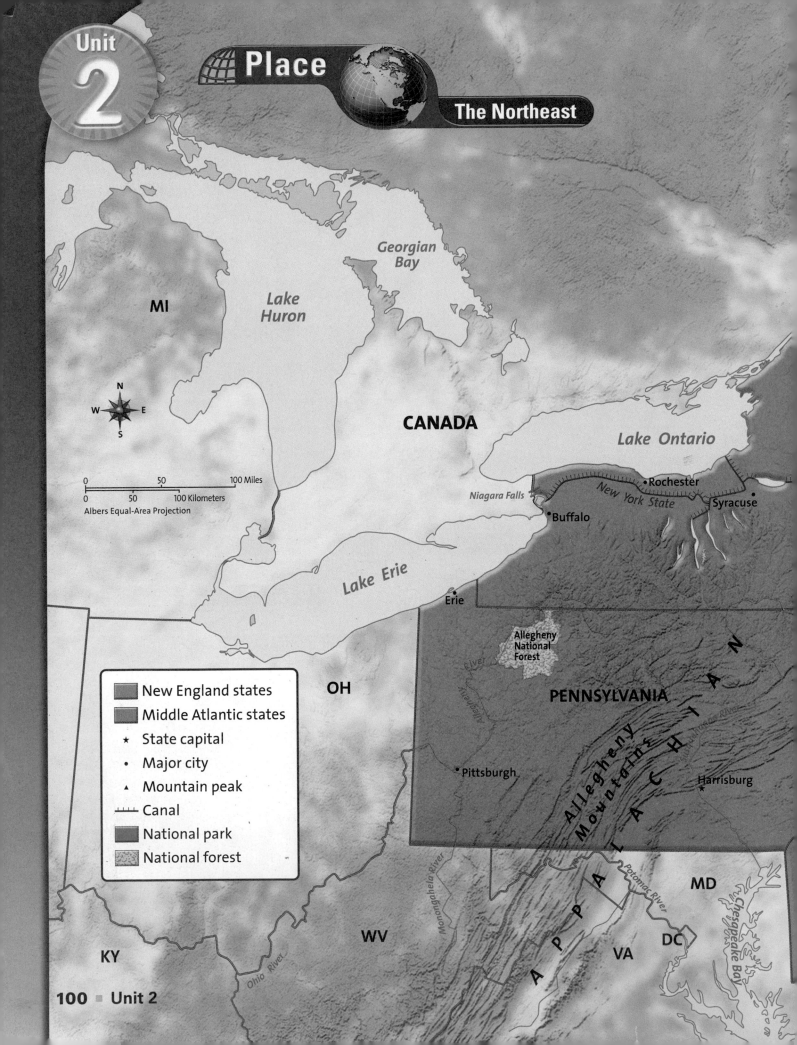

MI

Georgian Bay

Lake Huron

CANADA

Lake Ontario

Rochester

New York State

Syracuse

Niagara Falls

Buffalo

Lake Erie

Erie

N
W — E
S

0   50   100 Miles
0   50   100 Kilometers
Albers Equal-Area Projection

Allegheny National Forest

PENNSYLVANIA

OH

New England states
Middle Atlantic states
★ State capital
•   Major city
▲ Mountain peak
┼┼┼ Canal
National park
National forest

Pittsburgh

Harrisburg

Allegheny Mountains

APPALACHIAN

Monongahela River

Potomac River

MD

Chesapeake Bay

WV

KY

Ohio River

VA

DC

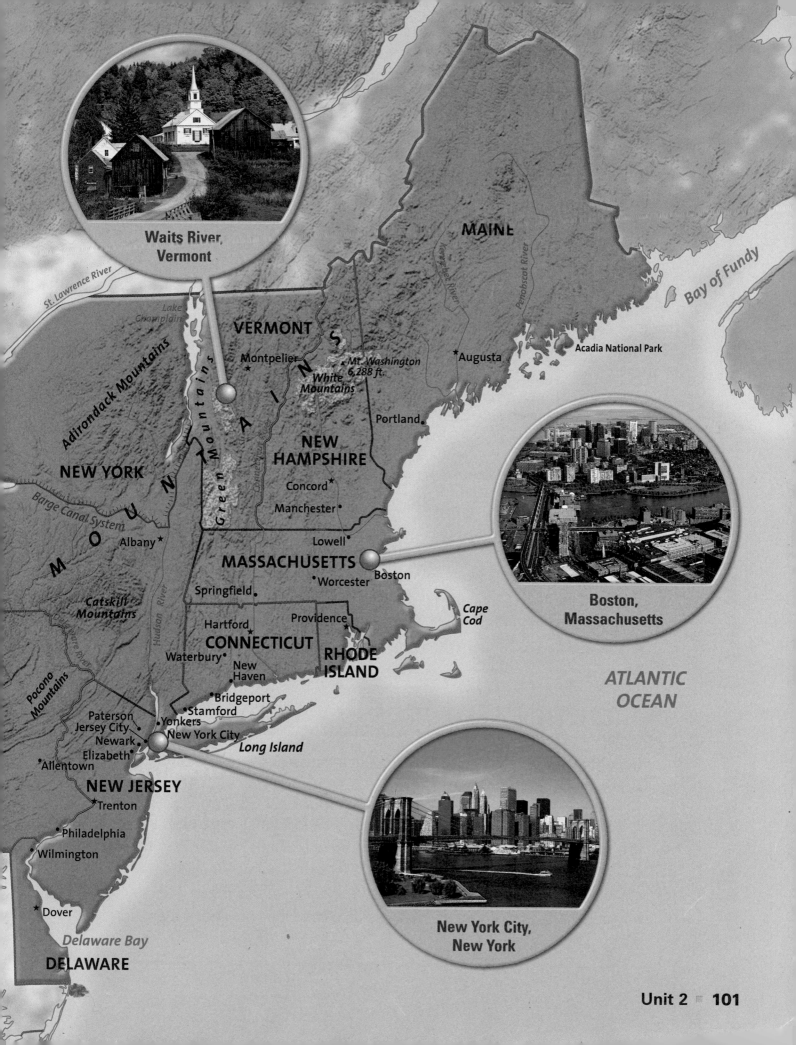

Waits River,
Vermont

St. Lawrence River

Lake
Champlain

MAINE

Bay of Fundy

Kennebec River

Penobscot River

Adirondack Mountains

VERMONT

Montpelier ★

White
Mountains

Mt. Washington
6,288 ft.

★ Augusta

Acadia National Park

Green Mountains

NEW YORK

NEW
HAMPSHIRE

Portland •

Barge Canal System

Concord ★

Manchester •

Albany ★

Lowell •

MASSACHUSETTS

Boston

ATLANTIC
OCEAN

Catskill
Mountains

Springfield •

Worcester •

Hudson River

Hartford ★

Providence ★

Cape
Cod

Boston,
Massachusetts

CONNECTICUT

Waterbury •

RHODE
ISLAND

New
Haven

Pocono
Mountains

Bridgeport •

Stamford •

Paterson •

Yonkers •

Jersey City •

New York City

Newark •

Long Island

Elizabeth •

Allentown •

NEW JERSEY

Trenton ★

Philadelphia •

Wilmington •

Dover ★

Delaware Bay

DELAWARE

New York City,
New York

Reading Social Studies

Focus Skill Cause and Effect

Why It Matters Understanding cause and effect can help you see why events and actions happen.

❯ LEARN

A **cause** is an action or event that makes something happen. An **effect** is what happens as the result of the cause.

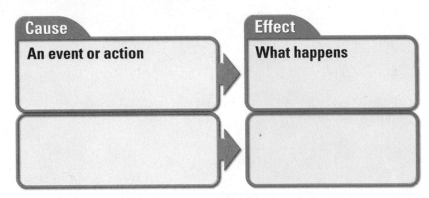

Cause	Effect
An event or action	**What happens**

- Words and phrases such as *because, since, so,* and *as a result* are clues that help identify causes and effects.
- Sometimes the effect may be stated before the cause.
- A cause can have more than one effect.

❯ PRACTICE

Read the paragraphs that follow. Find one cause and one effect in the second paragraph.

Cause The Northeast is a region with many people in a small area. Its cities are large, and many people drive cars. Because of this, the air is sometimes polluted. **Effect**

People work to prevent air pollution. Some people use trains, buses, and subways instead of cars. As a result, some cities now have cleaner air than they had in the past.

Read the paragraphs, and answer the questions.

Winter in the Northeast

Winters are cold in the Northeast. This affects the way people in the region live. For example, people have to keep their houses warm. Some people heat their houses with electric furnaces. Others use furnaces that burn oil or other fuels. Still others might burn firewood in stoves.

Electricity and fuels used for heating can be costly. Cutting and splitting firewood is hard work. For these reasons, some people keep the temperature in their houses low during the winter.

Travel can be difficult in winter. Very cold weather may cause car batteries to fail. In winter storms, snow and ice may cover roads. Since snow and ice make roads slippery, more accidents occur.

To prevent accidents, most towns and cities in the Northeast have snowplows. Snowplows remove the snow from the roads. Some towns put sand or salt on the roads. Sand makes roads less slippery, and salt helps melt snow and ice.

Because fuel can be costly and travel can be dangerous in winter, many schools in the Northeast have several "snow days" each year. Snow days are days when there is heavy snow, so the school district decides that it is better for students to stay home than to come to school. Students must make up these days later in the school year.

The Great Blizzard of 1888 hit many cities in the Northeast hard. Schools all over the region were closed. Public buildings and businesses were closed for days. Trains were not running. Carts and carriages were buried in snow. As a result, cities began to plan better to remove snow before it became a problem.

⭐ Focus Skill Cause and Effect

1. What causes some people to keep the temperature in their houses low during the winter?
2. For what reasons do schools decide to close schools on days when it snows heavily?
3. What are some effects of the Great Blizzard of 1888?

ROAD MAY
BE ICY
IN AREAS

A RIVER RAN WILD

written and illustrated by Lynne Cherry

Native Americans were the first people to live in the Northeast region of the United States. One group, the Nashua (NA•shu•wuh), settled along a river they called the Nash-a-way. It flows through lands known today as the states of Massachusetts and New Hampshire. By this river, the Nashua fished, farmed, and gathered plants.

Then Europeans began to settle this area. The new settlers brought with them different ways of life. They cleared the forests and plowed the land. They built mills and factories along the river. Read now about ways people have depended on the river over the years.

LONG AGO a river ran wild through a land of towering forests. Bears, moose, and herds of deer, hawks and owls all made their homes in the peaceful river valley. Geese paused on their long migration and rested on its banks. Beavers, turtles, and schools of fish swam in its clear waters.

One day a group of native people, searching for a place to settle, came upon the river valley. From atop the highest mountain, known today as Mt. Wachusett, they saw the river nestled in its valley, a silver sliver in the sun.

They came down from the mountain, and at the river's edge they knelt to quench their thirst with its clear water. Pebbles shone up from the bottom.

"Let us settle by this river," said the chief of the native people. He named the river Nash-a-way—River with the Pebbled Bottom.

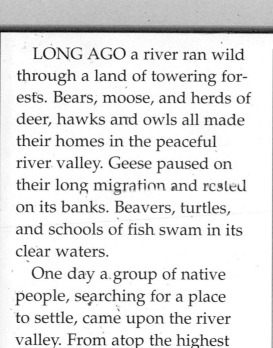

By the Nash-a-way, Chief Weeawa's people built a village. They gathered cattails from the riverbanks to thatch their dwellings. In the forest they set fires to clear brush from the forest floor. In these clearings they planted corn and squash for eating. They made arrows for hunting and canoes for river travel.

When the Indians hunted in the forest or caught salmon in the river, they killed only what they needed for themselves for food and clothing. They asked all the forest creatures that they killed to please forgive them.

The Nashua people saw a rhythm in their lives and in the seasons. The river, land, and forest provided all they needed.

The Nashua had lived for generations by the clear, clean, flowing river when one day a pale-skinned trader came with a boatload full of treasures. He brought shiny metal knives, colored beads, and cooking kettles, mirrors, tools, and bolts of bright cloth. His wares seemed like magic. The Nashua welcomed him, traded furs, and soon a trading post was built.

In the many years that followed, the settlers' village and others like it grew and the Nash-a-way became the Nashua. The settlers worked together to clear land by cutting down the forests, which they thought were full of danger—wilderness that they would conquer. They hunted wolves and beaver, killing much more than they needed. Extra pelts were sent to England in return for goods and money.

The settlers built sawmills along the river, which the Nashua's current powered. They built dams to make the mill-ponds that were used to store the water. They cut down the towering forest and floated tree trunks down the river. The logs were cut up into lumber, which was used for building houses.

The settlers built fences for their pastures, plowed the fields, and planted crops. They called the land their own and told the Indians not to trespass. Hunting land disappeared as the settlers cleared the forest. Indian fishing rights vanished as the settlers claimed the river.

The Indians' ways were disrupted and they began to fight the settlers. The wars raged for many years but the Indians' bows and arrows were no match against gunpowder, and so the settlers' rifles drove the Indians from the land.

Through a hundred years of fighting, the Nashua was a healthy river, sometimes dammed for grist and saw-mills, but still flowing wild and free. Muskrats, fish, and turtles still swam from bank to bank. Deer still came to drink from the river, and owls, raccoons, and beaver fed there.

Response Corner

1 (Focus Skill) **Cause And Effect** How did the environment shape Nashua ways of life?

2 **Make It Relevant** What were some long-lasting effects that the Europeans had on the environments?

STUDY SKILLS

USE A K-W-L CHART

A K-W-L chart can help you focus on what you already know about a topic and what you want to learn about it.

- **Before you read, use the K column to list things you know about a topic.**

- **Before you read, use the W column to list things you want to know about the topic.**

- **After you read, use the L column to list things you have learned about the topic.**

Exploring the Northeast

What I Know	What I Want to Know	What I Learned
The Northeast has many natural resources.	How do people use the region's resources?	_____ _____

PREVIEW VOCABULARY

glacier p. 111   **revolution** p. 121   **waterway** p. 127

Exploring the Northeast

Harbor at Rockport, Maine

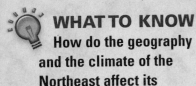
Geography of the Northeast

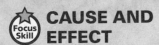 **WHAT TO KNOW**
How do the geography and the climate of the Northeast affect its economy?

VOCABULARY

harbor p. 111
glacier p. 111
blizzard p. 112
quarry p. 113

PLACES

Coastal Plain
Delaware Bay
Appalachian Mountains
Great Lakes

 **CAUSE AND EFFECT**

Cause	Effect

YOU ARE THERE

You hang on tight to the railing as your boat rises and falls over the waves. The wind has made the sea choppy today.

"This feels more like a roller coaster than a sailboat!" you shout to your mother.

"We'd better head in!" she calls back.

As you near land, you watch the white cliffs lining the shore. Behind them, you see the forests of tall green trees covering the distant hills.

This is the last day of your vacation in Maine. You can hardly wait until next year, when you can sail again along the Northeast coast.

Coasts to Countryside

The Northeast is the smallest region in the United States in terms of size. Yet, the area is made up of a variety of different physical features.

A Varied Landscape

The Atlantic Ocean forms the eastern border of the Northeast region. The northern coast of the region is rocky and jagged. It also has many harbors. A **harbor** is a protected area of water where ships can dock safely. Farther south, the flat **Coastal Plain** hugs the coast all the way to **Delaware Bay.**

Inland from the coast, green valleys and rolling hills spread across the land. Farther west, the **Appalachian Mountains** cut through the region. Beyond the mountain valleys, two of the **Great Lakes** separate the Northeast region from Canada.

Shaping the Northeast

Glaciers (GLAY•sherz) shaped many of the physical features of the Northeast. A **glacier** is a huge, slow-moving mass of ice. During an Ice Age, long ago, glaciers covered more of Earth than today. As glaciers moved across parts of the Northeast, they eroded, or wore down landforms. Sometimes, the glaciers carved deep basins into the land.

In time, the glaciers melted, and some of the basins filled with water. Many lakes in the Northeast formed in this way thousands of years ago.

Glaciers also had other effects on the region. In the northern coastal areas, they scraped away the topsoil, or the fertile upper layers of soil. This scraping left behind mostly poor, rocky soil.

READING CHECK ☙ **CAUSE AND EFFECT**
What caused many lakes to form in the Northeast?

▶ **HARBORS** Fishing boats and pleasure boats line one of the many harbors in the Northeast.

Climate

The climate in the Northeast varies across the region. It also changes from season to season.

Four Seasons

The Northeast has four very different seasons. Winters are mostly cold and snowy. In spring, the weather is warm and sunny. Flowers bloom, and trees are covered with bright green leaves. Summers are often hot and rainy.

During the cool autumns, the leaves turn orange, red, and gold before they fall to the ground. This makes most trees bare during the winter season. However, some trees, such as pines, stay green throughout the year.

Variety

Even during the same season, the climate in the Northeast varies from place to place. In general, the region is colder in the north and warmer in the south. Also, coastal areas have warmer climates than inland areas, especially those in the high mountains.

Extreme Weather

At times, the Northeast's weather can be extreme. **Blizzards**, or snowstorms with strong winds, sometimes occur. These storms can block roads, knock down power lines, and damage buildings. In 2005, a blizzard brought record amounts of snow to the region.

READING CHECK ☼ **CAUSE AND EFFECT**
What effects can blizzards sometimes cause?

▶ **BLIZZARD** A snowplow clears the road after a blizzard hit this small town in the Northeast.

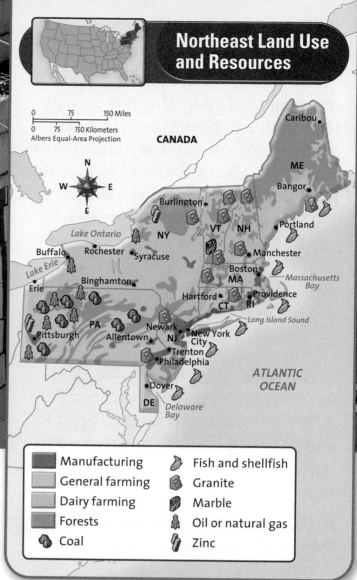

0 75 150 Miles
0 75 150 Kilometers
Albers Equal-Area Projection

Legend:
- Manufacturing
- General farming
- Dairy farming
- Forests
- Coal
- Fish and shellfish
- Granite
- Marble
- Oil or natural gas
- Zinc

MAP SKILL HUMAN-ENVIRONMENT INTERACTIONS
Workers (above) mine granite in a quarry.
Which state produces both granite and marble?

Natural Resources

The Northeast has many natural resources. Many people in the region use the resources to make a living.

Farming

The northern parts of the region have rocky soil and a cool climate. Yet, people still farm there. They grow potatoes, blueberries, and cranberries. They also use greenhouses to grow crops such as flowers and shrubs.

Farther south, on the more fertile soil of the Coastal Plain, farming is a larger industry. Corn and other vegetables are major crops.

The inland hills and valleys provide pasture grasses for dairy cows. Milk from the dairy cows is used to make products such as cheese and ice cream.

Mining Stone

Some people mine stone to earn a living. Every state in the region has stone quarries (KWAR•eez). A **quarry** is a large, open pit cut into the ground, from which stone is mined. Quarries in the region produce a large amount of granite and marble. New Hampshire and Vermont have many of these quarries. People use these stones to make buildings, bridges, roads, statues, and even kitchen counters.

Using Trees

The region's forests make logging an important industry. This is especially true in Maine, New Hampshire, and Vermont. People cut down trees to use as lumber. They also use trees to make products such as toothpicks and paper.

People also use trees to produce food. Many farmers grow fruits, such as apples and pears. Others collect sap, a liquid, from maple trees. Sap is used to make maple syrup.

Fishing

Fishing is an important industry for people living along the coast. The Atlantic Ocean provides cod, haddock, and plenty of oysters and lobsters. People also catch freshwater fish in the region's many lakes and rivers.

READING CHECK **MAIN IDEA AND DETAILS**
How do some people in the Northeast use trees to earn a living?

▶ **COLLECTING SAP** It takes more than 30 gallons of sap to make 1 gallon of maple syrup.

Summary

The Northeast has a varied landscape and a climate with four seasons. The region has many natural resources. People have used them to create important industries.

REVIEW

1. **WHAT TO KNOW** How do the geography and the climate of the Northeast affect its economy?

2. **VOCABULARY** Write a sentence that describes what happens in a **quarry**.

3. **GEOGRAPHY** Which mountains cut through the western part of the Northeast?

4. **CRITICAL THINKING** Why is farming a larger industry in the southern parts of the Northeast than in the northern parts of the region?

5. **MAKE A TABLE** Make a table titled *Using Resources*. In column one, list the Northeast's natural resources. In column two, describe how each resource is used.

6. **Focus Skill** **CAUSE AND EFFECT**

On a separate sheet of paper, copy and complete the graphic organizer below.

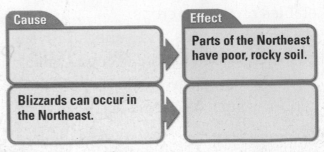

Cause	Effect
	Parts of the Northeast have poor, rocky soil.
Blizzards can occur in the Northeast.	

Katharine Lee Bates

Biography

Trustworthiness
Respect
Responsibility
Fairness
Caring
Patriotism

"*O beautiful for spacious skies,
For amber waves of grain,
For purple mountain majesties
Above the fruited plain!*"

Katharine Lee Bates used these words to begin her famous poem "America the Beautiful." In 1893, Bates took a trip through the western United States. She visited a high peak in the Rocky Mountains in Colorado. What she saw from the top of the mountain inspired her to write the poem.

Although Bates loved to travel, she spent most of her life in her home state, Massachusetts. Bates grew up in the coastal town of Falmouth. In 1880, she graduated from Wellesley College.

During her lifetime, Bates wrote many poems. She is best known for "America the Beautiful." Americans express their patriotism when they sing the words she wrote more than 100 years ago.

Why Character Counts

How does the title of Bates's poem "America the Beautiful" show patriotism?

Time

1859	1929
Born	Died

1880 Bates graduates from Wellesley College

1893 Bates writes "America the Beautiful"

1911 Bates publishes her book *America the Beautiful and Other Poems*

GO ONLINE For more resources, go to www.harcourtschool.com/ss1

Time

1500	1750	Present

1500
Native Americans are the only people living in the Northeast

1776
The 13 colonies declare independence from Britain

1783
The United States officially becomes a new nation

Early History of the Northeast

WHAT TO KNOW
What important role did the Northeast have in the early history of the United States?

VOCABULARY
confederation p. 117
colony p. 118
colonist p. 119
port p. 119
independence p. 120
declaration p. 120
revolution p. 121

PEOPLE
Algonquian
Iroquois
Hiawatha
Deganawida
Henry Hudson
Thomas Jefferson
Benjamin Franklin
John Adams
George Washington

PLACES
Boston
New York City
Philadelphia

CAUSE AND EFFECT

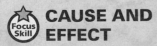

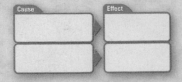

YOU ARE THERE

"They're back!" you hear people shout. You grab your basket of corn and run through the fields toward your village.

Everyone crowds around your father and the other hunters. One of them is carrying a deer! You know this means a big celebration tonight.

Your mother and the other women will prepare roasted venison and corn cakes. Then everyone will sit around the fire and feast together. You look forward to hearing the hunters' stories.

▶ AN IROQUOIS VILLAGE

Early People

Before the 1500s, Native Americans were the only people living in the Northeast. They included tribes from two language groups. These were the Iroquoian (IR•uh•kwoy•uhn) and the Algonquian (al•GAHN•kwee•uhn) languages. Most of the **Algonquian** tribes lived near the Atlantic Coast. Most of the **Iroquois** tribes lived farther inland.

Hunting, Gathering, and Farming

In most Native American villages in the Northeast, people shared the land and its resources. They hunted in the forests and fished in nearby waters. People gathered wild foods, such as roots, nuts, and berries. They also worked together to grow corn, beans, squash, melons, and other crops.

The forests of the Northeast were an important resource. Native Americans used wood to build their homes and villages. They made tools, weapons, and canoes with wood, too.

Joining Together

At times, Native American groups in the Northeast fought each other. Iroquois legend tells how two leaders came up with a plan for peace. These leaders were **Hiawatha** (hy•ah•WAW•thuh) and **Deganawida** (deh•gahn•uh•WEE•duh). They convinced five of the largest Iroquois tribes to join a **confederation**, or a group of governments that work together. Deganawida wanted the five tribes to act as "only one body, one head, and one heart."

READING CHECK ☼ CAUSE AND EFFECT
What caused the Iroquois peoples to unite?

The Colonies

In the 1500s, Europeans began to explore the Northeast. They sailed in ships across the Atlantic Ocean from England, France, and Holland.

Early Settlers

By 1610, the English explorer **Henry Hudson** had traveled along much of the Northeast coast. He sailed up what is now the Hudson River. There he described a region that was rich in natural resources.

In time, some Europeans decided to move to the Northeast. Most hoped to make money by selling the region's wood, fish, and furs in Europe. Some settlers, such as English Puritans and Quakers, came for religious freedom. They wanted to build colonies where they could worship as they pleased. A **colony** is a settlement that is ruled by a faraway government. Other settlers came to make a better life for themselves.

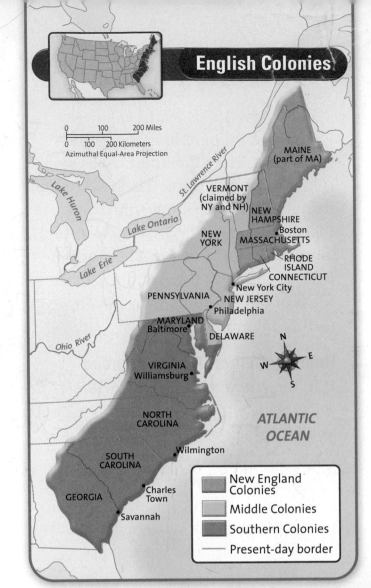

English Colonies

New England Colonies
Middle Colonies
Southern Colonies
Present-day border

MAP SKILL **REGIONS** People divide the 13 English colonies into three large regions. Which colonies made up each region?

▶ **COLONIAL LIFE** People today can visit this re-creation of the Plymouth Colony in Massachusetts.

▶ **COLONIAL JOBS** This reenactment shows a colonist at work in his wood shop.

The Northeast Colonies

During the 1600s, English settlers founded eight colonies in the Northeast. The **colonists**, or people living in colonies, were from all over Europe. To build their colonies, they bought land or took it by force from Native Americans in the region.

As the colonies grew, so did their economies. Some coastal towns grew into port cities. A **port** is a trading center where goods are put onto and taken off ships. The three largest cities in the colonies—**Boston, New York City,** and **Philadelphia**—all grew up around ports.

Farmers and traders traveled to ports to sell their goods. They brought grain, flour, lumber, furs, dried meat, and salted fish. Ships carried most goods to England, where traders sold them. Later, the ships returned with goods to sell in the colonies.

Self-Government

By 1733, England — or Britain, as it became known after 1707 — had 13 colonies along the Atlantic coast. The colonists had to follow British laws. However, they governed themselves in many ways. Each colony set up its own government. Each colony elected most of its leaders. Colonists also wrote their own laws. One law gave some colonists the freedom to practice any religion.

READING CHECK ⏺ **CAUSE AND EFFECT**
Why did port cities grow?

Young Patriots

Children played an important role in the American Revolution. Many girls made cloth for the colonies. This cloth enabled colonists to avoid buying British cloth, which was taxed. Later, during the war, girls made clothing and blankets for soldiers.

Some children also fought as soldiers or worked as spies. In most battles, a drummer boy led the way. Some boys, such as 13-year-old Andrew Jackson, delivered messages between troops. Jackson grew up to become the seventh President of the United States.

Make It Relevant Would you have been willing to work in support of the American Revolution?

Forming a Nation

The British colonists elected their own colonial leaders. However, they did not have representation in the British government in England.

New Laws in the Colonies

In the 1760s, Britain started passing laws for the colonies. Some laws forced colonists to pay taxes. Others made it difficult for them to trade. These laws angered many colonists. They shouted,

> **❝No taxation without representation!❞**

Some colonists wrote newspaper articles to speak out against the laws.

Others refused to buy British goods. Some colonists even began to talk about **independence**, or the freedom to govern oneself. They wanted the 13 colonies to form their own country.

The Declaration of Independence

In 1775, fighting started between colonists and British soldiers in Massachusetts. Representatives from all but one of the colonies gathered in Pennsylvania to decide what to do.

The representatives decided to write a **declaration**, or official statement, of independence. Virginian **Thomas Jefferson** did most of the writing. **Benjamin Franklin** and **John Adams** also helped. In July 1776, colonial leaders signed the Declaration of Independence.

Fighting for Independence

The American Revolution had officially begun. A **revolution** is a major, sudden change in government or in people's lives. This revolution meant war. It caused hardships for everyone. Yet, **George Washington**, the leader of the American army, never gave up.

After eight years of fighting, the colonists defeated the British. A treaty, signed in 1783, officially ended the war. The colonists had formed a new nation—the United States of America.

READING CHECK ✪ **CAUSE AND EFFECT**
What was a major effect of the American Revolution?

Summary

Native Americans were the only people living in the Northeast when explorers arrived in the 1500s. Years after, settlers built colonies and later fought for and won their independence.

▶ **GEORGE WASHINGTON** was elected the first President of the United States in 1789.

REVIEW

1. **WHAT TO KNOW** What role did the Northeast have in our nation's early history?

2. **VOCABULARY** Use the terms **declaration** and **independence** in a sentence.

3. **GEOGRAPHY** What were the eight English colonies in the Northeast?

4. **CRITICAL THINKING MAKE IT RELEVANT** How might your life be different today if the colonists had not fought for independence?

5. ✎ **WRITE A NEWSPAPER ARTICLE** Tell why the colonies should be independent.

6. (Focus Skill) **CAUSE AND EFFECT**

On a separate sheet of paper, copy and complete the graphic organizer below.

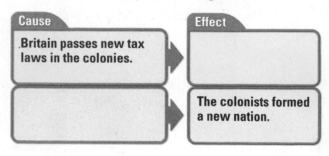

Cause		Effect
Britain passes new tax laws in the colonies.	▶	
	▶	The colonists formed a new nation.

Read a Time Line

Why It Matters Knowing the order of events and the amount of time between them can help you understand how events are connected.

▶ LEARN

A **time line** can show events that took place during one day, one month, one year, one decade, or longer. A **decade** is a period of ten years. On a time line, the earliest date is at the far left. The latest date is at the far right.

This time line shows events in the early history of the Northeast. The space between each mark stands for one **century**, or a period of 100 years. The first part of the time line shows events that happened during the seventeenth century—from 1601 to 1700. What centuries do the last two parts of the time line show?

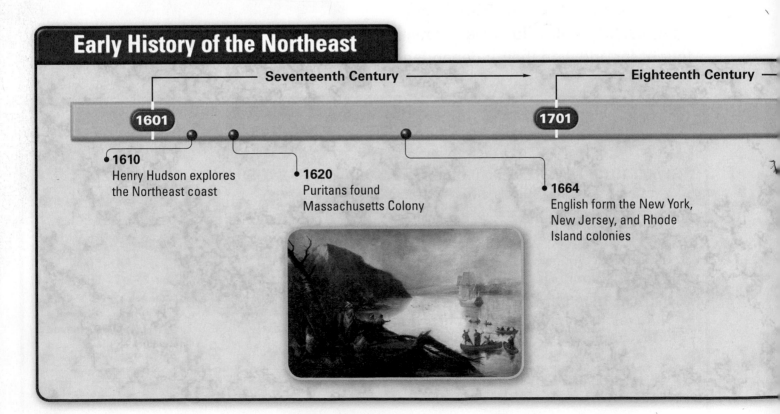

Early History of the Northeast

Seventeenth Century → Eighteenth Century

1601   **1701**

1610
Henry Hudson explores the Northeast coast

1620
Puritans found Massachusetts Colony

1664
English form the New York, New Jersey, and Rhode Island colonies

◗ PRACTICE

Use the time line to answer these questions.

1 When did Puritans establish the Massachusetts Colony?

2 Which English colonies in the Northeast were formed in 1664?

3 In what year did the United States become a country?

◗ APPLY

Make It Relevant Make a time line that shows the twentieth and twenty-first centuries. Label the first and last years of both centuries. Label the year in which you were born. Mark the year you will graduate from high school. Also mark other important years in both the past and the future. Add photographs or drawings, and share your time line with classmates.

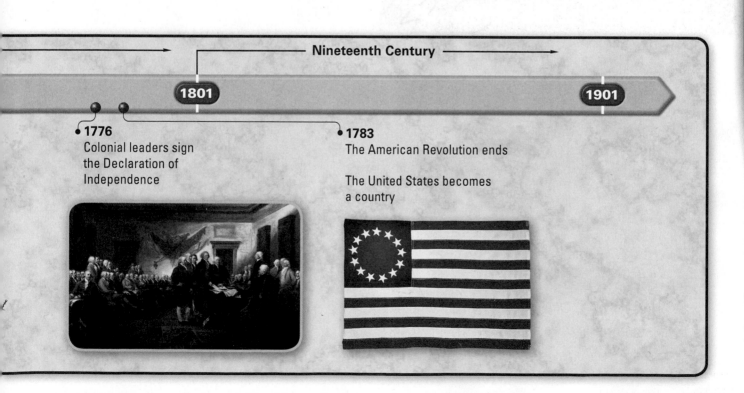

Nineteenth Century

1801   1901

1776
Colonial leaders sign
the Declaration of
Independence

1783
The American Revolution ends

The United States becomes
a country

The Declaration of Independence

Background In 1776, fifty-six representatives signed the Declaration of Independence in Philadelphia, Pennsylvania. Today, Americans celebrate this event as the birth of our nation. The Declaration is a symbol of our nation's history and liberty.

DBQ **Document-Based Question** Study these primary sources and answer the questions.

THE DECLARATION

On the final draft of the Declaration, John Hancock's signature is the largest and easiest to read.

DBQ **1** Why was it important for the representatives to sign the Declaration?

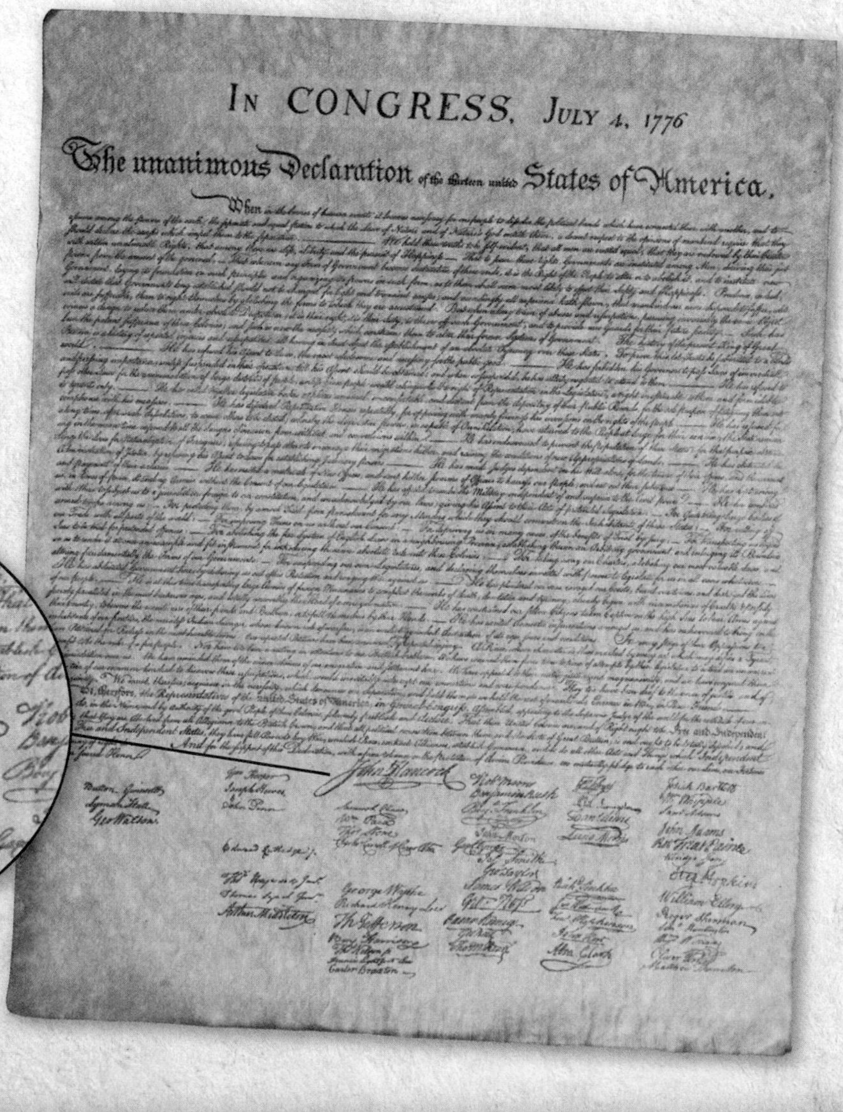

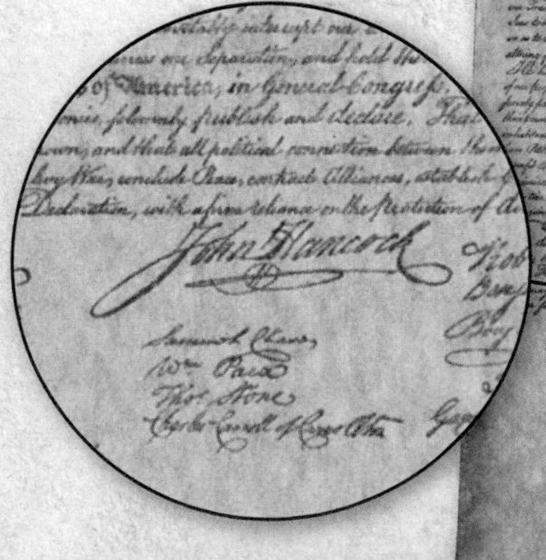

John Hancock's signature

JEFFERSON'S DESK

Thomas Jefferson wrote most of the Declaration of Independence.

DBQ ❷ Why do you think Jefferson needed a travel desk?

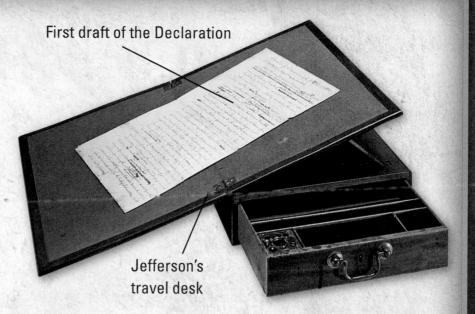

First draft of the Declaration

Jefferson's travel desk

INDEPENDENCE HALL

Representatives debated and signed the Declaration in this room at Independence Hall in Philadelphia.

DBQ ❸ Why might it be important for the representatives to meet in one room?

CENTENNIAL MEDAL

In 1876, medals were made to celebrate the one-hundredth anniversary of the Declaration of Independence.

DBQ ❹ Why do you think Liberty is pointing to 13 stars?

13 stars

A woman represents liberty.

WRITE ABOUT IT

What do these primary sources tell you about the Declaration of Independence? Write a paragraph that describes them.

GO ONLINE For more resources, go to www.harcourtschool.com/ss1

Lesson 3 Growth of the Northeast

WHAT TO KNOW
What changes helped the Northeast grow?

VOCABULARY
waterway p. 127
navigable p. 127
canal p. 127
Industrial Revolution p. 128
textile mill p. 128
urban growth p. 129
metropolitan area p. 130
megalopolis p. 130

PEOPLE
Thomas Edison
Alexander Graham Bell

PLACES
Philadelphia
Boston
Trenton
Erie Canal
Buffalo
Troy
New York City
Ellis Island
Pittsburgh
Newark

CAUSE AND EFFECT

Cause	Effect

YOU ARE THERE

It's 1800. "We'll be lucky if we make it in two weeks," your father says as he finishes loading the wagon. This is your family's first long trip—from **Philadelphia** to **Boston**!

In the city, the bumpy cobblestone streets make your teeth rattle. Outside the city, the dirt road is full of big holes, tree stumps, and mud.

When you finally stop for the night in **Trenton,** New Jersey, your body aches. You lie in the back of the wagon, trying to fall asleep, but you can't stop thinking—250 more miles to go.

▶ **TRANSPORTATION** In the 1800s, improved transportation helped cities like Trenton grow.

Early Transportation

In our nation's early history, people had two choices for transportation—road or water. Most roads were rough dirt paths. Traveling on them by horse and wagon was hard and slow. Water travel was often faster.

Northeast Waterways

The Northeast had many **waterways**, or bodies of water that boats can use. Deep harbors lined the Atlantic coast in the east. The Great Lakes lay to the west. **Navigable** rivers—rivers deep enough and wide enough for ships to use—flowed across the region.

Not all of these waterways connected, however. The Appalachian Mountains separated waterways in the eastern part of the Northeast from those in the western part.

Linking Waterways

In 1817, state leaders in New York came up with a plan to link the Great Lakes and the Atlantic Ocean. They had workers build a **canal**, a waterway dug across land. The new canal, the **Erie Canal**, was completed in 1825. It connected the New York cities of **Buffalo,** on Lake Erie, and **Troy,** on the Hudson River. From Troy, ships traveled down the Hudson River to **New York City** on the Atlantic coast.

By the early 1900s, better roads and miles of railroads connected much of the Northeast. In many places, people used these instead of canals. Even so, people continued to build large canals, such as the Saint Lawrence Seaway, for transportation and shipping.

READING CHECK ŎCAUSE AND EFFECT
Why was the Erie Canal built?

▶ **TEXTILE MILLS** Many children worked in textile mills in the Northeast.

Industrial Revolution

As transportation improved in the Northeast, so did its industries. People replaced machines powered by hand with new sources of power. The new machines allowed people to make more goods faster. This period is known as the **Industrial Revolution**.

Machines and Power

In the early 1800s, factories that used machines powered by moving water opened along rivers. Textile mills were the first factories to use these machines. A **textile mill** is a factory that uses machines to weave cloth.

In the mid-1800s, steam engines began to power machines in factories. Steam engines had already improved transportation. They provided power for boats and trains.

In 1882, **Thomas Edison** opened the world's first electric power plant in New York City. In time, power plants provided electricity across the country. They led to the spread of other inventions, including Edison's light bulb and **Alexander Graham Bell**'s telephone. By the early 1900s, the United States was a leading industrial nation.

READING CHECK ◌ **CAUSE AND EFFECT**
Why were most early factories built along rivers?

Immigrants

During the 1800s and early 1900s, millions of immigrants came to the United States. Most came by boat from Europe, arriving in New York. Their first stop was **Ellis Island,** the nation's largest immigration center.

Immigrants came to the United States for different reasons. Most had difficult lives in their homeland. Many were poor. Some had been treated badly because of their race or religion. Here, immigrants hoped to make a better life. For them, the United States was the land of opportunity. A person who worked hard could be a success.

Immigrants moved to every part of the nation. However, millions stayed in the Northeast to work in factories. Most settled in cities, such as New York City, Trenton, or Boston. The result was enormous **urban growth,** or growth of cities, in the region.

New immigrants settled mostly in crowded neighborhoods with others from their countries. To make a living, most new immigrants worked long hours in factories. Some immigrants started businesses, such as restaurants and shops. Others helped build bridges, buildings, and roads.

READING CHECK ⚙ **CAUSE AND EFFECT**
How did immigration help cause urban growth?

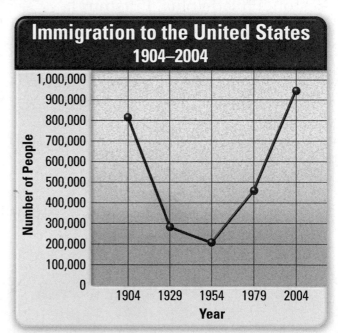

GRAPH Millions of immigrants arrived at Ellis Island (below), a small island in New York Harbor. In which year was immigration the lowest?

Cities Grow and Connect

Improved transportation, growing industries, and immigration helped cities in the Northeast grow. Today, the Northeast is one of the most crowded regions in the United States.

A Region of Cities

The Northeast's big cities include Boston, Philadelphia, **Pittsburgh, Newark,** and New York City. In fact, New York City has more people than any other city in the United States.

As Northeast cities grew, so did the suburbs around them. The result was the growth of metropolitan areas.

A **metropolitan area** is a large city together with its suburbs. A metropolitan area often stretches across state borders. The largest metropolitan area in the nation covers parts of New York and New Jersey.

Most metropolitan areas in the Northeast grew along the Atlantic coast. Over time, their boundaries grew closer together. Eventually, the metropolitan areas formed a long chain of cities stretching from New Hampshire to Virginia. These cities make up the nation's largest megalopolis (meh•guh•LAH•puh•lihs). A **megalopolis** is an urban region formed when two or more metropolitan areas grow together.

❱ **TRANSPORTATION** High-speed trains carry passengers between major cities in the Northeast.

Traveling Between Cities Today

Today, people can travel easily between cities in the Northeast. Modern highways, including turnpikes, or toll roads, crisscross the region. Airlines make many flights each day between major cities. Passenger trains also run many times daily, connecting Boston, New York City, Philadelphia, and other Northeast cities.

READING CHECK **MAIN IDEA AND DETAILS**
What forms of transportation link cities in the Northeast today?

Summary

Changes in transportation and power helped cities in the Northeast grow and connect during the Industrial Revolution. Immigrants also contributed to urban growth. Today, people and goods move more easily from one city to another.

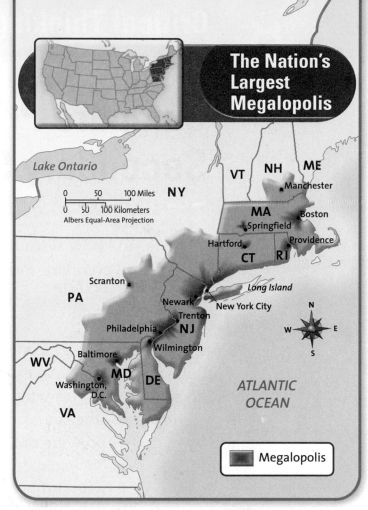

The Nation's Largest Megalopolis

ATLANTIC OCEAN

■ Megalopolis

MAP SKILL **REGIONS** The largest megalopolis in the United States is mostly in the Northeast. Which large cities in Massachusetts are part of the megalopolis?

REVIEW

1. **WHAT TO KNOW** What changes helped the Northeast grow?

2. **VOCABULARY** How are the terms **metropolitan area** and **megalopolis** related?

3. **GEOGRAPHY** Why did the state of New York build the Erie Canal?

4. **CRITICAL THINKING** How was early road travel in the Northeast different from road travel in the region today?

5. ✏ **WRITE A LETTER** Imagine that you are living in the Northeast in 1827. Write a letter to your cousin. Explain how life in the Northeast changed after the Erie Canal was built.

6. **CAUSE AND EFFECT**

On a separate sheet of paper, copy and complete the graphic organizer below.

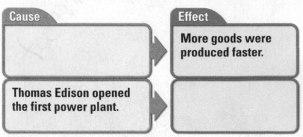

Cause	Effect
	More goods were produced faster.
Thomas Edison opened the first power plant.	

Compare Primary and Secondary Sources

Why It Matters To know what actually happened in the past, people study and compare sources of information.

❯ LEARN

A **primary source** is a record made by people who took part in or saw an event. An example might be a letter, a diary, an interview, a drawing, or a photograph.

A **secondary source** is a record of an event that was made by people who were not there. An encyclopedia is a secondary source. Newspaper stories and magazine articles written by people who did not take part in the event are also secondary sources. So, too, are paintings and drawings by artists who did not see the event.

❯ **PRIMARY SOURCES** This photograph Ⓐ, lantern Ⓑ, and list of toll rates Ⓒ are all primary sources related to the Erie Canal.

▶ PRACTICE

Examine the images on these two pages. Then answer the following questions.

1 How are items *A* and *D* alike and different?

2 Which sources show objects that people actually used for traveling on the Erie Canal?

3 Why might secondary sources *E* and *F* also be considered primary sources? Explain your answer.

▶ APPLY

Work with a partner to find primary and secondary sources in your textbook. Discuss what makes each source you selected a primary or a secondary source.

▶ **SECONDARY SOURCES** This painting **D**, Erie Canal website **E**, and book **F** are all secondary sources related to the Erie Canal.

Visual Summary

1500
Only Native Americans live in the Northeast

1600s
England starts eight colonies in the Northeast

Summarize the Chapter

Cause and Effect Complete this graphic organizer to show that you understand the causes and effects of growth in the Northeast.

Cause

People found new sources of power for machines.

Effect

Cause

Effect

During the 1800s and early 1900s, Northeastern cities grew crowded.

Vocabulary

Identify the term from the word bank that correctly matches each definition.

1. a loosely united group of governments that work together

2. a major, sudden change in government or in people's lives

3. a waterway dug across land

4. a huge, slow-moving mass of ice

5. a trading center where goods are put onto and taken off ships

6. a body of water that boats can use

7. a protected area of water where ships can dock safely

8. a settlement that is ruled by a faraway government

> ### Word Bank
>
> **harbor** p. 111   **port** p. 119
>
> **glacier** p. 111   **revolution** p. 121
>
> **confederation** p. 117   **waterway** p. 127
>
> **colony** p. 118   **canal** p. 127

1750   1875   Present

1775
The American
Revolution begins

Time Line

Use the chapter summary time line above to answer these questions.

9. How many colonies did England start in the Northeast during the 1600s?

10. In what year did the American Revolution begin?

Facts and Main Ideas

Answer these questions.

11. What are three physical features that are found in the Northeast?

12. Who was Henry Hudson?

13. What were two reasons why immigrants came to the Northeast?

Write the letter of the best choice.

14. Which of the following is mined in Northeast quarries?
   A gold
   B diamonds
   C granite
   D copper

15. Which group formed a confederation among tribes fighting in the Northeast?
   A the Iroquois
   B the Puritans
   C the British
   D the Wampanoag

Critical Thinking

16. How would the geography of the Northeast be different if glaciers had not once covered the region?

17. What did the phrase "no taxation without representation" mean to British colonists?

Skills

Read a Time Line

18. Make a time line that shows centuries. On the time line, show when Europeans began to explore the Northeast. Then show three more important events leading up to the twenty-first century.

writing

✏ **Write a Paragraph** Write a paragraph describing important events that happened during the Industrial Revolution. Name at least three changes that occurred during this time period.

✏ **Write a Song** Write a song about the geography and climate of the Northeast. Describe the region's physical features and its weather. You may set your words to the tune of "America the Beautiful" or another song you know.

STUDY SKILLS

TAKE NOTES

Taking notes can help you remember important ideas.

■ **Write down only important facts and ideas. Use your own words. You do not have to write in complete sentences.**

■ **One way to organize notes is in a chart. Write down the main ideas in one column and facts in another.**

The Northeast Today	
Main Ideas	Facts
Lesson 1: New England States • New England is a region of variety. • _____	• Southern New England has several large cities, including Boston, Providence, and Hartford. • _____
Lesson 2: Middle Atlantic States • _____ • _____	• _____ • _____

PREVIEW VOCABULARY

candidate p. 141   **skyscraper** p. 147   **urban sprawl** p. 148

The Northeast Today

The city of Pittsburgh, Pennsylvania

Lesson 1

New England States

WHAT TO KNOW
What features of life in New England today came from the region's past?

VOCABULARY

specialize p. 140

candidate p. 141

campaign p. 141

ballot p. 141

volunteer p. 141

PEOPLE

Robert Frost

Winslow Homer

Norman Rockwell

Louisa May Alcott

PLACES

Boston

Providence

Hartford

Portland

CAUSE AND EFFECT

YOU ARE THERE

While visiting your cousin in **Boston**, you walk through Boston Common, a big, grassy park in the middle of the city. People in the park are playing soccer and having picnics. A crowd gathers around a woman who is urging everyone to vote in a coming election.

"Most New England cities and towns have a place like this," your cousin says. "A common is like a big backyard that we all share!"

FAST FACT

Boston Common is one of the nation's oldest public parks. When Massachusetts was a colony, the Common was a place where colonists could let their cows graze.

▶ **NEWFANE VILLAGE** Many small, historic towns like Newfane, Vermont, can be found throughout the New England countryside.

A View of New England

New England is one of two smaller regions that make up the Northeast. New England includes Connecticut, Massachusetts, Maine, Rhode Island, New Hampshire, and Vermont.

Cities and Towns

Most New Englanders live in cities along the Atlantic coast. Boston, Massachusetts, is the region's biggest city by far. Other large cities in New England include **Providence**, Rhode Island, and **Hartford**, Connecticut.

Small towns are scattered all across New England. Many have a town common, surrounded by small stores, homes, and old churches.

People of New England

Many places in New England were founded in the colonial period. New Englanders take great pride in their colonial history. They preserve historic sites so that important events, people, and places will not be forgotten.

New England's history and beauty have inspired many artists. **Robert Frost** wrote poems about the region's peaceful countryside. **Winslow Homer** painted scenes of the rocky coastline of Maine. While **Norman Rockwell** painted scenes of life in small towns, **Louisa May Alcott** described growing up in one in her novel *Little Women*.

READING CHECK ☼ **CAUSE AND EFFECT**
How has New England affected artists?

The Economy Today

Like its cities and towns, many of New England's industries have a long history. Other industries are new.

A Changing Economy

Shipping and fishing have long been important industries in New England. After all, every New England state, except Vermont, borders the ocean. **Portland**, Maine, handles more goods than any other port in the region.

New England was once the nation's manufacturing center. During the past 50 years, however, many textile mills and other factories have moved. They have moved to places where their products can be made more cheaply.

Still, new kinds of factories have opened in New England. They make computer parts, scientific equipment, and other products. These factories need workers who specialize. People who **specialize** do one kind of job well.

Most New Englanders work in service industries, such as health care, insurance, and technology. Many people have jobs in hotels, museums, and restaurants. They serve the millions of people who visit New England.

Education is a large employer in New England, too. The region is known around the world for its top-rated colleges and universities.

READING CHECK ☼ **CAUSE AND EFFECT**
Why have some factories left New England?

▶ **EDUCATION** Massachusetts Institute of Technology, in Cambridge, Massachusetts, helps students specialize in computers and science.

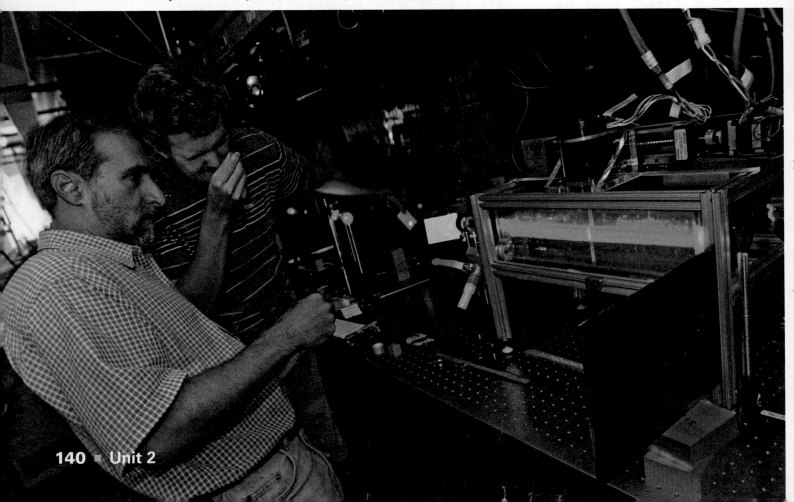

▶ **TOWN MEETING** Many New Englanders attend town meetings so they can take part in community decisions.

Citizenship

Town meetings have been a part of life in New England since colonial times. At town meetings, citizens gather to discuss and vote on important community issues.

Voting and Elections

Voting is the foundation of our nation's democracy. It gives people the power to rule. Citizens use this power when they vote to elect their local, state, and national leaders. The people who run for office in elections are called **candidates**.

Before an election, most candidates carry out **campaigns** to encourage people to vote for them. They display signs, make speeches, and talk to voters. They may advertise on television and set up Internet sites.

On election day, the names of all the candidates for each office are listed on a ballot. A **ballot** is either a sheet of paper on which votes are marked or another method used to record votes.

Helping the Community

As in all regions, people in New England help their communities by being volunteers. A **volunteer** is a person who works for no pay. Some volunteers clean up litter or work in hospitals. In some small towns, even the elected leaders are volunteers.

READING CHECK **MAIN IDEA AND DETAILS**
Why is voting important?

Global Connection

Many early European settlers in New England came from England. They named many New England towns and cities after places in England. For example, Hartford, Connecticut, was named after Hertford, England. Today, these two cities are "sister cities." They offer youth and teacher exchange programs, and they hold celebrations.

READING CHECK ☼**CAUSE AND EFFECT**
What is one effect that English settlers have had on the United States?

▶ **SISTER CITIES** A view of Hertford (above) and a statue in Hartford (left), showing one of its English founders

Summary

New England has big cities and small historic towns. Most people in the region work in service industries. Like all United States citizens, people in New England elect their leaders and vote to make decisions.

REVIEW

1. **WHAT TO KNOW** What features of life in New England today came from the region's past?

2. **VOCABULARY** Use the term **candidate** in a sentence about a **campaign**.

3. **GEOGRAPHY** Where do most people in New England live?

4. **CRITICAL THINKING MAKE IT RELEVANT** Why is voting both a right and a responsibility of citizenship?

5. **WRITE AN EXPLANATION** Think of a job you would like to do as a volunteer. Write a paragraph about how that job would help your community.

6. **CAUSE AND EFFECT**
On a separate sheet of paper, copy and complete the graphic organizer below.

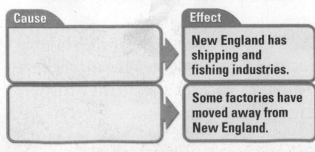

Cause	Effect
	New England has shipping and fishing industries.
	Some factories have moved away from New England.

Theodor Geisel

Biography

Trustworthiness
Respect
Responsibility
Fairness
Caring
Patriotism

*"The more that you read,
the more things you will know.
The more that you learn,
the more places you'll go."*

You may not know the name Theodor Geisel. That is because nearly everyone knows him as Dr. Seuss! Born in Springfield, Massachusetts, Dr. Seuss always loved to read. After college, he started writing magazine articles, drawing cartoons, and creating children's books.

In 1954, a report claimed that children had trouble learning to read because they were not interested in their books. A publisher asked Dr. Seuss to write a funny and exciting children's book. The result was the now-famous book *The Cat in the Hat*.

Dr. Seuss continued to write lively children's books. Many of these books have been translated into 15 different languages. His books have entertained and helped educate millions of children all over the world.

Why Character Counts

How do Dr. Seuss's books show that he cared about children?

Time

1904			1991
Born			Died

1937 Dr. Seuss's first children's book is published

1957 *The Cat in the Hat* is published

1984 Dr. Seuss wins an honorary Pulitzer Prize

GO ONLINE For more resources, go to www.harcourtschool.com/ss1

Should the School Year Be Longer?

In 1647, Massachusetts leaders passed the first public school law in what is now the United States. Today, most American students follow the same school calendar used in colonial days. They attend school for about 180 days a year and have summers off. However, some people want the school year to be longer. Others disagree.

1

GRACE LEAVITT

Grace Leavitt is a Spanish teacher in Cumberland, Maine. She believes the school year should be longer.

66 We are trying to fit the needs of today's students into a traditional calendar developed decades ago.... Our students simply need to know more. 99

2

SHANE FLYNN

Shane Flynn is a fourth-grade student in Columbia, Maryland. He does not believe the school year should be longer.

66 I love school. But I learn a lot during summer vacation, too. Last summer, my family went to the Grand Canyon. I learned about it in social studies. 99

3

DOROTHY MOODY

Dorothy Moody is a math and science teacher in Rialto, California. She does not believe the school year should be longer.

"Students, like teachers, are only human. They can handle only so much education before suffering information overload.... Our students need the summer to relax, play, and act like children. "

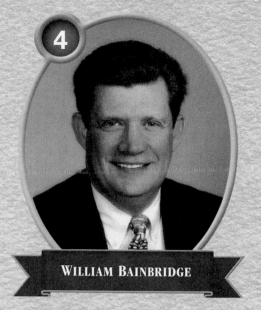

4

WILLIAM BAINBRIDGE

William Bainbridge is a professor at the University of Dayton in Ohio. He believes the school year should be longer.

"American students have a shorter school year than those living in 12 of the world's other wealthiest nations. . . . It is unreasonable to expect American students to learn as much as their overseas peers in half the time. "

It's Your Turn

Compare Points of View Summarize each person's point of view. Then answer the questions.

1. Who seems to support a longer school year?

2. How are Shane Flynn's and Dorothy Moody's points of view alike? How are they different?

3. Who provides facts to support his or her opinion? What are those facts?

Make It Relevant What do you think? Explain why one argument is more persuasive to you than another.

Lesson 2

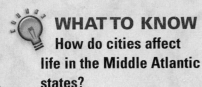

Middle Atlantic States

WHAT TO KNOW
How do cities affect life in the Middle Atlantic states?

VOCABULARY
skyscraper p. 147
commute p. 148
urban sprawl p. 148
pollution p. 149

PEOPLE
Rudolph Giuliani
Nydia M. Velázquez
Alvin Ailey

PLACES
New York City
Philadelphia
Pittsburgh
Wilmington
Newark

CAUSE AND EFFECT

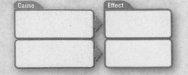

Cause	Effect

YOU ARE THERE

This is your first trip to **New York City**. Today, you are visiting Jackson Heights, a section of the city. It is one of the most culturally diverse neighborhoods in the United States. People from more than 80 nations live here. The streets are lined with restaurants offering the foods of India, China, Argentina, and other countries. After exploring Jackson Heights, you feel as if you have seen the world!

▶ **NEW YORK HARBOR** The Statue of Liberty stands on Liberty Island in the middle of New York Harbor.

New York City

The Middle Atlantic states are Delaware, New Jersey, New York, and Pennsylvania. This region has many big cities. In fact, New York City is the largest city in the United States.

A Global City

The former mayor of New York City, **Rudolph Giuliani**, once said, "We are a city of immigrants." He meant that people from all over the world have made their home in New York City. One New Yorker, **Nydia M. Velázquez**, came from Puerto Rico. In time, she became the first Puerto Rican woman elected to Congress.

New York City is a world-famous center for the arts. Residents and visitors enjoy museums, Broadway shows, and concerts. Groups such as the **Alvin Ailey** American Dance Theater train dancers and perform worldwide.

New York City is a global center for business, too. It is a leader in banking, publishing, fashion, entertainment, and other industries. Many industries fill the city's **skyscrapers**, or very tall buildings. On September 11, 2001, two of the city's tallest skyscrapers were destroyed in attacks. These buildings were part of the World Trade Center.

Another skyscraper in the city is the headquarters of the United Nations, or UN. Representatives from nearly every nation gather there. They help member nations work together to solve problems ranging from hunger to war.

READING CHECK ◌CAUSE AND EFFECT
What effect does the United Nations have?

Jackson Heights

City Life

New York City is not the only big city in the Middle Atlantic states. About four out of five people in the region live in urban areas.

Major Cities

Philadelphia and **Pittsburg** are two major cities in Pennsylvania. Philadelphia is a center of culture, education, and publishing.

Pittsburgh has a long history as a steelmaking center. However, today, only one major steel mill operates in the city. Medical research is a newer, growing industry there.

South of Philadelphia is **Wilmington**, the largest city in Delaware. Many big companies have headquarters there.

Newark is the largest city in New Jersey. It has a central location, highways, a port, and an international airport. These make Newark a transportation center for the region.

Growth and Services

In the past, workers needed to live close to where they worked. Because transportation has improved, people today can live farther from work. Many people live in the suburbs and **commute**, or travel back and forth between work and home. As a result, metropolitan areas have grown larger. New businesses, houses, and shopping centers have grown up around cities. This spreading of urban areas is called **urban sprawl**.

ILLUSTRATION In cities, buildings are often built close together. Why do you think many subways are built underground?

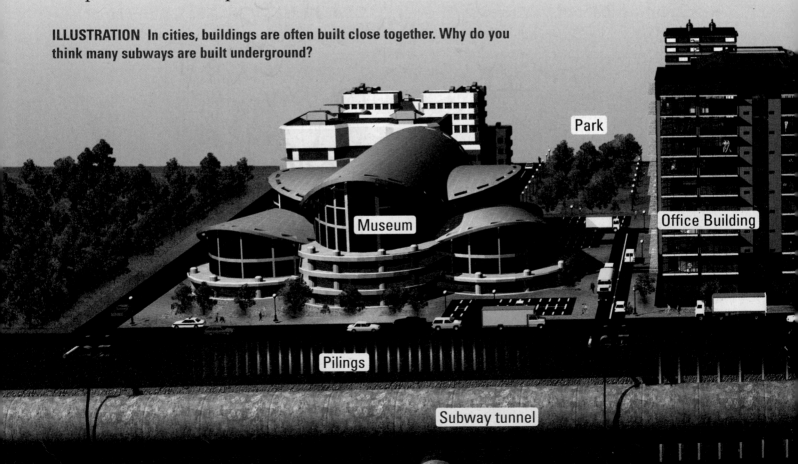

Park

Museum

Office Building

Pilings

Subway tunnel

Living in cities comes with both problems and benefits. Overcrowding can cause many problems. It can make housing hard to find and expensive. It can cause traffic jams and pollution. **Pollution** is anything that makes a natural resource dirty or unsafe to use. To help reduce traffic and pollution, most cities have public transportation, such as buses, trains, and subways. The benefits of living in cities include access to work, cultural, and educational opportunities.

City governments provide their citizens with many services. They provide water, electricity, schools, police protection, and trash removal. They keep streets, bridges, sewers, and pipes repaired. To provide these services, city governments hire many workers. This costs a lot of money. As a result, most cities have higher taxes than rural areas have.

READING CHECK ○CAUSE AND EFFECT
What are some problems that overcrowding causes in cities?

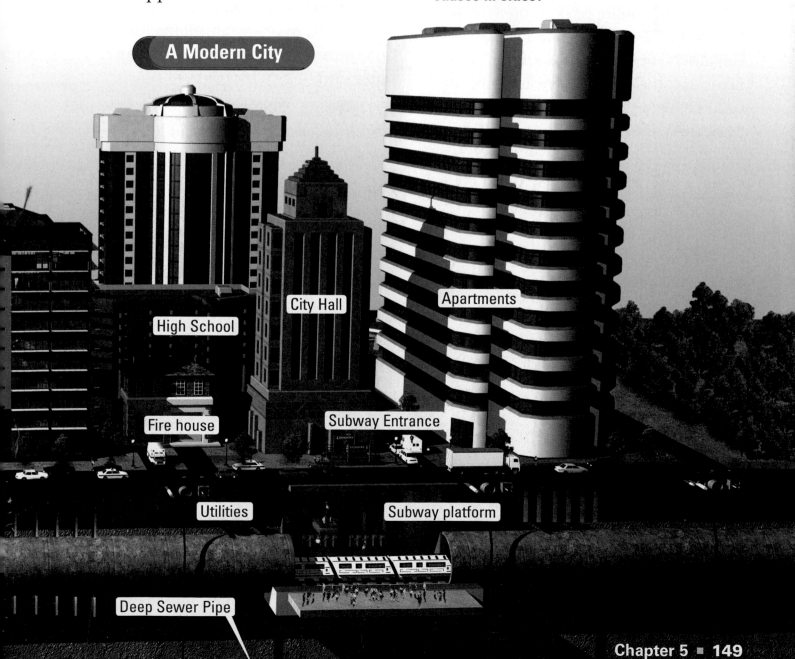

A Modern City

High School

City Hall

Apartments

Fire house

Subway Entrance

Utilities

Subway platform

Deep Sewer Pipe

Places to Visit

Many people who live in cities enjoy getting away from them now and then. Some places in the Middle Atlantic states are favorites for city dwellers to visit.

Upstate New York

Many New Yorkers divide their state into two parts. "The city" is the area around New York City. "Upstate" is the rest of the state.

The largest state park in the United States is Adirondack State Park, in upstate New York. It has 6 million acres and includes the western shore of Lake Champlain. Visitors to the park can canoe, hike, ski, ice-skate, and even dogsled!

The Jersey Shore

The Jersey Shore is a 127-mile-long area of beaches. It has amusement parks and other attractions along the New Jersey coast. In the summer, millions of people from nearby cities go to the Jersey Shore to have fun.

Pennsylvania Dutch Country

The Pennsylvania Dutch Country, in the southeastern part of the state, is known for its communities of Amish and Mennonite farmers. Because of their religious beliefs, these groups live simply. Many wear plain clothing, do not use electricity, and travel by horse and buggy.

READING CHECK ☼ **CAUSE AND EFFECT**
Why do the Amish and Mennonites live as they do?

> ⚡ *FAST FACT*
>
> Most Amish in Pennsylvania have German ancestors. People started calling the region Pennsylvania Dutch Country because they misunderstood the word *Deutsch*, which means "German."

Global Connection

Countries all over the world face challenges caused by urban growth and urban sprawl. Many workers in Tokyo, Japan's capital, commute long distances to and from work. These workers have found clever ways to deal with the long commute. Some rent sleeping capsules in the city during the week. This allows them to avoid the long commute on most days. Others commute by high-speed trains called bullet trains. Once in the city, about 10 million people use Tokyo's trains and subways each day.

READING CHECK ✪ **SUMMARIZE**
How do people in Tokyo deal with their long commutes to work?

Summary

Immigration has helped make the Middle Atlantic states a region of large cities. Urban growth creates problems for people and government to solve.

REVIEW

1. **WHAT TO KNOW** How do cities affect life in the Middle Atlantic states?

2. **VOCABULARY** What clues can you use to remember **skyscraper**'s meaning?

3. **GOVERNMENT** Where is the United Nations based, and what does it do?

4. **CRITICAL THINKING** What do you think are the main advantages and disadvantages of living in cities?

5. 🖌 **MAKE A PRESENTATION** Work with a partner to think of a problem that cities face today. Describe the problem to your class in a presentation.

6. ⭐ Focus Skill **CAUSE AND EFFECT**
On a separate sheet of paper, copy and complete the graphic organizer below.

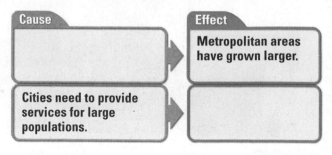

Cause	Effect
	Metropolitan areas have grown larger.
Cities need to provide services for large populations.	

Read a Population Map

Why It Matters Reading a population map helps you understand where in a city, state, or country people live.

❱ LEARN

The map on page 153 is a population map of the United States. It uses colors to show population density. **Population density** is the number of people who live in an area of a certain size. This map tells how many people live in 1 square mile and in 1 square kilometer.

To find the population density of an area, look to see what color that area is on the map. Then look at the map key to find that color. It tells you how many people live in each square mile and square kilometer. For example, the area around Newark, New Jersey, is purple. This color means that more than 500 people live in each square mile of that area. More than 200 people live in each square kilometer.

❱ **NEW JERSEY** New Jersey has both crowded cities (left) and small towns (right).

Newark

Cape May

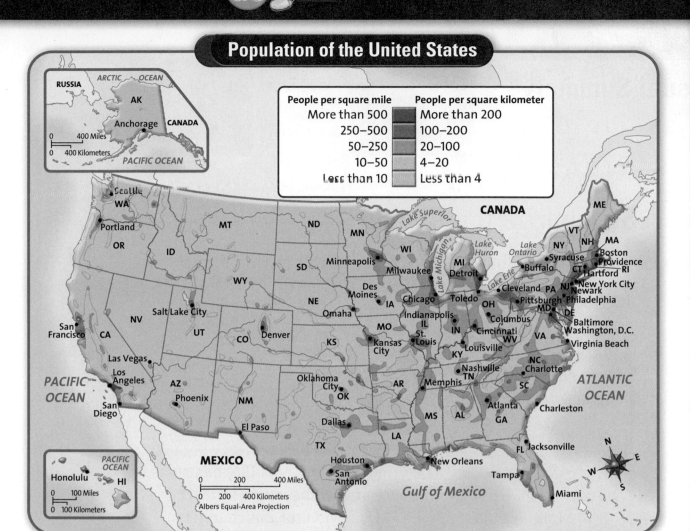

Population of the United States

People per square mile | People per square kilometer
More than 500 | More than 200
250–500 | 100–200
50–250 | 20–100
10–50 | 4–20
Less than 10 | Less than 4

PRACTICE

Use the map above to answer these questions.

1 Which color on the map shows the areas that are the most crowded? the least crowded?

2 How does this map show that the Northeast region is one of the most crowded parts of the United States?

APPLY

Make It Relevant Study a population density map of your state. Then write about how you think the different population densities affect the way people live.

Map and Globe Skills

Visual Summary

Boston Common is one of the nation's oldest parks.

Many historic towns lie in the New England countryside.

Summarize the Chapter

Focus Skill **Cause and Effect** Complete this graphic organizer to show that you understand the causes and effects of the past on life in the Northeast today.

Cause

Many early settlers in New England came from England.

Effect

Effect

New York City has some of the nation's most diverse communities.

 Vocabulary

Identify the term from the word bank that correctly matches each definition.

1. a person who runs for office in an election

2. to do one kind of job well

3. to travel back and forth between work and home

4. a person who works for no pay

5. the spreading of urban areas

6. anything that makes a natural resource dirty or unsafe to use

7. a very tall building

8. a method used to record votes

Word Bank

specialize p. 140	**skyscraper** p. 147
candidate p. 141	**commute** p. 148
ballot p. 141	**urban sprawl** p. 148
volunteer p. 141	**pollution** p. 149

People from more than 80 nations live in Jackson Heights.

Pennsylvania Dutch Country is known for its Amish community.

 Facts and Main Ideas

Answer these questions.

9. Which states are the New England states?

10. Why have some factories moved from New England to other places?

11. Which states are the Middle Atlantic states?

12. Why is Newark, New Jersey, considered a transportation center for the Northeast?

Write the letter of the best choice.

13. Which New England state has no coastline?
    A Maine
    B Vermont
    C Rhode Island
    D New Hampshire

14. Which person said that New York City is a "city of immigrants"?
    A Alvin Ailey
    B Rudolph Giuliani
    C Robert Frost
    D Theodor Geisel

15. Which is the largest city in the United States?
    A Newark, New Jersey
    B Wilmington, Delaware
    C Philadelphia, Pennsylvania
    D New York City, New York

 Critical Thinking

16. Why does New England have more historic sites than some other regions?

17. Why do people who live in cities enjoy visiting places away from urban areas?

 Skills

Read a Population Map

18. Study the map on page 153. Which areas of the United States, besides the Northeast, have high population densities?

writing

✎ **Write a Slogan** Imagine that your job is to persuade people to visit New England. Write a slogan that will make people want to spend their vacations in the region.

✎ **Write a Letter** Imagine that you live in New York City. Write a letter to a friend who lives in another region. Describe the sights and sounds of New York City.

Fun with Social Studies

Just the Facts

Go from Start to Finish along the path that has its facts straight about the Northeast. Circled letters will spell the answer to the riddle below.

START

Borders the Atlantic Ocean — **R**

Native Americans were the first to live here — **O**

English settlers founded colonies during 1600s — **C**

No navigable rivers — **T**

American Revolution brought independence — **K**

Pollution is a big problem — **N**

Most of the people live in urban areas — **I**

New York is the largest city in the U.S. — **S**

Immigration was a cause of urban growth here — **M**

Known for its top-rated schools — **U**

Shipping and fishing are important industries — **C**

No farming here — **E**

Has only one large city — **L**

FINISH

What do quarry workers listen to on the radio ?

Secret State

Which northeastern state's name is hiding in the rhymes? Find out by filling in the missing letters and unscrambling them.

Lonesome Valley
Sally's Ranch
Bill's Ranch
Big City

Rancher Bill and Rancher Sally
Lost their sheep herds in a blizza__d.
Some __urned up in Lonesome Valley.
Were they h__rs? Or was it his herd?

Who would like to __olunteer
For wind__w washing way up high
Where buildings __early scrape the sky?
We really do a lot of this
In our __egalopolis.

Online Adventures

GO ONLINE

Eco has a hot-air balloon that is floating through different times and places in the Northeast. Play the online game to face challenges in Plymouth Colony, at a battle of the American Revolution, and in the Northeast today. At the end of the game, you will get your first clue card and move one step closer to solving the mystery. Play now at **www.harcourtschool.com/ss1**

Review and Test Prep

THE BIG IDEA

Cities and Growth The early settlement of the Northeast helped give it the second-largest population of any region in the United States today.

Reading Comprehension and Vocabulary

The Northeast

The Northeast has a variety of physical features and climates. It has many natural resources, including farmland, stone, trees, and fish.

Native Americans in the region were hunters, gatherers, and farmers. European explorers began arriving in the 1500s. Soon settlers started colonies. Years later, in 1783, <u>colonists</u> won the American Revolution and gained independence from Britain.

In the 1800s, many changes took place. Canals, better roads, and railroads improved transportation. In addition, new power sources and machines led to the Industrial Revolution. During this time, immigrants came to the Northeast to work in factories.

New England is the northern part of the Northeast. It has a few big cities and many small historic towns. Most people work in service industries.

The Middle Atlantic States are home to many big cities, including New York City. People who live in big cities enjoy services such as museums, parks, and entertainment. They also face challenges, such as crowding and <u>pollution</u>.

Read the summary above. Then answer the questions that follow.

1. Who ruled the colonists before the American Revolution?
   - **A** France
   - **B** Britain
   - **C** Spain
   - **D** Native Americans

2. A <u>colonist</u> is—
   - **A** an early settler.
   - **B** an early hunter.
   - **C** a settlement that is ruled by a faraway government.
   - **D** a settlement in the Americas.

3. Most people in New England work in which industry?
   - **A** fishing
   - **B** farming
   - **C** service industry
   - **D** manufacturing industry

4. <u>Pollution</u> is—
   - **A** the growth of cities.
   - **B** the spreading of urban areas.
   - **C** the freedom to govern oneself.
   - **D** anything that makes a natural resource dirty.

Facts and Main Ideas

Answer these questions.

5. What are three crops that farmers grow in the Northeast?

6. Why did the Iroquois tribes form a confederation?

7. What is a textile mill?

8. What happens at a town meeting?

9. What have many large cities done to help reduce traffic and pollution?

10. What are two favorite vacation areas for people who live in cities in the Middle Atlantic states?

Write the letter of the best choice.

11. Which of these shaped many of the Northeast's physical features?
    A granite
    B marble
    C basins
    D glaciers

12. Where did most early European settlers in the Northeast come from?
    A France
    B England
    C Canada
    D Holland

13. The Erie Canal connects the Great Lakes to the—
    A Atlantic Ocean
    B Gulf of Mexico
    C Mississippi River
    D St. Lawrence Seaway

14. The largest city in New England is—
    A Boston
    B Portland
    C Providence
    D Philadelphia

Critical Thinking

15. What was one cause of the American Revolution?

16. What effect did the Industrial Revolution have on the United States?

Skills

Read a Population Map

Use the map below to answer these questions.

17. What is the population density of Manhattan?

18. Which area has a higher population density, Staten Island or Brooklyn?

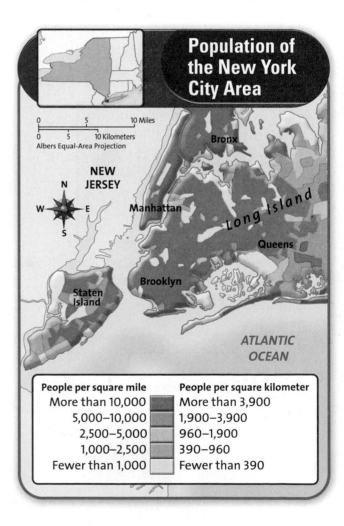

Population of the New York City Area

0   5   10 Miles
0   5   10 Kilometers
Albers Equal-Area Projection

People per square mile	People per square kilometer
More than 10,000	More than 3,900
5,000–10,000	1,900–3,900
2,500–5,000	960–1,900
1,000–2,500	390–960
Fewer than 1,000	Fewer than 390

Show What You Know

Unit Writing Activity

Write an Explanation Write a paragraph that explains how the past shaped the Northeast.

- Describe the Northeast today.
- Include important details.
- Explain how the past shaped life in the Northeast today.

Unit Project

Build a Museum Display Create a museum display about the Northeast.

- Choose people, places, and events to include in your display.
- Write brief reports about the people, places, and events.
- Create artifacts, drawings, time lines, maps, and journal entries to go with your reports.

Read More

- *A New England Scrapbook* by Loretta Krupinski. HarperCollins.
- *Liberty Rising: The Story of the Statue of Liberty* by Pegi Dietz Shea. Henry Holt.
- *Journey to Ellis Island: How My Father Came to America* by Carol Bierman. Hyperion.

GO ONLINE For more resources, go to www.harcourtschool.com/ss1

The Southeast

The Big Idea

Growth and Change

The Southeast is experiencing changes that give it one of the fastest-growing populations of any region in the United States today.

What to Know

- ✓ What is the geography of the Southeast?
- ✓ What important events took place in the Southeast during our nation's early history?
- ✓ How do ports in the Southeast affect the region and the United States?
- ✓ What is the Southeast like today?

Time

The Southeast

1565 St. Augustine—the first settlement in the Southeast—is built in what is now Florida, p. 186

1607 The Jamestown colony is founded in what is now Virginia, p. 186

1500 **1600** **1700**

At the Same Time

1524 Northeast Giovanni da Verrazano sails into what is now New York Bay

1608 French explorer Samuel de Champlain founds Quebec

The Southeast

1775 Daniel Boone and others clear a path for wagons through the Cumberland Gap, p. 187

1861 The Civil War begins, p. 189

Present The port of South Louisiana is the busiest port on the Gulf Coast, p. 195

1800

1900

Present

1760 **Northeast** About 16,000 people live in Boston, making it the largest city in New England

1850 **West** California becomes a state

1999 Most European Union countries begin to use a form of money called the euro

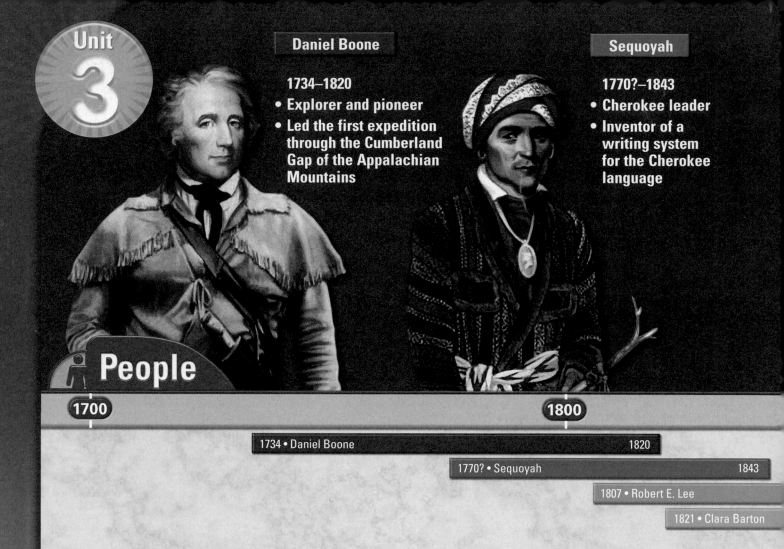

Daniel Boone

1734–1820
- Explorer and pioneer
- Led the first expedition through the Cumberland Gap of the Appalachian Mountains

Sequoyah

1770?–1843
- Cherokee leader
- Inventor of a writing system for the Cherokee language

People

1700

1800

1734 • Daniel Boone   1820

1770? • Sequoyah   1843

1807 • Robert E. Lee

1821 • Clara Barton

Thurgood Marshall

1908–1993
- Leader of the Civil Rights Movement
- First African American to serve on the United States Supreme Court

Bill Monroe

1911–1996
- Singer and songwriter
- Known as the Father of Bluegrass music
- Entered the Country Music Hall of Fame in 1970

Robert E. Lee

1807–1870

- Confederate General from Virginia
- Led Southern forces in the Civil War
- Defeated in the Battle of Gettysburg, Pennsylvania

Clara Barton

1821–1912

- Teacher and Civil War nurse
- Founder of the American Red Cross
- Supported equal rights for women and African Americans

1900　　　　　　　　　　　　　　　　　　　　　　　　PRESENT

1870

1912

1908 • Thurgood Marshall　　　　　　　　　1993

1911 • Bill Monroe　　　　　　　　　1996

1913 • Rosa Parks　　　　　　　　　2005

1929 • Dr. Martin L. King, Jr.　1968

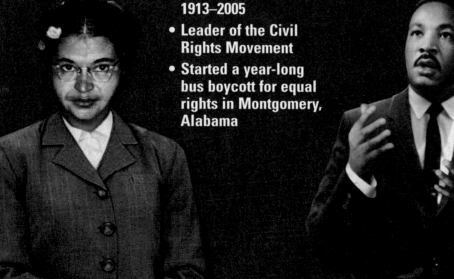

Rosa Parks

1913–2005

- Leader of the Civil Rights Movement
- Started a year-long bus boycott for equal rights in Montgomery, Alabama

Dr. Martin Luther King, Jr.

1929–1968

- African American minister who helped lead the Civil Rights Movement
- Awarded the Nobel Peace Prize for his work

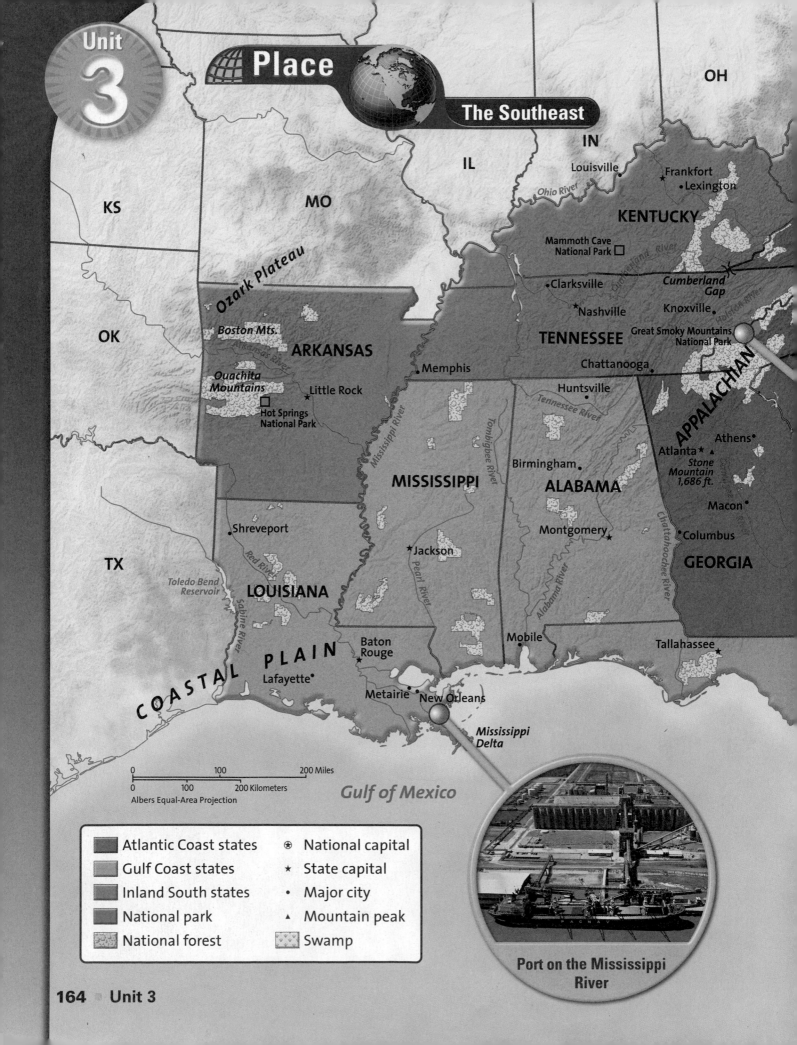

OH

IN

IL

Louisville • Frankfort • Lexington

Ohio River

KS

MO

KENTUCKY

Ozark Plateau

Mammoth Cave National Park □

Cumberland River

Cumberland Gap

• Clarksville

Knoxville •

OK

Boston Mts.

Arkansas River

ARKANSAS

★ Nashville

TENNESSEE

Great Smoky Mountains National Park

Holston River

Ouachita Mountains

□ • Little Rock

Hot Springs National Park

Chattanooga •

Memphis •

Huntsville •

APPALACHIAN

Tennessee River

Mississippi River

Tombigbee River

Birmingham •

Athens •

Atlanta ★ ▲

Stone Mountain 1,686 ft.

MISSISSIPPI

ALABAMA

Macon •

Shreveport •

Montgomery ★

• Columbus

Red River

★ Jackson

Alabama River

GEORGIA

TX

Toledo Bend Reservoir

Pearl River

Chattahoochee River

Sabine River

LOUISIANA

Mobile •

Tallahassee ★

Baton Rouge ★

C O A S T A L   P L A I N

Lafayette •

Metairie • • New Orleans

Mississippi Delta

0 ___ 100 ___ 200 Miles
0 ___ 100 ___ 200 Kilometers
Albers Equal-Area Projection

Gulf of Mexico

▨ Atlantic Coast states	⊛ National capital
▨ Gulf Coast states	★ State capital
▨ Inland South states	• Major city
▨ National park	▲ Mountain peak
▨ National forest	▨ Swamp

Port on the Mississippi River

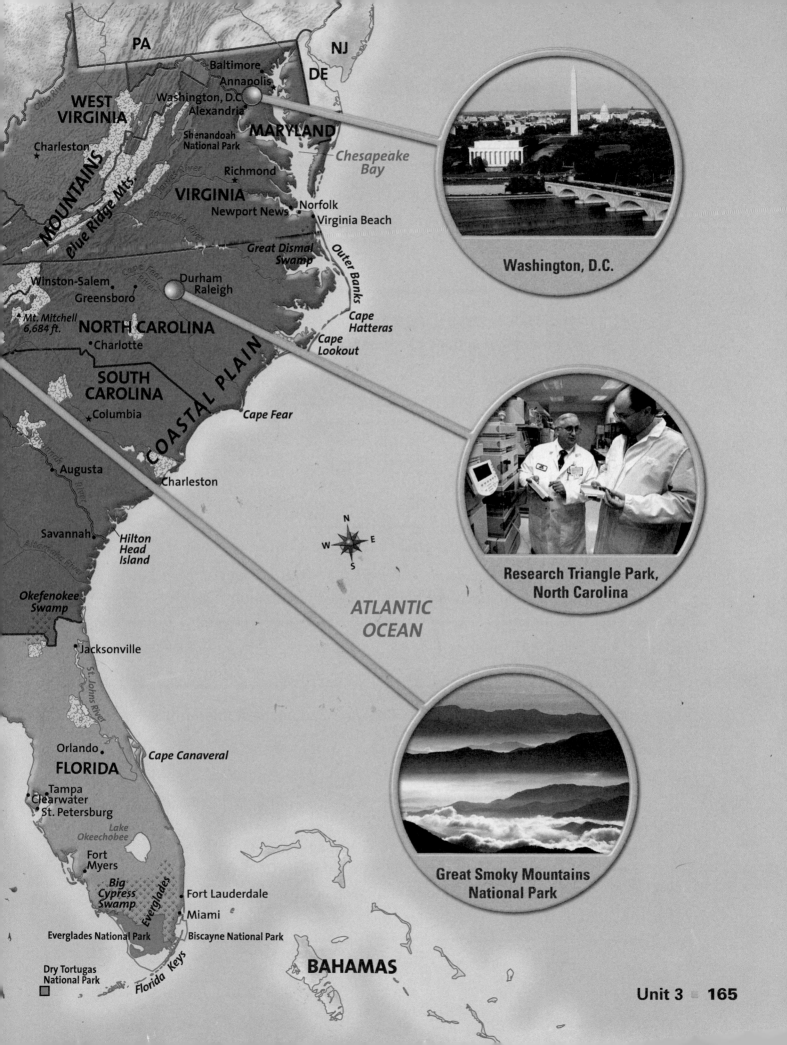

Washington, D.C.

Research Triangle Park,
North Carolina

Great Smoky Mountains
National Park

Reading Social Studies

(Focus Skill) Compare and Contrast

Why It Matters Comparing and contrasting can help you understand how things are alike and how they are different.

▶ LEARN

When you **compare,** you think about how two or more items are alike. When you **contrast,** you think about how two or more items are different.

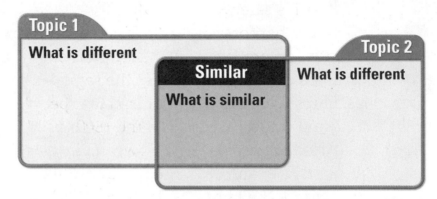

- *Like, alike, both, also, same,* and *similar* are words that compare.
- *Different, instead, however,* and *but* are words that contrast.

▶ PRACTICE

Read the paragraphs that follow. Compare and contrast the information in the second paragraph.

Similar
Different

Coal and oil are both fuels that are found in the Southeast. The region's largest coal deposits are in the Appalachian Mountains. Its largest oil deposits, however, are in Louisiana.

Coal is a solid fuel, but oil is a liquid. Mining companies dig deep holes called shafts to reach underground coal deposits. Oil deposits are also located underground. Instead of shafts, oil companies drill wells to pump oil to the surface.

Read the paragraphs, and answer the questions.

Lighthouses

Many lighthouses stand along the shores of the Southeast. They can be found both on the Atlantic coast and around the Gulf of Mexico. People along these coasts built many lighthouses in the 1700s and 1800s. Beams of light from light-house towers guided ships safely into and out of ports and harbors. This was important for settlers who depended on ships carrying food and supplies. Ships were also important for travel and trade.

Early lighthouses used lanterns to produce beams of light. The lanterns burned fish oil. Sometimes the light was not bright enough to be seen from a distance or on a foggy night. In the 1800s, people found a way to solve this problem. They shined the light through a special lens that made the beam brighter.

Ships rarely depend on light-houses today. Modern ships use electronic navigation systems instead. As a result, most light-houses in the Southeast are no longer used. Many have been pre-served because of their historic value. Tourists enjoy visiting these lighthouses to learn about the past.

Lighthouses that are still active use the same kind of lens that people in the 1800s used. However, instead of oil-burning lanterns, today's lighthouses use electricity.

Compare and Contrast

1. **How would you contrast the purpose of lighthouses in the past with their main use today?**
2. **What is one difference between lighthouses of the past and lighthouses that are still used today?**
3. **What is one technology that is the same for light-houses from the 1800s and lighthouses that are still used today?**

Tanya's Reunion

by **Valerie Flournoy**
illustrated by **Jerry Pinkney**

Tanya is excited to travel with her grandmother to her family's Virginia farm for a big family reunion. After all, her grandmother has promised her "special days" on the farm.

When they arrive, Tanya is disappointed. All she sees is a dusty road and an old farmhouse. This changes as Tanya's grandmother shares family stories about the people who built, worked, and loved the farm. Read now how the farm earns a special place in Tanya's heart, too.

The sun rose slowly in the morning sky as Tanya watched all her familiar places vanish behind her. Past her schoolyard and the park. Past row after row of houses and traffic lights.

And still they traveled on and on. They stopped only to switch from one bus to another. Tanya listened while Grandma spoke about "going home" to the great land of Virginia that "borned four of the first five Presidents of these United States."

And still they traveled on and on. Until the bright sunny sky grew cloudy and gray and the highway turned into never-ending dirt roads that seemed to disappear into the fields and trees, down into the "hollers," the valleys below. Tanya could barely keep her eyes open.

And still they traveled on and on . . . until finally the bus crawled to a stop.

Grandma shook Tanya gently. "We're here, Tanya honey, wake up." Tanya rubbed her eyes awake. "We're home."

Standing on the last step of the bus, Tanya spied a car, trailing clouds of dust, coming toward them. In the distance were a farmhouse and barn.

"I've been sitting for the past eight . . . nine hours," Grandma told Uncle John, who'd come to get them, "so I think I'll just let these old limbs take me the rest of the way."

Tanya watched Grandma walk slowly but steadily up the familiar roadway.

"Memories die hard," Uncle John whispered to Tanya.

Tanya wasn't certain what her great-uncle meant. She only knew that if Grandma was going to walk, she would walk too. And she raced to the old woman's side.

"Take care, honey," Grandma said. "August weather down here's meant to be eased on through, not run through."

Tanya looked up at Grandma as she stared off into the distance, a faraway look in her eyes. What Tanya saw didn't look like the pictures in her schoolbooks or magazines or the pictures in her head.

There wasn't a horse in sight and the farmhouse was just a faded memory of its original color. Tanya noticed clouds of dust floating about her ankles, turning her white socks and sneakers a grayish-brown color.

"Just open your heart to it," Grandma said. "Can't you feel the place welcomin' ya?"

Tanya didn't feel anything but hot and tired and disappointed. The farm wasn't what she expected. No, it wasn't what she expected at all.

A dog's bark drew Tanya's gaze back to the farmhouse. Stepping off the porch, a large dog at her side, was Grandma's baby sister, Kay.

"Watchin' you walk up that road, Rose Buchanan," Aunt Kay began, then gave Grandma a hug.

"Yes, on summer days like this it's as if time were standing still just a bit," Grandma finished for her.

Aunt Kay turned to her great-niece, smothering her in a welcoming hug full of warmth and softness that reminded Tanya of Grandma.

A summer breeze suddenly blew across the land, pushing the scattered gray clouds together. Tanya felt rain drops.

"Looks like it's comin' up a cloud," Uncle John said, hurrying the women onto the back porch and into the house. "I think it's *finally* gonna rain!"

Tanya was swept into the house by the laughing, talking grownups. Inside the kitchen Tanya met her cousin Celeste and her children, baby Adam and seven-year-old Keisha. The room was filled with wonderful aromas that made Tanya's mouth water—until she noticed the fly strip hanging above the kitchen table.

When Tanya went to bed that night, she was miserable. She barely touched her supper, until Uncle John thought to remove the fly strip dangling overhead. She missed her own room. She missed Mama and Papa, even Ted and Jim. Cousin Keisha and baby Adam were nice. But he was too small to really play with, and Keisha refused to leave her mother's side all night.

Grandma helped Aunt Kay tuck the children in. "What happened to our special days, Grandma?" whispered Tanya.

"Seems to me our first one went just fine," said Grandma. "The land needed the rain and it's finally gettin' it. Makes today kinda special, don't you think?"

Tanya sighed. "I wanna go home," she murmured into her pillow. . .

* * *

"Did you *really* like living on this farm, Grandma?" Tanya asked. "Weren't you *ever* lonely?"

Grandma laughed again. "No, Tanya, I wasn't lonely. Back then, this whole farmyard: the barn, the pasture, fields, and orchard beyond"— she stretched out her arm—"this place was filled with activity. We had the land and the land had us. We worked over it, tilled and planted it. Then harvested it when it was ready. In turn the land gave us water, food, clothing, and a roof over our heads."

"If you weren't lonely, Grandma, why did you leave?" Tanya persisted.

Grandma looked out over the land, remembering. "It was after the second World War. My Isaac—your grandpa Franklin—and many other people thought we'd find better opportunities, better jobs closer to the cities up north. And we did. But we still kept the land and paid taxes on it. Sometimes let other people pay to work it, 'til Kay and John came back. But this will always be home."

Response Corner

1. **(Focus Skill) Compare And Contrast** How was the farm different from how Tanya expected it to be?

2. **Make It Relevant** Why do you think people like to visit places from their past?

STUDY SKILLS

MAKE AN OUTLINE

An outline is a good way to record main ideas and details.

- **Use Roman numerals to identify topics.**
- **Use capital letters to show main ideas about each topic.**
- **Use numbers to identify details about each main idea.**

Exploring the Southeast

I. Geography of the Southeast
  A. Coastal Areas
    1. Low, flat lands of the Coastal Plain
    2. Beaches
  B. Marshes and Swamps
    1. _____
    2. _____

PREVIEW VOCABULARY

peninsula p. 177   **fall line** p. 178   **raw material** p. 196

Exploring the Southeast

GREAT SMOKY MOUNTAINS NATIONAL PARK, TENNESSEE

Lesson 1 Geography of the Southeast

WHAT TO KNOW
What are the major physical features of the Southeast?

VOCABULARY
peninsula p. 177
wetland p. 177
piedmont p. 178
fall line p. 178
growing season p. 179
hurricane p. 179
fertilizer p. 180

PLACES
Great Dismal Swamp
Coastal Plain
Florida Peninsula
Okefenokee Swamp
Everglades
Appalachian Mountains
Piedmont
Cumberland Plateau
Ozark Plateau
Mississippi River
Chesapeake Bay

COMPARE AND CONTRAST

YOU ARE THERE

You can hardly believe that you're riding a bike through a swamp! The dirt road is mostly dry, but water is all around you. Tall trees block the sunlight. Frogs croak, and birds make strange-sounding calls.

Your tour guide points out a big snake sleeping on a log nearby. "Deer, foxes, and bears live here, too," she says.

You're touring the **Great Dismal Swamp** on the border between Virginia and North Carolina. It's part of the long **Coastal Plain** found in the Southeast.

▶ **LIGHTHOUSE** A lighthouse along the coast of North Carolina

Coastal Wildlife

ILLUSTRATIONS Swamps, such as Okefenokee Swamp, have a wide variety of life.

1 Sunfish
2 Wood duck
3 Cypress tree
4 Great blue heron
5 Great egret
6 Opossum
7 Red belly turtle
8 Alligator

What are some of the birds that live in a swamp?

Coastal Areas

The Southeast has two long coast-lines. The Atlantic Ocean forms its eastern boundary. The Gulf of Mexico forms its southern border.

The Coastal Plain

The flat Coastal Plain covers more than half of the Southeast. In fact, the plain makes up the entire **Florida Peninsula**. A **peninsula** is land that is almost surrounded by water.

Parts of the Southeast coast have wetlands. A **wetland** is an area of low land that is partly covered with slow-moving or still water. In some wetlands, only short plants grow. These wetlands are called marshes. They cover large coastal areas of Maryland, Virginia, and the Carolinas.

Wetlands with bushes and trees are called swamps. One of the largest swamps in the United States is **Okefenokee** (oh•kuh•fuh•NOH•kee) **Swamp**. It lies in parts of southern Georgia and northern Florida.

The **Everglades** in southern Florida has marshes and swamps. This wetland covers more than 1 million acres.

READING CHECK ŏ**COMPARE AND CONTRAST**
How are all wetlands in the Southeast alike?

Inland Areas

Inland from the Coastal Plain, the Southeast has different features. Here there are hills, mountains, plateaus, plains, and a mighty river.

Hills and Mountains

The **Appalachian Mountains** run through the middle of the Southeast. To the east of them is a hilly region called the **Piedmont** (PEED•mahnt). A **piedmont** is an area of high land at the foot of mountains.

Where the Piedmont meets the Coastal Plain, the land drops sharply. Geographers call this area the Fall Line. A **fall line** is a place where rivers drop from higher to lower land, causing waterfalls and rapids to form.

MAP SKILL **PLACE** Waterfalls at the Fall Line blocked early settlers from traveling upstream by boat. As a result, many early cities formed along the Fall Line. On the map, which cities formed along the Fall Line?

Plateaus and Plains

West of the Appalachians are the **Cumberland Plateau**, in Kentucky and Tennessee, and the **Ozark Plateau**, in Arkansas. From the plateaus, the land lowers to the Central Plains. The **Mississippi River**, which flows here, often floods. The floodwaters deposit silt on the land, making the soil fertile. As a result, the Mississippi River valley is an important farming region.

READING CHECK **CAUSE AND EFFECT**
What causes waterfalls to form on many rivers in the Southeast?

The Fall Line

ATLANTIC OCEAN

0   100   200 Miles
0   100   200 Kilometers
Azimuthal Equal-Area Projection

—— Fall Line
• City

▶ REBUILDING A worker (right) rebuilds in New Orleans (above) after Hurricane Katrina hit in 2005.

Climate

The Southeast is famous for its mild climate. Thousands of people visit or move there each year to enjoy it.

Warm, Sunny, and Wet

The Southeast has a warm, sunny climate. The farther south you travel, the warmer the climate becomes. This gives much of the Southeast a long growing season. A **growing season** is the time during which the weather is warm enough for plants to grow.

Although the Southeast has plenty of sunshine, it also gets lots of rain. Every state in the region gets more than 40 inches of rain in most years.

In winter, the Appalachian Mountains get plenty of snow, too.

Hurricanes strike the Southeast almost every year between June and November. A **hurricane** is a huge tropical storm. It has heavy rain and winds of more than 73 miles per hour. Hurricanes form above warm ocean water. After they form, however, they may move over land, causing terrible damage.

Several major hurricanes hit the Southeast in 2004 and 2005. Besides damaging buildings and trees, their heavy rains caused flooding in the region.

READING CHECK ⏱ COMPARE AND CONTRAST
How does the climate in the Southeast differ from north to south?

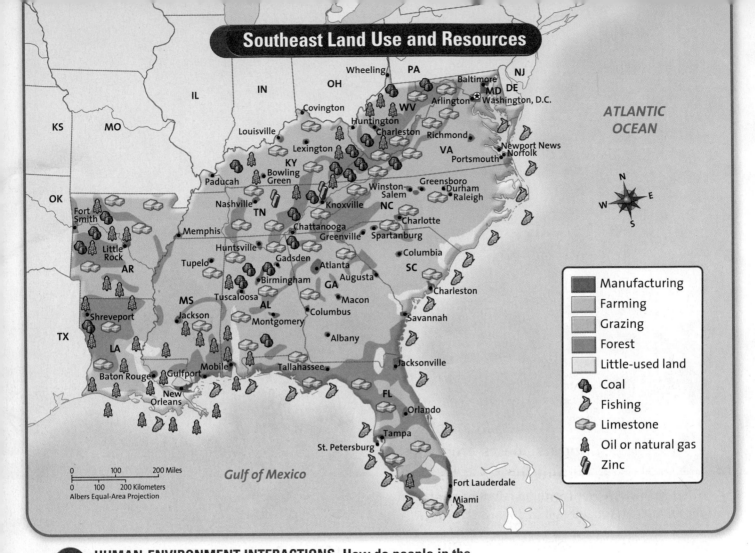

Southeast Land Use and Resources

Legend:
- Manufacturing
- Farming
- Grazing
- Forest
- Little-used land
- Coal
- Fishing
- Limestone
- Oil or natural gas
- Zinc

MAP SKILL HUMAN-ENVIRONMENT INTERACTIONS How do people in the Southeast use most of the land?

Natural Resources

The Southeast has many natural resources. People in the region depend on those resources to make a living.

The Land

A sunny climate, plentiful rainfall, and flat land make the Southeast a good place for farming. Cotton, soybeans, rice, peanuts, vegetables, and tobacco are major crops. Farmers in the hottest, wettest areas grow oranges, grapefruit, and sugarcane.

Many farmers in the region raise pigs, dairy cows, and other animals.

Georgia and Arkansas are the nation's largest producers of chickens.

Trees also grow well in the region. Pine forests cover the Piedmont and the Appalachians. In Arkansas, pine, elm, and maple trees grow on the Ozark Plateau. Louisiana has large forests of cypress and oak.

The region has mineral and fuel resources, too. Florida has minerals that are used to make fertilizers. **Fertilizers** are materials that are added to soil to make it more fertile. In the Appalachians, coal mining is an important industry. Louisiana is the nation's fourth-largest oil-producing state.

The Waters

The Southeast's long coastlines make fishing an important industry. **Chesapeake Bay**, in Maryland and Virginia, provides fish, oysters, clams, and crabs. In the Gulf of Mexico, fishers from Florida, Alabama, Mississippi, and Louisiana catch shrimp, crabs, red snapper, and tuna.

READING CHECK **CAUSE AND EFFECT**
Why is the Southeast a good region for farming?

Summary

The Southeast has a variety of physical features. Along its coasts are plains and wetlands. Farther inland, it has mountains and plateaus. The climate is warm and wet. Rich soil, trees, fish, coal, and oil are some of the region's natural resources.

▶ **COTTON** People use cotton plants to produce many items, including clothing and cooking oil.

REVIEW

1. **WHAT TO KNOW** What are the major physical features of the Southeast?

2. **VOCABULARY** Use the term **piedmont** to explain the **fall line** in the Southeast.

3. **GEOGRAPHY** What bodies of water form the eastern and southern boundaries of the Southeast?

4. **CRITICAL THINKING** Why is the warm climate of the Southeast a key feature of the region?

5. **WRITE A LIST** Write a list of five jobs that depend on natural resources found in the Southeast. For each job, explain how that job depends on natural resources.

6. **Focus Skill** **COMPARE AND CONTRAST**

On a separate sheet of paper, copy and complete the graphic organizer below.

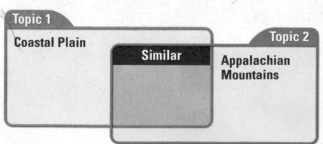

Topic 1: Coastal Plain — Similar — Topic 2: Appalachian Mountains

READ ABOUT

Land Between The Lakes

THE HOMEPLACE is a living history farm. It recreates what life might have been like in the 1850s.

In 1963, the federal government created a new park in western Kentucky and Tennessee. The park covers a narrow strip of land between two lakes—Kentucky Lake and Lake Barkley. For this reason, the park was named Land Between the Lakes.

This park is a national recreation area. This means that one purpose of the park is to offer people lots of fun activities. Visitors can swim, boat, fish, water-ski, hike, or ride horseback in the park.

Education is another purpose of the park. At the nature station, visitors can learn about the park's protected wildlife. They can tour Homeplace and see how people lived during the mid-1800s. They can even stargaze at the park's planetarium.

FIND

Land Between the Lakes

KENTUCKY

TENNESSEE

HOMEPLACE

WATER LILLIES

BOATING AT SUNSET

BARN OWL

SHEEP AT HOMEPLACE

A VIRTUAL TOUR

GO ONLINE For more resources, go to www.harcourtschool.com/ss1

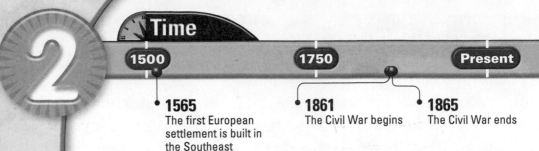

Time

| 1500 | 1750 | Present |

1565
The first European settlement is built in the Southeast

1861
The Civil War begins

1865
The Civil War ends

WHAT TO KNOW
What important events took place in the Southeast during its early history?

VOCABULARY
plantation p. 186
slavery p. 186
cash crop p. 188
abolish p. 189
Union p. 189
secede p. 189
Confederacy p. 189
civil war p. 189

PEOPLE
Daniel Boone
Henry Clay
Abraham Lincoln
Robert E. Lee
Ulysses S. Grant
George Washington Carver

PLACES
St. Augustine
Jamestown
New Orleans
Cumberland Gap
Charleston

COMPARE AND CONTRAST

Early History of the Southeast

YOU ARE THERE
The year is 1500. While others are bringing the huge tree trunk into the village, you search for dry twigs to fuel a fire. You're going to help make a canoe. Over many days, you and some other villagers will slowly burn and scrape out the inside of the tree trunk. When the canoe is finished, it will be used for fishing and for traveling to nearby villages.

Early Peoples

In 1500, Native Americans were living in all parts of the Southeast. The Powhatan (pow•uh•TAN) lived near the coasts. The Cherokee had settled in the Appalachians. The Shawnee and other tribes had made their homes west of the mountains.

Village Life

Most Native Americans of the Southeast built villages along rivers or lakes. They used these waters to provide fresh water, food, and transportation routes. In their canoes, they often traveled great distances to trade. They used wood from forests to build their homes. The Cherokee wove branches together to make frames that they covered with mud or clay.

Everyone in the village had a job. The women grew corn, beans, and squash. They wove baskets from plant parts. They used baskets for collecting and storing crops and for gathering acorns and other wild foods.

While the women did most of the farming and gathering, the men hunted and fished. They carved stone, wood, and bones to make tools and weapons. They used the weapons to hunt wild deer, turkeys, and other animals. They also made nets for catching fish.

READING CHECK ☼**COMPARE AND CONTRAST**
How were the jobs of men and women different?

▶ **CHEROKEE VILLAGE Many activities took place in the village's center.**

Anyokah

At age 6, many children are just learning to write. Anyokah, a Cherokee, was helping to invent a writing system! Anyokah lived in the Appalachian Mountains in the early 1800s. She helped her father, Sequoyah (sih•KWOY•uh), create the Cherokee's first written language. Anyokah helped Sequoyah identify each syllable, or unit of sound, in the Cherokee language. Then Sequoyah made symbols for all the syllables. Anyokah also helped Sequoyah show the other Cherokee how the writing system worked.

Thanks to Anyokah and Sequoyah, the Cherokee were able to write down their stories so they would never be forgotten.

Make It Relevant **How does writing improve your life?**

Colonies and Settlers

In the early 1500s, explorers from Spain, England, and France claimed land in the Southeast. Settlers soon followed to set up colonies.

Early Coastal Settlements

Europeans built their earliest settlements in the Southeast along the Atlantic coast. In 1565, the Spanish built **St. Augustine**, in Florida. In 1607, the English founded **Jamestown**, in Virginia. The French built **New Orleans** on the Mississippi River in 1718.

Many European settlers began to develop large farms known as **plantations**. To get workers, they forced Native Americans into slavery.

Slavery is making one person the property of another. Enslaved people had no freedom and were forced to work without pay. In time, Europeans began bringing millions of Africans to the Americas as enslaved workers.

Settlers Move West

By the late 1700s, farms and towns covered the Coastal Plain. To start farms inland, settlers had to cross the Appalachian Mountains. Few made the trip until a pass, or opening between mountains, was found. This pass was the **Cumberland Gap**. In time, thousands of people used it to travel to Kentucky and Tennessee.

READING CHECK **MAIN IDEA AND DETAILS**
What is the Cumberland Gap?

Life in the Highlands

Most settlers who crossed the Appalachian Mountains wanted land to farm. Some also sought adventure in an unsettled region.

Appalachian Culture

Imagine a mountain region in a time before modern roads. Travel was slow and difficult. Transporting goods into and out of the region was even harder. How did this affect life in the region?

The history of Appalachia, or the Appalachian region, tells the answer. Early settlers there made almost everything they needed. This included their homes, clothing, and furniture. They even made their own entertainment.

Some people became storytellers. Others developed a new style of music and made instruments to play it. In these ways, the people of Appalachia created their own culture.

Settling Arkansas

In 1819, Arkansas became a territory of the United States. To open up land for settlers, the United States government then forced many Native Americans to leave Arkansas. Soon after, some settlers from Appalachia began moving west to Arkansas. Many grew cotton and other crops along the Mississippi and Arkansas Rivers.

READING CHECK **MAIN IDEA AND DETAILS**
How did settlers in Appalachia make their own entertainment?

> **WILDERNESS ROAD** In 1775, Daniel Boone (center) and others cleared a path through the Cumberland Gap for wagons. This path became known as the Wilderness Road.

The Nation Divided, 1861

Union state
Border state
Confederate state
Territory

MAP SKILL **REGIONS** Border states allowed slavery but remained part of the Union. Which states were border states?

A Divided Nation

By the early 1800s, the United States had two major economic regions—the North and the South. These regions grew in different ways.

Different Economies

The South's economy was based on agriculture. Many farmers grew cash crops, such as cotton and rice, on large plantations. **Cash crops** are crops raised to be sold. Enslaved African Americans did most of the work on plantations. This made the South's economy depend on slavery.

The North's economy was made up of small farms, manufacturing, and other businesses. It did not depend on slave labor. In fact, by 1819, slavery was outlawed in all Northern states.

The Missouri Compromise

In 1819, the 11 Southern states allowed slavery. The 11 Northern states did not. In that year, Missouri asked to join the United States as a slave state. This would give the nation more slave states than free states.

Congress debated the issue. Then, in 1820, **Henry Clay**, a member of Congress from Kentucky, found a solution. Missouri would join the nation as a slave state. Maine would join as a free state. In this way, the balance would be kept.

The plan also allowed slavery in new states formed in the South. It would not be allowed in states formed in the North. Clay's plan became known as the Missouri Compromise.

READING CHECK **CAUSE AND EFFECT**
What caused the Missouri Compromise?

The Civil War

The Missouri Compromise did not end conflicts over slavery. Many Northerners still wanted to **abolish**, or end, slavery in all the states.

In 1860, **Abraham Lincoln** was elected President. He said that slavery should not be allowed in any new states that joined the **Union**, or the United States. Many people in the South feared that President Lincoln would try to end slavery everywhere. As a result, the 11 Southern states decided to **secede** from, or leave, the Union. Those states formed a new country, the Confederate States of America. People also called it the **Confederacy**.

On April 12, 1861, fighting broke out between Confederate and Union soldiers in **Charleston**, South Carolina. This event marked the beginning of the Civil War. A **civil war** is a war fought between groups of people in the same country.

For the next four years, the Union and the Confederacy fought a terrible war in which more than 600,000 soldiers died. On April 9, 1865, the leader of the Confederate army, **Robert E. Lee**, surrendered to Union general **Ulysses S. Grant**. The war was over, and more than 4 million enslaved African Americans were freed.

READING CHECK **CAUSE AND EFFECT**
What was one effect of the Civil War?

> **BATTLE OF GETTYSBURG** The Union victory at Gettysburg, in Pennsylvania, ended the Confederacy's attempts to invade the North.

Social Changes

Manufacturing continued to grow in the North after the Civil War. Agriculture, however, remained a big part of the South's economy.

To earn a living, many freed slaves rented land to raise crops. Because they had no money, they paid for the land with part of the crops they grew. Other freed slaves moved to cities in the South and the North.

Even though African Americans were now free, life was difficult for most of them. They were still not treated as equals to white Americans. Even so, many African Americans continued to make important contributions to society.

READING CHECK ⟳**COMPARE AND CONTRAST**
How did the lives of African Americans change once they were freed?

▶ **GEORGE WASHINGTON CARVER was a scientist whose work led to advances in agriculture.**

Summary

People in the North and the South had different economies and disagreed about slavery. This led to the Civil War. After the war, enslaved people became free but did not gain equal rights.

REVIEW

1. **WHAT TO KNOW** What important events took place in the Southeast during its early history?

2. **VOCABULARY** How are the terms **cash crop** and **plantation** related?

3. **HISTORY** Which European countries started colonies in the Southeast?

4. **CRITICAL THINKING** How did the Missouri Compromise please people in both the North and the South?

5. ✏️ **MAKE A TIME LINE** While reviewing the lesson, record some important dates and events in the Southeast's history. Then make a time line of those events. Be sure to label your time line.

6. ⭐ **COMPARE AND CONTRAST**

   On a separate sheet of paper, copy and complete the graphic organizer below.

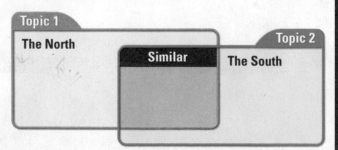

Topic 1 — The North — Similar — Topic 2 — The South

Sequoyah

Biography

Trustworthiness

Respect

Responsibility

Fairness

Caring

Patriotism

"I thought [writing] would be like catching a wild animal and taming it."

Cherokee leader Sequoyah was born in the late 1700s in what is now eastern Tennessee. At that time, the Cherokee had no written language. Sequoyah had seen English writing and understood why writing was important. He decided to develop a writing system for the Cherokee language.

The job took 12 years. Sequoyah first tried to make a symbol for every word, but there were thousands of words. With the help of his daughter Anyokah, he then made a symbol for each syllable in the spoken Cherokee language. This way, he needed only 85 symbols. The system worked!

Within a few months, thousands of Cherokee had learned Sequoyah's writing system. In 1824, the leaders of the Cherokee Nation voted to award Sequoyah a silver medal. They did so to honor the great contribution Sequoyah had made to Cherokee culture and history.

Why Character Counts

How did Sequoyah show respect for Cherokee culture?

Time

1770 — Born?

1843 — Died

1814 Sequoyah fights on the side of the United States in the War of 1812

1821 Sequoyah completes the Cherokee writing system

GO ONLINE For more resources, go to www.harcourtschool.com/ss1

RULE OF LAW

"I have a dream that my four little children will one day live in a nation where they will not be judged by the color of their skin, but by the content of their character."

—Dr. Martin Luther King, Jr.

Dr. King was an African American minister from Georgia. He and many others worked for **justice**, or fairness. They wanted to gain equal rights for African Americans.

The Civil War ended slavery, but African Americans struggled to have equal rights. Congress passed laws meant to provide these rights. The laws, however, were not always carried out. African Americans

❯ DR. KING (below) received the Nobel Peace Prize (left) in 1964.

❯ **A PEACEFUL MARCH**

were often kept from voting. Some companies refused to hire African Americans. Some stores and restaurants refused to serve them.

Beginning in the 1950s, African Americans and others worked together to end these unfair ways. Their work became known as the Civil Rights movement. **Civil rights** are the rights of citizens to equal treatment. Dr. Martin Luther King, Jr., was an important leader in the Civil Rights movement. He gave speeches and led peaceful marches and protests to help win civil rights.

The Civil Rights movement brought about many changes. New laws were passed that promised equal rights for African Americans and for women. This time, the government took action to carry out the new laws.

Make It Relevant Why do you think one of the major goals of the Civil Rights movement was to protect people's right to vote?

❯ **ROSA PARKS** (below) refused to give up her bus seat to a white passenger in 1955. At a museum, children sit on the bus (left) behind a statue of Parks.

Ports of the Southeast

WHAT TO KNOW
How are ports important to the Southeast's economy?

VOCABULARY
raw material p. 196
international trade p. 196
import p. 196
export p. 197

PLACES
Baltimore
Charleston
Savannah
New Orleans
Miami

COMPARE AND CONTRAST

YOU ARE THERE Huge ships float at the ends of concrete piers. Cranes lift giant containers as if they were toys. All around you, people enter information into handheld computers.

You are visiting the Port of **Baltimore**, in Maryland. It is one of the largest, busiest ports in the United States. More than 16,000 people come to work here each day. At least 30 million tons of goods come and go every year.

"What do you think of the place where I work?" your mom asks you.

"It's terrific!"

▶ **BALTIMORE** A view of downtown Baltimore and the Inner Harbor of Chesapeake Bay

A Region of Ports

The Southeast has two long coastlines and many navigable rivers. Because of this, the region is known for its busy ports.

Old Ports

The first cities in the Southeast grew around ports near the mouths of major rivers. Colonial port cities along the Atlantic coast include Baltimore, Maryland; **Charleston**, South Carolina; and **Savannah**, Georgia. **New Orleans**, Louisiana, has been a major Gulf coast port since 1718.

Plantation owners and other farmers used rivers to send their cash crops to port cities. From there, most of the crops were shipped to Europe to be sold. The ships then returned with manufactured goods from Europe.

New Ports

Most of the colonial ports in the Southeast still operate today. Newer ports have also been built, such as the Port of South Louisiana. This port is the busiest port in the United States.

Most ports handle only goods, but some are also used for passenger ships. **Miami** and Port Everglades, in Florida, are two of the nation's largest cruise-ship ports. Passengers board ships there that take them to places around the world.

READING CHECK ☼COMPARE AND CONTRAST
What are two things that Baltimore and Savannah have in common?

Busiest Ports in the Southeast, 2003

ATLANTIC COAST	GULF COAST
Baltimore, MD	South Louisiana, LA
Norfolk Harbor, VA	New Orleans, LA
Charleston, SC	Baton Rouge, LA
Savannah, GA	Plaquemines, LA
Port Everglades, FL	Lake Charles, LA
Jacksonville, FL	Mobile, AL

TABLE Why do you think the busiest Gulf coast ports are in Louisiana?

Shipping Goods

Many ships that use the Southeast's ports carry goods from one part of the United States to another. Some ships carry **raw materials**, or natural resources used to make products. Raw materials, such as crops and minerals, are taken from the places where they are grown or mined to factories. Factories use the raw materials to make finished products.

Arriving Ships

Many ports in the Southeast are also important for **international trade**, or trade among different countries. Ships from around the world bring imports to ports in the Southeast. An **import** is a good brought into one country from another country.

The United States imports products, such as automobiles and electronics from Japan. Clothing and furniture come from China and other countries.

Containers

Silos

Warehouse

The United States also imports some agricultural products. Rubber and beef from South America and bananas from Central America are examples of such products.

Departing Ships

As ships arrive carrying imports, other ships leave carrying exports. An **export** is a good shipped from one country to be sold in another. Ships leaving the Southeast's ports carry goods east to Europe and Africa, south to South America, and west to Asia. Canada and Mexico are also important trading partners of the United States.

The states in the Southeast export both crops and food products. For example, Florida exports grapefruit and other citrus fruits. The Southeast also exports steel, machinery, chemicals, automobiles, textiles, and many other products.

READING CHECK ⦿ **COMPARE AND CONTRAST**
How are imports and exports different?

Cranes

Container ship

Tugboat

A Modern Port

ILLUSTRATION Modern ports provide a low-cost and organized way to ship goods around the world. Why do you think two cranes are used on each ship?

Container Shipping

In recent years, big changes have come to the shipping industry. A new way of shipping, called container shipping, saves both time and money.

Shipping in the Past

First, think about how shipping worked in the recent past. Imagine a big truck in China arriving at a port. The truck is filled with furniture to be shipped to the United States. Workers must carry the furniture, piece by piece, from the truck to the ship. When the ship arrives in the United States, workers must unload the furniture and carry it to another truck. All this loading and unloading takes a lot of time, for which workers must be paid.

Shipping Today

Today, furniture is brought to the port in a container that fits on a truck bed. A crane then lifts the whole container from the truck onto the ship! When the ship docks in the United States, another crane lifts the container onto a truck of the right size.

Containers come in standard sizes, and a lot of them fit in a ship. A container that fits on a truck in China or Brazil will also fit on a truck in the United States. Containers also protect

▶ **CONTAINER SHIPPING** has helped increase international trade.

FAST FACT

About nine-tenths of all goods shipped today are shipped in containers.

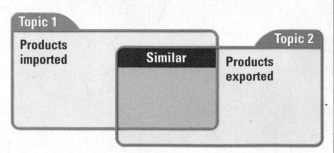
▶ TRADE Through international trade, Japanese shoppers can buy oranges from the United States.

the goods inside them, and prevent them from being handled by many workers. Because fewer workers are needed to load and unload ships, container shipping is a less expensive way to ship goods.

READING CHECK Ŏ COMPARE AND CONTRAST
How is container shipping different from the older way of shipping?

Summary

The Southeast has major ports on both the Atlantic coast and the Gulf coast. Ships carrying goods to and from other parts of the United States and other countries visit these ports. Container shipping has made shipping goods faster, easier, and cheaper.

REVIEW

1. **WHAT TO KNOW** How are ports important to the Southeast's economy?

2. **VOCABULARY** How does each word in **international trade** relate to the meaning of the entire term?

3. **HISTORY** During colonial days, where were most cash crops shipped?

4. **CRITICAL THINKING** Why do you think many major ports are located at the mouths of rivers?

5. ✎ **WRITE A STORY OUTLINE** Write an outline for a short story that takes place on a ship. Describe your story's setting, characters, and main events.

6. ⭐(Focus Skill) **COMPARE AND CONTRAST**
On a separate sheet of paper, copy and complete the graphic organizer below.

Topic 1		Topic 2
Products imported	Similar	Products exported

Read a Double-Bar Graph

Why It Matters A **double-bar graph** shows comparisons of two different things. By comparing the lengths of the bars, you can quickly compare the amounts they represent.

❱ LEARN

Follow these steps to use a double-bar graph.

Step 1 Read the title of the graph on page 201. Then read the labels along the bottom and sides. In the graph, the dollar amounts shown on the left side stand for the value of the products exported.

Step 2 Read the graph key to see what each bar stands for. The red bars stand for computer products. The yellow bars stand for crops.

Step 3 Choose one state, and compare its two bars. In this graph, you can see whether a certain state exports more computer products or more crops.

Step 4 To find the amount of money a bar stands for, put your finger on the top of the bar. Then read the number at the left that is closest to the top of the bar.

▶ PRACTICE

Use the double-bar graph to answer these questions.

1 Which states exported more computer products than crops?

2 Which state exported more crops than computer products?

3 How did Virginia's exports of computer products compare with its exports of crops in 2004?

4 What was the value of Virginia's crop exports?

▶ APPLY

Make It Relevant Make a double-bar graph of your test scores in social studies and in another subject. Remember to use a different color for each subject.

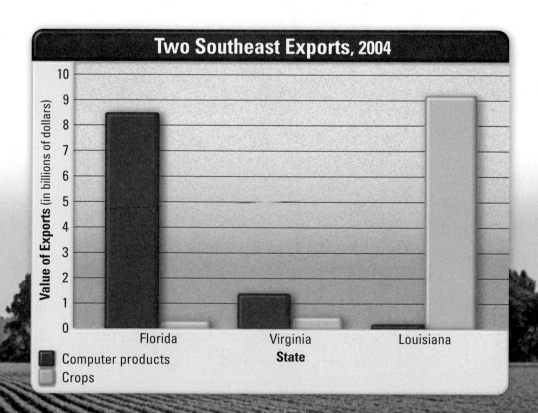

Chart and Graph Skills

Time

1500
The Cherokee live
in the Appalachians

Visual Summary

Summarize the Chapter

Focus Skill **Compare and Contrast** Complete this graphic organizer to
show that you understand how the Southeast states are alike
and how they are different.

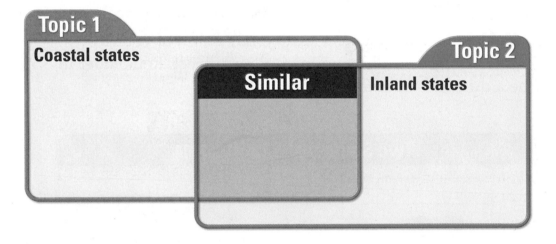

Topic 1

Coastal states

Similar

Topic 2

Inland states

Vocabulary

**Identify the term from the word bank that
correctly matches each definition.**

1. to end

2. a good that is brought into one country
   from another

3. land that is almost completely surrounded
   by water

4. materials that are added to soil to make it
   more fertile

5. a good that is shipped from one country to
   be sold in another

6. to leave

7. an area of high land near the foot of mountains

8. a huge farm where cash crops are grown

Word Bank	
peninsula p. 177	**abolish** p. 189
piedmont p. 178	**secede** p. 189
fertilizer p. 180	**import** p. 196
plantation p. 186	**export** p. 197

1750   1875   Present

1775
Wilderness
Road opens

1863
The Battle of
Gettysburg is
fought during
the Civil War

 Time Line

Use the chapter time line above to answer these questions.

9. When did the Wilderness Road open?

10. In which century did the Battle of Gettysburg take place?

 Facts and Main Ideas

Answer these questions.

11. When do most hurricanes strike the Southeast?

12. Whom did Europeans enslave as workers in the Southeast?

13. What was the Missouri Compromise?

14. What are two cash crops grown in the Southeast today?

Write the letter of the best choice.

15. Which of these Southeast physical regions is a wetland?
    A the Everglades
    B the Fall Line
    C the Piedmont
    D the Ozark Plateau

16. Which of these cities grew around a port on the Gulf Coast?
    A Baltimore, Maryland
    B Charleston, South Carolina
    C Miami, Florida
    D New Orleans, Louisiana

 Critical Thinking

17. Why is the Southeast a good region for farming?

18. How did Native Americans in the Southeast use natural resources?

19. How did finding the Cumberland Gap affect life in the Southeast?

20. What were one cause and one effect of the Civil War?

 **Skills**

Read a Double-Bar Graph

21. Study the bar graph on page 201. Which state exported the most crops in 2004? How can you tell by reading the graph?

writing

🖊 **Write a Narrative** Imagine it is the early 1800s. You are moving with your family from the Atlantic coast of the Southeast to the Appalachian region. Write a story describing your journey and why you are making it.

🖊 **Write a Report** Write a short report explaining what happens at a typical port in the Southeast. Be sure to describe the goods that are shipped in and out of the port, the people who work there, and the kinds of machines they use.

STUDY SKILLS

CONNECT IDEAS

A web organizer can help you organize information and connect ideas.

- List important themes in the ovals in the web's center.

- Add ovals showing main ideas that support each theme.

- Add bubbles for the details that support each main idea.

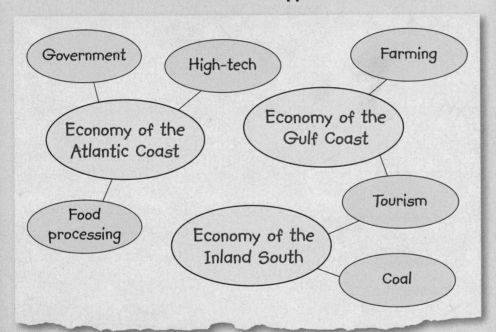

Government

High-tech

Farming

Economy of the Atlantic Coast

Economy of the Gulf Coast

Food processing

Tourism

Economy of the Inland South

Coal

PREVIEW VOCABULARY

food processing p. 209

tourism p. 214

habitat p. 223

The Southeast Today

The city of Atlanta, Georgia

Lesson **1** Atlantic Coast States

WHAT TO KNOW

What are some important industries in the Atlantic Coast states?

VOCABULARY

state legislature p. 208
governor p. 208
food processing p. 209
pulp p. 209
high-tech p. 209

PEOPLE

Clara Barton

PLACES

Myrtle Beach
Atlanta
Charlotte
Norfolk
Baltimore
Washington, D.C.
High Point
Raleigh
Durham
Chapel Hill

COMPARE AND CONTRAST

YOU ARE THERE

As the ferryboat approaches Ocracoke Island, you're thinking about pirates. You know that long ago, the dreaded pirate Blackbeard hid on this island when he wasn't attacking ships.

The ferryboat captain is talking about a different kind of danger. "The sea is wild out beyond the island," he says. "Storms and sandbars have sunk more treasure than pirates ever stole. More than 600 ships lie wrecked below these waters."

You had no idea North Carolina was such an interesting place!

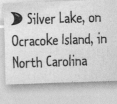

▶ Trainer and whale at the National Aquarium, in Baltimore, Maryland

▶ Silver Lake, on Ocracoke Island, in North Carolina

> The city of Atlanta, Georgia, at dusk

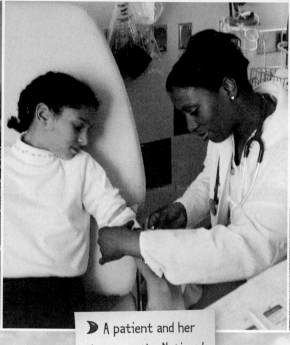

> A patient and her doctor at the National Institutes of Health, in Bethesda, Maryland

> Tourists viewing homes in Charleston, South Carolina

Beaches and Cities

The Atlantic Coast states are Maryland, Virginia, North Carolina, South Carolina, and Georgia. These states have big cities and beach towns.

Adventure on the Coast

For many years, lighthouses along the shores of the Atlantic Coast states have helped sailors avoid dangers. These dangers include sudden storms, hidden rocks, and sandbars.

Today, the region's coast attracts many visitors. Wide beaches have made **Myrtle Beach**, South Carolina, a favorite vacation spot. Islands off the coast of Georgia and North Carolina are popular places to visit, too.

Business in the Cities

Cities are economic centers in the Atlantic Coast states. For example, many banks and other businesses have main offices in **Atlanta**, Georgia, and **Charlotte**, North Carolina.

Every branch of the United States military has at least one base in the **Norfolk**, Virginia, area. Shipbuilding is another important industry there.

Baltimore, Maryland, is the most-populated city in the Atlantic Coast states. Many people in Baltimore work in health care and education. Others commute to **Washington, D.C.**, where they work for the federal government.

READING CHECK ⚪ **COMPARE AND CONTRAST**
How are Atlanta and Charlotte alike?

Centers of Government

You may not see the government as an industry, but it is a kind of service industry. It employs millions of workers who provide services for citizens.

Federal Government

Nearly 250,000 people work for the federal government in Washington, D.C. People who work at military bases in the Atlantic Coast states also work for the federal government.

Many charities are based in the region because they work closely with the federal government. For example, the American Red Cross has its headquarters in Washington, D.C. **Clara Barton**, of Maryland, founded the charity in 1881. Today, the American Red Cross helps people in emergencies all over the world.

State Governments

Many people in the region also work for their state's government. Often they work in their state's capital city.

Like the federal government, state governments have three branches. The legislative branch, or **state legislature**, makes laws for the state. The executive branch, led by the **governor**, carries out state laws. The judicial branch, made up of state courts, makes sure laws are carried out fairly.

READING CHECK ♂COMPARE AND CONTRAST
How are state governments like the federal government?

❱ **MARYLAND STATE HOUSE** In Annapolis, students listen to a speaker at the Maryland State House, the nation's oldest state house still in use.

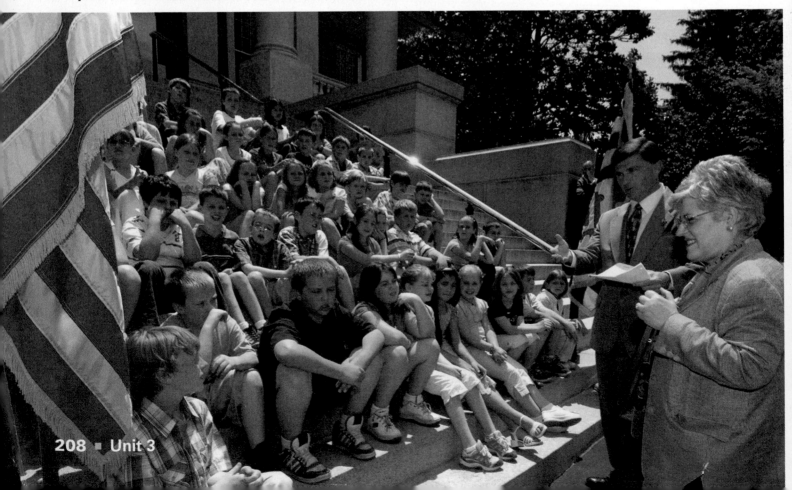

▶ **INDUSTRIES** Atlantic Coast industries range from peanut farming in Georgia (above) to cancer research in North Carolina (left).

Other Industries

The Atlantic Coast states have both old and new industries. Some older industries use natural resources and crops grown on the region's farms. Some newer industries depend more on human resources.

Products from Farms and Forests

Food-processing industries are important in the Atlantic Coast states. **Food processing** is the cooking, canning, drying, freezing, or packaging of food products. For example, peanuts grown in the region go through food processing to make peanut butter.

Manufacturers in Georgia produce lumber and wood pulp. **Pulp** is a soft mixture of ground-up wood chips and chemicals. It is used to make paper and cardboard. Factories in **High Point**, North Carolina, use lumber to make furniture.

Computers and Electronics

High-tech, or high-technology, industries are growing in the Atlantic Coast states. **High-tech** industries invent, build, or use computers and other electronic equipment. Companies in these industries need many workers with special training and skills.

North Carolina has one of the nation's largest high-tech centers. It is a triangle-shaped area formed by three cities—**Raleigh, Durham,** and **Chapel Hill**. This area is called Research Triangle Park because many businesses, universities, and government agencies do high-tech research there. Thousands of people work within Research Triangle Park. They work in areas such as computers, medical care, and communications.

READING CHECK ☼**COMPARE AND CONTRAST**
How are high-tech industries different from food-processing industries?

▶ **INDIA** An Indian scientist works in the city of Bangalore, the high-tech center of India.

Global Connection

India's high-tech industries, like those in the United States, are grouped in cities. Many workers in those cities speak English. This ability enables them to work with companies in other English-speaking countries.

READING CHECK ○ **COMPARE AND CONTRAST**
How are India's high-tech industries like those in the United States?

Summary

The Atlantic Coast states have both big cities and small towns. The federal government, in Washington, D.C., is a major employer in the region. As in other regions, many people in the Atlantic Coast states work for their state's government. High-tech and food-processing industries are also important in the region.

REVIEW

1. **WHAT TO KNOW** What are some important industries in the Atlantic Coast states?

2. **VOCABULARY** What is the main role of a **governor** in state government?

3. **ECONOMICS** What are three products that workers in the Atlantic Coast states make from natural resources?

4. **CRITICAL THINKING** Why do you think many high-tech companies are in cities that have colleges and universities?

5. **WRITE A DESCRIPTION** Use what you have read in this lesson to write a summary describing the economy of the Atlantic Coast region.

6. **COMPARE AND CONTRAST**

On a separate sheet of paper, copy and complete the graphic organizer below.

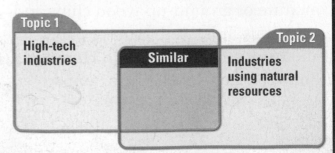

Topic 1
High-tech industries
Similar
Topic 2
Industries using natural resources

Thurgood Marshall

Biography

Trustworthiness
Respect
Responsibility
Fairness
Caring
Patriotism

"I want to be remembered for doing the best I could with what I had."

Thurgood Marshall had an important job in government as a United States Supreme Court justice. In fact, he was the first African American to have that job.

Marshall was born in Baltimore, Maryland. He studied law in Washington, D.C. Then he worked as a lawyer for the National Association for the Advancement of Colored People (NAACP). In 1954, Marshall presented a case to the United States Supreme Court. The case is known as *Brown v. Board of Education of Topeka*. Marshall argued that African American children have the right to go to the same schools that white children attend. The Supreme Court agreed, and Marshall won the case.

A few years later, President Lyndon B. Johnson appointed Marshall to the Supreme Court. Marshall served as a justice for 23 years.

Why Character Counts

How did **Thurgood Marshall** show that he cared about others?

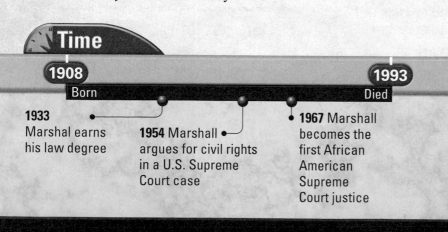

Time

1908		1993
Born		Died

1933 Marshal earns his law degree

1954 Marshall argues for civil rights in a U.S. Supreme Court case

1967 Marshall becomes the first African American Supreme Court justice

GO ONLINE For more resources, go to www.harcourtschool.com/ss1

Gulf Coast States

WHAT TO KNOW
How do the coasts affect life in the Gulf Coast states?

VOCABULARY
Sun Belt p. 213
tourism p. 214
resort p. 214
barrier island p. 216
mainland p. 216
wildlife refuge p. 216
coral p. 216
reef p. 216

PEOPLE
Walt Disney

PLACES
New Orleans
Orlando
Natchez
Huntsville
Miami Beach
Dauphin Island
Key West

COMPARE AND CONTRAST

YOU ARE THERE You and your grandmother walk along the beach near her new home. You are visiting her for the first time since she moved to the Mississippi coast. You are surprised that it is so warm in December.

"I like it here, Grandma," you say.

"I do, too," she answers. "Tomorrow you will meet my friends. We all volunteer one day a week. We paint houses for people who aren't able to do the job themselves."

▶ Children riding waves on a Gulf Coast beach

▶ A historic mansion in Natchez, Mississippi

The Sun Belt

The Gulf Coast states are Florida, Alabama, Mississippi, and Louisiana. They all lie in the **Sun Belt**—a wide area in the southern United States that has a mild climate all year. The Sun Belt stretches from Virginia in the east to California in the west.

History and Change

The Gulf Coast region has a long history of cultural diversity. African Americans have been important to that history. They helped create blues and jazz music. **New Orleans**, Louisiana, is often called the Birthplace of Jazz.

Louisiana's Cajun (KAY•juhn) culture began in the mid-1700s, when many French Catholic settlers left Canada. They moved to the bayous, or swamps, of southern Louisiana, where they became known as Cajuns. Cajuns speak a form of French and maintain their unique culture to this day.

The Gulf Coast states continue to attract new residents. Today, as in other parts of the United States, Hispanics make up the fastest-growing group in the region.

Many older people from northern states move to the Gulf Coast region when they retire, or stop working. They enjoy the warm weather and outdoor activities of the region. In fact, Florida has the oldest population of all states. About one in five Floridians is over the age of 65.

READING CHECK ŎCOMPARE AND CONTRAST
How does Florida's population differ from the populations of other states?

❱ The French Quarter, in New Orleans, Louisiana

❱ A blues artist singing with children in Mississippi

❱ A view of downtown Birmingham, Alabama

Tourism

Warm weather and beaches bring new residents as well as visitors to the Gulf Coast states. These people are important to the region's economy.

From Beaches to Space

The region's tourism industry started with its beaches. **Tourism** is the selling of products and services to people who visit a place for fun. Each year, millions of tourists visit the region's beach **resorts**, or places for fun and recreation.

People also can enjoy museums, golf courses, riverboat rides, and theme parks. **Walt Disney**, a cartoonist, opened the first of his famous Florida theme parks in 1971. The park helped make **Orlando** one of the top tourism destinations in the world.

People who are interested in history can drive along the Natchez Trace Parkway from Nashville, Tennessee, to **Natchez**, Mississippi. This road follows a path used long ago by Native Americans and settlers. Along the route are many Civil War battlefields and other historic sites.

Tourists who are interested in space can visit the United States Space and Rocket Center, in **Huntsville**, Alabama. Others might go see a space shuttle launch from the John F. Kennedy Space Center, in Florida.

READING CHECK **MAIN IDEA AND DETAILS**
What are some tourist attractions in the Gulf Coast states?

> **SPACE** Tourists to the Gulf Coast states can watch a shuttle launch in Florida (above left) or learn about space in Alabama (left).

▶ **FISH FARMING** Workers collect catfish in a net at a catfish farm on the Mississippi Delta, or land at the river's mouth.

Fish and Farms

In addition to its oil industry, the Gulf Coast has a thriving fishing industry. Farther inland, farms cover much of the region.

Fishing

Gulf Coast fishers catch a variety of fish and shellfish. They harvest shrimp and oysters in the waters off all four states in the region. Louisiana is a leading provider of these shellfish.

Fish farming is a large industry in the region. A fish farm is a closed-off area of water in which people raise fish to sell. Mississippi is a leading state for farm-raised catfish.

Farming

Farmers in the region grow cotton, corn, and soybeans. Some of the corn and soybeans are turned into food for farm-raised catfish.

Florida's top crops include oranges, grapefruit, and other citrus fruits. Florida farmers also grow sugarcane, vegetables, and flowers.

Mississippi leads the nation in tree farms. Trees growing in your school-yard or in your yard at home may have been grown from seeds on a Mississippi tree farm.

READING CHECK **DRAW CONCLUSIONS**
Why do people in the Gulf Coast states have fish farms?

Islands and Keys

Hundreds of islands ring the Gulf Coast states. No two islands are the same.

Protecting the Coast

Many **barrier islands** lie just off the Atlantic and Gulf coasts. They are islands made of sand, soil, and shells deposited over time by waves. They block the mainland from ocean waves and winds. The **mainland** is the continent or the part of a continent nearest an island.

Some barrier islands have big cities, like **Miami Beach**, Florida. Others, like **Dauphin Island**, Alabama, have parks and wildlife refuges. A **wildlife refuge** is a place set aside to protect wild animals and plants.

The Florida Keys

The Florida Keys are a chain of islands that stretch 150 miles out to sea. They are made of limestone and coral. **Coral** is a stone like material made of skeletons of tiny sea animals. Coral reefs lie near some of the Keys. A **reef** is an underwater ridge of rocks, sand, or coral near the surface of the sea.

Key West is the largest city in the Keys, but this island is only about 4 miles long and 1 mile wide. Even so, more than 25,000 people live there. Key West is also the southernmost island in the Keys. The Overseas Highway connects Key West and the other Keys to the mainland.

READING CHECK ⟳ **COMPARE AND CONTRAST**
How do barrier islands and the Keys differ?

▶ **SEVEN MILE BRIDGE** The Seven Mile Bridge is one of the 42 bridges that connect the Florida Keys.

216

▶ **PARADE** A crowd watching a parade waves flags while celebrating Cuban culture.

Global Connection

Cuba is a small island nation in the Caribbean Sea. It lies just 90 miles south of Key West.

Many Cubans have immigrated to the United States. In fact, Florida now has the largest Cuban American population in the nation.

READING CHECK ᚛**COMPARE AND CONTRAST**
How are Cuba and Key West alike?

Summary

The Gulf Coast states lie in the Sun Belt. These states have a diverse population. Hispanics make up the fastest-growing group in the Gulf Coast states. Retired people also make up a large part of the population in some Gulf Coast states, such as Florida. Tourism, fishing, and farming are some of the leading industries in the region.

REVIEW

1. **WHAT TO KNOW** How do the coasts affect life in the Gulf Coast states?

2. **VOCABULARY** Write a sentence to explain how the terms **tourism** and **resort** are related.

3. **GEOGRAPHY** How do barrier islands protect the mainland?

4. **CRITICAL THINKING** Why do you think many immigrants from Latin American countries settle in the Gulf Coast states?

5. **PLAN A TRIP** Plan a one-week trip through the Gulf Coast states. In your plan, list each day and each stop.

6. **(Focus Skill) COMPARE AND CONTRAST**
On a separate sheet of paper, copy and complete the graphic organizer below.

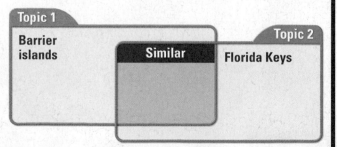

Topic 1
Barrier islands   Similar   Topic 2   Florida Keys

Read a Map Scale

Why It Matters Maps show large places in a smaller scale. A **map scale** compares a distance on a map with a distance in the real world.

⟩ LEARN

You can use the map scale on page 219 to find the length of the Natchez Trace Parkway. You can also find the distance between any two places along the parkway.

Step 1 Use a ruler to measure the exact length of the scale bar in inches.

Step 2 Read the scale's label. How many miles does that length stand for?

Step 3 Use your ruler to measure the distance between any two points.

Step 4 Multiply the number of inches by the number of miles each inch represents in the map scale.

⟩ **NATCHEZ TRACE PARKWAY** Split-rail fences line parts of the parkway.

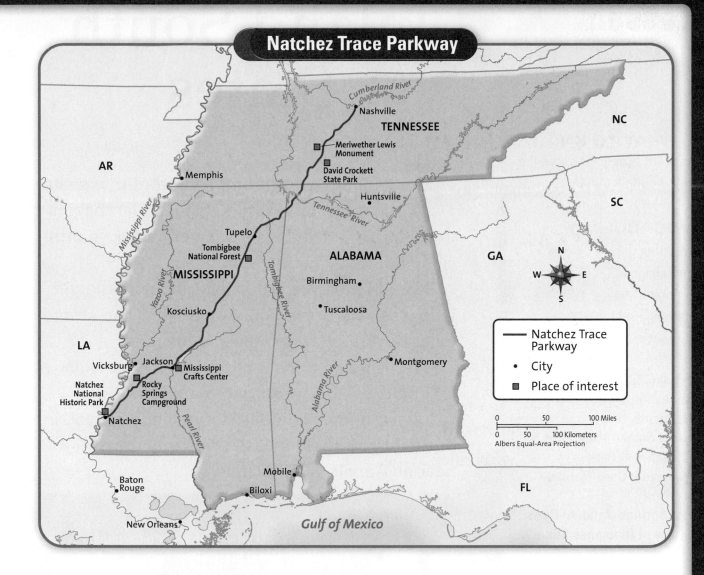

Natchez Trace Parkway

➤ PRACTICE

Use the map to answer these questions.

1 About how many miles long is the parkway?

2 About how many miles of the parkway run through Alabama?

3 About how far is Tupelo, Mississippi, from Nashville, Tennessee?

➤ APPLY

Make It Relevant Use a map of your state to find the distances between your city and three other cities.

Map and Globe Skills

Lesson  3 Inland South States

 WHAT TO KNOW
What is special about the Inland South states?

VOCABULARY

tradition p. 221

reclaim p. 222

habitat p. 223

endangered p. 224

extinct p. 224

PLACES

Jonesborough
Nashville
Great Smoky Mountains
   National Park
Mammoth Cave National
   Park
Hot Springs National Park
Crater of Diamonds State
   Park

 COMPARE AND CONTRAST

YOU ARE THERE You and your mom have front-row seats in a theater. On the stage, a man begins to speak. On most days, he is your school's principal, but today he is a storyteller.

"I want to tell you all a story about a little girl who was very brave and very clever," the storyteller begins. "Her name was Mustmag."

"This is going to be a good story," you whisper.

"I think so, too," your mom answers.

You are at the National Storytelling Festival, in **Jonesborough**, Tennessee, and you are about to hear an Appalachian folktale.

STORYTELLER A storyteller entertains a crowd at the National Storytelling Festival, in Tennessee.

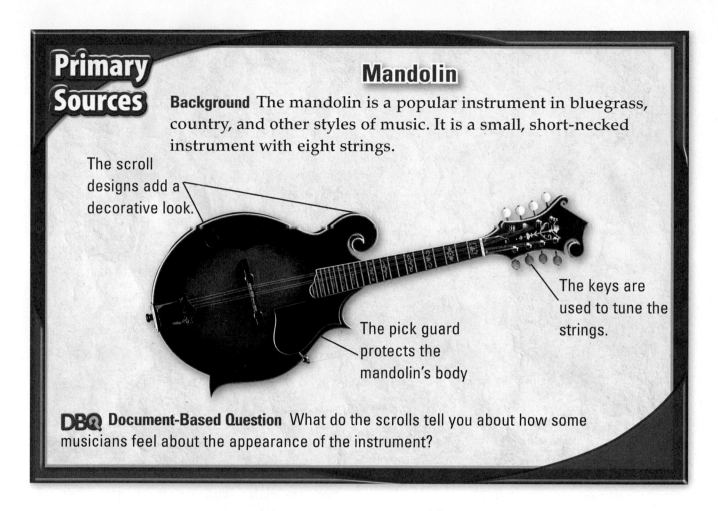

Mandolin

Background The mandolin is a popular instrument in bluegrass, country, and other styles of music. It is a small, short-necked instrument with eight strings.

The scroll designs add a decorative look.

The keys are used to tune the strings.

The pick guard protects the mandolin's body

DBQ Document-Based Question What do the scrolls tell you about how some musicians feel about the appearance of the instrument?

The Highlands Today

The Inland South states are West Virginia, Tennessee, Kentucky, and Arkansas. All except Arkansas are part of Appalachia, an area in and around the Appalachian Mountains. In Arkansas, the Ozark Mountains and the Ouachita (WAH•shuh•taw) Mountains give much of the land a geography that is similar to Appalachia's.

Traditions and Tourism

The people of the Inland South have built a tourism industry based on **traditions**, or customs continued from the past. In Appalachia, museums and festivals celebrate the skills and crafts of Native Americans and early settlers.

The mountain areas of Arkansas offer tourists similar experiences. Visitors to Arkansas's Ozark Folk Center State Park, for example, see reenactments of early settlers' lives.

People also come to the Inland South states to hear music. Visitors enjoy bluegrass music, the folk music that began with early Appalachian settlers. Most of those settlers sang about the rural areas in which they lived. People can also hear country music. Today, **Nashville**, Tennessee, is often called the Capital of Country Music.

READING CHECK ⟳**COMPARE AND CONTRAST** How are the mountain areas of Arkansas and the Appalachia region alike?

Mountains of Coal

Most coal deposits in the eastern United States are in the Appalachian Mountains. So coal mining has long been an industry in the Inland South.

Appalachian Ranges

Several ranges of the Appalachians are found in the Inland South. Parts of the Blue Ridge and the Allegheny mountains extend into West Virginia. The Cumberland Mountains lie in the eastern parts of Kentucky and Tennessee. The Great Smoky Mountains extend into eastern Tennessee.

Many of these ranges contain coal. In fact, mines in Kentucky and West Virginia provide about one-fourth of the nation's coal. Most of that coal is used to make electricity.

Shaft Mines and Strip Mines

When coal is found deep inside Earth, miners use machines to dig holes called shafts to reach it. Miners go down one shaft and send coal up another.

When coal is near Earth's surface, bulldozers strip away the trees and plants to reach the coal. This kind of mining is called strip mining.

Strip mining is hard on land. Once trees and plants are removed, the soil washes away. Then nothing can grow. Laws now require mining companies to reclaim strip-mined land. To **reclaim** land means that the companies must return the land to its natural state by putting back soil, trees, and plants.

READING CHECK ☼ **COMPARE AND CONTRAST**
How are shaft mines and strip mines different?

CHANGES IN
COAL-MINING TECHNOLOGIES

> Young miners with horses and mules at a mine entrance

1895

> A miner rides a small train into a mine

1930s

> A view of reclaimed strip-mined land

2004

▶ GREAT SMOKY MOUNTAINS A sign (left) leads visitors into the 800 square miles of Great Smoky Mountains National Park.

National Parks

The Inland South has many national parks. These parks protect land, water, wildlife, culture, and history.

Mountains and Caves

Great Smoky Mountains National Park is located on the border between Tennessee and North Carolina. It gets more visitors than any other national park in the United States.

The park's warm lowlands and cool highlands provide a wide range of habitats. A **habitat** is a region in which a plant or an animal naturally grows or lives. Protected wildlife in Great Smoky Mountains National Park includes black bears, elk, and owls.

One of the most popular attractions in Kentucky is **Mammoth Cave National Park**. This park protects the longest cave system in the world.

Hot Springs and Diamonds

Hot Springs National Park, in Arkansas, was one of the first areas in the United States to be protected. It is named for its 47 natural hot springs. Some people believe the water in the springs is good for their health.

Arkansas has another very special state park. **Crater of Diamonds State Park** holds the only working diamond mine in the United States. Visitors can keep any diamonds they find.

READING CHECK ⭕COMPARE AND CONTRAST
What do all national parks have in common?

Global Connection

Kruger National Park is the largest and most-visited park in South Africa. Like many national parks, Kruger provides a safe place for endangered animals. **Endangered** animals are ones whose numbers are very limited. Without parks and wildlife refuges, endangered animals may become extinct. Animals are **extinct** when all of their kind have died out.

READING CHECK ⎙ **COMPARE AND CONTRAST**
What is the difference between an endangered animal and an extinct animal?

Summary

The traditions of the Inland South and its popular national parks have helped this region build a tourist industry. Coal mining is another important industry.

▶ **WILDLIFE** Kruger National Park is home to elephants, lions, zebras, hippopotamuses, and other animals.

REVIEW

1. **WHAT TO KNOW** What is special about the Inland South states?

2. **VOCABULARY** What is a **habitat**?

3. **GEOGRAPHY** How is Arkansas like Appalachia?

4. **CRITICAL THINKING** Why do you think it is important for people to protect the environment?

5. 🖌 **DESIGN A COVER** Design a cover for a brochure titled "Visit the Southeast" that features one of the parks in this lesson. Include artwork and captions.

6. (Focus Skill) **COMPARE AND CONTRAST**

On a separate sheet of paper, copy and complete the graphic organizer below.

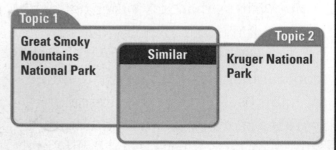

Topic 1
Great Smoky Mountains National Park

Similar

Topic 2
Kruger National Park

Bill Monroe

Biography

Trustworthiness

Respect

Responsibility

Fairness

Caring

Patriotism

"It's plain music that tells a good story. . . . Bluegrass is music that matters."

Bill Monroe is known as the Father of Bluegrass. He did not invent bluegrass, but he made it famous all over the world.

Monroe was born in Kentucky. He grew up hearing the folk music of Appalachia. This music blends songs that settlers from Scotland, Ireland, and places in Africa had brought with them. Monroe traveled around the country playing this music. He named his band the Blue Grass Boys after Kentucky's nickname, the Bluegrass State. The music they played became known as blue-grass music.

Monroe wrote songs about Kentucky, too. His "Blue Moon of Kentucky" is the official bluegrass state song.

Today, bluegrass is so popular that you can hear it in movie soundtracks and on TV shows. Bands as far away as Russia play bluegrass music, too!

Why Character Counts

How did Bill Monroe show respect for the traditions of the region where he grew up?

Time

1911				1996
Born				Died

1939 Monroe names his band the Blue Grass Boys

1970 Monroe enters the Country Music Hall of Fame

1993 Monroe wins a Lifetime Achievement Grammy

GO ONLINE For more resources, go to www.harcourtschool.com/ss1

225

Visual Summary

In the Atlantic Coast states, farmers grow crops for the food-processing industries.

Fish farming is an important industry in the Gulf Coast states.

Summarize the Chapter

Focus Skill **Compare and Contrast** Complete this graphic organizer to show that you understand how to compare and contrast the economies of the Southeast states.

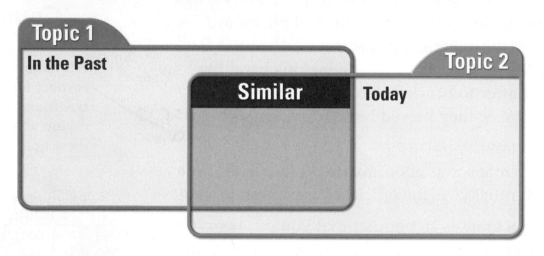

Topic 1

In the Past

Similar

Today

Topic 2

Vocabulary

Identify the term from the word bank that correctly matches each definition.

1. a place for fun and recreation

2. an island made by sand, soil, and shells deposited over time by waves

3. no longer in existence

4. the continent or part of a continent nearest an island

5. the selling of products or services to people who visit a place for fun

6. the head of the executive branch of state government

7. a state's legislative branch

Word Bank

state legislature p. 208

governor p. 208

tourism p. 214

resort p. 214

barrier island p. 216

mainland p. 216

extinct p. 224

The Overseas Highway connects the Florida Keys to the mainland.

The Inland South states have many national parks.

 Facts and Main Ideas

Answer these questions.

8. What kinds of jobs do people have in high-tech industries?

9. How do food-processing industries depend on farms?

10. What are three tourist attractions in the Southeast states?

11. How do people reclaim land that has been strip-mined?

Write the letter of the best choice.

12. Which city in the Atlantic Coast states has the largest population?
    A Atlanta, Georgia
    B Baltimore, Maryland
    C Charlotte, North Carolina
    D Norfolk, Virginia

13. New Orleans, Louisiana, is often called the birthplace of what kind of music?
    A bluegrass
    B country
    C jazz
    D rock

14. Which of these physical features is found in all the Inland South states?
    A deserts
    B islands
    C mountains
    D swamps

 Critical Thinking

15. How did state and federal governments help many cities in the Southeast grow?

16. How has geography affected the cultural traditions that have developed in the Inland South states?

17. What factors are contributing to the rapid population growth in many parts of the Southeast today?

 **Skills**

Read a Map Scale

18. Study the map on page 219. About how many miles does the Natchez Trace Parkway run through Tennessee?

writing

✎ **Write a Comparative Report** Write a report in which you compare and contrast the federal government and state governments in the United States. Be sure to describe the three branches of each level.

✎ **Write a Persuasive Article** Write a newspaper article explaining why you think national parks and wildlife refuges are important. Include facts to support your opinions.

Fun with Social Studies

Vacation Station

These travelers have lost their luggage! Use what you have learned to decide which suitcase these travelers should have.

St. Augustine

Nashville

Chesapeake Bay

Raleigh-Durham

Everglades

Under Construction

VOCABULARY

Finish building the terms on the left by adding the word blocks on the right.

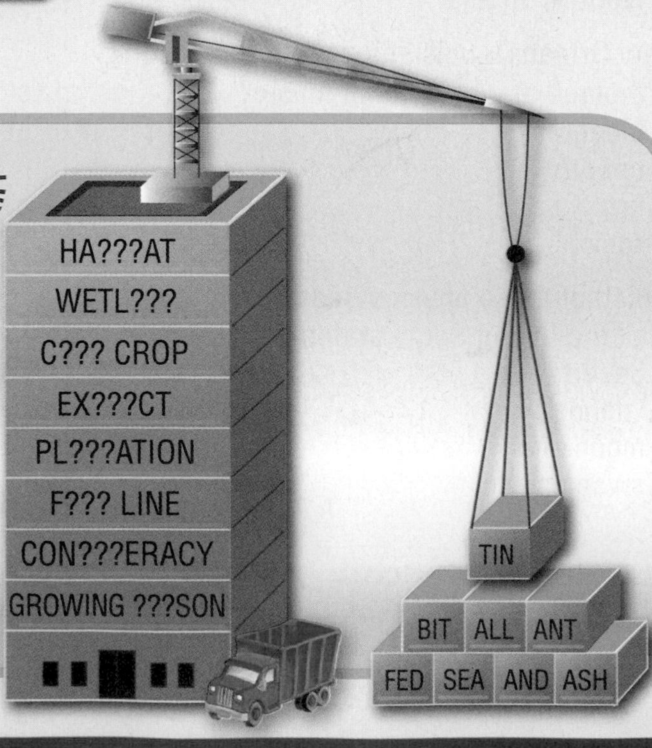

HA???AT

WETL???

C??? CROP

EX???CT

PL???ATION

F??? LINE

CON???ERACY

GROWING ???SON

TIN

BIT   ALL   ANT

FED   SEA   AND   ASH

If they'd had the Internet

Which famous people in Unit 3 might have written these e-mails?

FROM:
symbolwriter@my_GA_home.com
TO:
listenswell@my_GA_home.com
SUBJECT:
Sound System

FROM:
ilovenursing@imahelper.org
TO:
david@coolmail.net
SUBJECT:
I founded it!

FROM:
mountainman@newwayfinder.net
TO:
jeremiah@stillbackeast.com
SUBJECT:
Through the Gap

Online Adventures

GO ONLINE

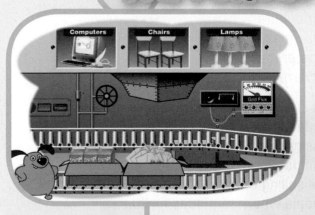

It's time to move on to the Southeast. In this online game, Eco is on the way to a Native American village long ago. With Eco, you'll have to do things in different places and times, including starting a business in the Southeast today. If you can do it, you'll catch one of the suspects and ask about the missing American symbol. Play now at **www.harcourtschool.com/ss1**

Review and Test Prep ✔

🔆 THE BIG IDEA

Growth and Change The Southeast is experiencing changes that give it one of the fastest-growing populations of any region in the United States today.

Reading Comprehension and Vocabulary

Old and New in the Southeast

The 13 Southeast states make up a large region with a varied geography. Fertile plains stretch from the coasts. Inland are tree-covered hills and mountains, plateaus, and river valleys.

Most Native Americans and early European settlers in the Southeast were farmers. Some settlers built plantations where they grew cash crops. Enslaved African Americans did much of the work. In the 1860s, most of the Southeast states joined the Confederacy. They fought against the Union during the Civil War.

After the war ended in 1865, the Southeast rebuilt its economy. Agriculture remained important, but newer industries also grew. These included coal mining and food processing. Today, tourism, government, and high-tech industries employ many people in the Southeast.

Attracted by its growing economy and warm climate, many people have moved to the Southeast in recent years. Its states and cities are growing fast. Yet, the Southeast remains a region of strong traditions.

Read the summary above. Then answer the questions that follow.

1. What kind of landform covers most of the eastern half of the Southeast?
   A hills
   B mountains
   C plains
   D plateaus

2. A civil war is a war fought between whom?
   A people who speak the same language
   B groups of people in the same country
   C people who follow different religions
   D groups of people in bordering countries

3. Which of these industries developed first in the Southeast?
   A agriculture
   B coal mining
   C food processing
   D government

4. What is the meaning of the word tourism?
   A a place people visit for fun
   B businesses that invent, build, or use computers and other electronics
   C the selling of products and services to people who visit places for fun
   D methods of transportation

Answer these questions.

5. What causes waterfalls to form along the Fall Line?

6. Why did most Native Americans in the Southeast build their villages along rivers or lakes?

7. What are some goods that are exported from the Southeast?

8. What role is climate playing in the Southeast's population growth?

9. Why do Americans create national parks and wildlife refuges?

Write the letter of the best choice.

10. In which part of the Southeast region did Europeans first settle?
    A the Appalachian Mountains
    B the Central Plains
    C the Coastal Plain
    D the Piedmont

11. What is the main job of state legislatures?
    A to carry out state laws
    B to make sure state laws are fair
    C to make state laws
    D to choose state judges

12. Which of these areas is best described as a high-tech center?
    A Appalachia
    B the Florida Keys
    C the Research Triangle
    D the Sun Belt

13. Which of these physical features is most related to the Cajun culture that developed in the Southeast?
    A deserts
    B islands
    C mountains
    D bayous

14. How are farming and manufacturing industries in the Southeast interdependent?

15. What are some of the advantages and disadvantages of rapid growth in the Southeast states?

Read a Map Scale

Use the map on this page to answer the following questions.

16. About how many miles is it from Little Rock to Hot Springs National Park?

17. About how many miles does the Arkansas River flow through Arkansas?

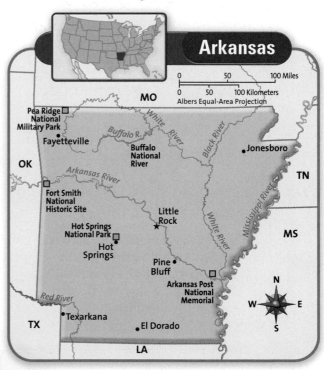

Activities

Show What You Know

 Unit Writing Activity

Write a Summary Write a summary explaining why and how the Southeast region has changed over time.

- Describe ways in which the region has changed.
- Explain causes and effects of those changes.
- Summarize the main ideas.

Unit Project

Design a Southeast Travel Brochure
Design a travel brochure about the Southeast.

- Include places such as national parks, cities, and other points of interest you have read about.
- Illustrate your brochure with drawings, maps, and magazine pictures.
- Provide a brief description of each place you include.

Read More

- *An Island Scrapbook: Dawn to Dusk on a Barrier Island* by Virginia Wright-Frierson. Simon and Schuster Books for Young Readers.

- *Rosa* by Nikki Giovanni. Henry Holt.

- *The Journal of Jesse Smoke: A Cherokee Boy, The Trail of Tears, 1838* by Joseph Bruchac. Scholastic.

GO ONLINE For more resources, go to www.harcourtschool.com/ss1

The Big Idea

Transportation, Land, and Cities

Mighty waterways, busy highways, and fertile lands stretch between cities of the Midwest region today.

What to Know

- ✓ What is the geography of the Midwest?
- ✓ How did the settlement of the Midwest change over time?
- ✓ How did changes in transportation affect the early economy of the Midwest?
- ✓ What is the Midwest like today?

Time

The Midwest

1673 Jacques Marquette and Louis Joliet explore what is now the Midwest, p. 256

1700s Sioux Indians live on the Great Plains, p. 254

1500   1600   1700

At the Same Time

1535 New Spain is formed in North America

1664 Northeast The New Jersey Colony is established

The Midwest

1783 Part of the Midwest becomes a territory of the United States, p. 256

1803 The United States makes the Louisiana Purchase, p. 258

Present Some of the nation's busiest airports are in the Midwest, p. 277

1800

1900

Present

1836 Southeast Arkansas becomes the twenty-fifth state

1982 Canada gains its independence from Britain

Unit 4 ■ 233

Abraham Lincoln

1809–1865
- Sixteenth President of the United States
- Signed the Emancipation Proclamation
- Led the Union to win the Civil War

Samuel Clemens

1835–1910
- Missouri writer better known as Mark Twain
- Author of *The Adventures of Tom Sawyer* and *Life on the Mississippi River*

 People

1800   1850

1809 • Abraham Lincoln   1865

1835 • Samuel Clemens

1842? • Crazy Horse   1877

1863 • Henry Ford

1867 • Laura Ingalls Wilder

Laura Ingalls Wilder

1867–1957
- Children's book author who wrote about her pioneer childhood
- Writer of *Little House in the Big Woods* and *Little House on the Prairie*

Thomas Hart Benton

1889–1975
- Painter and art teacher
- He painted murals of life in the rural Midwest, including *History of Missouri* in the Missouri State House

Crazy Horse

1842?–1877
- Chief of the Oglala Sioux
- Led Sioux warriors at the Battle of the Little Bighorn

Henry Ford

1863–1947
- Entrepreneur
- Inventor of assembly line for making automobiles
- Designed, built, and sold Model T automobiles in 1908

1900   **1950**   **PRESENT**

1910

1947

1957

1889 • Thomas Hart Benton   1975

1951 • Benjamin S. Carson

1954 • Oprah Winfrey

Benjamin S. Carson

1951–present
- Doctor and leader, born in Detroit
- Started a scholarship that helps students across the United States pay for their college education

Oprah Winfrey

1954–present
- Entertainment industry leader and entrepreneur
- First African American woman to own a major television production company and the first to become a billionaire

Place

The Midwest

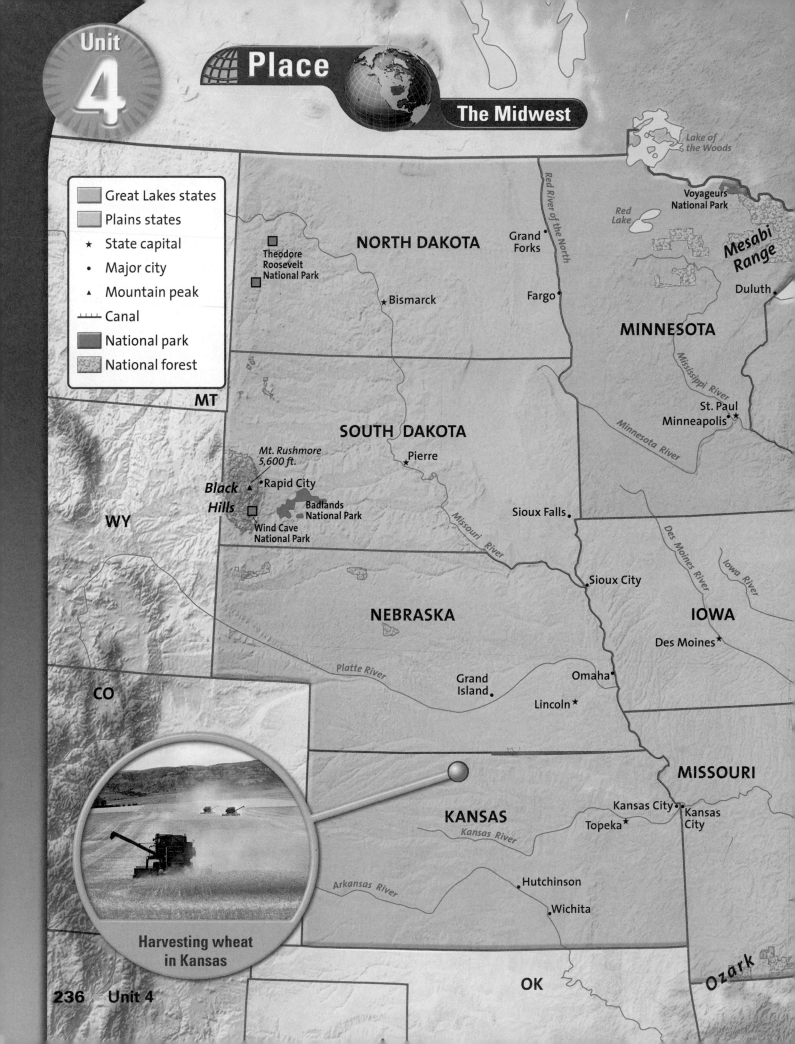

Map Legend
- Great Lakes states
- Plains states
- ★ State capital
- • Major city
- ▲ Mountain peak
- Canal
- National park
- National forest

NORTH DAKOTA
- Theodore Roosevelt National Park
- Grand Forks
- Fargo
- ★ Bismarck

MINNESOTA
- Lake of the Woods
- Red Lake
- Voyageurs National Park
- Mesabi Range
- Duluth
- St. Paul ★
- Minneapolis •
- Red River of the North
- Mississippi River
- Minnesota River

MT

SOUTH DAKOTA
- Mt. Rushmore 5,600 ft.
- Black Hills
- ▲ Rapid City
- Wind Cave National Park
- Badlands National Park
- ★ Pierre
- Sioux Falls •
- Missouri River

WY

NEBRASKA
- Platte River
- Grand Island •
- Omaha •
- Lincoln ★
- Sioux City •

IOWA
- Des Moines ★
- Des Moines River
- Iowa River

CO

MISSOURI
- Kansas City •
- Kansas City

KANSAS
- Topeka ★
- Kansas River
- Hutchinson •
- Wichita •
- Arkansas River

Harvesting wheat in Kansas

OK

Ozark

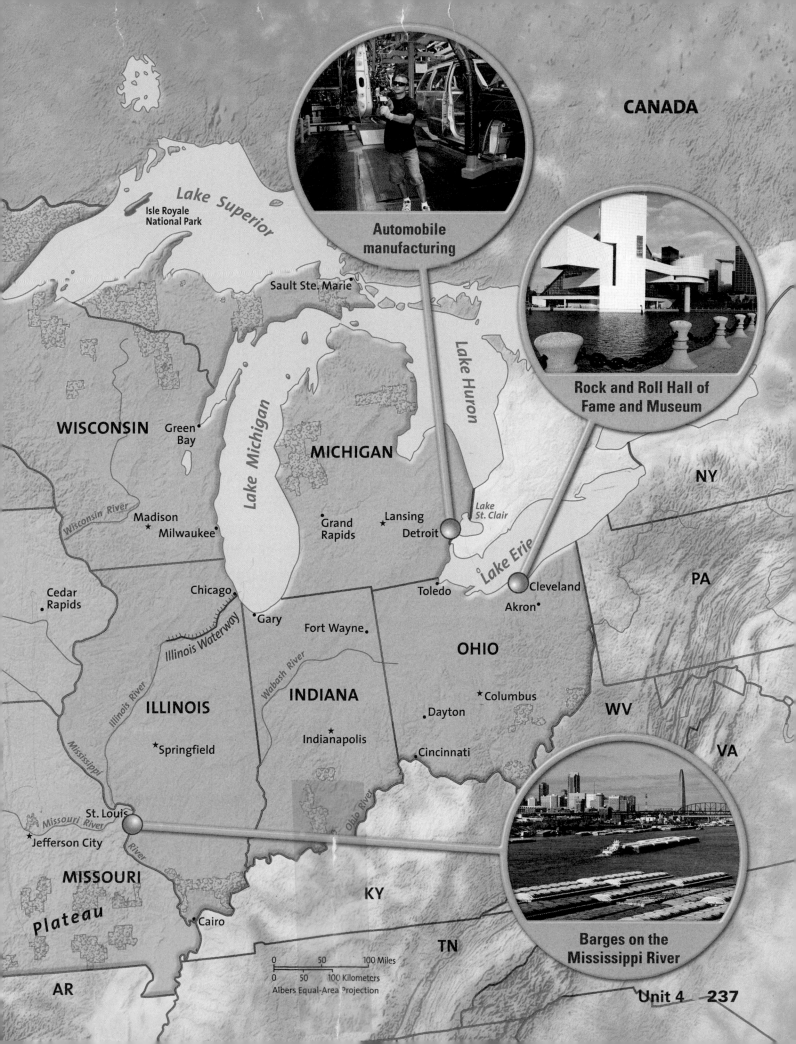

CANADA

Lake Superior

Isle Royale National Park

Automobile manufacturing

Rock and Roll Hall of Fame and Museum

Sault Ste. Marie

Lake Huron

WISCONSIN

Green Bay

Lake Michigan

MICHIGAN

Lake St. Clair

NY

Wisconsin River

Madison
★Milwaukee

Grand Rapids

★Lansing
Detroit

Lake Erie

PA

Cedar Rapids

Chicago

Gary

Fort Wayne

Toledo

Cleveland

Akron•

Illinois Waterway

Wabash River

OHIO

WV

Illinois River

ILLINOIS

INDIANA

★Columbus

•Dayton

VA

Mississippi

★Springfield

Indianapolis★

•Cincinnati

Ohio River

Missouri River

St. Louis

River

★Jefferson City

MISSOURI

KY

Plateau

•Cairo

Barges on the Mississippi River

AR

TN

0   50   100 Miles

0   50   100 Kilometers

Albers Equal-Area Projection

Reading Social Studies

(Focus Skill) Summarize

Why It Matters Summarizing what you read can help you understand and remember the most important information.

⟩ LEARN

When you **summarize**, you state in your own words a shortened version of what you read.

Key Facts	Summary
Important idea from the reading	Important information you read, shortened and written in your own words
Important idea from the reading	

- A summary includes only the most important ideas from what you have read.
- Always use your own words when you summarize.

⟩ PRACTICE

Read the paragraphs that follow. Write a summary of the second paragraph.

Facts

The Great Lakes are very important to the United States. Through rivers and canals, the Great Lakes connect with the Mississippi River and the Atlantic Ocean. Boats and barges use them to transport grain, minerals, and manufactured products to distant places. (The Great Lakes are important because they are used to transport items to distant places.)

Summary

Many people think of Detroit as the place where cars are made. However, many other things are produced there. Some of Detroit's important but less well-known products include steel, paint, and medicines.

Read the paragraphs, and answer the questions.

The Mississippi River

Long before Europeans and others came to America, Native Americans lived along the Mississippi River. In fact, the name *Mississippi* is a Native American word for "big river." The Mississippi River valley had rich soil and was full of life. Native Americans enjoyed the foods that the river and its valley provided. They also used the river for travel by canoe.

Spanish explorers were the first Europeans to see the Mississippi River. Later, French and English explorers traveled along it. All the explorers understood that a river this large would be useful in many ways. At different times, Spain, France, and Britain each claimed the Mississippi River and the lands of its valley.

In time, the United States gained control of the Mississippi. The river became important to the nation's transportation and trade. Cities and towns sprang up along the river. Soon, faster boats were built, and they began traveling the river. Some children dreamed of taking trips to distant places. A few of those children ended up working on boats on the river.

Today, many large cities still thrive on the banks of the Mississippi River. Their people and businesses use the river as a source of water, as a means of transportation, and as a place to have fun.

 Summarize

1. How would you describe the Native Americans' reasons for settling in the Mississippi River valley?
2. Why was the Mississippi River important to the United States?
3. Why is the Mississippi River important today?

ON THE BANKS OF

Plum Creek

written by Laura Ingalls Wilder
illustrated by Garth Williams
embroidery by Nancy Freeman

Laura Ingalls Wilder is best known as the author of the Little House books, stories based on her pioneer childhood. In 1874, when Laura was just eight years old, her family set out to go west in a covered wagon. Laura traveled with her ma and pa, her sisters, Mary and Carrie, and the family's dog, Jack, from Wisconsin to Walnut Grove, a tiny pioneer village in Minnesota. Read now how Laura explored her family's new home—a dugout carved into a hillside on the banks of Plum Creek.

Ma picked up Carrie and said: "Come, Mary. Let's go look at the dugout."

Jack got to the door first. It was open. He looked in, and then he waited for Laura.

All around that door green vines were growing out of the grassy bank, and they were full of flowers. Red and blue and purple and rosy-pink and white and striped flowers all had their throats wide open as if they were singing glory to the morning. They were morning-glory flowers.

Laura went under those singing flowers into the dugout. It was one room, all white. The earth walls had been smoothed and whitewashed. The earth floor was smooth and hard.

When Ma and Mary stood in the doorway the light went dim. There was a small greased-paper window beside the door. But the wall was so thick that the light from the window stayed near the window.

That front wall was built of <u>sod</u>. Mr. Hanson had dug out his house, and then he had cut long strips of prairie sod and laid them on top of one another, to make the front wall. It was a good, thick wall with not one crack in it. No cold could get through that wall.

Ma was pleased. She said, "It's small, but it's clean and pleasant." Then she looked up at the ceiling and said, "Look, girls!"

<u>sod</u> a layer of soil held together by the roots of grasses

The ceiling was made of hay. Willow boughs had been laid across and their branches woven together, but here and there the hay that had been spread on them showed through.

"Well!" Ma said. They all went up the path and stood on the roof of that house. No one could have guessed it was a roof. Grass grew on it and waved in the wind just like all the grasses along the creek bank.

"Goodness," said Ma. "Anybody could walk over this house and never know it's here."

But Laura spied something. She bent over and parted the grasses with her hands, and then she cried: "I've found the stovepipe hole! Look, Mary! Look!"

Ma and Mary stopped to look, and Carrie leaned out from Ma's arm and looked, and Jack came pushing to look. They could look right down into the whitewashed room under the grass.

They looked at it till Ma said, "We'll brush out the place before Pa comes back. Mary and Laura, you bring the water-pails."

Mary carried the large pail and Laura the small one, and they went down the path again. Jack ran ahead and took his place by the door.

Ma found a willow-twig broom in a corner and she brushed the walls carefully. Mary watched Carrie to keep her from falling down into the creek, and Laura took the little pail and went for water.

She hoppity-skipped down the stair-steps to the end of a little bridge across the creek. The bridge was one wide plank. Its other end was under a willow tree.

The tall willows fluttered slender leaves up against the sky, and little willows grew around them in clumps. They shaded all the ground, and it was cool and bare. The path went across it to a little spring, where cold, clear water fell into a tiny pool and then ran trickling to the creek.

Laura filled the little pail and went back across the sunny footbridge and up the steps. She went back and forth, fetching water in the little pail and pouring it into the big pail set on a bench inside the doorway.

Then she helped Ma bring down from the wagon everything they could carry. They had moved nearly everything into the dugout when Pa came rattling down the path. He was carrying a little tin stove and two pieces of stovepipe.

"Whew!" he said, setting them down. "I'm glad I had to carry them only three miles. Think of it, <u>Caroline</u>! Town's only three miles away! Just a nice walk. Well, Hanson's on his way west and the place is ours. How do you like it, Caroline?"

"I like it," said Ma. "But I don't know what to do about the beds. I don't want to put them on the floor."

"What's the matter with that?" Pa asked her. "We've been sleeping on the ground."

"That's different," Ma said. "I don't like to sleep on the floor in a house."

"Well, that's soon fixed," said Pa. "I'll cut some willow boughs to spread the beds on, for tonight. Tomorrow I'll find some straight willow poles, and make a couple of <u>bedsteads</u>."

<u>**Caroline**</u> Mrs. Ingalls

<u>**bedsteads**</u> are frames for beds

Response Corner

1. ⭐ **Focus Skill** **Summarize** Each member of the Ingalls family found something to like about their new home. What was special about the Ingalls' new home?

2. **Make It Relevant** What kinds of things make your home or community a good place to live?

STUDY SKILLS

USE AN ANTICIPATION GUIDE

An anticipation guide can help you anticipate, or predict, what you will learn as you read.

- Look at the lesson titles and section titles for clues.

- Preview the Reading Check questions. Use what you know about the topic of each section to predict the answers.

- Read to find out whether your predictions were correct.

Great Lakes to Great Plains

Reading Check	Prediction	Correct?
How would you describe the geography of the Midwest?	The Midwest is flat, with fertile plains and many large lakes.	✓

Climate

Reading Check	Prediction	Correct?

PREVIEW VOCABULARY

prairie p. 247   **pioneer** p. 258   **assembly line** p. 267

Exploring the Midwest

CHAPTER 8

▶ Split Rock Lighthouse on Minnesota's Lake Superior shore

Geography of the Midwest

WHAT TO KNOW
How do the geography and climate of the Midwest affect the ways people use the land?

VOCABULARY
prairie p. 247
tornado p. 249
drought p. 249
ore p. 250

PLACES
Interior Plains
Great Lakes
Central Plains
Great Plains
Corn Belt
Black Hills

SUMMARIZE

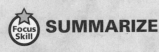

It's still dark outside when you crawl out of bed, but you're used to that. During harvesttime, you always help out on the weekends.

"Let's go!" your dad yells over the sound of the combine's engine.

You climb into the cab of the huge harvesting machine. It's already hot outside, so the air conditioning feels good. You sing along with your favorite song as your dad steers the combine toward the field. Rows of tall, ripe corn stretch to the horizon. You have a lot of work to do today.

Great Lakes to Great Plains

Fields of corn, wheat, and other crops are common sights in the Midwest. The **Interior Plains** are the main reason why. These flat, fertile plains cover the entire Midwest region.

Shaping the Plains

The Interior Plains formed thousands of years ago. They took shape as glaciers pushed south over North America. As the glaciers moved, they flattened hills and filled in valleys.

Glaciers also formed the region's **Great Lakes**. They carved out five huge holes in low areas. Then the climate warmed. The melted ice from glaciers slowly filled the holes.

A Sea of Grass

As the climate warmed, miles and miles of prairie (PRAIR•ee) were left in the Interior Plains. A **prairie** is an area of flat or rolling land covered mostly with grasses and wildflowers.

When early settlers saw the **Central Plains**, or the eastern part of the Interior Plains, they described it as a sea of grass. That is because the prairie grasses grew very tall. However, on the drier **Great Plains** to the west, the prairie grasses did not grow as tall.

Today, crops such as corn and wheat have replaced most of the tallgrass prairies in the Midwest. The fertile soil that once helped the grasses grow now helps crops grow.

READING CHECK ⵔSUMMARIZE
How would you describe the geography of the Midwest?

▶ **PRAIRIES** Corn (inset) and other crops have replaced most prairies in the Midwest. The few prairies that still exist often lie in protected areas, such as Nachusa Grassland, in Illinois.

Climate

In the Midwest, the climate gets drier as you move from east to west. As a result, taller grasses and more trees grow on the Central Plains than on the Great Plains.

Winds from the North and South

The entire region shares some climate features. The Midwest is located far from the oceans. As a result, strong winds off the oceans cannot reach the region from the east or west.

However, strong winds blowing from the north and south do reach the region. In summer, warm, moist air flows north from the Gulf of Mexico. It brings hot, rainy weather. In winter, cold air moves south from Canada. It can bring snowstorms and hailstorms.

The Lake Effect

The Great Lakes affect the areas that border them. These large bodies of water absorb heat in summer. They release this heat in winter. Even so, the surface of the Great Lakes can freeze in the coldest months. Also in winter, cold winds pick up moisture from the lakes. The moisture causes snowfall to be heavier in some nearby areas. This event is known as the "lake effect."

❱ **THE GREAT LAKES** A boy and his father (below) ice-fish on one of the five Great Lakes. The image at left shows the lakes from space.

❯ **TWISTER** A powerful tornado, or twister, moves across an area of the Great Plains known as Tornado Alley.

Earth's Strongest Winds

When masses of warm air and cold air meet over the flat Interior Plains, tornadoes can form. A **tornado** is a funnel-shaped, spinning windstorm.

Tornadoes are common in the Midwest in spring and summer. They move over the land quickly, often destroying everything in their paths. At the center of some tornadoes, wind speeds can reach more than 300 miles per hour! After a tornado struck his community, one Ohio resident said,

❝ Just a few hours ago, this was a nice, [quiet] suburban neighborhood. Now it looks like a war zone. ❞

Dry Times

Droughts (DROWTZ) are another danger in the Midwest. A **drought** is a long period of little or no rain. In the 1930s, the southern Great Plains had the worst drought in the history of the United States. For nearly ten years, there was too little rain for farmers to grow crops there.

The drought caused the soil to dry up. Then strong winds blew the dry soil away in huge dust storms. These storms filled homes with dirt and destroyed farms. The entire area became known as the Dust Bowl.

READING CHECK ⟳ **SUMMARIZE**

What happened during the worst drought in the history of the United States?

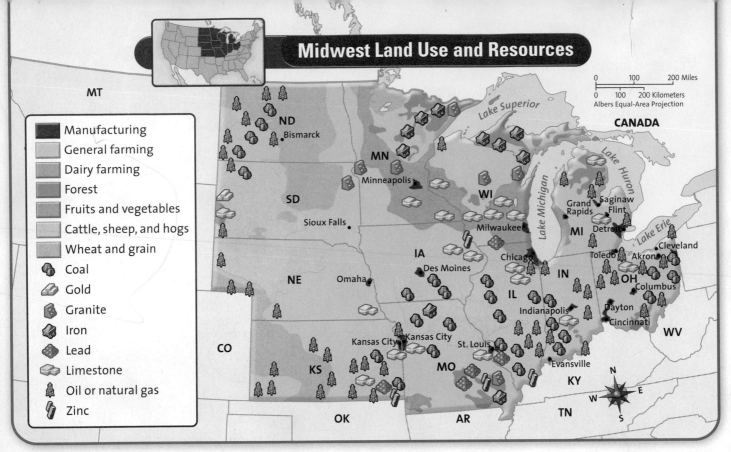

Midwest Land Use and Resources

Legend:
- Manufacturing
- General farming
- Dairy farming
- Forest
- Fruits and vegetables
- Cattle, sheep, and hogs
- Wheat and grain
- Coal
- Gold
- Granite
- Iron
- Lead
- Limestone
- Oil or natural gas
- Zinc

0 100 200 Miles
0 100 200 Kilometers
Albers Equal-Area Projection

MAP SKILL **HUMAN-ENVIRONMENT INTERACTIONS** The Midwest is rich in natural resources. In fact, South Dakota has the largest gold mine in the country. **What is the main land use for most of North Dakota?**

Natural Resources

People use most of the Midwest's land for farming and ranching. The Midwest is one of the nation's major agricultural regions.

Land Resources

The climate and soil of the Central Plains are perfect for growing crops. Corn has long been an important crop. In fact, much of the region is known as the **Corn Belt**. Farmers there grow soybeans, too. In the Great Plains, the drier climate and harder soil are good for growing wheat. Most of this wheat is used to make flour. Because of this, the Great Plains are sometimes called America's breadbasket.

Raising livestock is also important in the region. On the Central Plains, farmers raise dairy cows in the valleys of Wisconsin and Minnesota. On the Great Plains, ranching is an important industry. Ranching is especially important in Kansas and Nebraska. Cattle and sheep graze on land that is too dry for farming.

The Midwest has other resources, too. In forested areas, such as South Dakota's **Black Hills**, workers produce lumber. Workers in the region also mine for minerals. Much of the nation's iron ore comes from the Midwest. **Ore** is rock that has one or more kinds of minerals. The region also has oil. Kansas and Illinois are two of the top ten oil-producing states.

Water Resources

The Midwest also has valuable water resources. People fish in and use the water from the region's rivers. These include the Mississippi, Missouri, and Illinois Rivers. The Great Lakes also provide for people's needs. The lakes contain nearly one-fifth of the world's fresh surface water.

READING CHECK ☝SUMMARIZE
Besides land used for farming and ranching, what other resources are found in the region?

Summary

Fertile plains make the Midwest a major agricultural region. Corn and wheat are two leading crops. Because of its location, the Midwest can face extreme weather, such as tornadoes.

❯ **WISCONSIN** is one of the nation's leading producers of dairy products such as cheese.

REVIEW

1. **WHAT TO KNOW** How do the geography and climate of the Midwest affect the ways people use the land?

2. **VOCABULARY** Write a short description of a **tornado**.

3. **GEOGRAPHY** Why do the Central Plains and the Great Plains have different kinds of vegetation?

4. **CRITICAL THINKING MAKE IT RELEVANT** How might a long drought in the Midwest affect you and your family?

5. ✎ **WRITE A PERSUASIVE ARTICLE** Write an article to try to persuade people to buy land in the Midwest. Include a list of the natural resources found in the region.

6. (Focus Skill) **SUMMARIZE**

On a separate sheet of paper, copy and complete the graphic organizer below.

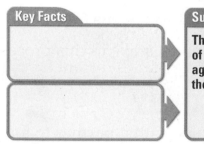

Key Facts	Summary
	The Midwest is one of the most important agricultural regions in the United States.

Read a Flowchart

Why It Matters Sometimes a process is easier to understand if it is presented in a diagram or a drawing.

❯ LEARN

A **flowchart** is a diagram that shows the steps in a process. The flowchart on page 253 shows how people use wheat to make bread. Follow these steps to understand the flowchart.

Step 1 Read the title of the flowchart. The title tells you what process the chart explains.

Step 2 Follow the direction of the arrows. The arrows tell you the order of the steps.

Step 3 Read through the entire chart. Read each label or text box. Think about how the pictures relate to the words.

Step 4 Pay attention to the order of the steps. On some flowcharts, one step can lead to more than one possible result.

❯ PRACTICE

Use the flowchart to answer the questions.

1 Where does wheat go after it is harvested?

2 What happens after the flour is made into dough?

3 Which steps in this process require shipping?

❯ APPLY

Work with a partner to make a flowchart. Write each step on a strip of paper. Find or draw a picture to show each step. Then paste the words and pictures, in order, onto a sheet of posterboard. Connect the steps with arrows, and give your flowchart a title.

How Wheat is Made Into Bread

1. Farmers use machines to harvest wheat in late spring or early summer. Then they ship the wheat grains to a flour mill.

2. At the mill, machines clean the wheat grains and grind them into flour. The flour is bagged and shipped to a bread factory.

3. At the bread factory, bakers make the flour into dough. They shape it into loaves and bake the loaves in huge ovens.

4. Sliced and packaged bread is shipped to grocery stores in trucks. At the grocery stores, people buy the bread to make sandwiches and other foods.

Chart and Graph Skills

Lesson

Time

1500   1750   Present

1783
The Central Plains
become part of
the United States

1787
The Northwest
Ordinance
is passed

1803
The Louisiana Purchase
makes the Great Plains
part of the United States

WHAT TO KNOW
How did the Midwest's environment affect early people there?

VOCABULARY
adapt p. 255
survey p. 256
township p. 256
ordinance p. 256
frontier p. 257
pioneer p. 258
self-sufficient p. 258
sod p. 258

PEOPLE
Jacques Marquette
Louis Joliet
Sieur de la Salle
Jean Baptiste Pointe du Sable
Tecumseh
Abraham Lincoln

PLACES
Central Plains
Great Plains
Northwest Territory

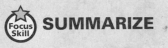

SUMMARIZE

Key Facts	Summary

Early History of the Midwest

YOU ARE THERE

The year is 1700. You and your little brother sit together in your family's tepee. You feel the ground shaking beneath you.

"Do you hear that noise?" your brother asks.

"It's the buffalo," you whisper. You know this sound well. It's the pounding hooves of thousands of buffalo running from your tribe's hunters.

If the hunters are successful, there will be meat to cook and hides to prepare for clothing.

▶ **SIOUX CAMPS** on the Great Plains in the 1700s might have looked like the one in this illustration.

Early People

Long ago, millions of buffalo roamed the Interior Plains. For many Native Americans there, buffalo was an important natural resource.

Adapting to Change

The Sioux (SOO) were one of the many Native American groups in what is now the Midwest. They lived in villages along the rivers and lakes of the **Central Plains**. There, they fished the waters and hunted in the forests. Some also farmed.

In time, European settlers came to the area. The Lakota and many other Sioux tribes moved west to the **Great Plains**. They had to **adapt**, or change their ways of life, to survive in the new environment.

There are few rivers on the Great Plains, so the Sioux could no longer use canoes to travel. Instead, they captured wild horses and learned to ride them. Horses were first brought to the Americas by European explorers.

The Sioux did not build permanent villages or farms on the Great Plains. They moved from place to place, following herds of buffalo. At each place, they set up tepees.

Like other Great Plains groups, the Sioux used buffalo for most of their needs. They ate buffalo meat. They used the skins to make tepees, clothing, and blankets. They also made tools, needles, and arrowheads from the bones and horns.

READING CHECK ⚙ **SUMMARIZE**
How did the Sioux depend on the buffalo?

Exploring the Midwest

1673
Jacques Marquette and Louis Joliet explore the upper Mississippi River and Lake Michigan

1682
Sieur de la Salle travels down the Mississippi River to its mouth at the Gulf of Mexico

1764
French fur traders found St. Louis in what is now Missouri

1784
Jean Baptiste Pointe du Sable builds the first permanent settlement in the Chicago area

Time

1600 — 1700 — 1800

TIME LINE When was the first permanent settlement built in the Chicago area?

The Old Northwest

European explorers and traders began traveling to the Central Plains in the 1600s. They built forts along the region's waterways so they could trade with the Native Americans.

The Northwest Territory

Over the years, different European countries fought wars over control of the Central Plains and its resources. In 1783, most of the region became part of the United States. The northern Central Plains became known as the **Northwest Territory.** The Ohio River, the Mississippi River, and the Great Lakes formed its boundaries.

Thousands of settlers rushed to settle on the territory's fertile lands. Sometimes, two settlers claimed the same land and arguments broke out.

United States leaders decided to control the settling of the Northwest Territory. First, they sent workers to **survey**, or measure, the territory. Then, the government divided the land into squares called **townships**. Each township was divided into 36 smaller square sections to be sold to settlers.

In 1787, the government passed the Northwest Ordinance. The **ordinance**, or set of laws, described how the territory's government would work. It also explained how new states could be formed there.

Life on the Frontier

At this time, the Northwest Territory was part of the nation's **frontier**, or the lands beyond settlement. Like Native Americans in the region, settlers had to use the resources around them to survive in this wilderness.

Much of the Northwest territory had thick forests of oak and hickory. Settlers chopped down some of these trees to build log cabins. After building their cabins, settlers cleared more trees and bushes to make room for crops. Corn and other crops grew well in the fertile soil of the Central Plains. Livestock grazed on the tall grasses. Settlers also hunted deer, rabbits, and other animals in the forests.

Settlers and Native Americans

As many settlers took land from Native Americans, fights broke out. The United States sent troops to help settlers fight the Native Americans. Some tribes joined together to fight them. Shawnee Chief **Tecumseh** said,

> **"A single twig breaks, but the bundle of twigs is strong."**

Over time, the Native Americans lost most of their land to settlers or treaties. Many moved out of the region, ending traditional ways of life. Frontier settlements spread across the entire Interior Plains.

READING CHECK ᐧᔕSUMMARIZE

Where was the Northwest Territory?

Children IN HISTORY

Growing Up on the Frontier

Everyone on the frontier had to work to survive—including children. **Abraham Lincoln** and his parents moved to the Northwest Territory in 1816. They settled in what is now Indiana. "It was a wild region, with many bears and other wild animals still in the woods," Lincoln later remembered. Even though he was only seven years old, Abe did a lot of work. He cleared trees and bushes and split logs for firewood. He helped his father build their log cabin and helped plant and harvest their crops. Many people today think Lincoln's frontier experiences helped him become a great President.

Make It Relevant How might hard work help make a good leader?

Pioneer Spirit

In 1803, the United States bought a huge territory from France. The Louisiana Purchase, as it became known, doubled the size of the United States. The nation now owned much of the Great Plains.

Attracting Settlers

At first, few settlers wanted to move to the Great Plains. Most thought the region was too dry to farm or to live in. It was also far away from most cities and other settled areas.

To attract settlers, the United States government passed the Homestead Act in 1862. This law gave land to any head of a family who was over 21 years old and who would live on the land for five years. Thousands of pioneers soon headed to the Great Plains. A **pioneer** is a person who first settles a place.

Life on the Great Plains

Most pioneers lived far from towns and stores. Their closest neighbors were often miles away. For these reasons, pioneer families had to be **self-sufficient**—they had to do almost everything for themselves.

Pioneers made just about everything they needed. With few trees available, most people used sod to build their houses. **Sod** is a layer of soil held together by the roots of grasses. Pioneers slept on mattresses filled with straw or cornhusks. To make fires, they burned corncobs, straw, and dried manure.

Pioneers grew their own food, too, including corn, beans, and potatoes.

➤ **SOD HOUSE** This photograph from the 1880s shows a pioneer family in front of their sod house.

From their farm animals, they had milk, meat, eggs, wool, hides, and materials to make soap and candles. To get water on the dry Great Plains, settlers dug deep wells. They built large windmills to pump the water.

READING CHECK **☼SUMMARIZE**
Why did early settlers on the Great Plains need to be self-sufficient?

Summary

By 1803, most of the Central Plains and the Great Plains were part of the United States. The government passed laws to encourage people to settle in those frontier regions. Once there, most pioneers had to rely on themselves to survive.

❯ **PIONEER LIFE** Every year, people across the country get together to relive pioneer life.

REVIEW

1. **WHAT TO KNOW** How did the Midwest's environment affect early people there?

2. **VOCABULARY** How are the terms **survey** and **ordinance** related to the settlement of the Northwest Territory?

3. **GEOGRAPHY** How did Native Americans and settlers adapt to living on the Great Plains?

4. **CRITICAL THINKING** Why do you think many pioneers were willing to settle on the frontier in the Midwest?

5. **✎ MAKE AN ADVERTISEMENT** Imagine that you work for the United States government in the 1860s. Make an advertisement for the Homestead Act to attract settlers to the Midwest. Include a drawing, such as a pioneer wagon, in your advertisement.

6. **☆ SUMMARIZE** (Focus Skill) On a separate sheet of paper, copy and complete the graphic organizer below.

Key Facts		Summary
	➤	The United States government encouraged pioneers to settle on the frontier.
	➤	

Compare Historical Maps

Why It Matters Comparing historical maps can help you understand how places change over time.

❱ LEARN

A **historical map** shows information about a place at a certain time in history. Follow these steps to compare the historical maps on pages 260 and 261.

Step 1 Read the title of each map. The title tells the place and time the map shows.

Step 2 Study the map key for each map. The colors show which areas were states, territories, or disputed.

Step 3 Look at the labels on each map. The labels tell you when each state or territory was formed.

Step 4 Compare the two maps to see how the borders of the United States changed from 1791 to 1803.

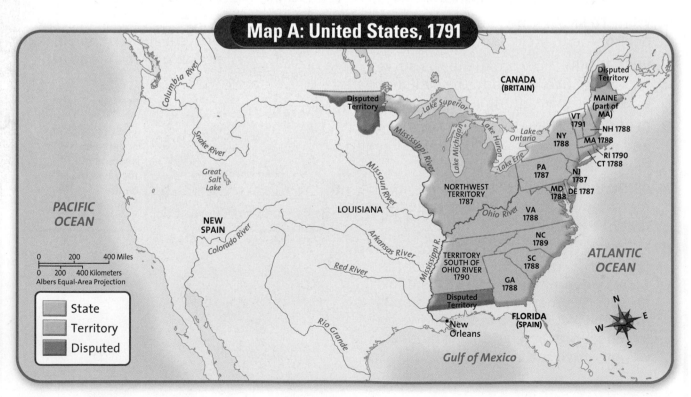

Map A: United States, 1791

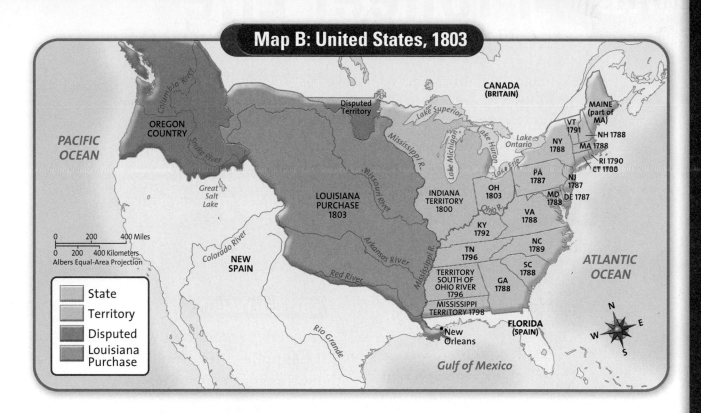

Map B: United States, 1803

PRACTICE

Use Maps A and B to answer these questions.

1 What formed the borders of the United States in 1791?

2 How did the Louisiana Purchase change the borders of the United States?

3 What new states formed between 1791 and 1803? Which of those states were in the Midwest?

APPLY

Compare Map B on this page to the map of the United States on pages R10 and R11. Write to describe how the borders of the United States have changed during the past 200 years.

Map and Globe Skills

Pioneer Life

Background As pioneers traveled west, some settled in the Great Plains. Others continued across the plains to lands even farther west. They made the journey in covered wagons. On the frontier, pioneers used what they brought and the natural resources they found around them to make most of what they needed.

 Document-Based Question Study these primary sources and answer the questions.

Watertight canvas bonnet

Hardwood bows to hold bonnet

COVERED WAGON

Pioneers packed their wagons with the supplies they would need to start a new life on the frontier.

DBQ ❶ Why was it important that the wagon and bonnet be watertight?

Watertight wagon box

CORN HUSK DOLL

Making dolls like this was a craft learned from Native Americans.

DBQ ❷ What natural resource did pioneers use to make dolls?

Doll's dress

IRON

Flatirons were heated and then used to press clothes.

DBQ ❸ Why might a pioneer bring an iron to the frontier?

WOODEN CRADLE

Small children often slept in cradles.

DBQ ❹ What are the rockers for?

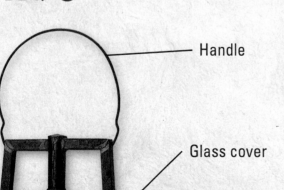

Handle

Glass cover

LANTERN

Pioneers brought items such as lanterns to use along their journey.

DBQ ❺ Why would pioneers need to carry a lantern from place to place?

WRITE ABOUT IT

What do these primary sources tell you about traveling and living on the Great Plains? Write a paragraph that describes daily life on the Great Plains.

GO ONLINE For more resources, go to www.harcourtschool.com/ss1

Lesson 3

Transportation in the Midwest

WHAT TO KNOW
How did changing transportation affect the Midwest?

VOCABULARY
flatboat p. 264
migration p. 265
steamboat p. 265
entrepreneur p. 266
stockyard p. 266
assembly line p. 267
mass production p. 267
industrial economy p. 268

PEOPLE
Robert Fulton
Joseph McCoy
Henry Ford
Madam C. J. Walker

PLACES
Topeka
Kansas City
Omaha
Chicago
St. Louis
Cincinnati
Minneapolis
Cleveland
Detroit

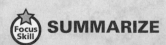

SUMMARIZE

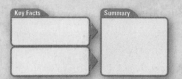

YOU ARE THERE

The year is 1870. For hours, you watch workers load cargo onto the **flatboats**—large rafts made of boards tied together. Then they lead your family's cows, pigs, dogs, and horses on board. Finally, you and the other passengers step aboard.

It seems impossible that the flatboat can carry such a heavy load all the way down the Ohio River! You feel better knowing that thousands of other settlers have already made this trip.

▶ **WATERWAYS** The Mississippi River was an important transportation route for many settlers going to the Midwest.

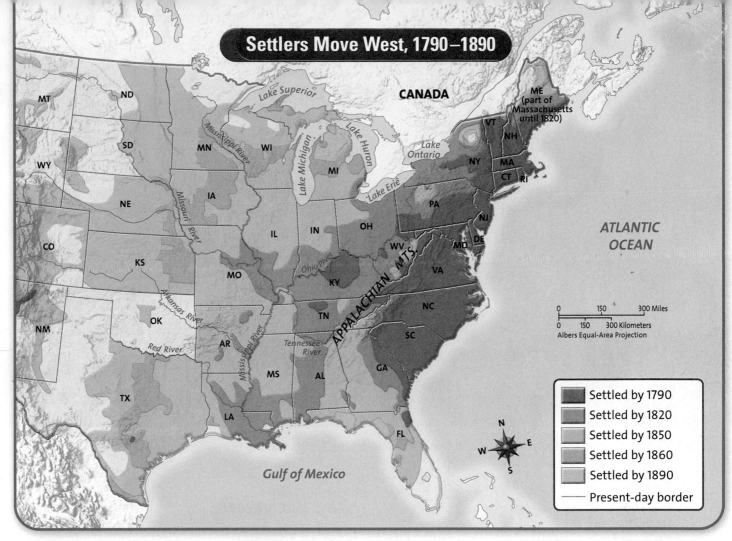

Settlers Move West, 1790–1890

MT | ND | Lake Superior | CANADA | ME (part of Massachusetts until 1820)

Legend:
- Settled by 1790
- Settled by 1820
- Settled by 1850
- Settled by 1860
- Settled by 1890
- Present-day border

ATLANTIC OCEAN

Gulf of Mexico

MAP SKILL **MOVEMENT** Most of the Midwest was settled by 1890. By what year was all of Ohio settled?

River Highways

In the late 1700s, settlers began to use Midwest rivers for migration to the west. A **migration** is the movement of people from one place to another.

Moving West

Most pioneers traveled west by wagon. When they reached the Ohio River, many took flatboats. Each flatboat was about 40 feet long and could be used in shallow rivers. Flatboats had no power, so they only traveled downstream. At the end of a trip, flatboats were sold for their lumber.

In the late 1700s and early 1800s, **Robert Fulton** and others developed the steamboat. A **steamboat** is a boat powered by a steam engine. The engine turns the boat's large paddle wheel, causing the boat to move.

Steamboats could travel upstream. They also traveled downstream much faster than flatboats. Trips that took weeks or months by flatboat took only days by steamboat. The cost of shipping goods dropped, and river travel increased.

READING CHECK ⦵ **SUMMARIZE**
How did steamboats change river travel?

▶ **RAILROADS** attracted new people and businesses to towns located along the train routes in the Midwest.

Railroads

Beginning in the mid-1800s, railroad companies built miles of train tracks across the Midwest. The new railroads helped the region grow even more.

Railroad Towns

Railroads provided an easier way for settlers to reach the Midwest. As more people arrived, new towns grew up along the tracks. Also, older towns grew larger. These included **Topeka** in Kansas, **Kansas City** in Missouri, and **Omaha** in Nebraska.

By 1856, **Chicago**, Illinois, had become one of the world's busiest railroad centers. The city connected ten major railroad lines and about 3,000 miles of track. Every day, nearly 100 trains arrived to or left from the city.

New Businesses

The railroad towns attracted many **entrepreneurs** (ahn•truh•pruh•NERZ), or people who start new businesses. Entrepreneurs opened businesses to serve the region's growing population.

Some cattle traders opened stockyards in the towns. A **stockyard** is a place where livestock is bought, sold, and held before shipment. In Abilene, Kansas, **Joseph McCoy** opened one of the largest stockyards in the region.

Texas and Oklahoma ranchers drove their herds in cattle drives to McCoy's and other stockyards. So did ranchers in the Midwest. From the stockyards, railroad cars took the cattle to cities to be prepared for markets in the East.

READING CHECK ☼**SUMMARIZE**
How did railroads change the Midwest?

Industries Grow

Better transportation helped cities and industries in the Midwest grow. Boats and trains brought raw materials to these cities. They also carried finished products to buyers.

Port Cities

The region's largest cities grew near ports. River ports included **St. Louis**, Missouri; **Cincinnati**, Ohio; and **Minneapolis**, Minnesota. Port cities that grew along the Great Lakes included Chicago, Illinois; **Cleveland**, Ohio; and **Detroit**, Michigan.

| Automobiles in the United States, 1900–2004 ||
YEAR	NUMBERS OF AUTOMOBILES
1900	8,000
1925	17,481,001
1950	40,339,077
1975	106,705,934
2004	136,430,651

The Automobile Industry

In the early 1900s, Detroit became the center of the nation's automobile industry. One reason for this was the city's location on the Great Lakes. The region's steel industry was another reason. Mills in Gary, Indiana, and other nearby cities provided the steel needed to make automobiles.

Henry Ford and others helped the automobile industry grow. In 1913, Ford set up an assembly line in his Detroit factory. An **assembly line** is a line of workers along which a product moves as it is put together one step at a time. It is a form of **mass production**, in which a product is made more quickly and cheaply by using machines.

TABLE Mass production allowed automobiles to be made more cheaply. In turn, more people could afford to buy them. Between which two years did the number of automobiles increase the most?

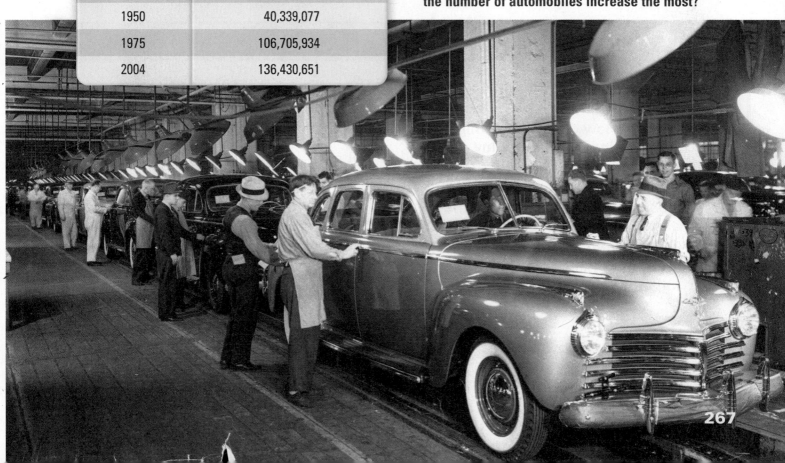

Mass Production Grows

Other industries in Midwest cities also started using mass production. Factories made furniture, food products, steel products, and more. By the mid-1900s, an industrial economy had developed in parts of the Midwest, especially along the Great Lakes. In an **industrial economy**, most goods are made by machines and in factories.

READING CHECK ⊙ **SUMMARIZE**
What is mass production?

Summary

In the 1800s, steamboats and railroads added to the growth of cities and industries in the Midwest. The region's largest cities developed around ports. During the 1900s, the automobile industry and other manufacturing industries grew in many of those cities.

▶ **MADAM C.J. WALKER** started a manufacturing company in Indianapolis, Indiana, that made beauty products for women across the nation.

REVIEW

1. **WHAT TO KNOW** How did changing transportation affect the Midwest?

2. **VOCABULARY** How does the meaning of each word in **industrial economy** relate to the meaning of the whole term?

3. **ECONOMY** How did the invention of the steamboat affect the economy of the Midwest?

4. **CRITICAL THINKING** Why do you think settlers in the United States kept moving farther west?

5. ✏ **WRITE A NEWSPAPER STORY** Imagine that you are a reporter in 1913. Write a newspaper story about Henry Ford's new assembly line. Research what an early automobile looked like and include a drawing of one.

6. ⭐ **SUMMARIZE**

On a separate sheet of paper, copy and complete the graphic organizer below.

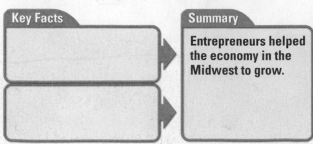

Key Facts		Summary
	▶	Entrepreneurs helped the economy in the Midwest to grow.
	▶	

Samuel Clemens

"I supposed—and hoped—that I was going to follow the river the rest of my days."

Samuel Clemens grew up in Hannibal, Missouri, a small town on the Mississippi River. After his father's death in 1847, young Clemens worked as a printer's assistant. For the next ten years, he worked in printing shops in Hannibal and several cities in the East.

In 1857, Clemens took a job on a Mississippi River boat. He eventually became a riverboat pilot. For four years, Clemens traveled every bend and curve of the Mississippi River from St. Louis to New Orleans. He later described his experiences in his book *Life on the Mississippi*.

By that time, Clemens was already a world-famous author. He wrote his books under the name Mark Twain, a term used by riverboat pilots.

Many of Mark Twain's stories are about growing up in Missouri during the 1800s. The Mississippi River plays an important role in many of them. Some people think the river is like a character in Twain's books.

Why Character Counts

How did Samuel Clemens show that he cared about the Mississippi River?

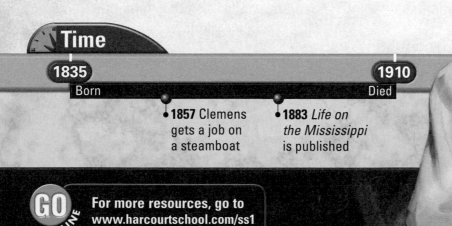

Time

| 1835 | | | 1910 |
| Born | | | Died |

1857 Clemens gets a job on a steamboat

1883 *Life on the Mississippi* is published

GO ONLINE For more resources, go to www.harcourtschool.com/ss1

269

About 1650
The Sioux begin to adapt to new ways of life on the Great Plains

Visual Summary

Summarize the Chapter

Focus Skill **Summarize** Complete this graphic organizer to show that you understand how to summarize information about the Midwest.

Key Facts

Boats carried raw materials to factories and finished products to market.

River ports helped St. Louis, Cincinnati, and other cities grow.

Summary

Vocabulary

Identify the term from the word bank that correctly matches each definition.

1. to measure

2. a long period of little or no rain

3. a person who starts a new business

4. the movement of people from one place to another

5. to change in order to survive in a new environment

6. a funnel-shaped, spinning windstorm

7. an area of flat or rolling land covered with grasses and wildflowers

8. a set of laws

> **Word Bank**
>
> **prairie** p. 247   **survey** p. 256
>
> **tornado** p. 249   **ordinance** p. 256
>
> **drought** p. 249   **migration** p. 265
>
> **adapt** p. 255   **entrepreneur** p. 266

1750   1875   Present

1850
Railroads link the Midwest frontier with Eastern states

1950
Midwest cities have growing industrial economies

Time Line

Use the chapter summary time line above to answer these questions.

9. When did railroads link the Midwest with the east?

10. What made the Midwest's cities grow in 1950?

Facts and Main Ideas

Answer these questions.

11. What two physical features of the Midwest were created by glaciers?

12. What were three ways in which Native Americans of the Great Plains used the buffalo?

13. How did Henry Ford change the auto industry?

Write the letter of the best choice.

14. Which mineral is plentiful in the Midwest region?
    A gold
    B coal
    C iron ore
    D sulfur

15. What did most early settlers on the Great Plains use to build their homes?
    A sod
    B wood
    C stone
    D bricks

Critical Thinking

16. What ways of life changed for the Sioux once they moved to the Great Plains?

17. Why were railroads important to the growth of the Midwest?

Skills

Read a Flowchart

18. Study the flowchart on page 253. What happens to wheat after it is ground into flour?

writing

✏ **Write a Persuasive Letter** Imagine that you are a settler on the Great Plains in the 1800s. Write a letter to a railroad company. Try to persuade the company to bring the railroad to your town.

✏ **Write a Journal Entry** Write a journal entry about something you learned about the Midwest. Write questions or thoughts you have in response to what you read.

STUDY SKILLS

PREVIEW AND QUESTION

Identifying main ideas and asking questions about them can help you find important information.

- **To preview a passage, read the title. Look at the pictures, and read their captions. Try to get an idea of the main topic. Think of questions you have about it.**

- **Read to find the answers to your questions. Then recite, or say, the answers aloud. Finally, review what you have read.**

The Midwest Today

Preview	Questions	Read	Recite	Review
Lesson 1 Years of immigration have brought a mix of people and cultures to the Great Lakes region.	What attracted immigrants to the Great Lakes region in the 1900s?	✓	✓	✓
Lesson 2				

PREVIEW VOCABULARY

architecture p. 276   **barge** p. 277   **urbanization** p. 285

MILLENIUM PARK, CHICAGO, ILLINOIS

Lesson 1

Great Lakes States

 WHAT TO KNOW
In what ways are the Great Lakes states centers of industry and culture?

VOCABULARY
architecture p. 276
hub p. 277
barge p. 277
freight p. 277

PEOPLE
Oprah Winfrey
Frank Lloyd Wright

PLACES
Chicago
Detroit
Milwaukee
Indianapolis
Cleveland
Minneapolis
St. Paul

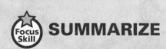 **SUMMARIZE**

YOU ARE THERE

You and your friends wander among the food stands in **Chicago**'s Grant Park. Some of the vendors sell Mexican quesadillas (kay•sah•DEE•ahz). Some sell Lebanese falafel sandwiches. Others offer Polish sausages, Irish stew, and Thai chicken satays. Of course, many serve Chicago's famous deep-dish pizza and barbecued ribs.

Today, you are visiting the Taste of Chicago festival. Like the city where it is held, this yearly festival celebrates some of the many cultures of the Great Lakes states.

▶ Polish Fest in Milwaukee, Wisconsin

▶ Sculpture in Detroit, Michigan, honoring African American history

Regional Culture

The Great Lakes states are Illinois, Indiana, Michigan, Minnesota, Ohio, and Wisconsin. Years of immigration have brought diverse groups of people and cultures to these states.

From Many Places

In the late 1800s, the region's industrial economy created jobs, especially in factories. Those jobs attracted many immigrants. Most immigrants came from Ireland, Poland, Italy, Greece, and other European countries.

In about 1910, many African Americans began to migrate from the South to cities in the North for work. So many African Americans came that the movement became known as the Great Migration.

More recently, immigrants have come to the Great Lakes states from Latin America, mostly from Mexico. Other immigrants have come from countries in Asia. In fact, Michigan has the nation's largest Arab American community.

All these different groups shaped life in the region. African Americans created **Detroit**'s "Motown sound" and Chicago's blues and jazz music. Irish immigrants started the St. Patrick's Day parade in Chicago. In **Milwaukee**, Wisconsin, many people celebrate at the Polish Fest. People from these and other groups have also made important political and economic contributions to the region.

READING CHECK 🔖**SUMMARIZE**
Why are the Great Lakes states diverse?

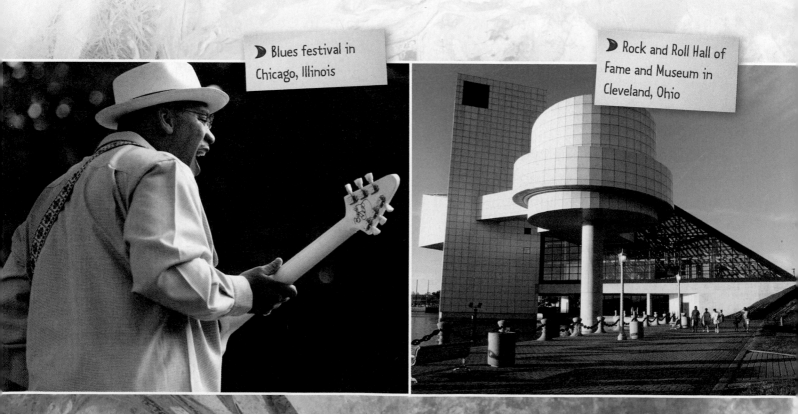

▶ Blues festival in Chicago, Illinois

▶ Rock and Roll Hall of Fame and Museum in Cleveland, Ohio

> ► ARCHITECTURE Chicago is home to the Sears Tower (left) and to the Robie House (above), which was designed by Frank Lloyd Wright.

A Changing Economy

In the past, factory jobs brought many people to the Great Lakes states. Today, however, service industries are growing in the region.

Growing Services

The automobile industry has been important to the region since the early 1900s. Today, workers there still design and make new automobiles. However, in recent years, many automobile factories have moved to places where labor is cheaper.

In contrast, service industries are growing in the region. Banking and real estate have long been important to the region. Others, such as entertainment and tourism, are more recent. For example, **Oprah Winfrey**'s company in Chicago makes popular television programs, movies, and magazines. **Indianapolis** hosts a popular auto race—the Indianapolis 500.

Many tourists also come to see the region's **architecture**, or building styles. Chicago is famous for its skyscrapers. Other tourists come to see **Frank Lloyd Wright's** Prairie Style of architecture. His flat-roofed buildings reflect the region's flat prairies. People also enjoy the building and tours of **Cleveland**'s Rock and Roll Hall of Fame and Museum.

READING CHECK **MAIN IDEA AND DETAILS**
What are some service industries in the Great Lakes states today?

Travel and Shipping

The Great Lakes region is important to our nation's transportation system. Its central location makes it an ideal place for connecting different parts of the United States and Canada.

Land and Air Transportation

Busy highways and railroads criss-cross the Great Lakes states. The region also has busy airports. In fact, Chicago, Detroit, and the twin cities of **Minneapolis** and **St. Paul** have three of the nation's ten busiest airports. All those cities are air transportation hubs. A **hub** is a center of activity.

Shipping Goods

The Great Lakes are among the most important waterways in North America. Many rivers flow into and out of the Great Lakes. Barges carry goods on the rivers and lakes. A **barge** is a large boat with a flat bottom. A single barge can carry tons of **freight**, or transported goods. Some barges carry freight south on the Mississippi River to the Gulf of Mexico. Others carry freight east on the St. Lawrence Seaway to the Atlantic Ocean. At ocean ports, the freight is then shipped to ports all around the world.

READING CHECK ⊘**SUMMARIZE**
Why are the region's rivers and lakes important?

Airline Passengers, 2004

AIRPORT	CITY	NUMBER OF PASSENGERS
O'Hare International	Chicago, IL	🧍🧍🧍🧍🧍🧍🧍🧍
Midway Airport	Chicago, IL	🧍🧍
Minneapolis–St. Paul Airport	Minneapolis and St. Paul, MN	🧍🧍🧍🧍
Detroit Metro	Detroit, MI	🧍🧍🧍🧍

🧍 = 10 million people

TABLE About how many passengers did Detroit Metro Airport (below) have in 2004?

Global Connection

Waterways are major transportation routes around the world. In Europe, the Rhine River is the most important inland waterway. Like the Mississippi River, the Rhine connects inland industries to ocean ports. The Rhine River starts in Switzerland. It flows through Germany to the Netherlands. There, the Rhine empties into the North Sea at the ocean port of Rotterdam.

READING CHECK **COMPARE AND CONTRAST**
How is the Rhine River, in Europe, like the Mississippi River?

Summary

The Great Lakes states have a diverse population and a diverse economy. Entertainment and tourism are growing industries. In addition, the region is a transportation center.

▶ **THE RHINE RIVER is one of the busiest inland waterways in the world.**

REVIEW

1. **WHAT TO KNOW** In what ways are the Great Lakes states centers of industry and culture?

2. **VOCABULARY** What does it mean to say that Chicago is a **hub**?

3. **HISTORY** What was the Great Migration, and when did it begin?

4. **CRITICAL THINKING** What kinds of goods do you think are shipped on barges from the Great Lakes states?

5. **MAKE A BROCHURE** Make a brochure to advertise one of the cities, events, or attractions that you read about in this lesson.

6. **SUMMARIZE**

On a separate sheet of paper, copy and complete the graphic organizer below.

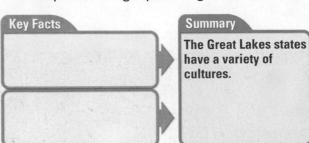

Key Facts		Summary
	▶	The Great Lakes states have a variety of cultures.
	▶	

Benjamin S. Carson

Biography

Trustworthiness
Respect
Responsibility
Fairness
Caring
Patriotism

"We can take charge of our own lives."

Benjamin S. Carson is a doctor known for having "gifted hands." For many years, he has helped children with brain injuries from all around the world.

Carson was born in Detroit, Michigan. In school, he had a difficult time making high grades. To improve his grades, he started reading more and more. He soon began to love learning and reading and did not want to stop. After finishing college, Carson got a job at Johns Hopkins University in Maryland. There, he became skilled in medicine.

Carson never forgot how hard it was for him as a young boy. In addition to writing books, he started the Carson Scholars Fund. This group rewards fourth graders who help out in their communities and do well in school. It is Dr. Carson's dream to have a Carson Scholar student in every school.

Why Character Counts

How did Carson take responsibility for his own success?

Time

1951		Present
Born		

1977 Carson receives a medical degree from University of Michigan

1992 Carson publishes *THINK BIG!*

1994 The Carson Scholars Fund is started

GO ONLINE For more resources, go to www.harcourtschool.com/ss1

Critical Thinking Skills

Solve a Problem

Why It Matters Learning how to solve problems is an important skill that you can use now and in the future.

❯ LEARN

Here are some steps you can use to help you solve a problem.

Step 1 Identify the problem and the cause of the problem.

Step 2 Gather information, and list possible solutions to the problem.

Step 3 Think of the advantages and disadvantages of each solution.

Step 4 Choose the best solution. Plan how to carry it out.

Step 5 Follow your plan. Then think about how well your solution worked. Did it solve the problem? If not, try other solutions until the problem is solved.

❯ **SOLAR POWER** This vehicle is powered by energy from the sun.

▶ NEW FUELS are being studied, such as hydrogen (above) and cooking oil (above right).

▶ PRACTICE

In the lesson, you read that workers in the Great Lakes states design new automobiles. Since gasoline shortages sometimes occur, they are looking at new ways to power automobiles. Citizens, too, can act to help prevent gasoline shortages. Think about all the solutions to this problem. Then answer these questions.

1 What problems might a gasoline shortage cause in the lives of people?

2 How might people decrease the amount of gasoline they use in automobiles?

3 What do you think is a wise solution to prevent any future gasoline shortages? Explain.

▶ APPLY

Make It Relevant Identify a problem in your community. Then use the steps to solve this problem. Share your ideas with your classmates.

Critical Thinking Skills

Lesson 2

Plains States

WHAT TO KNOW

 In what ways do people in cities, on farms, and on ranches in the Plains states depend on one another?

VOCABULARY

urbanization p. 285
meatpacking p. 285

PEOPLE

Willa Cather
Thomas Hart Benton
Crazy Horse
Joyce C. Hall

PLACES

Grand Forks
Fargo
Jefferson City
St. Louis
Kansas City
Omaha
Des Moines
Branson

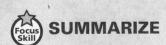 SUMMARIZE

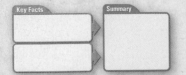

YOU ARE THERE

What a terrific day! You're going to **Grand Forks**, in North Dakota. This is one of your favorite trips. Not only do you get to visit your cousins, but you get to see how the land changes as you travel. Once you and your family drive away from the city of **Fargo**, you see wide-open farmland. As you gaze out the window, you see farmers harvesting their crops.

As you near Grand Forks, the land changes again. More and more buildings and homes begin to dot the landscape. Then, once again, you're in a city.

Open Spaces

The Plains states are Iowa, Kansas, Missouri, Nebraska, North Dakota, and South Dakota. Large stretches of mostly flat plains, farmland, and ranches separate the cities and towns in the region.

Natural Attractions

The open spaces of the Plains states offer many interesting views. In some places, wild buffalo and wild horses roam freely. In Nebraska, a grassland area called the Sand Hills covers about one-fourth of the state.

Not all of the Plains region is flat. Forested mountains cover the Ozark Plateau, in southern Missouri. In the Badlands of South Dakota, spectacular colored rock formations are found.

Inspiration on the Plains

The open spaces of the Plains states have inspired many artists. **Willa Cather** wrote *O Pioneers!* and other books about pioneers who settled on the Nebraska frontier. **Thomas Hart Benton** painted rural scenes in the region. One of his murals now hangs in the Missouri State Capitol in **Jefferson City**.

Some artists use the landforms of the Plains in their artwork. Mount Rushmore National Memorial, for example, is carved into the side of a mountain in South Dakota's Black Hills. Just a few miles away, artists are now creating a similar memorial to the Lakota Sioux leader **Crazy Horse.**

READING CHECK   **SUMMARIZE**
How have the Plains states inspired artists?

▶ **PLAINS** Wide, open plains, such as this one in North Dakota, cover much of the Plains states.

Changes in Farming

Farming in the Plains states has changed greatly since the days of the early settlers. Today's farmers have new technology and new crops.

New Tools and New Crops

Farmers use modern farm machines to help them grow and harvest more crops in less time. Many farmers also use computers to help them decide what crops to plant; when to plant, fertilize, and harvest; and where to get the best prices for their crops.

Plains farmers have learned that growing several kinds of crops, instead of just one, has many benefits. Varying crops helps keep the soil fertile. It also reduces the numbers of pests that damage crops. Besides growing corn and wheat, Plains farmers now grow barley, canola, flax, soybeans, and sunflowers.

Bigger Farms, Bigger Harvests

Using new farming methods enables farmers to grow more crops on each acre of land. These new ways also make it possible for farmers to plant larger areas of land. In fact, most farms in the region today are about three times larger than they were 100 years ago.

Most farms in the Plains region are now owned by large companies. These farms are like huge factories. Machines do much of the work on these large farms.

READING CHECK ⚙SUMMARIZE
What is farming in the Plains states like today?

▶ HI-TECH EQUIPMENT in farm machines (right) helps farmers during harvest (below).

▶ **ST. LOUIS, Missouri, is a center of industry, education, and culture in the Plains region.**

Cities

New technology means that farms and ranches need fewer workers, so some people have moved to cities to work. This shift of people to cities from rural areas is called **urbanization**.

Linking Farms, Ranches, and Cities

People who live in cities need food. They need the crops grown on farms and the cattle raised on ranches. In turn, farmers and ranchers use goods and services from the city.

Some city industries depend on the region's farms and ranches. One such industry is food processing. Factories use crops of corn and wheat to make flour, breads, pastas, and margarine. **Meatpacking** companies prepare cattle from ranches for market.

Not all city industries are related to agriculture. In **Kansas City**, Missouri, **Joyce C. Hall** started a business in 1910 that has become the world's largest greeting card company. **Omaha**, Nebraska, and **Des Moines**, Iowa, have major insurance industries. In Missouri, **Branson** is a center of entertainment and tourism.

READING CHECK ○̬SUMMARIZE

How do city industries depend on farms and ranches?

Global Connection

Plains are found all over the world. In South America, a plains region called the Pampas covers much of the country of Argentina.

The Pampas has much in common with the Plains states. Farmers in both regions grow wheat and corn. In addition, cattle ranching and meatpacking are major industries.

READING CHECK **COMPARE AND CONTRAST**
How are the Pampas and the Plains states alike?

Summary

Farms and ranches cover much of the Plains states. Cities are growing, however, as machines do more of the work on farms. People and many industries depend on farms and ranches.

▶ **THE PAMPAS** covers about one-fifth of Argentina.

REVIEW

1. **WHAT TO KNOW** In what ways do people in cities, on farms, and on ranches in the Plains states depend on one another?

2. **VOCABULARY** Use the term **urbanization** in a sentence to explain it.

3. **ECONOMICS** Why is Joyce C. Hall an example of an entrepreneur?

4. **CRITICAL THINKING** Why are most farms in the Plains region larger today than they were in the past?

5. ✎ **WRITE A POEM** Study the photograph on pages 282 and 283. Then write a short poem describing the scene or telling how you might feel if you were there.

6. (Focus Skill) **SUMMARIZE**

On a separate sheet of paper, copy and complete the graphic organizer below.

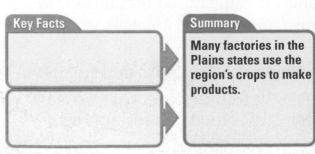

Key Facts

Summary

Many factories in the Plains states use the region's crops to make products.

286 ▪ Unit 4

Laura Ingalls Wilder

Biography

Trustworthiness
Respect
Responsibility
Fairness

Caring

Patriotism

"*It is the simple things in life that make living worthwhile.*"

Laura Ingalls Wilder lived in many places in the Midwest during her long life. Born in Wisconsin in 1867, she and her family traveled by wagon to Missouri, Kansas, Minnesota, and Iowa. They finally settled in South Dakota, where her father started a small farm.

As an adult, Wilder moved to Mansfield, Missouri. There, she decided to record her childhood memories. Wilder wrote about growing up on the frontier, the hardships her family faced, and the closeness her family shared.

The stories Wilder wrote became the much-loved Little House series of children's books. The books were later made into the popular television series "Little House on the Prairie." People around the world have read Wilder's books and watched "Little House on the Prairie."

Why Character Counts

How did Laura Ingalls Wilder show that she cared about her family's history?

Time

1867		1957
Born		Died

1894 Wilder settles in Mansfield, Missouri

1932 Wilder's first book, *Little House in the Big Woods*, is published

GO ONLINE For more resources, go to www.harcourtschool.com/ss1

287

Crazy Horse Memorial

Since 1948, workers have been carving a huge sculpture into a mountain in South Dakota's Black Hills. They are creating a memorial to Crazy Horse. Crazy Horse was a Lakota Sioux warrior and leader who lived in the Plains region during the 1800s. Some Native Americans think the memorial is an excellent way to honor Crazy Horse. Others think that it is not a good idea.

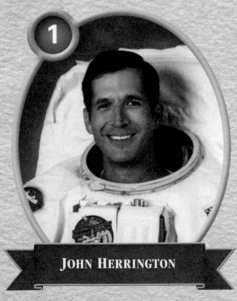

1 — JOHN HERRINGTON

John Herrington is an astronaut and a member of the Chickasaw Nation. He supports the project.

"The story of Crazy Horse is one of a true American hero. I think it's the nation's responsibility to hold him up as an example. . . . Having this monument is an inspiration."

2 — AVIS LITTLE EAGLE

Avis Little Eagle is Vice Chairman of the Standing Rock Sioux Tribe. She is against the project.

"It's a monument of exploitation [unfair use]. Many promises were made to the Lakota when the monument was begun, but few of them have been kept."

3

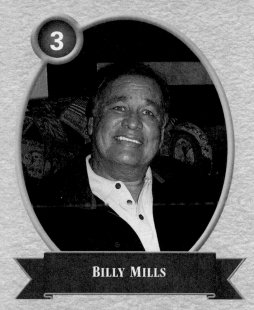

BILLY MILLS

Billy Mills is an Olympic gold medalist in Track and Field and a member of the Sioux Nation. He supports the project.

"Crazy Horse challenged me to follow my dreams. . . . It honors me to know that I can bring my grandchildren back someday and I can show them my hero."

4

CHARMAINE WHITE FACE

Charmaine White Face is a writer and a member of the Sioux Nation. She does not approve of the project.

"Instead of . . . blowing up mountains in a total violation of the beliefs that he held, . . . why don't they try to have the land returned to Crazy Horse's people?"

It's Your Turn

Compare Points of View Summarize each person's point of view. Then answer the questions.

1. Who seems to be against the building of the monument?

2. How are the points of view of Billy Mills and John Herrington alike?

3. Which person offers an idea for a different way to honor Crazy Horse? What is that idea?

Make It Relevant What do you think? Explain why one argument is more persuasive to you than the others.

Visual Summary

The Great Lakes states are known for their diversity.

Summarize the Chapter

Focus Skill **Summarize** Complete this graphic organizer to show that you understand how to summarize information about the Midwest.

Key Facts

In the late 1800s, immigrants from Europe moved to the Great Lakes states.

About 1910, African Americans from the South moved to the region.

Summary

 Vocabulary

Identify the term from the word bank that correctly matches each definition.

1. a center for an activity, such as the transportation industry

2. the shift of people to cities from rural areas

3. building styles

4. a large boat with a flat bottom

5. preparing cattle from ranches for market

6. transported goods

Word Bank

architecture p. 276   **freight** p. 277

hub p. 277   **urbanization** p. 285

barge p. 277   **meatpacking** p. 285

The Great Lakes are important to our nation's transportation system.

Open plains and farmlands stretch across the Plains states.

 Facts and Main Ideas

Answer these questions.

7. Where do most immigrants to the Great Lakes states come from today?

8. What kinds of transportation make many cities in the Great Lakes region hubs?

9. What is Thomas Hart Benton known for?

10. How are farms in the Plains states different today than they were 100 years ago?

Write the letter of the best choice.

11. Which state has the nation's largest Arab American community?
    A Illinois
    B Michigan
    C Minnesota
    D Ohio

12. Which industries are growing in the Great Lake states?
    A agricultural industries
    B manufacturing industries
    C service industries
    D agricultural and manufacturing industries

13. Which part of the Plains states is mountainous?
    A the Ozark Plateau
    B the Pampas
    C the Badlands
    D the Sand Hills

 Critical Thinking

14. How are the entertainment industry and the tourism industry linked in the Great Lakes states?

15. Why do you think state fairs are important events to many people in the Plains states?

 Skills

Make a Thoughtful Decision

16. **Make It Relevant** Imagine that you are a farmer in the Plains states. You must decide whether to continue farming or move to the city. What information would you gather to help you make your decision?

writing

Write a Report Write a report about the Midwest today. Tell about the people and the economies of the Great Lakes states and of the Plains states.

Write a Letter Write a letter to the owner of a business in the Midwest. Choose a business that you read about in the chapter. In your letter, ask five questions that you have about the business.

Fun with Social Studies

Make a Match

Can you make eight matches?

Henry Ford	Writer	Architect	Abraham Lincoln
Sioux Leader	Frank Lloyd Wright	Crazy Horse	Painter
Willa Cather	United States President	Steamboat	Joseph McCoy
Robert Fulton	Stockyards	Thomas Hart Benton	Assembly Line

Rhyme Time

Read each riddle and find a vocabulary word rhyme.

What do you call. . . ?

VOCABULARY

- a big boat with a flat bottom? *a large* __?__

- a person who talks on and on about rock that contains minerals? *an* __?__ *bore*

- transported goods that don't arrive on time? *late* __?__

- a person who protects livestock before shipment? *a* __?__ *guard*

- a farm of milk cows on flat or rolling land? *a* __?__ *dairy*

Midwest Museum

Which two pictures do not belong in this museum exhibit?

Online Adventures

GO ONLINE

Have you ever traveled on a steamboat? Eco has a ticket for you to ride on one of the early steamboats in the Midwest. In an online game, the boat stops at three different places. At each place, you'll have to complete a challenge to stay on board. Complete all three, and the steamboat will take you straight to the next clue card. Play now at **www.harcourtschool.com/ss1**

Review and Test Prep

🔆 THE BIG IDEA

Transportation, Land, and Cities Mighty waterways, busy highways, and fertile lands stretch between cities of the Midwest region today.

Reading Comprehension and Vocabulary

The Midwest

The Interior Plains cover the entire Midwest. The climate becomes drier as you travel from east to west across the region. Wheat and corn are the region's main crops.

The Sioux and many other Native Americans lived in the Midwest before settlers arrived in the 1600s. By 1783, most of the Central Plains was part of the United States. The northern Central Plains was known as the Northwest Territory. Much of the Great Plains was added to the United States in the Louisiana Purchase of 1803. The government encouraged people to settle on the frontier.

In the 1800s, steamboats and railroads helped the region grow. Cities and factories grew up around ports and train stops. Today, big cities in the Great Lakes states are still transportation hubs. Entertainment and tourism are growing industries in this region. These states also have a diverse population.

Farms and ranches cover much of the Plains states. Many industries in the region's cities depend on farm and ranch products.

Read the summary above. Then answer the questions that follow.

1. A frontier is—
   - **A** a set of laws.
   - **B** a Sioux village.
   - **C** an area beyond settlements.
   - **D** a person who first settles a new place.

2. What is the main physical feature in the Midwest?
   - **A** hills
   - **B** plains
   - **C** plateaus
   - **D** mountains

3. A hub is—
   - **A** a building style.
   - **B** a large boat with a flat bottom.
   - **C** a trading center where ships are loaded and unloaded.
   - **D** a center of activity.

4. What is the economy of the Plains states based on?
   - **A** mining and fishing
   - **B** tourism and entertainment
   - **C** farming and ranching
   - **D** manufacturing and steel products

Answer these questions.

5. What is the eastern part of the Interior Plains called?

6. When do tornadoes form?

7. Where did European traders build the first forts in the Midwest?

8. What did the Northwest Ordinance describe?

9. What was the Great Migration?

Write the letter of the best choice.

10. Which city was a steel-making center in the early 1900s?
    A Gary
    B Omaha
    C St. Louis
    D Kansas City

11. Which of these is growing in the Great Lakes states?
    A mining
    B ranching
    C manufacturing
    D service industries

12. Which of these Plains states industries depends on agriculture?
    A mining
    B insurance
    C meatpacking
    D entertainment

Critical Thinking

13. How did frontier life in the Northwest Territory differ from frontier life on the Great Plains?

14. Name three ways in which immigrants have shaped life in the Great Lakes states.

Compare Historical Maps

Use the maps below to answer these questions.

15. Which waterways formed most of the boundary of the Northwest Territory in 1800?

16. By 1900, which new states in the Midwest included land that was once part of the Northwest Territory?

Map A: Midwest, 1800

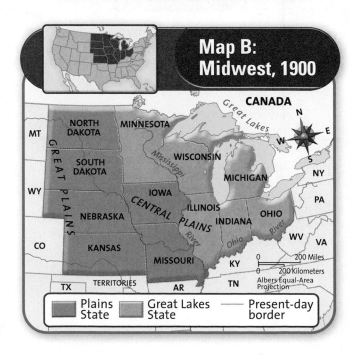

Map B: Midwest, 1900

Show What You Know

 Unit Writing Activity

Write an Information Report Write a brief report about the Midwest.

- Tell about the region's past.
- Explain how the Great Lakes states and the Plains states differ.
- Describe life in the Midwest today.

Unit Project

Publish a Newspaper Put together a newspaper that tells about some of the important events that took place in the Midwest during the late 1800s and early 1900s.

- Choose people and events to feature in articles, editorials, and cartoons.
- Illustrate your newspaper with drawings and advertisements of the time.

Read More

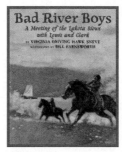

- *On Sand Island* by Jacqueline Briggs Martin. Houghton Mifflin.

- *Bad River Boys: A Meeting of the Lakota Sioux with Lewis and Clark* by Virginia Driving Hawk Sneve. Holiday House.

- *Mark Twain and the Queens of the Mississippi* by Cheryl Harness. Simon and Schuster Books for Young Readers.

 For more resources, go to www.harcourtschool.com/ss1

The Southwest

The Big Idea

People and Resources

People have learned to use both the abundant and limited resources of the Southwest to develop the region.

What to Know

✓ What is the geography of the Southwest?

✓ How did control of the Southwest's lands change over time?

✓ How have people in the Southwest developed its resources?

✓ What is the Southwest like today?

Time

The Southwest

● **1540** Francisco Vásquez de Coronado claims the Southwest for Spain, p. 320

● **1610** The city of Santa Fe, in New Mexico, is built, p. 320

1500   **1600**   **1700**

At the Same Time

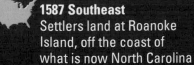 **1587 Southeast** Settlers land at Roanoke Island, off the coast of what is now North Carolina

 1681 Northeast William Penn founds the colony of Pennsylvania

The Southwest

• 1848 The United States wins the Mexican-American War, p. 321

• 1912 By this time, the territories in the Southwest had gained statehood, p. 323

• Present Oil remains one of the Southwest's most important products, p. 341

1800

1900

Present

1821 Mexico wins its independence from Spain

1896 The modern Olympic Games begin in Athens, Greece

1913 Midwest Henry Ford sets up an assembly line in his Detroit, Michigan, factory

People

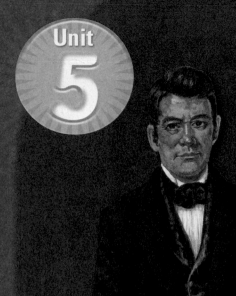

John Ross

1790–1866
- Chief of the Cherokee Nation
- Led the Cherokee people on the journey known as the Trail of Tears

Stephen F. Austin

1793–1836
- Lawyer, leader, and pioneer
- Founded a colony in the Mexican territory of Texas

1700

1800

1790 • John Ross

1793 • Stephen F. Austin   1836

1834 •

Lady Bird Johnson

1912–present
- Environmentalist and First Lady of the United States from 1963–1969
- Led Texas to adopt a highway program that planted wildflowers alongside roadways

Cesar Chavez

1927–1993
- Leader of the United Farm Workers
- Led peaceful protests to improve working conditions for migrant workers

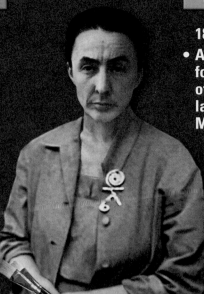

John Wesley Powell

1834–1902
- Scientist and explorer of the American West
- Explored the Colorado River and the Grand Canyon in 1869

Georgia O'Keeffe

1887–1986
- Artist best known for her paintings of flowers and landscapes of New Mexico
  - National Women's Hall of Fame

1900 ————————————————————————————————— **PRESENT**

1866

John Wesley Powell   1902

1887 • Georgia O'Keeffe   1986

1912 • Lady Bird Johnson

1927 • Cesar Chavez   1993

1945 • Wilma Mankiller

1956 • Mae C. Jemison

Wilma Mankiller

1945–present
- Former Native American chief and author
- First woman to be elected principal Chief of the Cherokee Nation

Mae C. Jemison

1956–present
- Scientist and space shuttle astronaut
- Teacher of space-age technology
- Started a science camp for children

NV

UT

CO

ROCKY MOUNTAINS

Lake Mead

Colorado River

Hoover Dam

Colorado Plateau

Grand Canyon National Park

▲ Wheeler Peak 13,161 ft.

Bullhead City

Painted Desert

Gallup

★ Santa Fe

Flagstaff

Albuquerque

CA

Petrified Forest National Park

NEW MEXICO

Clovis

ARIZONA

Sun City

Salt River

Phoenix ★

Mesa

Gila River

Roswell

Yuma

Gila River

Casa Grande

Rio Grande

Sonoran Desert

Tucson

Las Cruces

Carlsbad Caverns National Park

Pecos

Saguaro National Park

Chihuahuan Desert

El Paso

Guadalupe Mountains National Park

River

Wildflowers blooming in the desert

A Native American ceremony

Big Bend National Park

MEXICO

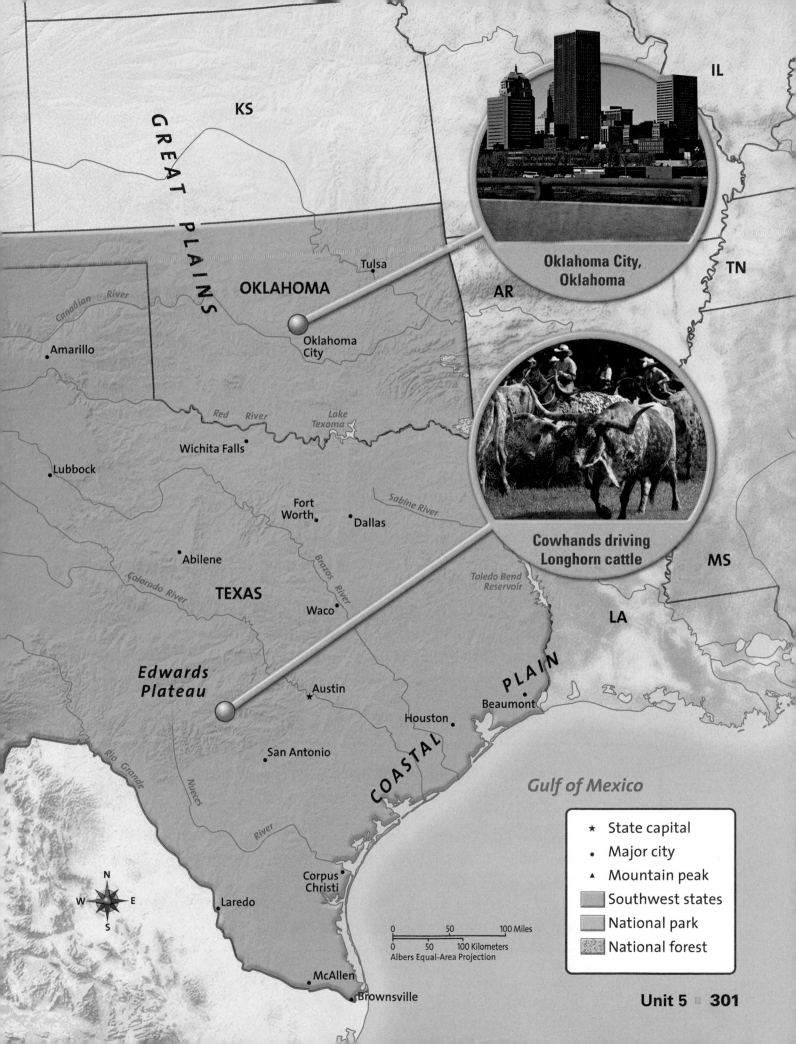

KS

GREAT PLAINS

OKLAHOMA

Tulsa

AR

TN

IL

Oklahoma City, Oklahoma

Canadian River

Amarillo

Oklahoma City

Red River

Lake Texoma

Wichita Falls

Lubbock

Sabine River

Fort Worth

Dallas

Cowhands driving Longhorn cattle

MS

Abilene

Colorado River

Brazos River

TEXAS

Waco

Toledo Bend Reservoir

LA

Edwards Plateau

Austin

PLAIN

Rio Grande

San Antonio

Houston

Beaumont

COASTAL

Gulf of Mexico

Nueces River

Corpus Christi

Laredo

McAllen

Brownsville

★	State capital
•	Major city
▲	Mountain peak
	Southwest states
	National park
	National forest

0   50   100 Miles
0 50 100 Kilometers
Albers Equal-Area Projection

Reading Social Studies

(Focus Skill) Draw Conclusions

Why It Matters Being able to draw conclusions can help you better understand what you read.

❯ LEARN

A **conclusion** is a general statement about an idea or event. To draw a conclusion, you use evidence, or what you learn from reading, along with knowledge, or what you already know.

Evidence	Knowledge
What you learn	What you already know

Conclusion

A general statement about an idea or event

- Think about the new facts you read about a subject.
- Think about the facts you already know about that subject.
- Combine the new facts with those you already know to draw a conclusion.

❯ PRACTICE

Read the paragraphs that follow. Draw a conclusion for the second paragraph.

Evidence Knowledge Conclusion

The desert is a place with little water. Desert plants are quite different from plants in other places. (Plants need a lot of water to grow. Desert plants only need small amounts of water.)

Hiking in the desert is a wonderful experience, but you must be careful. You will see amazing plants but probably not a drop of water.

Read the paragraphs, and answer the questions.

Searching for Cíbola

After the Spanish took control of Mexico in 1521, they heard stories about the lands that lay to the north. One story described seven great cities filled with gold! The Spanish called those cities Cíbola (SEE•boh•lah).

The Spanish explorer Álvar Núñez Cabeza de Vaca (AHL•vahr NOON•yes kah•BAY•sah day VAH•kah) and the African Estevanico or Estéban (es•TAY•bahn) were among the first to report that Cíbola might be in what is now the Southwest region. After arriving by ship in Florida, they and others traveled over land to meet up with their ship farther west. They looked for the ship along the Gulf coast but never found it. Eventually, they wandered through what is now Texas and northern Mexico. In 1536, only four survivors, including Cabeza de Vaca and Estéban, reached Mexico City.

Spanish leaders in Mexico soon sent explorers to find Cíbola. In 1540, Francisco Vásquez de Coronado (kawr•oh•NAH•doh) led the largest group of explorers across the Rio Grande. They traveled into what is now Arizona, New Mexico, Texas, and Oklahoma. However, they never found Cíbola—or any gold at all. Tired and disappointed, the group headed home.

Coronado arrived back in Mexico City in 1542. He had claimed nearly the entire Southwest region for Spain. Even so, the Spanish leaders decided that his trip had been a failure.

Draw Conclusions

1. What conclusion can you draw about the hardships Coronado and his group must have faced during the early part of their journey?

2. What conclusion can you draw about why Spanish leaders thought that Coronado's trip was a failure?

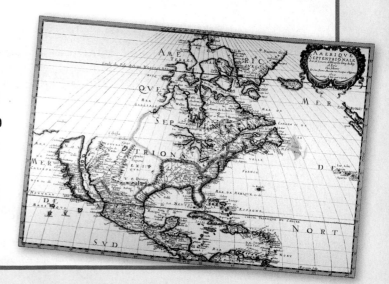

Cactus Hotel

BY BRENDA Z. GUIBERSON
ILLUSTRATED BY MEGAN LLOYD

The Sonoran Desert of the Southwest is home to plants and animals that can stand the heat. For example, the great saguaro (suh•WAR•oh) cactus does well in a desert climate. The story below tells about the growth of one saguaro cactus and the animals that move into this desert hotel.

On a hot, dry day in the desert, a bright-red fruit falls from a tall saguaro cactus. *Plop*. It splits apart on the sandy floor. Two thousand black seeds glisten in the sunlight.

When the air cools in the evening, an old pack rat comes out and eats the juicy fruit. Then he skitters across the sand. A seed left clinging to his whiskers falls off under a paloverde tree.

glisten shine   skitters moves lightly and quickly
paloverde small desert tree with thorns

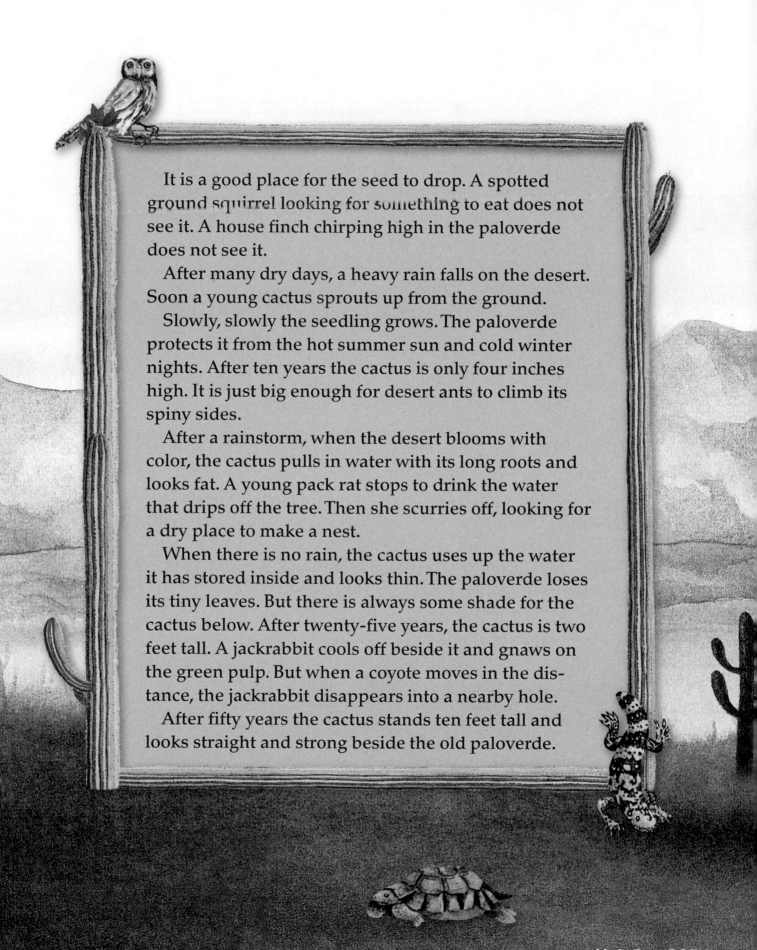

It is a good place for the seed to drop. A spotted ground squirrel looking for something to eat does not see it. A house finch chirping high in the paloverde does not see it.

After many dry days, a heavy rain falls on the desert. Soon a young cactus sprouts up from the ground.

Slowly, slowly the seedling grows. The paloverde protects it from the hot summer sun and cold winter nights. After ten years the cactus is only four inches high. It is just big enough for desert ants to climb its spiny sides.

After a rainstorm, when the desert blooms with color, the cactus pulls in water with its long roots and looks fat. A young pack rat stops to drink the water that drips off the tree. Then she scurries off, looking for a dry place to make a nest.

When there is no rain, the cactus uses up the water it has stored inside and looks thin. The paloverde loses its tiny leaves. But there is always some shade for the cactus below. After twenty-five years, the cactus is two feet tall. A jackrabbit cools off beside it and gnaws on the green pulp. But when a coyote moves in the distance, the jackrabbit disappears into a nearby hole.

After fifty years the cactus stands ten feet tall and looks straight and strong beside the old paloverde.

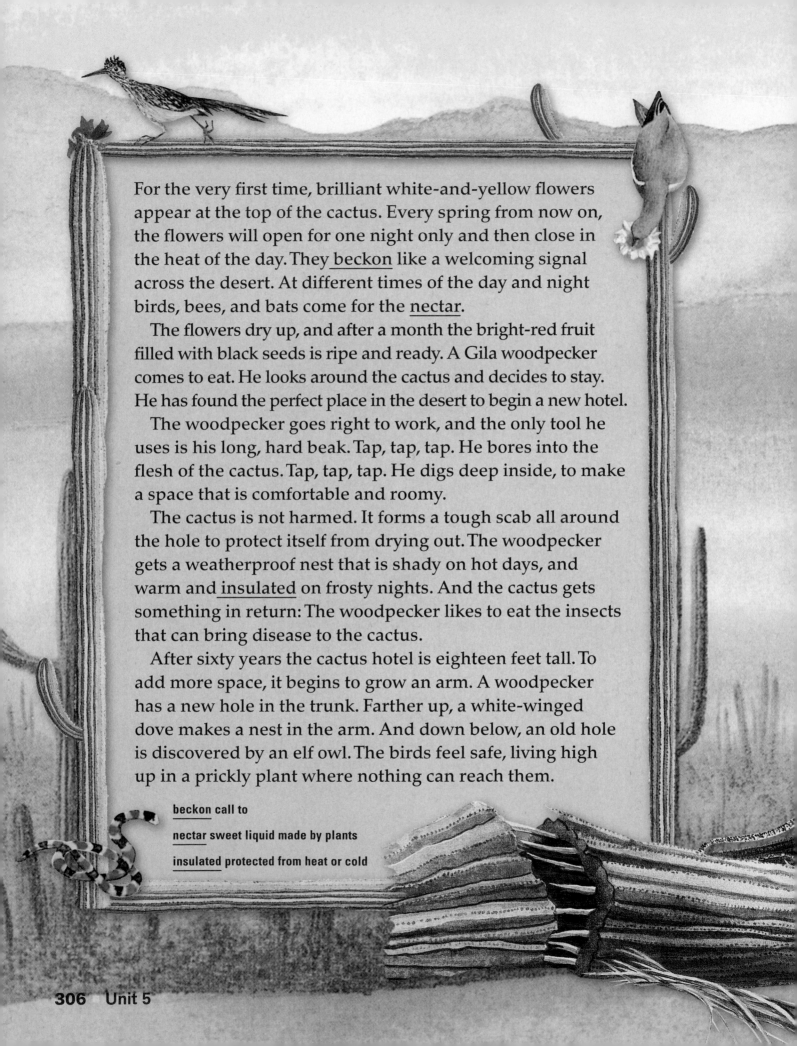

For the very first time, brilliant white-and-yellow flowers appear at the top of the cactus. Every spring from now on, the flowers will open for one night only and then close in the heat of the day. They <u>beckon</u> like a welcoming signal across the desert. At different times of the day and night birds, bees, and bats come for the <u>nectar</u>.

The flowers dry up, and after a month the bright-red fruit filled with black seeds is ripe and ready. A Gila woodpecker comes to eat. He looks around the cactus and decides to stay. He has found the perfect place in the desert to begin a new hotel.

The woodpecker goes right to work, and the only tool he uses is his long, hard beak. Tap, tap, tap. He bores into the flesh of the cactus. Tap, tap, tap. He digs deep inside, to make a space that is comfortable and roomy.

The cactus is not harmed. It forms a tough scab all around the hole to protect itself from drying out. The woodpecker gets a weatherproof nest that is shady on hot days, and warm and <u>insulated</u> on frosty nights. And the cactus gets something in return: The woodpecker likes to eat the insects that can bring disease to the cactus.

After sixty years the cactus hotel is eighteen feet tall. To add more space, it begins to grow an arm. A woodpecker has a new hole in the trunk. Farther up, a white-winged dove makes a nest in the arm. And down below, an old hole is discovered by an elf owl. The birds feel safe, living high up in a prickly plant where nothing can reach them.

<u>beckon</u> call to

<u>nectar</u> sweet liquid made by plants

<u>insulated</u> protected from heat or cold

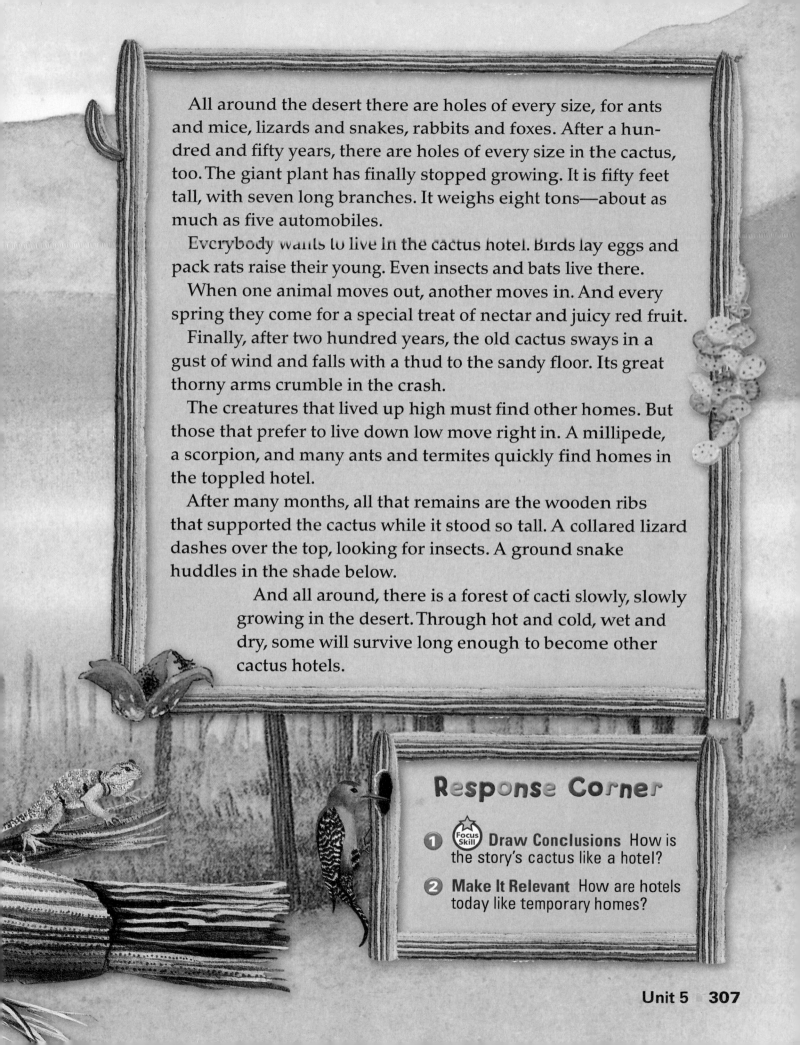

All around the desert there are holes of every size, for ants and mice, lizards and snakes, rabbits and foxes. After a hundred and fifty years, there are holes of every size in the cactus, too. The giant plant has finally stopped growing. It is fifty feet tall, with seven long branches. It weighs eight tons—about as much as five automobiles.

Everybody wants to live in the cactus hotel. Birds lay eggs and pack rats raise their young. Even insects and bats live there.

When one animal moves out, another moves in. And every spring they come for a special treat of nectar and juicy red fruit.

Finally, after two hundred years, the old cactus sways in a gust of wind and falls with a thud to the sandy floor. Its great thorny arms crumble in the crash.

The creatures that lived up high must find other homes. But those that prefer to live down low move right in. A millipede, a scorpion, and many ants and termites quickly find homes in the toppled hotel.

After many months, all that remains are the wooden ribs that supported the cactus while it stood so tall. A collared lizard dashes over the top, looking for insects. A ground snake huddles in the shade below.

And all around, there is a forest of cacti slowly, slowly growing in the desert. Through hot and cold, wet and dry, some will survive long enough to become other cactus hotels.

Response Corner

1. **Focus Skill** **Draw Conclusions** How is the story's cactus like a hotel?

2. **Make It Relevant** How are hotels today like temporary homes?

STUDY SKILLS

WRITE TO LEARN

Writing about what you read can help you understand and remember information.

- **Many students write about their reading in learning logs. The writing in a learning log can be both creative and personal.**

- **Writing about the text leads you to think about it.**

- **Writing your reactions to the text makes it more meaningful to you. This makes you more likely to remember it.**

Geography of the Southwest	
What I Learned	My Response
Though plains, mountains, and plateaus are found in the Southwest, deserts cover much of the region. The climate there is mostly hot and dry.	This probably means that farming is difficult in the region and that other industries are more important.

PREVIEW VOCABULARY

mesa p. 311

irrigation p. 314

pueblo p. 319

CHAPTER 10

Exploring the Southwest

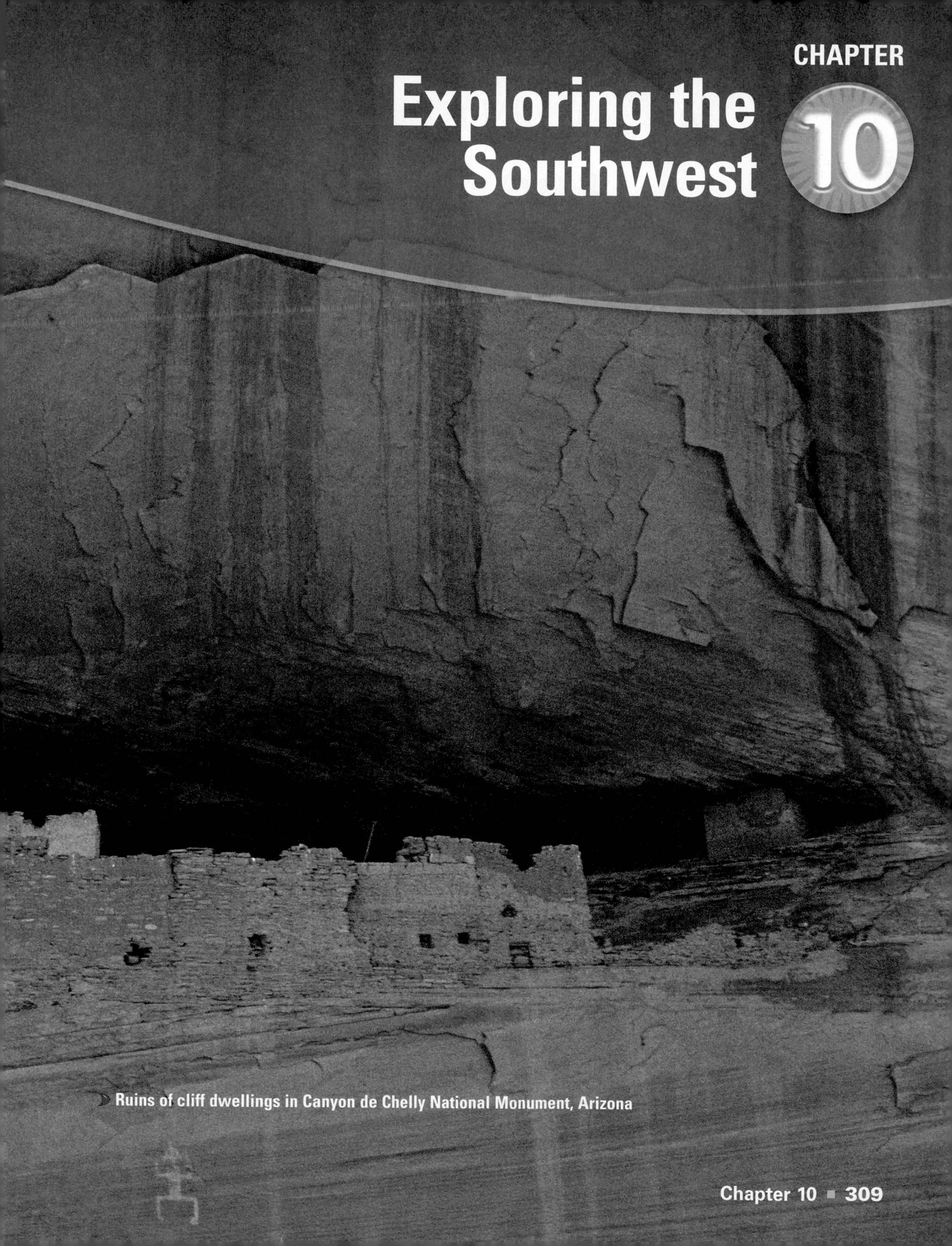

Ruins of cliff dwellings in Canyon de Chelly National Monument, Arizona

Geography of the Southwest

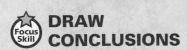 **WHAT TO KNOW**
What are the land and the climate of the Southwest like?

VOCABULARY
mesa p. 311
butte p. 311
rain shadow p. 312
cloudburst p. 312
arroyo p. 312
aquifer p. 313
reservoir p. 313
aqueduct p. 313
irrigation p. 314

PEOPLE
Lady Bird Johnson

PLACES
Sandia Mountains
Chihuahuan Desert
Rio Grande
Colorado River
Sonoran Desert
Colorado Plateau
Hoover Dam

 **DRAW CONCLUSIONS**

Evidence · Knowledge

Conclusion

YOU ARE THERE With a jolt, the giant hot-air balloon lifts off. It takes you high into the blue skies above Albuquerque, New Mexico. You see the **Sandia Mountains** towering above the city. The **Chihuahuan** (chee•WAH•wahn) **Desert** spreads to the south. Cottonwood trees and low bushes line the banks of the **Rio Grande**. You know this river flows all the way to the Gulf of Mexico. What a great way to see the Southwest!

❯ **ALBUQUERQUE** Riders in a hot-air balloon get a view of the city.

▶ **COCONINO NATIONAL FOREST,** in Arizona, offers many recreational activities to visitors.

Plains and Deserts

The Southwest includes only four states—Texas, Oklahoma, New Mexico, and Arizona. Still, the region stretches from the Gulf of Mexico in the east to the **Colorado River** in the west.

Texas and Oklahoma

The Southwest has a variety of landforms. In Texas, the lowest and wettest lands lie along the Gulf of Mexico. This area is part of the Coastal Plain. Inland parts of the Central Plains reach into Oklahoma.

Farther west, the land gets higher. The high, dry grasslands of the Great Plains extend to western Texas. There, low ranges of the Rocky Mountains surround the Chihuahuan Desert.

New Mexico and Arizona

The Chihuahuan Desert spreads north from Mexico into Texas and southern New Mexico. Farther west, the **Sonoran** (suh•NOHR•uhn) **Desert** covers southern Arizona. In fact, deserts cover much of New Mexico and Arizona.

The northern parts of New Mexico and Arizona share the **Colorado Plateau.** Over time, wind and water have eroded mesas (MAY•suhz) and buttes (BYOOTS) into the plateau. A **mesa** is a hill with a flat top and steep sides. A **butte** is a steep hill of rock with a flat top, like a mesa, but smaller.

READING CHECK ⟳**DRAW CONCLUSIONS**
Which state has the most varied land?

Desert Wildlife

ILLUSTRATION Many plants and animals have adapted to desert environments.

1 Saguaro cactus **3** Collared lizard **5** Roadrunner **7** Prickly pear cactus
2 Gila woodpecker **4** Century plant **6** Barrel cactus **8** Tarantula

What other plants and animals do you recognize in this illustration?

Climate

Climate varies in the Southwest. The Gulf Coast has a hot, humid climate. The mountain areas can be cold and snowy in winter. Still, most of the Southwest has a hot and dry climate.

The Rain Shadow

The mountains in the west are the main reason that the Southwest is so dry. The mountains block moist ocean air from reaching the region. The Southwest lies in the **rain shadow**, or the drier side of the mountains.

When rain comes to the desert, it often comes in a **cloudburst**, or a sudden, heavy rain. The rain quickly fills the dry beds of rivers and streams. It also flows through **arroyos** (uh•ROY•ohz), deep ditches carved over time by running water.

Desert Plants

During spring, wildflowers bloom in the deserts and on the plains of the Southwest. Former First Lady **Lady Bird Johnson** founded the National Wildflower Research Center in Texas. Its goal is to use native plants to protect the Southwest environment.

READING CHECK ŎDRAW CONCLUSIONS
What do you think happens in the desert after a cloudburst?

Sources of Water

There are many challenges to life in the desert. Finding enough water for a growing population is one of the biggest. In the Southwest, people have found different ways to overcome the scarcity, or limits, of this resource.

Groundwater and Rivers

Most parts of Arizona and New Mexico have little rainfall, and there is little surface water. However, in many places in these states there is water in **aquifers**. This groundwater collects in layers of sand and rock beneath Earth's surface. To reach the water in aquifers, people drill wells.

The large rivers in these states include the Colorado River in Arizona and the Rio Grande and the Pecos River in New Mexico. People use dams to control the flow of these rivers. A reservoir forms upstream from a dam. A **reservoir** is a human-made lake. Water from the reservoir is released downstream as it is needed.

In many places, aqueducts (A•kwuh•duhkts) carry the water from dams and wells to places where it is needed. An **aqueduct** is a large pipe or canal built to carry water.

READING CHECK ⚡DRAW CONCLUSIONS
How might dams help farmers and others during long periods of dry weather?

▶ **HOOVER DAM** (right) lies on the border between Nevada and Arizona. It controls the flow of the Colorado River. Its reservoir, Lake Mead (below), provides much of Arizona's water.

Natural Resources

The Southwest has many kinds of land resources. These natural resources include minerals, fuels, and forests.

Minerals and Fuels

The Southwest states are among the nation's top producers of minerals and fuels. Great amounts of oil and natural gas lie buried beneath the land in Texas, Oklahoma, and New Mexico. The region also has coal, copper, and uranium deposits. Uranium is a metal used as a fuel in some power plants.

Forests

Some parts of the Southwest get enough rainfall for forests to grow. Eastern Texas and Oklahoma have forests of pine, oak, and hickory. Ponderosa pine trees cover parts of northern New Mexico and Arizona.

Farms and Ranches

Although some parts of the Southwest get enough rain to grow crops, most farmers in the region must use irrigation to water crops. **Irrigation** is the use of canals, ditches, or pipes to bring water to dry places. Farmers in the Southwest grow cotton, wheat, vegetables, and citrus fruits each year.

Ranching is also an important industry in the region, especially in the

Southwest Land Use and Resources

Legend:
- Manufacturing
- General farming
- Forest
- Fruits and vegetables
- Cattle and sheep
- Wheat and grain
- Little-used land
- Coal
- Gold
- Iron
- Oil or natural gas
- Copper
- Silver
- Potash
- Uranium

Map labels: NV, UT, CO, KS, MO, Oklahoma City, Tulsa, Santa Fe, ARIZONA, Albuquerque, OKLAHOMA, AR, NEW MEXICO, CA, Phoenix, Tucson, El Paso, Dallas, Ft. Worth, LA, TEXAS, Beaumont, Austin, San Antonio, Houston, MEXICO, Gulf of Mexico

Scale: 0 150 300 Miles / 0 150 300 Kilometers / Albers Equal-Area Projection

MAP SKILL **HUMAN-ENVIRONMENT INTERACTIONS** Many farmers in the Southwest use irrigation for farming. Which state has the least farming?

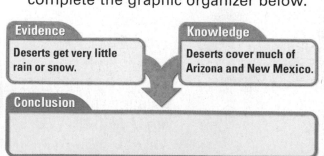

> **PEPPERS** are grown in the Southwest. They are commonly used in Southwestern cooking.

drier areas. Livestock can graze on the grassy land that is too dry for farming. Beef cattle are the largest source of income for ranchers in the Southwest. Sheep and goats are also raised on Southwestern ranches.

READING CHECK **MAIN IDEA AND DETAILS**
How do most Southwest farmers get water?

Summary

Plains, deserts, mountains, and plateaus cover the Southwest region. Much of the region has a hot, dry climate. The region's natural resources include forests, minerals, fuels, and land for farms and ranches.

REVIEW

1. **WHAT TO KNOW** What are the land and the climate of the Southwest like?

2. **VOCABULARY** How are a **mesa** and a **butte** alike? How are they different?

3. **GEOGRAPHY** In general, how do elevations in the Southwest change as you move from east to west?

4. **CRITICAL THINKING** How do you think irrigation has affected the population of the desert Southwest?

5. **DESIGN A COVER** Review the information in this lesson. Then design a cover for a scrapbook titled "The Southwest."

6. **DRAW CONCLUSIONS**

On a separate sheet of paper, copy and complete the graphic organizer below.

Evidence	Knowledge
Deserts get very little rain or snow.	Deserts cover much of Arizona and New Mexico.

Conclusion

Tell Fact from Fiction

Why It Matters It is important to know whether what you are reading is fact or fiction. A **fact** can be proved true. **Fiction** is made-up writing.

⟩ LEARN

One way to check facts is to look for the same information in a reference source. For example, you could use a dictionary, an encyclopedia, or another nonfiction book, such as a textbook. Other sources of facts are newspaper articles, letters, and diaries.

From a newspaper article in the *Hastings Tribune* written on May 11, 1934

"A gigantic cloud of dust 1,500 miles long, 900 miles across and two miles high buffeted [surrounded] and smothered almost one-third of the nation today. For more than 36 hours arid winds . . . swirled tons of sand and grit eastward. Cattle in parched fields sickened and died as dust blanketed grass and fodder [animal feed]. Thousands of persons suffered from eye and nose irritations."

⟩ **A DUST STORM** hits a farm in the 1930s.

The Dust Storm

Dad and I stared at the dark mountain moving from the west toward our farm. Like a monster, it kept changing shape as it swallowed one farm after another.

First it was the Loves' place. Bob Love had had enough money to get his family out before the dust blew in. Now, as we watched, the few cattle he had left behind disappeared inside the mountain. Next it would be the Jensens' place, and then it would be our turn.

I looked up at my dad and saw the sadness written on his face. The few dust storms that had blown through in '32 had been warnings. Mom had wanted us to leave then, but Dad had always been hopeful that things would get better. Now we stood with fast-blinking eyes as fingers of the mountain reached out to sting our faces. We ran for the house.

❯ PRACTICE

The two passages are both about dust storms in the 1930s. Read the passages, and answer the questions.

❶ How are the passages alike? How are they different?

❷ Which passage tells only facts? Which is fiction? Explain.

❯ APPLY

Compare the two passages. What facts are in both? How would you check the facts?

Lesson

Time

1500   1750   Present

Early 1500s
The Spanish
conquer Mexico

1848
The Mexican-
American
War ends

1889
The Indian Territory is
opened to settlers

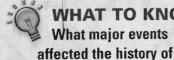

WHAT TO KNOW
What major events
affected the history of
the Southwest?

VOCABULARY

pueblo p. 319
adobe p. 319
nomad p. 319
mission p. 320
land grant p. 322

PEOPLE

Francisco Vásquez de
  Coronado
Stephen F. Austin
John Ross

PLACES

Taos Pueblo
Santa Fe
Indian Territory

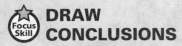
**DRAW
CONCLUSIONS**

Early History of the Southwest

YOU ARE THERE

It is the 1500s. You are
in your village—**Taos
Pueblo** (PWEH•bloh) in what is
now New Mexico. You're watching
the adults perform the Corn Dance.
The men and the women stand in two lines. The
men sound out the beat of the dance, with rattles
made from gourds. The women hold feathers
and pine branches. Together, the two lines move
across the plaza.

Early Peoples

In the 1500s, Native Americans lived all over the Southwest. Some groups lived in **pueblos**, or villages, and farmed. Others traveled the region's grasslands and deserts.

Farmers

The Caddo (KAD•oh) and the Pueblo peoples were two groups that farmed in the Southwest. Corn was their main crop. The Caddo lived in eastern Texas and Oklahoma, where there was plenty of rain for farming. The Pueblo people lived in the deserts of Arizona and New Mexico. They had to use irrigation to get water for their crops.

The Caddo used wood from the nearby forests to build large, round houses. Since few trees grow in the desert, the Pueblo used mud, rocks, and adobe (uh•DOH•bee) to build their homes. **Adobe** is a mixture of sandy clay and straw that is dried into bricks.

Nomads

Some Native Americans in the Southwest did not farm. They were nomads. A **nomad** is a person who moves from place to place and does not have a permanent home. Some groups of nomads lived together in communities.

The Apache were nomads on the region's Great Plains. They traveled on foot to hunt deer and buffalo. They used all parts of the animals they hunted.

READING CHECK ○ **DRAW CONCLUSIONS**
Why do you think the Pueblo people used adobe to build their homes?

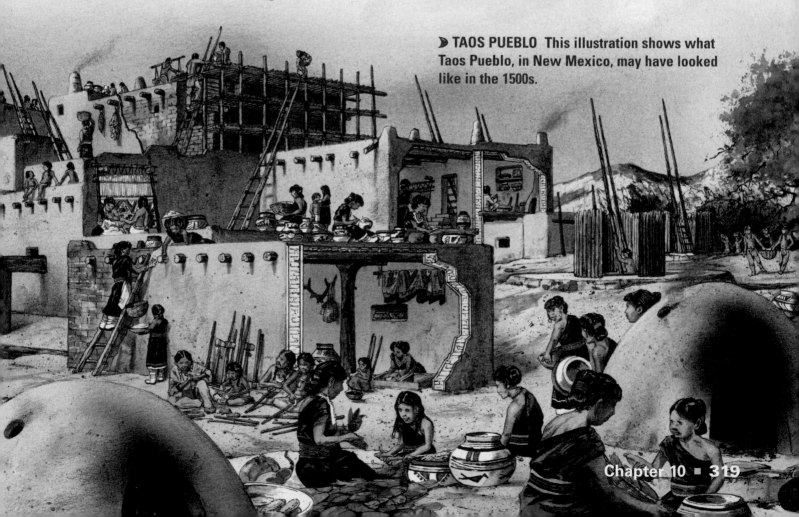

▶ **TAOS PUEBLO** This illustration shows what Taos Pueblo, in New Mexico, may have looked like in the 1500s.

The Spanish Arrive

In the early 1500s, the Spanish conquered Mexico. Soon after, Spanish explorers traveled north across the Rio Grande. They searched for gold and more lands to claim.

Settling the Southwest

In 1540, **Francisco Vásquez de Coronado** left Mexico with more than 1,300 soldiers, workers, and priests. He spent the next two years exploring much of the Southwest. Coronado claimed these lands for Spain.

To protect their new lands, the Spanish built forts in the Southwest. By 1610, the Spanish were building the city of **Santa Fe,** in New Mexico. They also built **missions**, or religious settlements.

Most Spanish missions had a school, a church, and workshops. Catholic priests taught Native Americans about Christianity and Spanish culture. Often, they forced Native Americans to work on the mission farms and ranches. They would also not let some practice their own religion.

The Spanish and Native Americans learned from one another. The Spanish introduced metal tools, horses, cattle, sheep, wheat, and orange trees to the Southwest. The Native Americans taught the Spanish how to build with adobe and how to use native plants as medicine. They also taught the Spanish new irrigation methods.

READING CHECK ☼ **DRAW CONCLUSIONS**
How do you think Native Americans felt about the missions?

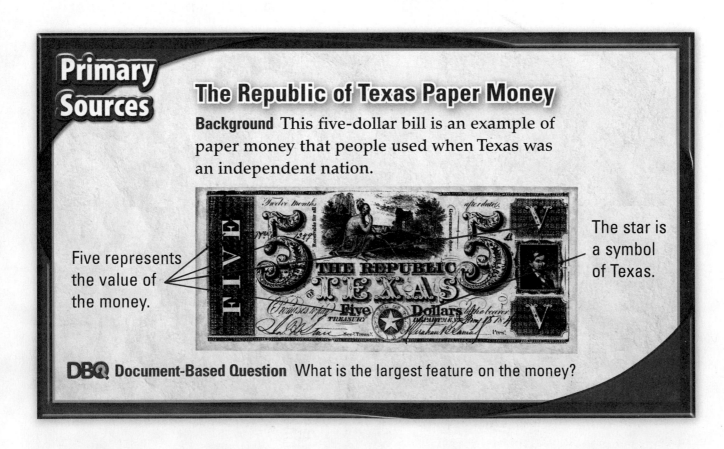

Primary Sources

The Republic of Texas Paper Money

Background This five-dollar bill is an example of paper money that people used when Texas was an independent nation.

Five represents the value of the money.

The star is a symbol of Texas.

DBQ Document-Based Question What is the largest feature on the money?

The Mexican-American War

May 1846
President Polk asks Congress to declare war on Mexico

January 1847
The signing of the Treaty of Cahuenga ends the fighting in California

September 1847
General Winfield Scott and the United States Army capture Mexico City

February 1848
Treaty of Guadalupe Hidalgo ends the Mexican-American War

Time

1846   1847   1848   1849

TIME LINE How long after the Treaty of Cahuenga was signed was the Treaty of Guadalupe Hidalgo signed?

Toward Statehood

The Spanish controlled most of the Southwest region for more than 200 years. Then, in 1821, Mexico won its independence from Spain.

Texas

Texas was now part of Mexico. Yet most settlers there were from the United States. Then the Mexican government passed new laws. One law raised taxes in Texas. Another law limited American settlement there. Many Texans thought those laws were unfair. Texas leader **Stephen F. Austin** declared,

> 66 We must defend our rights, ourselves, and our country. 99

War soon broke out. In 1836, the Texans won the war. Texas became an independent nation, the Republic of Texas. In 1845, Texas became the twenty-eighth state.

Arizona and New Mexico

At that time, other lands in the Southwest and West were still part of Mexico. Then, from 1846 to 1848, the United States fought Mexico to take control of these lands. The war was known as the Mexican-American War.

In 1848, the United States won the war. Many Americans soon moved west. Arizona and New Mexico both became states in 1912.

READING CHECK ŏDRAW CONCLUSIONS
Why do you think Texas eventually became a part of the United States?

Oklahoma Statehood

What is now Oklahoma became part of the United States with the Louisiana Purchase of 1803. In 1830, the government gave most of present-day Oklahoma to the Native Americans. This area was known as the **Indian Territory**.

The Trail of Tears

Many Cherokee Indians refused to give up their land and move to the Indian Territory. To push them out, the government gave their land to settlers. Cherokee Chief **John Ross** fought against the government in court, but he did not succeed.

In 1838, soldiers forced most of the Cherokee to move to the Indian Territory. More than 4,000 Cherokee died along the way. They died from sickness, cold, and lack of food. Their long journey became known as the Trail of Tears.

Land Rush

In 1889, the government opened parts of the Indian Territory to settlers. To get settlers to move there, it offered free land, called **land grants**, to anyone who settled in the territory. To claim a piece of land, a person had to be the first one to occupy it.

April 22, 1889, was the first day of the land grant program in the Indian Territory. About 50,000 people stood at the territory's border. At noon, the signal was given. People rushed toward the land they wanted.

▶ **THE TRAIL OF TEARS Many Cherokee died on the 800-mile journey to the Indian Territory.**

FAST FACT

Boomers rushed to claim land in the Indian Territory. Some rode horses, others drove wagons, and some just ran to the land they wanted to claim.

These settlers were called Boomers because they were part of a land boom—a quick and sudden development of land. What had been the Indian Territory began to fill with settlers from the East. In 1907, Oklahoma became a state.

READING CHECK ☼ **DRAW CONCLUSIONS**

Why do you think so many people wanted land in what became Oklahoma?

Summary

The Spanish were the first Europeans in the Southwest. They brought Spanish culture to the region and learned from the Native Americans there. The Spanish also forced many Native Americans to work against their will. The lands in the Southwest gained statehood between 1845 and 1912.

REVIEW

1. **WHAT TO KNOW** What major events affected the history of the Southwest?

2. **VOCABULARY** What was the purpose of **land grants** in the Indian Territory?

3. **HISTORY** Which Southwest state was once an independent nation?

4. **CRITICAL THINKING** Why do you think the Cherokee journey to the Indian Territory became known as the Trail of Tears?

5. **WRITE A LETTER** Imagine that you were at the Oklahoma land rush in 1889. Write a letter to a friend back East. Describe the scene.

6. (Focus Skill) **DRAW CONCLUSIONS**

   On a separate sheet of paper, copy and complete the graphic organizer below.

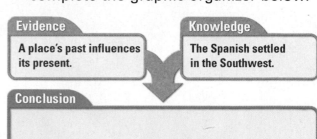

Evidence

A place's past influences its present.

Knowledge

The Spanish settled in the Southwest.

Conclusion

FIELD TRIP

READ ABOUT

About 1,000 years ago, Chaco (CHAH•koh) Canyon was the center of a complex Native American culture. Ancestors of the Pueblo peoples built large settlements there. More than 5,000 people may have lived in those settlements.

Ancient Puebloans built homes of stone and adobe below the canyon's towering rock walls. Some buildings had hundreds of rooms. People came from all directions to attend ceremonies and trade at Chaco Canyon.

Today, people can visit the Chaco Culture National Historical Park. There, they can learn how the Ancient Puebloans lived in the Southwest long ago.

FIND

Chaco Canyon

NEW MEXICO

CHACO CANYON

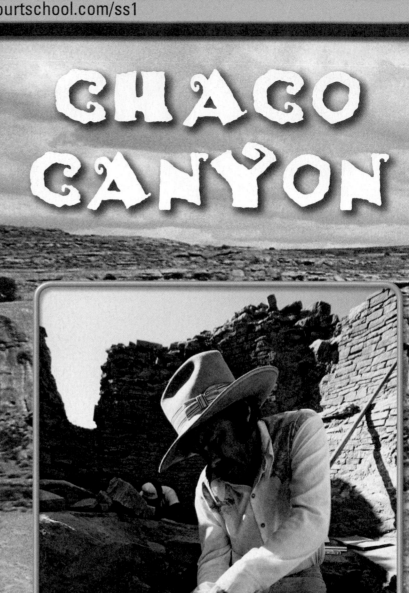

CHACO CANYON RESEARCH A scientist (above) digs for artifacts at the site of Chaco Canyon (right).

CHACO STYLE POTTERY

ROCK CARVINGS

DANCER PERFORMING A CEREMONY

A ROCK FORMATION

RUINS OF A CEREMONIAL ROOM

A VIRTUAL TOUR

GO ONLINE   For more resources, go to
www.harcourtschool.com/ss1

Identify Multiple Causes and Effects

Why It Matters Some events in history have more than one cause and more than one effect. A cause is an event that makes something else happen. What happens is an effect.

❱ LEARN

Use these steps to help you identify multiple causes and effects.

Step 1 Look for the effects. Decide whether there is more than one effect.

Step 2 Look for the causes of the effects.

Step 3 Think about how the causes and effects are related.

❱ PRACTICE

The diagram on page 327 shows some important events linked to the Mexican-American War. Use the diagram to answer these questions.

❶ What is the first cause shown on the diagram? What is the effect of that cause?

❷ Which event had more than one effect?

❱ **MEXICAN-AMERICAN WAR** This painting shows a battle from the Mexican-American War.

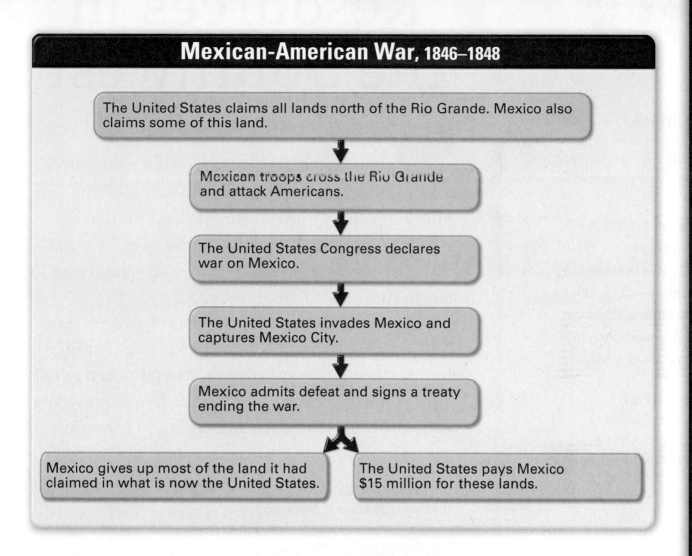

Mexican-American War, 1846–1848

The United States claims all lands north of the Rio Grande. Mexico also claims some of this land.

Mexican troops cross the Rio Grande and attack Americans.

The United States Congress declares war on Mexico.

The United States invades Mexico and captures Mexico City.

Mexico admits defeat and signs a treaty ending the war.

Mexico gives up most of the land it had claimed in what is now the United States.

The United States pays Mexico $15 million for these lands.

3 Identify one event that is both a cause and an effect.

4 What was one effect of the treaty that ended the Mexican-American War?

▶ APPLY

Turn to pages 120–121 in your textbook. With a partner, make a diagram showing causes and effects of the American Revolution.

Critical Thinking Skills

Resources in the Southwest

WHAT TO KNOW
How have people in the Southwest developed the region's resources?

VOCABULARY

arid p. 329

migrant worker p. 329

commercial p. 330

conflict p. 330

compromise p. 331

cooperate p. 331

PEOPLE

Cesar Chavez

Dolores Huerta

Frank Phillips

PLACES

Rio Grande

Presidio

Mexico

Bartlesville

Houston

Dallas

Oklahoma City

Tulsa

Gulf of Mexico

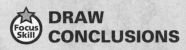

DRAW CONCLUSIONS

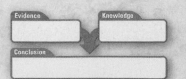

YOU ARE THERE
It is the 1850s. All during the cattle drive through Texas, your dad has told you about the **Rio Grande.** He told you that, in Spanish, *rio grande* means "large river." He said that the Rio Grande is one of the longest rivers in North America.

Now, you are surprised by what you see. Here in **Presidio,** Texas, the Rio Grande is beautiful, but it is just a narrow stream. You pick up a small stone and make your best throw. The stone lands with a thud on the opposite bank—in **Mexico**.

❯ THE RIO GRANDE forms about two-thirds of the boundary between the United States and Mexico.

Children IN HISTORY

Teddy Abbott

In the late 1800s, many boys in the United States wanted to be cowhands. They dreamed of driving herds of cattle from ranches in Texas north to the railroads. Cattle drives meant riding horseback all day and sleeping under the stars.

Teddy Abbott joined his first cattle drive when he was just 10 years old. When he was 15, he survived a stampede. Teddy once explained that cowhands sang to their cattle at night to prevent stampedes: "The singing was supposed to soothe them, and it did . . ."

Make It Relevant Why is it important to work hard at whatever task you have?

Land

In the Southwest, people have learned to use the region's land. They used the more **arid**, or dry, land for ranching and the more fertile land for farming.

Ranches

The Spanish brought cattle and sheep to the Southwest and started the region's first ranches. Their herds grazed freely on the open land. In time, ranchers hired cowhands to move herds of cattle to market. During these cattle drives, cowhands guided cattle across hundreds of miles of open country.

By the 1800s, railroads had come to the region. This made ranching a more profitable industry. Trains gave ranchers an easier and quicker way to get their cattle to market.

Migrant Workers

Ranches and farms spread across the Southwest and farther west. Now those places needed more workers. Many jobs, however, were temporary, especially those for harvesting crops.

Migrant workers began to fill the need for temporary workers. A **migrant worker** is someone who moves from place to place, doing one job after another. Migrant workers might round up cattle in Texas and then move to New Mexico to harvest crops.

The life of a migrant worker was difficult. In the 1960s, **Cesar Chavez** and **Dolores Huerta** began to work for the rights of migrant workers and others. Since then, the lives of migrant workers have improved.

READING CHECK ⚙ **DRAW CONCLUSIONS**
Why might some farmwork be temporary?

Oil and Water

In the 1890s, people began to use the region's oil to supply the nation's growing industries. People also needed water for the region's growing populations.

Building the Oil Industry

In 1897, Oklahoma produced its first commercial oil, or oil that was to be sold. Then, in 1901, workers struck oil at Spindletop, in Texas. New Mexico began producing oil in the 1920s.

Oil brought a new industry and more people to the region. **Frank Phillips** was a barber in Iowa before he moved to **Bartlesville,** Oklahoma.

There, he started an oil company that became a worldwide company. The oil industry also affected the growth in cities. **Houston** and **Dallas,** in Texas, and **Oklahoma City** and **Tulsa,** in Oklahoma, grew due to the oil industry.

The Rio Grande

The Rio Grande has long been a major source of water for people in the Southwest and Mexico. The river starts in Colorado and crosses New Mexico. It forms the border between Texas and Mexico before emptying into the **Gulf of Mexico.** Along its way, people use the river's water for farms, cities, and industries.

As more people use the water of the Rio Grande, the water becomes more scarce. At times, water shortages have led to **conflicts**, or disagreements, between the United States and Mexico.

To settle these conflicts, both countries have worked to compromise.

❭ SPINDLETOP The discovery of oil at Spindletop attracted thousands of people to the Southwest.

In a **compromise**, people on each side of a conflict agree to give up something. The United States agreed to build a dam that allows a fixed amount of water to flow to Mexico each month. In return, Mexico agreed to give up some of that water during periods of drought in the United States.

The United States and Mexico have also learned other ways to **cooperate**, or work together. They have cleaned up the Rio Grande and passed laws to prevent pollution of the river.

READING CHECK ☼ **DRAW CONCLUSIONS**
Why is it important to protect the Rio Grande?

Summary

People in the Southwest have developed the region's resources. They use the drier land for ranches and more fertile land for farms. They also use and protect the oil and water resources.

❱ **BIG BEND NATIONAL PARK** offers visitors many activities on the Rio Grande.

REVIEW

1. **WHAT TO KNOW** How have people in the Southwest developed the region's resources?

2. **VOCABULARY** Explain how people can **cooperate** to end a **conflict**.

3. **GEOGRAPHY** Which border does the Rio Grande form?

4. **CRITICAL THINKING** Why do farmers in the Southwest depend on rivers more than farmers do in some other parts of the country?

5. ✏️ **WRITE A PARAGRAPH** Describe in a short paragraph how the railroads helped ranching grow.

6. (Focus Skill) **DRAW CONCLUSIONS**

On a separate sheet of paper, copy and complete the graphic organizer below.

Evidence	Knowledge
The United States and Mexico use the Rio Grande.	The Rio Grande forms their border.

Conclusion

Resolve Conflicts

Why It Matters One way to **resolve**, or settle, a conflict is to learn how to compromise.

❱ LEARN

Follow these steps to resolve a conflict through compromise.

Step 1 Identify the conflict.

Step 2 Have both sides explain what they want to happen. Discuss the differences.

Step 3 Think of possible compromises. Choose one that both sides agree on.

Step 4 Follow the best compromise. Plan to make sure that the compromise works.

❱ **FLAG** of the United States (above) and of Mexico (right)

▶ **THE CHAMIZAL NATIONAL MEMORIAL** in Texas honors the resolution of one of several conflicts the United States and Mexico have had over the Rio Grande.

▶ PRACTICE

From the lesson, think about how the United States and Mexico resolved their conflict over the Rio Grande.

1 What caused the conflict?

2 How did the two countries compromise to resolve the conflict?

3 Do you think that both parties cooperated fairly and equally? Explain.

▶ APPLY

Make It Relevant With a partner, think of a conflict that two students might have. You and your partner should take opposite sides in the conflict. Then use the steps on page 332 to figure out ways you can compromise to resolve the conflict.

Time

Visual Summary

1500
Some Native Americans build pueblos

Summarize the Chapter

(Focus Skill) **Draw Conclusions** Complete this graphic organizer to show that you understand how the geography of the Southwest affects life in the region.

Evidence

Deserts cover much of Arizona and New Mexico.

Knowledge

Water is a scarce resource in deserts.

Conclusion

Vocabulary

Identify the term from the word bank that best replaces the underlined text in each sentence. One of the terms will not be used.

1. The use of canals, ditches, or pipes to bring water to dry places is necessary to farm in many parts of the Southwest.

2. Some places may get half of their yearly precipitation in one sudden, heavy rain.

3. In general, Arizona and New Mexico have a hot and dry climate.

4. Lake Mead is a human-made lake.

5. When it rains in the desert, the water often fills deep ditches that have been carved over time by running water.

Word Bank

cloudburst p. 312	**aqueduct** p. 313
arroyos p. 312	**irrigation** p. 314
reservoir p. 313	**arid** p. 329

1838
Cherokee people journey
on the Trail of Tears

1901
Oil is discovered
in Texas

 Time Line

Use the chapter time line above to answer these questions.

6. In what century did Cherokee people journey on the Trail of Tears?

7. In what year was oil discovered in Texas?

 Facts and Main Ideas

Answer these questions.

8. Where in the Southwest would you see many buttes and mesas?

9. What nonrenewable resources does the Southwest have?

10. What was the Trail of Tears?

11. What kind of jobs do most migrant workers do in the Southwest?

Write the letter of the best choice.

12. Which Native Americans in the Southwest were nomads?
    A the Apache
    B the Caddo
    C the Cherokee
    D the Pueblo

13. What forms much of the border between the Southwest region and Mexico?
    A the Colorado River
    B the Gulf of Mexico
    C the Rio Grande
    D the Sandia Mountains

 Critical Thinking

Answer these questions.

14. Why are most farms and ranches in the Southwest located in different places?

15. How might some Native Americans in the Southwest have felt about Spanish missions? Explain.

16. Why is it necessary for people, states, and countries to cooperate when they share natural resources?

 Skills

Identify Multiple Causes and Effects

17. What were two causes of the war between Texas and Mexico in 1836?

18. What were two effects of the Oklahoma land rushes?

writing

Write a Narrative Imagine you traveled through the early Southwest. Use the illustration on pages 318–319 to help you describe a visit to Taos Pueblo.

Write a Summary Write a summary explaining how people in the Southwest have resolved conflicts over scarce water resources.

STUDY SKILLS

SKIM AND SCAN

Skimming and scanning are two ways to learn from what you read.

- **To skim, quickly read the lesson title and the section titles. Look at the pictures and read the captions. Use this information to identify the main topics.**

- **To scan, look quickly through the text for specific details, such as key words or facts.**

SKIM	SCAN
Lesson: Texas and Oklahoma **Main Idea:** Texas and Oklahoma have people from many different cultures, as well as ranches, astronauts, and oil. **Titles/Headings:** Old and New, Many Cultures, Oil **Visuals:** _____	Key Words and Facts • immigrants • aerospace industry • oil • _____ • _____ • _____

PREVIEW VOCABULARY

aerospace p. 339   **crude oil** p. 341   **refinery** p. 341

The Southwest Today

A VIEW OF DOWNTOWN DALLAS, TEXAS

Texas and Oklahoma

WHAT TO KNOW
What is special about Texas and Oklahoma today?

VOCABULARY
aerospace p. 339
reservation p. 340
crude oil p. 341
refinery p. 341
dredge p. 341

PEOPLE
Mae C. Jemison

PLACES
Houston
Tulsa
Oklahoma City

DRAW CONCLUSIONS

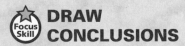

YOU ARE THERE You and your family are visiting a cattle ranch in Oklahoma. You ask a cowhand, "Where are all the cattle? Don't you keep them fenced in?" as he helps you onto your horse.

"Sure we do," he replies, "but they have more than 10,000 acres to roam in. We may not find them until after lunch."

He yells, "Let's ride out!" As he heads down the trail on his horse, you and the others follow. You're riding the range!

▷ OKLAHOMA CAPITOL BUILDING

▶ **JOHNSON SPACE CENTER** workers oversee space shuttle flights.

Old and New

Life in Texas and Oklahoma is a mixture of old and new ways of life. Most people live in cities and work in service and manufacturing industries. Still, people farm and run ranches.

Using the Land

Food production is a large industry in the region. Texas has more farms than any other state, and Oklahoma raises huge crops of wheat.

Most ranchers raise cattle for beef. Texas is the nation's leading beef producer. Oklahoma is one of the top five beef-producing states. Many ranch workers still use horses to round up cattle, but some use helicopters!

Working in Cities

Most Texans and Oklahomans live in cities. **Houston** is Texas's largest city and the nation's fourth-largest city. More than one-half of all Oklahomans live in **Tulsa** and **Oklahoma City.**

Some people in both states work for the aerospace industry. **Aerospace** is the building of aircraft and equipment for air and space travel. Astronauts train at the Johnson Space Center in Houston. Workers there oversee the space shuttle flights. Former NASA astronaut **Mae C. Jemison** founded two aerospace companies in Houston. She was the first African American woman to travel into space.

READING CHECK ⌁**DRAW CONCLUSIONS**
Which industries in the region rely on the land?

Many Cultures

Over the years, people from all over the world have moved to Texas and Oklahoma. They have added a variety of cultures to the region.

A Diverse Population

Texas and Oklahoma both have large European American populations. Many of their ancestors came to the United States in the 1800s from Germany, Ireland, Britain, the Netherlands, and France.

Today, about one out of every ten Oklahomans is African American. Some of their ancestors came to the region in the 1800s as cowhands, settlers, and farmers.

Many Native Americans also live in the region. In fact, Oklahoma has the second-largest Native American population in the nation. Most Native Americans live on **reservations**— land set aside for Native Americans. The Osage Nation Reservation in Oklahoma covers more than one million acres.

Hispanics have long made up a large part of the region's population. In fact, about one-third of all Texans are Hispanic.

Immigrants from Vietnam have also moved to the region. Many came to Texas in the 1970s to escape war in their home country.

READING CHECK ♞ **DRAW CONCLUSIONS**
Why might so many Hispanics live in Texas?

> **CHEROKEE gather to drum and celebrate their culture.**

Oil

Today, the oil industry remains a leading industry in the region. Texas is the nation's largest producer of oil. Oklahoma is the sixth-largest producer.

Drilling for Oil

On land and in the Gulf of Mexico, huge drills move through layers of rock to reach deposits of **crude oil**, or natural oil. The crude oil is then pumped to the surface. Pipelines, trucks, or ships carry it to refineries. A **refinery** is a factory that turns crude oil into products, including gasoline.

Shipping Oil

Houston has the most oil refineries in the United States. It also has one of the nation's busiest ports for handling oil shipments. Ships called tankers carry crude oil into the port to be refined. Then tankers carry gasoline and other oil products out of the port to be sold around the world.

When Houston wanted to enlarge its port to handle more shipments of oil, it dredged the waterway between the city and the Gulf of Mexico. To **dredge** is to dig out the bottom and sides to make a waterway deeper and wider.

READING CHECK ŏ DRAW CONCLUSIONS
What jobs might oil workers do?

ILLUSTRATION Oil deposits are usually found in layers of rock. People use oil rigs to reach this oil. What is the drill bit attached to?

Oil Rig

Safety platform

Derrick

Storage tanks

Rotary table

Casing

Drill pipe

Rock layers

Drill bit

Oil

Global Connection

Saudi Arabia is the leading oil producer in the world. In fact, it has about one-fourth of all known oil deposits in the world. About one-seventh of all the oil imported to the United States is shipped from Saudi Arabia. Saudi Arabia is mostly desert. The nation covers most of the Arabian Peninsula, between the Persian Gulf and the Red Sea.

READING CHECK ⓈDRAW CONCLUSIONS
Why do you think the United States imports some of its oil?

Summary

Texas and Oklahoma have many industries, including farming, ranching, aerospace, and the oil industry. Both states have diverse populations.

▶ **THE OIL INDUSTRY** is the largest industry in Saudi Arabia. It provides jobs for many Saudis.

REVIEW

1. **WHAT TO KNOW** What is special about Texas and Oklahoma today?

2. **VOCABULARY** Write a sentence that describes one job that a person might have in the **aerospace** industry.

3. **CULTURE** Why do you think Oklahoma has such a large Native American population today?

4. **CRITICAL THINKING** How do you think the invention of the automobile affected the oil industry? Explain your answer.

5. ✎ **WRITE A BIOGRAPHY** Research more about the many achievements of Mae C. Jemison. Then write a short biography about her career.

6. ⭐(Focus Skill) **DRAW CONCLUSIONS** On a separate sheet of paper, copy and complete the graphic organizer below.

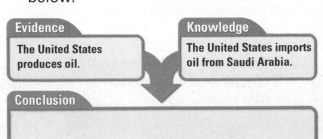

Evidence
The United States produces oil.

Knowledge
The United States imports oil from Saudi Arabia.

Conclusion

Wilma Mankiller

Biography

Trustworthiness
Respect
Responsibility
Fairness
Caring
Patriotism

"*One of the things my parents taught me . . . is to not ever let anybody else define me.*"

Wilma Mankiller was the first woman to be chief of the Cherokee. From 1985 to 1995, she was the leader of more than 140,000 Cherokee.

Mankiller was born in Tahlequah, Oklahoma, the capital of the Cherokee Nation. She grew up on land that had belonged to her family for 100 years. When she was 11 years old, however, the United States government forced her family and others to move to California.

As an adult, Mankiller moved back to Oklahoma. She soon began to work for the rights of Native Americans and women. As chief, Mankiller helped get better housing and better jobs for the Cherokee. She oversaw the building of schools and health clinics. She also helped preserve and honor Cherokee traditions.

Why Character Counts

How did Wilma Mankiller take responsibility for her people?

Time

1945			Present
Born			

1956 Mankiller and her family are forced to move to California

1985 Mankiller becomes chief of the Cherokee Nation

1993 Mankiller's life story, *Mankiller: A Chief and Her People,* is published

GO ONLINE

For more resources, go to
www.harcourtschool.com/ss1

Helping People in Need

"We will continue to do what it takes . . . to get through this together, as one American family."

—Rick Perry, Governor of Texas

When natural disasters occur, people need help from others to recover. In August 2005, Hurricane Katrina hit the coast of the Gulf of Mexico. Wind damage and flooding forced about one million Americans to leave their homes in the states of Louisiana and Mississippi.

Many of these people had only the clothes they were wearing. They traveled by car, bus, and airplane to other cities to find safety or to start new lives.

▶ **VICTIMS** of Hurricane Katrina comfort each other.

Most people who left the Gulf coast went to Texas and other nearby states. There, thousands of Americans were ready to help. They set up shelters. They provided food, clothing, and supplies. They helped people get new jobs and find new homes. They also welcomed children into their schools.

Citizens often work together to help others or to solve problems in their communities. Some natural disasters, such as Hurricane Katrina, are so damaging that Americans from all regions must work together. People from other countries help, too.

❯ **VOLUNTEERING** A volunteer sorts shoes.

Make It Relevant Why is it important to help others in times of need?

❯ **SHELTERS** The Astrodome (below) in Houston, Texas, served as a shelter for many victims of Hurricane Katrina. A group of students (right) from Louisiana take a bus to their first day of classes in Texas.

New Mexico and Arizona

WHAT TO KNOW
How do people in New Mexico and Arizona make the most of scarce water resources?

VOCABULARY
observatory p. 348
xeriscape p. 349
evaporation p. 350

PEOPLE
John Wesley Powell
Georgia O'Keeffe
Kate Cory

PLACES
Grand Canyon
Santa Fe
Taos
Phoenix
Albuquerque
Carlsbad Caverns
Tucson

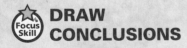

DRAW CONCLUSIONS

YOU ARE THERE
You are standing near the edge of the **Grand Canyon**, in northwestern Arizona. When you look down, you see a huge crack in Earth. It is more than a mile deep!

You try to imagine what it was like for **John Wesley Powell** when he first explored this canyon in 1869. How awesome to look up from the swirling rapids of the Colorado River and see mile-high cliff walls towering over you! Today, about to journey to the bottom of the canyon, you understand just how brave Powell was.

❯ **THE GRAND CANYON** provides beautiful scenery to visitors.

▶ **PUEBLO-STYLE HOUSES** are common in the region's cities, such as Santa Fe, New Mexico.

Moving to the Desert

Arizona and New Mexico make up the western part of the Sun Belt. They are two of the fastest-growing states.

Artists Lead the Way

In the early 1900s, many artists moved to the desert Southwest. They were drawn by the natural beauty of the land and the warm, dry climate.

Some artists, such as **Georgia O'Keeffe**, worked or lived in and around the cities of **Santa Fe** and **Taos** (TOWS) in New Mexico. Others, such as Hopi painter **Kate Cory**, lived on reservations. Cory painted pictures of the Hopi and of the Grand Canyon. Paintings and photographs by Southwest artists were the first pictures many Americans had seen of the region.

In time, more and more people traveled to Arizona and New Mexico. Some decided to stay. Soon new highways, railroads, and airplanes made travel to the region faster. Air-conditioning made life in the desert more comfortable. As more people moved to the desert, cities began to grow. Today, the region's largest cities are **Phoenix** (FEE•niks), Arizona, and **Albuquerque** (AL•buh•ker•kee), New Mexico.

READING CHECK ☼**DRAW CONCLUSIONS**
Why might early paintings and photographs have led to growth in the region?

Growing Economies

Ranching, farming, and mining have long been industries in Arizona and New Mexico. However, most people now work in newer industries.

Tourism

Tourism is a leading industry in the region. Natural attractions, such as the Grand Canyon in Arizona and **Carlsbad Caverns** in New Mexico, bring many tourists each year. The region's cities and diverse cultures also attract visitors. Tourists can shop for Native American arts and crafts in Santa Fe or tour a historic Spanish mission in **Tucson**, Arizona.

Manufacturing and Technology

Manufacturing is another major industry in Arizona and New Mexico. Both states make electronic equipment. New Mexico also makes processed foods and glass products.

People in both states work in high-tech jobs. Many New Mexicans work at Los Alamos or Sandia laboratories. Some Arizonans work at the Kitt Peak National Observatory in Tucson, Arizona. An **observatory** is a place where people use instruments, such as telescopes, for studying space.

READING CHECK **MAIN IDEA AND DETAILS**
In what industries do most people in Arizona and New Mexico work?

> **KITT PEAK NATIONAL OBSERVATORY** (below) has the world's largest collection of telescopes (inset).

How Much Water?	
USE	AMOUNT
Brushing teeth	1 to 2 gallons
Flushing a toilet	5 to 7 gallons
Running a dishwasher	9 to 12 gallons
Taking a shower	15 to 30 gallons
Washing dishes by hand	20 to 30 gallons

TABLE Xeriscaping (above) is one way people conserve water. How much water is used to brush your teeth?

Water Resources

With fast-growing populations, people in Arizona and New Mexico need more and more water. They are working to meet this challenge.

Supplying Water

People have found new ways to supply water to desert cities. They have drilled deeper and deeper wells into aquifers. They have built more pumping stations and aqueducts to carry water from aquifers and rivers to desert cities. However, some people worry that there may not be enough water to continue meeting the needs of this growing region.

Conserving Water

Although people have new sources of water, they are working hard to conserve water. In some places, people work together to decide how much water to use. In other places, laws require people to limit their use of water.

People have also learned to use less water in their yards. They use **xeriscape** (ZIR•uh•skayp), a landscaping method that conserves water. Instead of planting grass lawns that need watering, they plant desert plants. These plants can live with little water.

READING CHECK **MAIN IDEA AND DETAILS**
What are some ways in which people in the region conserve water?

Global Connection

Around the world, people who live in deserts find ways to make the most of scarce water. The farmers in Israel's Negev desert are one example. They collect rainwater in tanks. They also use aqueducts to carry fresh water from the Sea of Galilee to the desert.

In the desert, much water is lost through evaporation. **Evaporation** is the process in which the sun's heat turns liquid water into its gas form, water vapor.

Farmers in the Negev desert use different methods to limit the evaporation of water from crops. For example, they build greenhouses over crop fields. They also use underground pipes to carry water to the roots of their crops.

READING CHECK ⭘DRAW CONCLUSIONS

How do you think a greenhouse works to limit evaporation?

▶ **A GREENHOUSE IN THE NEGEV DESERT**

Summary

Arizona and New Mexico are two of the fastest growing states. Newer industries in the region include tourism, manufacturing, and high-tech industries. With growing populations, people are working to conserve their water resources.

REVIEW

1. **WHAT TO KNOW** How do people in New Mexico and Arizona make the most of scarce water resources?

2. **VOCABULARY** Use the term **evaporation** in a sentence that explains its meaning.

3. **ECONOMY** What are some important industries in Arizona and New Mexico?

4. **CRITICAL THINKING** How do you think the invention of air-conditioning affected population growth in the desert? Explain your answer.

5. **WRITE A WATER CONSERVATION PLAN** Think about all the ways in which you and your family use water. Then write a plan for conserving water.

6. **DRAW CONCLUSIONS** On a separate sheet of paper, copy and complete the graphic organizer below.

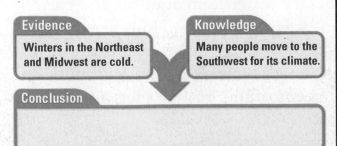

Evidence
Winters in the Northeast and Midwest are cold.

Knowledge
Many people move to the Southwest for its climate.

Conclusion

John Wesley Powell

Biography

Trustworthiness
Respect
Responsibility
Fairness
Caring
Patriotism

"We are ready to start our way down the great unknown. . . ."

John Wesley Powell was born on March 24, 1834, in New York. Even as a young boy, Powell had a sense of adventure.

Powell had many adventures in his life. In 1856, at the age of 22, he rowed the whole length of the Mississippi River! A year later, he repeated the feat on the Ohio River.

On one of his best-known adventures, Powell explored the Grand Canyon of the Colorado River. During this trip in 1869, Powell recorded information on the landscape and plant and animal life of the area. He also studied the cultures of Native Americans living there.

In 1881, Powell became director of the United States Geological Survey. This government agency studies land and resources. Today, people all over the world respect Powell for his knowledge and sense of adventure.

Why Character Counts

How did Powell earn many people's respect?

Time

1834		1902
Born		Died

1856 Powell explores the Mississippi River

1869 Powell explores the Grand Canyon

1881 Powell becomes director of the U.S. Geological Survey

GO ONLINE
For more resources, go to
www.harcourtschool.com/ss1

Read a Road Map

Why It Matters A road map shows the roads that connect places and the distances between those places. You can use a road map to find the best way to get somewhere.

❱ LEARN

Follow these steps to read a road map.

Step 1 Use the map key to see what kind of road each line color stands for. Knowing the kinds of roads helps you choose good routes.

Step 2 Use the map scale to find out how many miles are represented by 1 inch.

❱ PRACTICE

Use the road map on page 353 to answer these questions.

❶ What interstate highway connects Albuquerque and Las Cruces?

❷ What United States highways and state highways would you use to get from Grants to Silver City?

❱ **NEW MEXICO HIGHWAY**

Road Map of New Mexico

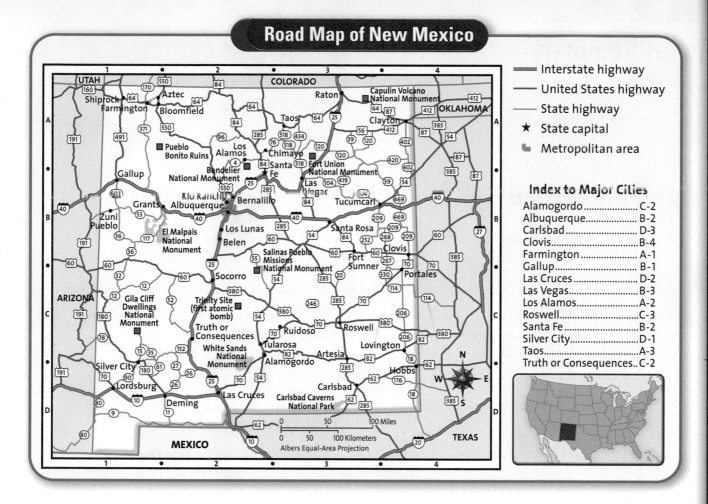

Road Map of New Mexico

Interstate highway
United States highway
State highway
★ State capital
Metropolitan area

Index to Major Cities

Alamogordo	C-2
Albuquerque	B-2
Carlsbad	D-3
Clovis	B-4
Farmington	A-1
Gallup	B-1
Las Cruces	D-2
Las Vegas	B-3
Los Alamos	A-2
Roswell	C-3
Santa Fe	B-2
Silver City	D-1
Taos	A-3
Truth or Consequences	C-2

3 About how many miles would you have to drive to get from Alamogordo to Carlsbad?

4 About how many miles is it from Santa Fe to Taos?

▶ APPLY

Make It Relevant Plan a road trip between two places in your state. Use a road map of your state to decide the best routes and to figure out the distance in miles.

Map and Globe Skills

Visual Summary

Aerospace and oil are important industries in Texas and Oklahoma.

Summarize the Chapter

Focus Skill **Draw Conclusions** Complete this graphic organizer to show that you understand how people and the environment interact in the Southwest.

Evidence

The population of the Southwest is growing fast.

Knowledge

All people use fresh water every day.

Conclusion

TEST PREP **Vocabulary**

Identify the term from the word bank that best completes each sentence. One of the terms will not be used.

1. People use huge drills and pumps to remove _____ from the ground.

2. Astronauts, engineers, and pilots are just some of the people who work in the Southwest's _____ industry.

3. Many Native Americans in the Southwest live and work on a _____.

4. Some farmers in the Southwest use greenhouses so that less water will be lost through _____.

5. To make room for large tankers, it was necessary to _____ the waterway that connects Houston to the Gulf of Mexico.

> ### Word Bank
>
> **aerospace** p. 339   **refinery** p. 341
>
> **reservation** p. 340   **dredge** p. 341
>
> **crude oil** p. 341   **evaporation** p. 350

Xeriscaping is one way people in Arizona and New Mexico conserve water.

The Grand Canyon provides beautiful scenery to visitors.

 Facts and Main Ideas

Answer these questions.

6. Where in the Southwest do most people live?

7. What Southwest state is the nation's largest producer of oil?

8. What are some tourist attractions in the Southwest?

9. What kind of jobs do people have in the Los Alamos and Sandia National Laboratories in New Mexico?

Write the letter of the best choice.

10. Which woman works in the Southwest's aerospace industry?
    A Kate Cory
    B Mae C. Jemison
    C Wilma Mankiller
    D Georgia O'Keefe

11. Taos is a famous center for artists in which Southwest state?
    A Arizona
    B New Mexico
    C Oklahoma
    D Texas

12. Which industry is considered a newer industry in the Southwest region?
    A mining
    B ranching
    C tourism
    D farming

 Critical Thinking

Answer these questions.

13. Why do you think many people in the Southwest today speak Spanish?

14. What features of the Southwest's geography make it a good region for studying planets and stars?

15. Do you think the actions people in the Southwest are taking to conserve water are effective? Why or why not?

 Skills

Read a Road Map

16. Study the road map on page 353. What highways could you use to get from Las Cruces to Carlsbad? About how many miles would you have to drive?

writing

Write a Persuasive Letter Write a letter to the editor of a newspaper, explaining why you think it is important to conserve oil resources. Include some ideas for ways people can use less oil.

Write a Report Choose a city in the Southwest, and write a short report about its special features. Include descriptions of the city's location as well as some of its industries and attractions.

Fun with Social Studies

Terrific Travels

Which picture is on the other side of each postcard?

Dear Grandma,
Whew! We drove for hours to get here. Today we saw the Rio Grande. Tomorrow, we will cross the river to visit Mexico.

Hi, Uncle David,
Wish you were here to see where the gasoline that runs your truck might have gotten its start! I heard on the radio that only five states produce more oil than Oklahoma.

Dear Ms. Washburn,
Remember when we studied the Southwest in art class? Right now, I am in a place that is perfect for artists. You should see the beautiful colors of the sunset behind the desert mesas near here and Albuquerque!

Hi, Emily!
This place is amazing! It is wider and deeper than I expected. I just cannot believe the colors. This must be the grandest canyon in the whole world!

Madeleine's Wish

VOCABULARY

Match each definition to a Unit 5 vocabulary word. Then unscramble the highlighted letters to see if Madeleine gets her wish.

DEFINITION

Disagreement
You'll find groundwater here.
Gasoline is made from it.
Dry climate
Religious settlement

VOCABULARY

c o n f l i c t
☐ ☐ ☐ ☐ ☐ ☐ ☐
☐ ☐ ☐ ☐ ☐   ☐ ☐ ☐
☐ ☐ ☐ ☐
☐ ☐ ☐ ☐ ☐ ☐ ☐

Madeleine was tired
    of the wandering life.
Always moving made her sad.
But when she asked Mom,
    "Could we please settle down?"
Her mother just told her,
    "☐☐ , ☐☐☐. We're nomadic."

Online Adventures

GO ONLINE

Eco's next adventure begins with a search for a hidden Native American village in the ancient Southwest. This time you'll pilot a blimp through a map of different historical places. Be careful, because it's hard to steer and you don't want to get lost! If you solve all the puzzles along the way, you can find the next suspect. Play now at **www.harcourtschool.com/ss1**

Review and Test Prep

💡 THE BIG IDEA

People and Resources People have learned to use both the abundant and limited resources of the Southwest to develop the region.

Reading Comprehension and Vocabulary

Resources of the Southwest

Until the 1500s, Native Americans were the only people in the Southwest. Some farmed. Others were <u>nomads</u>. Then the Spanish arrived with soldiers and priests. They built missions, forts, and towns in the Southwest. Over time, people from all over the world made the Southwest their home. Each group added part of its culture to the region.

As in the past, many people in the Southwest still depend on natural resources to earn a living. People use irrigation to farm on the region's plains and river valleys. In drier areas, they raise cattle and sheep on ranches. Thousands of people earn a living in the Southwest's oil industry. In recent years, manufacturing, tourism, high-tech, and aerospace industries have helped the Southwest's economy grow.

The region's population is growing, too. In fact, the Southwest is one of the fastest-growing regions in the United States. Such rapid growth can strain resources that are already scarce. For this reason, people in the Southwest have learned to use <u>xeriscape</u> to conserve natural resources.

Read the summary above. Then answer the questions that follow.

1. What is the meaning of the word <u>nomads</u>?
   A hunters
   B people who move from place to place and have no permanent homes
   C traders
   D people who make a living by raising cattle and other livestock

2. Who were the first Europeans to settle in the Southwest?
   A the British
   B the French
   C the Germans
   D the Spanish

3. Which of these industries developed most recently in the Southwest?
   A aerospace
   B farming
   C oil
   D ranching

4. What is the meaning of the word <u>xeriscape</u>?
   A building equipment for air and space travel
   B setting aside land for Native Americans
   C landscaping methods that conserve water
   D turning crude oil into gasoline

Answer these questions.

5. What is the rain shadow, and how does it affect the Southwest?

6. Why did people build missions in the Southwest?

7. What are two reasons people build wells in the Southwest?

8. Whioh city in the Southwest has the largest population?

9. What are some ways people in the Southwest conserve water?

Write the letter of the best choice.

10. What kind of landform covers most of Oklahoma?
    A deserts
    B plains
    C plateaus
    D mountains

11. The Hoover Dam controls the flow of what river?
    A the Colorado River
    B the Pecos River
    C the Rio Grande
    D the Red River

12. Which Southwest state was once part of an area called Indian Territory?
    A Arizona
    B New Mexico
    C Oklahoma
    D Texas

13. What happens at a refinery?
    A Machines turn the power of moving water into electricity.
    B Crops are turned into food products, such as sugar.
    C Crude oil is turned into useful products, such as gasoline.
    D People do scientific research.

14. What are some ways in which life in the Southwest today is similar to life in the region 100 years ago?

15. What are some of the challenges people in the Southwest are now facing because of the recent rapid growth in the region?

 **Skills**

Read a Road Map

Use the map on this page to answer the following questions.

16. What highway can you use to drive from Tucson to Phoenix?

17. About how many miles do you have to drive to get from Kingman to Flagstaff?

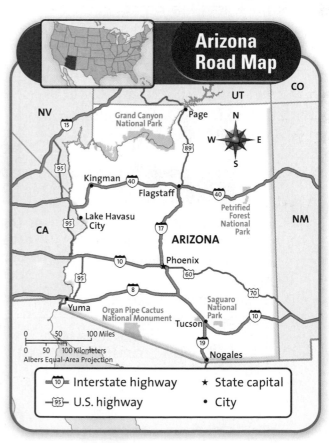

Show What You Know

 Unit Writing Activity

Write a Narrative Write a short story about one of the people or events in the Southwest described in this unit.

■ Tell where and when your story takes place.

■ Include facts about the person or event.

■ Use descriptive language and include details.

Unit Project

Design a Scrapbook Design a scrapbook that honors notable people, events, or achievements in the Southwest during the 1900s.

■ Write a short paragraph that summarizes each person, event, or achievement.

■ Include illustrations in your scrapbook.

Read More

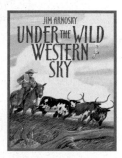

■ *Miss Lady Bird's Wildflowers* by Kathi Appelt. HarperCollins.

■ *Under the Wild Western Sky* by Jim Arnosky. HarperCollins.

■ *The Grand Canyon's Long-Eared Taxi* by Karen L. Taylor. Grand Canyon Association.

GO ONLINE For more resources, go to www.harcourtschool.com/ss1

The West

The Big Idea

Diversity

As the largest of the five regions of the United States, the West is a region of diversity.

What to Know

- ✓ What is the geography of the West?
- ✓ What events greatly increased the settlement of the West?
- ✓ How does control of much of the land in the West differ from other regions?
- ✓ What is the West like today?

Unit

6

Time

The West

● **1500s** The Shoshone, Paiutes, Yokuts, Pomo, and Makahs live in what is now the West, p. 383

1500   **1600**   **1700**

At the Same Time

1522 Ferdinand Magellan's crew completes a voyage around the world

1733 Southeast James Oglethorpe founds the Georgia Colony

The West

1805 Lewis and Clark reach the Pacific Ocean, p. 384

1869 The Transcontinental Railroad is completed, p. 386

1959 Alaska and Hawaii become states, p. 387

Present Silicon Valley, California, is one of the high-tech centers in the world, p. 411

1800

1900

Present

1803 Midwest Ohio becomes a state

1947 Southeast Henry Flager builds a railroad in Florida, from Miami to Key West

1990s The Internet becomes important in telecommunication

Meriwether Lewis

1774–1809
- **Explorer and soldier**
- **Led an expedition with William Clark to explore the Louisiana Purchase**

Sacagawea

1786?–1812
- **Shoshone guide and interpreter**
  - **Traveled with the Lewis and Clark expedition**

People

1750	1800	1850

1774 • Meriwether Lewis   1809

1786? • Sacagawea   1812

1801 • Brigham Young

1838 • Queen Liliuokalani

Margaret Murie

1902–2003
- **Known as the Grandmother of the Conservation Movement**
- **Awarded the Medal of Freedom for protecting the wilderness**

Eppie Archuleta

1922–present
- **Hispanic weaver and teacher**
- **Received the National Heritage Award for her handmade textiles**

Brigham Young

1801–1877
- Led a migration of Mormons to Salt Lake Valley, Utah
- First governor of the Territory of Utah

Queen Liliuokalani

1838–1917
- Last queen of the Hawaiian Islands
- Author of *Hawaii's Story by Hawaii's Queen*

1900	1950	PRESENT

1877

1917

1902 • Margaret Murie   2003

1922 • Eppie Archuleta

1953 • Antonio Villaraigosa

1955 • Bill Gates

Antonio Villaraigosa

1953–present
- First Hispanic mayor of Los Angeles since 1872
- In 2005, he won about 6 out of every 10 votes in the election

Bill Gates

1955–present
- Entrepreneur and computer software inventor
- Founder of the world's largest computer software company

CANADA

Puget Sound

North Cascades National Park

Olympic National Park

Seattle

Olympia ★   WASHINGTON

Grand Coulee Dam

Spokane

▲ Mt. Rainier National Park

Mt. Rainier 14,410 ft.

Portland ●

Columbia River

Coast Ranges

Cascade Range

Mt. Hood 11,235 ft.

Salem ★

Eugene ●   OREGON

IDAHO

Columbia Plateau

Crater Lake National Park

Boise ★

Snake River

Redwood National Park

Lassen Volcanic National Park

GREAT BASIN

Sierra Nevada

Sacramento River

Coast Ranges

Reno ●

Carson City ●   NEVADA

Great Basin National Park

San Francisco ●

San Joaquin River

Sacramento ★

San Jose ●

Yosemite National Park

Death Valley National Park

Kings Canyon National Park

Sequoia National Park

Mt. Whitney 14,495 ft.

Las Vegas ●

PACIFIC OCEAN

CALIFORNIA   Mojave Desert

Hoover Dam   Lake Mead

Channel Islands National Park

Joshua Tree National Park

Los Angeles ●

Salton Sea

San Diego ●

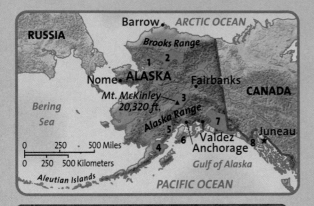

RUSSIA

Barrow ●   ARCTIC OCEAN

Brooks Range

1   2

Nome ●   ALASKA

Fairbanks ●   CANADA

Mt. McKinley 20,320 ft.   3

Bering Sea

Alaska Range

7

5   4   6   Valdez   8   Juneau ★

Anchorage ●

Gulf of Alaska

0   250   500 Miles
0   250   500 Kilometers

Aleutian Islands

PACIFIC OCEAN

ALASKA'S NATIONAL PARKS

1 Kobuk Valley National Park

2 Gates of the Arctic National Park

3 Denali National Park

4 Katmai National Park

5 Lake Clark National Park

6 Kenai Fjords National Park

7 Wrangell–St. Elias National Park

8 Glacier Bay National Park

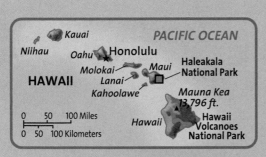

Kauai

Niihau   Oahu   Honolulu

PACIFIC OCEAN

Molokai   Maui   Haleakala National Park

HAWAII   Lanai

Kahoolawe   Mauna Kea 13,796 ft.

Hawaii

Hawaii Volcanoes National Park

0   50   100 Miles
0   50   100 Kilometers

Food processing

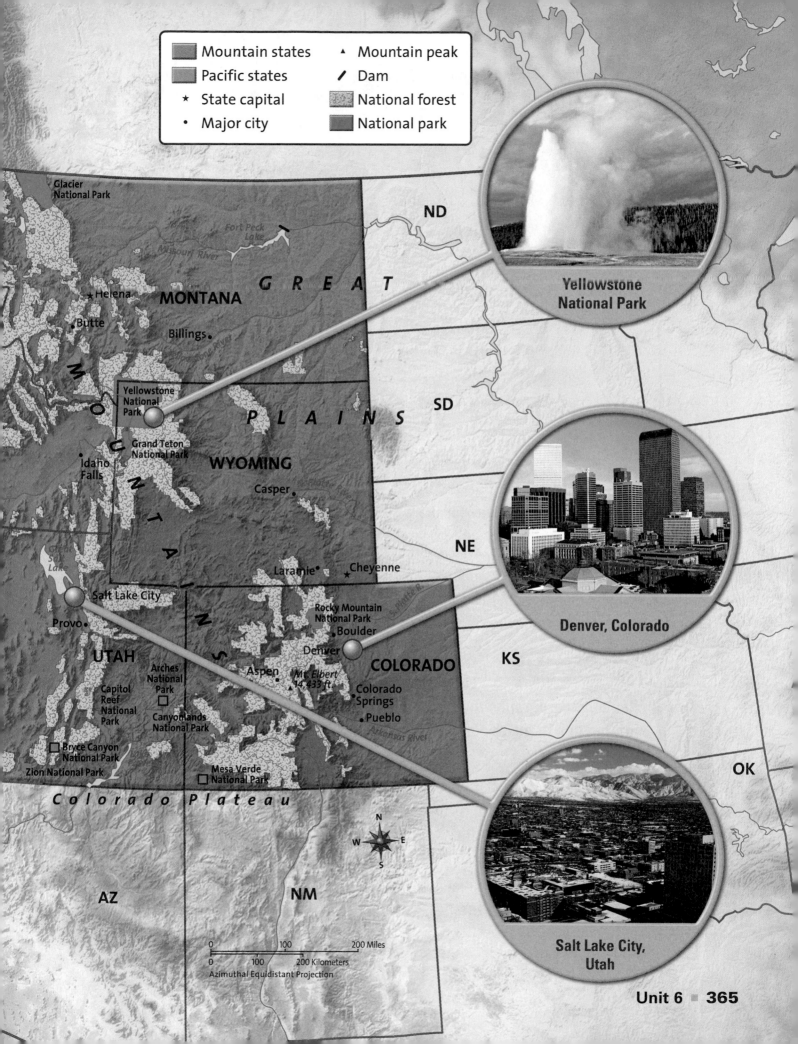

Mountain states
Pacific states
★ State capital
• Major city
▲ Mountain peak
/ Dam
National forest
National park

Glacier National Park

MONTANA
★ Helena
• Butte
Billings

GREAT

ND

Fort Peck Lake

Missouri River

Yellowstone National Park

Yellowstone National Park

P L A I N S

SD

Grand Teton National Park

WYOMING

Idaho Falls

Casper

Laramie• ★ Cheyenne

NE

Denver, Colorado

Great Salt Lake

Salt Lake City

Provo•

UTAH

Arches National Park

Capitol Reef National Park

Canyonlands National Park

Bryce Canyon National Park

Zion National Park

Rocky Mountain National Park
• Boulder

Denver •

COLORADO

Aspen •
▲ Mt. Elbert 14,433 ft.

Colorado Springs

• Pueblo

KS

South Platte R.

Arkansas River

Mesa Verde National Park

Colorado Plateau

AZ

NM

Salt Lake City, Utah

OK

N
W   E
S

0   100   200 Miles
0   100   200 Kilometers
Azimuthal Equidistant Projection

Reading Social Studies

(Focus Skill) Generalize

Why It Matters Being able to generalize can help you better understand what you read.

❯ LEARN

When you **generalize**, you make a broad statement. This statement summarizes a group of facts and shows how they are related.

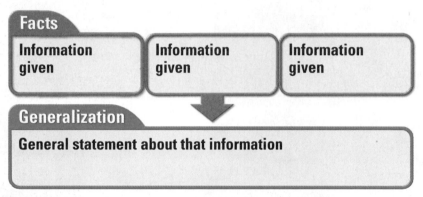

Facts

| Information given | Information given | Information given |

Generalization

General statement about that information

- A generalization is always based on facts.
- Signal words include *most, many, some, generally,* and *usually.*

❯ PRACTICE

Read the paragraphs that follow. Make a generalization based on the information in the second paragraph.

Facts   Pikes Peak, in the Rocky Mountains, was discovered by the explorer Zebulon Pike. The French mapmaker Samuel de Champlain discovered Lake Champlain. Josiah Whitney made a detailed map of Mount Whitney. **Generalization** (Places are sometimes named after the people who explore them.)

Christopher Columbus's first voyage to the Americas was paid for by the king and queen of Spain, who hoped to profit from what was found. Under President Thomas Jefferson, the United States government provided money for exploring the West.

Read the paragraphs, and answer the questions.

An Explorer's Life

An explorer's job was not easy. Explorers often traveled through unknown wilderness and desert regions. They had to survive extremely hot and cold weather. They risked hunger, sickness, and attacks from wild animals.

The explorer Sebastián Rodríquez Cermenho (sair•MAY•ayoh) was in a ship that hit rocks off the California coast. To get home, Cermenho and his crew built a smaller boat from what was left of the wreck. The English sailor Sir John Franklin explored farther north. His ship got trapped in ice, and some of the crew died.

Jedediah Smith became the first person who was not a Native American to reach California from the east. He crossed huge deserts in Utah, Nevada, and California along the way. He also traveled through these deserts on his return journey. The temperatures became so hot that he and his men buried themselves in sand to keep cool.

Explorers often got help from Native Americans. Kit Carson wanted to travel from Nevada to California in the winter of 1844. He spoke with Native Americans first. They warned him about the snowy mountains he would have to cross. Earlier, Native Americans in New Mexico helped Spanish explorer Juan de Oñate (ohn•YAH•tay). They showed Oñate and his men how to survive in the desert. Meriwether Lewis and William Clark explored the West in the early 1800s. They found help from a Native American guide named Sacagawea.

Generalize

Focus Skill

1. What generalization can you make about an explorer's life?

2. What generalization can you make about how explorers got along with Native Americans?

Two Bear Cubs

A Miwok Legend from California's Yosemite Valley

retold by Robert D. San Souci
illustrated by Daniel San Souci

The Miwok (MEE•wahk) are a Native American group from California's Yosemite Valley. They called their land *Ah-wah'-nee*. The Miwok often told a story about how El Capitan, one of the valley's landforms, came to be. According to the story, two bear cubs wandered away from their mother. While the cubs slept on a rock beside the Merced River, the rock grew higher—as high as a mountain.

Red-tailed Hawk spotted the cubs sleeping on top of the rock. Mouse, Badger, Gray Fox, Mother Deer, and Mountain Lion all tried to help Mother Grizzly rescue the two cubs, but none of the animals could reach them. Read now to find out how the cubs were rescued by Measuring Worm.

So Measuring Worm began to creep up the rock, curling himself into an arch, anchoring himself with his four short back legs, then stretching out his body until his six front legs could grasp another bit of stone. Curling and stretching, he inched his way up. While he climbed he chanted, *"Tú-tok! Tú-tok!"* When he curved his body, that was *"Tú,"* and when he stretched out, that was *"tok."*

As he went, he marked the safe path with a sticky thread, for Measuring Worm can make a string like a spider.

In time, he went even higher than Mountain Lion. The animals below could no longer see him, or hear his little song, *"Tú-tok! Tú-tok!"*

Up and up and up he went. Day turned to night over and over, and still he climbed. Beneath him, Mother Grizzly and the other animals kept anxious watch. Above, the cubs slept peacefully, wrapped in cloud-blankets.

Once Measuring Worm looked down and saw that the mighty river now seemed only a thin band of silver, decorated with sparkling rapids and green islands. The forests and meadows of the valley floor looked no bigger than bunches of twigs and moss. At this sight, Measuring Worm grew afraid. For a time, he could not move at all. But he found his courage again. He began to sing, *"Tú-tok! Tú-tok!"* as loudly as he could, and crept still higher up the wall.

Day after day, Measuring Worm climbed, until at last, early one morning, he reached the top of the vast stone. He softly whispered into the ears of the two cubs, "Wake up!" He was afraid that if he woke them too quickly, they might become frightened and fall off the slippery rock.

When they saw how high above the river they were, the cubs began to cry. But Measuring Worm comforted them. "Follow me," he said. "I will guide you safely down the mountain, for I have marked a safe path with my string."

To the brown cub Measuring Worm said, "Older Brother, you follow right behind me." Then, to the one with cinnamon-colored fur, he said, "Younger Brother, follow your brother and make your every step the same as his. Do this, and you will not fall."

Still the cubs were fearful. But Measuring Worm said, "Surely Mother Grizzly's children are not cowards, for she is the bravest creature in *Ah-wah'-nee*."

Then the two little bears puffed out their chests and said, "We are brave. We will follow you."

So they began the slow climb down, both cubs doing just what Measuring Worm told them.

After a long time, sharp-eyed Gray Fox spotted them. He told Mother Grizzly, "See! Your cubs are returning." Anxiously she looked where her friend was pointing. Sure enough, there she saw her cubs making their way down the face of the mountain, as Measuring Worm guided their every step and called encouragement to them.

At last the little bears and their rescuer reached the valley floor. Then how joyfully Mother Grizzly gathered her cubs to her heart and hugged them and scolded them for not minding her and then hugged them again. Loudly she praised Measuring Worm for his courage and resourcefulness.

Then all the animals decided to call the rock that grew to be a mountain *Tu-tok-a-nu-la*, which means Measuring Worm Stone, in honor of the heroic worm who had done what no other creature could do. And so the towering landmark was known for many years, until newcomers renamed the huge granite wall "El Capitan."

Response Corner

1. **(Focus Skill) Generalize** How was Measuring Worm able to rescue the bear cubs?

2. **Make It Relevant** How do people you know use stories, poems, and songs?

STUDY SKILLS

POSE QUESTIONS

Asking questions as you read can help you understand what you are learning.

- **Form questions as you read. Think about why and how events happened and how events and ideas are related.**

- **Use the questions to guide your reading. Look for the answers as you read.**

Exploring the West

Questions	Answers
What are some of the major landforms of the West?	The West has mountains, basins, deserts, and plateaus.

PREVIEW VOCABULARY

volcano p. 376   **telegraph** p. 386   **hydroelectricity** p. 392

Rockies to the Pacific

The Rocky Mountains run through North America from north to south. They mark the end of the Midwest and the beginning of the West.

Mountains and More

The Rocky Mountains are among the highest mountains in North America. An imaginary line runs north and south along their peaks. This line is called the **Continental Divide**. All rivers to the east of this line flow toward the Atlantic Ocean. All rivers west of this line flow toward the Pacific Ocean.

To the west of the Rockies, the Great Basin forms a huge desert. The Columbia Plateau lies to its north. The Colorado Plateau lies to its south. Farther west are mountain ranges that run parallel to the Pacific coast. They include the Sierra Nevada and the Cascade and Coast Ranges. Alaska and Hawaii have mountains, as well.

Highs and Lows

The highest land and the lowest land in the United States are both in the West. The highest is the 20,320-foot peak of Alaska's **Mount McKinley**. It is also known as Denali, which means "the great one" in a Native American language. The lowest is 282 feet below sea level in **Death Valley,** California.

READING CHECK **GENERALIZE**
What is the geography of the West like?

GRAND TETON is the highest peak of the Rockies that run through Wyoming. A rock climber (above) tests his skills in the mountains.

Big Changes

Long ago, changes happening deep inside Earth formed mountains in the West. The same kinds of changes are still going on today.

Fiery Mountains

Some of the West's mountains are volcanoes. A **volcano** is a mountain formed when erupted lava cools and hardens onto Earth's surface. **Lava** is melted rock. A bowl-shaped area called a **crater** can form at the volcano's top.

Most volcanoes in the West are in states that border the Pacific Ocean. These include Mauna Loa (MOW•nah LOH•uh) in Hawaii, Mount Rainier in Washington, and Mount Hood in Oregon.

Shaky Ground

Changes inside Earth can also cause earthquakes. An **earthquake** is a sudden shaking of the ground. This movement occurs along **faults**—cracks in Earth's outer layer. Small movements along faults can cause earthquakes that people do not feel. Large movements can damage entire cities or even larger areas.

Like volcanoes, most earthquakes in the West occur in states that border the Pacific Ocean. This is because the rock layers under the Pacific Ocean move against those of our continent.

READING CHECK Ŏ**GENERALIZE**
What generalization can you make about volcanoes and earthquakes?

⚡**FAST FACT**

Mount Saint Helens in Washington erupted in 1980. This event created one of the largest volcanic eruptions ever recorded in North America.

▶ **FOREST FIRES** can spread quickly in the dry areas of the West.

Climate

The West's climate varies. It ranges from the heat of the California desert to the frozen land of northern Alaska.

Mountains Affect Climate

Like other regions, the West has a warmer climate in the south than in the north. Its many tall mountains also affect its climate. As elevation increases, the temperature drops. A warm, rainy day in a valley may be a cold, snowy day on a nearby peak.

Climate changes on mountain slopes affect plant life, too. It is too cold for trees to grow above the **timberline**. Below the timberline, forests thrive.

Setting Records

The West's geography creates extreme climates. Death Valley is not only the country's lowest land but also its driest and hottest. Its average yearly rainfall is less than two inches. The highest temperature ever recorded there was 134°F in 1913. In contrast, the coldest temperature ever recorded in the United States was 80°F below zero at **Prospect Creek**, Alaska. In the country's rainiest place, **Mount Waialeale** (wy•ah•lay•AH•lay) in Hawaii, it rains about 335 days each year.

READING CHECK 🌀 **GENERALIZE**

What generalizations can you make about the West's climate?

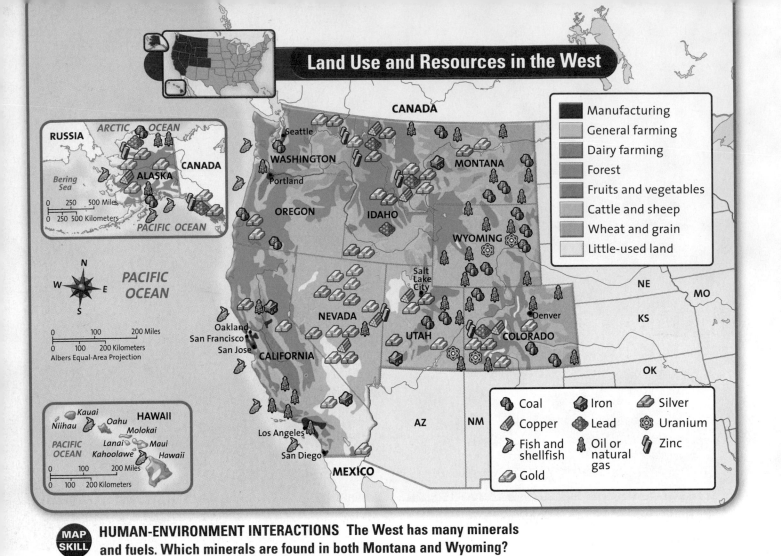

MAP SKILL HUMAN-ENVIRONMENT INTERACTIONS The West has many minerals and fuels. Which minerals are found in both Montana and Wyoming?

Natural Resources

A variety of natural resources can be found in the West. These resources include its land, forests, minerals, fuels, water, and fish.

Land

Much of the land in the West is either too mountainous or too dry for farming. However, states along the Pacific coast have huge agricultural industries. California has long been the nation's leading agricultural state. Most of the state's crops are grown on irrigated land. Farmers in Oregon produce a variety of crops. These crops include grains, vegetables, and fruits. Washington is the nation's leading producer of apples.

In the flatter, drier parts of states, such as in Montana and Wyoming, ranching is important. Ranchers in the region raise mostly cattle and sheep.

On the mountain slopes in the West, huge forests of pine, spruce, and fir grow. As in other regions, people harvest these trees to make lumber and paper products. In central California, giant trees called sequoias (sih•KWOY•uhz) grow. Redwoods, the tallest living trees, grow near the coast from central California to southern Oregon. Many redwoods are more than 300 feet tall!

Water

Although the West includes a lot of dry areas, the region has several major rivers. These include the Missouri, the Colorado, the Columbia, and many smaller rivers. Great Salt Lake, in Utah, is the largest natural lake west of the Mississippi River. The coastal waters of the northern Pacific Ocean are rich in fish and shellfish, including salmon, flounder, tuna, crabs, oysters, and clams.

READING CHECK **MAIN IDEA AND DETAILS**
What are some of the natural resources found in the West?

Summary

The West is a vast region of mountains, basins, plateaus, and deserts. It also has extreme elevations and climates. Its natural resources include forests, minerals, and fish.

❯ **FISHING is an important industry in Alaska.**

REVIEW

1. WHAT TO KNOW What landforms and natural resources does the West have?

2. VOCABULARY What is the **Continental Divide**, and how does it affect rivers?

3. GEOGRAPHY Where are most volcanoes found in the West?

4. CRITICAL THINKING What part of the West would be the best place to live? Give reasons to support your answer.

5. ✎ **MAKE A TABLE** Make a two-column table that describes places in the West. One column should list a place's name. The second column should use adjectives such as *highest, lowest, hottest, driest,* or *rainiest.*

6. (Focus Skill) **GENERALIZE** On a separate sheet of paper, copy and complete the graphic organizer below.

Facts		
The Rockies are high.	Death Valley is hot.	Mount Waialeale is wet.

Generalization

Read a Time Zone Map

Why It Matters Knowing how to read a time zone map will help you know what time it is anywhere in the world.

❯ LEARN

People divide Earth into 24 time zones. A **time zone** is a region in which all the people use the same clock time. The map on page 381 shows that the United States has 6 time zones. The clocks on the map show that each time zone has a time that is one hour earlier than the time zone to its east. You can add or subtract hours to figure out the time in different time zones.

Denver, Colorado, for example, is in the Mountain time zone. Miami, Florida, is in the Eastern time zone. The clocks on the map show that the Mountain time zone is two hours earlier than the Eastern time zone. So, if it is 3:00 P.M. in Denver, it is 5:00 P.M. in Miami.

❯ PRACTICE

Use the time zone map to answer these questions.

❶ Is the time in Seattle, Washington, earlier than, later than, or the same as the time in Boise, Idaho?

❷ If it is midnight in St. Louis, Missouri, what time is it in El Paso, Texas?

❸ How many time zones does the West region have?

❯ **IDAHO** People traveling from Idaho to Oregon might see this sign.

United States Time Zones

> APPLY

Make It Relevant Record the time it is in your own time zone. Then use the map to help you figure out what time it is in each of the other five time zones in the United States.

Map and Globe Skills

Lesson

Time

| 1500 | 1750 | Present |

1804
Lewis and Clark set out to explore the West

1869
The transcontinental railroad is completed

1959
Alaska and Hawaii become the 49th and 50th states

WHAT TO KNOW
Why did settlers move to the West?

VOCABULARY
barrier p. 384

wagon train p. 385

forty-niner p. 385

boomtown p. 385

telegraph p. 386

transcontinental railroad p. 386

PEOPLE
Meriwether Lewis
William Clark
Sacagawea

PLACES
The Dalles
South Pass
Sacramento
Helena
Denver
Promontory

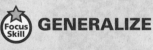

GENERALIZE

Facts		

Generalization

Early History of the West

YOU ARE THERE

It is the 1700s. You sit in the middle of a large canoe. Your father and mother are paddling. The canoe is loaded with dried salmon and whale oil to trade. Your brother paddles a new canoe next to yours. Your father will trade that canoe for furs and baskets.

As the canoes round a bend, you see the trading center ahead. On the shore, people of many tribes trade what they have for what they need.

▶ **THE MAKAH** and other groups lived along the Pacific coast. They caught fish such as cod and salmon. They also hunted whales and seals. They used whale oil and seal oil for fuel.

Early People

Long before Europeans arrived in the 1500s, many different Native American groups lived throughout the West. These groups included the Shoshone, Paiute, Yokuts, Pomo, and Makah.

Different Cultures

Each Native American group in the West had its own culture. People in the arid Great Basin, such as the Shoshone and Paiute, were nomads. They survived on small animals, nuts, seeds, and roots. The Pomo and Yokuts lived in what is now California. They made flour from acorns and hunted deer and rabbits.

Trading Networks

Rivers made long-distance travel possible. It was much faster to canoe on a river than to walk through dense forests. The people of the West used rivers to create trading networks.

The Dalles, a waterfall on the Columbia River, was a major trading center. People traveled great distances to trade goods that they had for those that they wanted. The Chinook (shuh•NUK) were among the most successful traders. They invented a language to help themselves communicate and trade with different groups.

READING CHECK ŎGENERALIZE
What generalization can you make about Native Americans of the West?

▶ **EXPLORATION** Sacagawea helped Lewis and Clark on their journey.

Exploring the West

Until the early 1800s, most people in the United States knew little about the West. Then, explorers began to push beyond the Rocky Mountains.

Lewis and Clark

In 1804, **Meriwether Lewis** and **William Clark** led a group to explore the West. They left from what is now St. Louis and traveled up the Missouri River to what is now North Dakota. From there, a Shoshone woman named **Sacagawea** (sa•kuh•juh•WEE•uh) joined them as a guide. In 1805, the group reached the Pacific Ocean.

The Way West

The Rockies were a barrier to westward travel. A **barrier** is something that blocks the way. The Rockies were steep and often covered in snow. In winter, temperatures were freezing.

At first, only a few explorers and fur trappers tried to cross the Rockies. Then, some trappers found a pass, or an opening between the mountains. They named it the **South Pass.** It is near where the states of Wyoming, Utah, and Colorado meet. The South Pass became a door to the West.

READING CHECK ⚙GENERALIZE
How were the Rockies a barrier to the West?

Settlers Head West

The South Pass was low enough that covered wagons could cross the Rockies. Starting in 1843, thousands of settlers drove wagons through the pass to start new lives in the West.

Beyond the Mountains

Most settlers joined wagon trains. A **wagon train** is a group of wagons, each pulled by horses, mules, or oxen.

Few newcomers settled in the mountains. There conditions were harsh. Many headed for the Oregon Country. That was their name for the land that is now Oregon, Washington, and parts of other states. This land had rich soil, a mild climate, and plenty of rain. Farmers were able to grow vegetables and fruit.

Gold!

In 1848, workers building a sawmill near **Sacramento**, California, found gold nuggets. As the news spread, people rushed to California hoping to get rich. In a short time, about 80,000 people arrived in California. These gold-seekers were called **forty-niners** because the first of them arrived in 1849.

Gold rushes occurred in other parts of the West, too. With each discovery, miners flocked to the area. New towns sprang up. They were called **boomtowns** because they grew so fast. **Helena**, Montana, and **Denver**, Colorado, started as boomtowns. Today they are state capitals.

READING CHECK **CAUSE AND EFFECT**
What caused boomtowns to spring up in the West?

Children IN HISTORY

Virginia Reed

Virginia Reed was the daughter of James Reed, a leader of a settler group called the Donner party. Virginia was 12 years old when her family set out for California from Missouri. At the Sierra Nevada, heavy snows trapped them. Virginia recalled that the snowstorms "often lasted ten days at a time." Virginia later wrote that the "children were crying with hunger, and the mothers were crying because they had so little to give their children."

Make It Relevant Do you think the Sierra Nevada is easier to cross today? Explain your answer.

The Transcontinental Railroad

June 28, 1861
Judah and the Big Four form the Central Pacific Railroad Company

October 27, 1863
The Central Pacific Railroad lays track eastward from Sacramento, California

July 1865
The Union Pacific Railroad lays track Westward from Omaha, Nebraska

May 10, 1869
The "Last Spike" is driven at a ceremony at Promontory, Utah

Time

1860   1865   1870

TIME LINE How many years did it take to build the transcontinental railroad?

Linking the Coasts

By 1860, many settlements had grown up along the Pacific coast. Vast, mountainous lands divided them from the rest of the nation.

Communication and Transportation

In 1860 and 1861, the Pony Express carried mail to the West. It began in Missouri, where the railroad ended. It worked like a relay race. Each rider carried mail for about 75 miles. Mail reached California in 10 days.

The telegraph soon ended the Pony Express. A **telegraph** is a machine that uses electricity to send messages over wires. The telegraph could send messages between coasts within minutes.

To improve transportation, the United States paid for a **transcontinental railroad**. In 1857, one engineer wrote,

> **❝It is the most magnificent project ever conceived [thought of].❞**

One company began laying track in Nebraska and headed west. Another started in California and headed east. The tracks met on May 10, 1869, in **Promontory,** Utah. Now, a trip from New York to California takes less than two weeks.

The railroad brought more settlers to the West. California, Oregon, and Nevada were already states. By 1896, Colorado, Washington, Montana, Wyoming, Idaho, and Utah were states.

States 49 and 50

The United States added new lands even farther west. It bought Alaska from Russia in 1867. Hawaii became a territory of the United States in 1898. Alaska and Hawaii became the forty-ninth and fiftieth states in 1959.

Today, the United States has other territories in the Pacific. These include Guam, American Samoa, and other Pacific islands.

READING CHECK 🔥**GENERALIZE**
What was the general direction of the settlement of the United States?

Summary

Native Americans of the West were fishers, hunters, gatherers, and traders. The discovery of the South Pass and gold brought many settlers to the region. The transcontinental railroad linked the West to the rest of the United States.

▶ **STATEHOOD** In 1959, this young girl in Hawaii showed her support for statehood.

REVIEW

1. WHAT TO KNOW Why did settlers move to the West?

2. VOCABULARY What was a **forty-niner**?

3. HISTORY When was gold discovered in the West?

4. CRITICAL THINKING How do you think the transcontinental railroad changed life in the West?

5. ✏️ **MAKE A TIME LINE** Make a time line using five important dates in the lesson. Illustrate two of your time line entries.

6. ⭐(Focus Skill) **GENERALIZE**
On a separate sheet of paper, copy and complete the graphic organizer below.

Facts		
Settlers begin to move to the West in 1843.	By 1860, many settlements exist in the West.	By 1896, many states exist in the West.

Generalization

Gold Miners

Background At the time of the gold rushes, much of the West was wilderness. Miners often lived in simple mining camps located many miles away from the nearest town. They needed sturdy tools to help them do their work. In time, the miners developed new tools that made searching for gold easier.

DBQ **Document-Based Question** Study these primary sources and answer the questions.

Gold nuggets

METAL PAN

Miners swirled metal pans filled with gold-bearing water. This process separated any gold from the water.

DBQ ❶ Why might it be easier to pan for gold on a sunny day?

Metal rivet

CLOTHES

Miners needed clothes that would be long lasting. In 1873, Levi Strauss and a partner designed pants that had metal rivets on the pockets to make them strong.

DBQ ❷ Why might long-lasting clothes have been so important to miners?

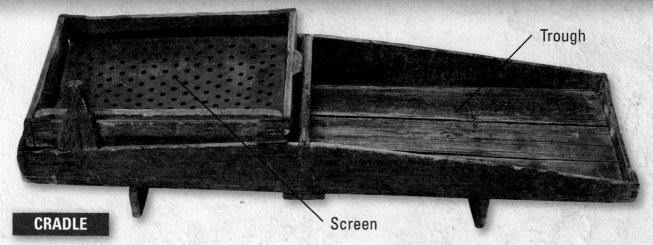

Trough

Screen

CRADLE

At least two people were needed to operate a cradle. With this tool, they used a rocking motion to separate gold from dirt and rocks.

DBQ **3** Why do you think this tool was called a cradle?

Iron head

ADVERTISEMENT

This advertisement is for a store that sold supplies to miners. Such stores also served as mail and banking centers.

DBQ **4** What are some items for sale at the store?

Handle

PICK

Miners dug for gold with picks like this one.

DBQ **5** Why do you think the iron head has two ends?

GOOD NEWS
FOR
MINERS.
NEW GOODS,
PROVISIONS, TOOLS,
CLOTHING, &c. &c.
GREAT BARGAINS!

WRITE ABOUT IT

What do these primary sources tell you about a gold miner's life? Select one item and write how it made a miner's life a little easier.

GO **ONLINE** For more resources, go to www.harcourtschool.com/ss1

Environment of the West

WHAT TO KNOW
How do people in the West use and protect the environment?

VOCABULARY
public land p. 391
hydroelectricity p. 392
ecosystem p. 393

PEOPLE
Theodore Roosevelt

PLACES
Wallace
Grand Coulee Dam
Yellowstone National Park
Muir Woods
Natural Bridges

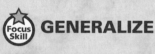

GENERALIZE

Facts

Generalization

YOU ARE THERE Today you are touring a real silver mine in **Wallace**, Idaho. Wearing a hard hat, you follow your guide into the mine.

The guide explains how miners remove silver from a mine. He knows just how it is done, because he is a retired miner.

"My father was a miner," he tells you, "and now my son is a miner. We never seem to run out of silver here in Idaho!"

> **WORKERS MINING IN IDAHO**

Public Lands of the United States

Public lands

Albers Equal-Area Projection

MAP SKILL REGIONS Which states have the most public land?

Natural Resources

In the 1800s, natural resources brought settlers to the West. These same resources are still important to the region's economy.

Managing Land

In the mid-1800s, the United States government encouraged people to settle all across the West. Early settlers there built an economy based on mining, farming, ranching, logging, and fishing.

In the late 1800s, government leaders decided to stop settlement on some lands that held valuable resources. They believed that the government should manage, or control, these resources. This was the beginning of **public land**, or land that is owned by the government.

Today, the United States government manages much of the land in the West where valuable resources are found. The government controls such economic activities as logging, ranching, and mining on these lands. It requires people to pay rent when they use the land for economic activities. The government also controls recreational use of these public lands.

READING CHECK ŎGENERALIZE
In the late 1800s, why did the government change which lands people could settle?

Dams in the West

People have built dams on some of the largest rivers in the West. They use these dams in many ways.

Controlling Rivers

When people build a dam across a river, water builds up behind the dam and forms a reservoir, or human-made lake. People then can take water from the reservoir to supply towns and cities and to irrigate farmland.

People also use dams to prevent damage caused by flooding. To do this, they use dams to hold back floodwater. Later, they can slowly release this water.

At times, the water downstream from a dam can become too low.

The water upstream from a dam can become too high. By opening or closing valves at the dam, workers can adjust the water levels.

Water Power

People can also use the water in a reservoir to produce electricity. They release water from the reservoir onto huge turbines, or engines with fanlike blades attached. The water turns the blades, causing the engine to produce electricity. Electricity produced by water power is **hydroelectricity**. The **Grand Coulee Dam** in Washington produces more electricity than any other dam in the United States.

READING CHECK **MAIN IDEA AND DETAILS**
What are two reasons why people in the West build dams?

Hydroelectric Dam

ILLUSTRATION What machines are used to make electricity?

water stored in reservoir

Pipe

Power Plant

Generator

Turbine

Power lines

Power lines

Water returns to the river

▶ **CLEANUP** Workers and volunteers clean up after an oil spill in Alaska.

The Environment

When people use resources, they change the environment. Some of these changes can harm the environment and ecosystems. An **ecosystem** is a community of living things in a natural area and its environment.

Waterways and Wildlife

All over the nation, people take steps to protect the environment. In the West, dams once kept salmon from swimming up the Columbia River to lay their eggs. Soon there were fewer salmon left in the river. To protect the salmon, people built fish ladders. A fish ladder is like a stairway of pools of water. Salmon can jump from one pool to the next to get over the dam.

Ships that carry oil may damage the environment. If an oil tanker has an accident and breaks open, oil can spill into the sea, killing wildlife. People have designed ships with two walls to make oil spills less likely. They have also invented ways to keep oil spills from spreading.

Limits on Land Use

People also protect the environment by setting limits on how some of the land can be used. Some public lands, such as national parks and national forests, are set aside mostly for tourism. **Yellowstone National Park,** founded in 1872, was the nation's first national park. It covers parts of Idaho, Wyoming, and Montana.

▶ OLD FAITHFUL in Yellowstone National Park.

President **Theodore Roosevelt** loved the outdoors. He strongly supported protecting the land. In the early 1900s, Roosevelt created many national monuments in the West and Southwest. Two such monuments are **Muir Woods** in California and **Natural Bridges** in Utah.

READING CHECK ☾GENERALIZE
What generalization can you make about using resources?

Summary

People in the West depend on natural resources, just as they did in the past. Many of these resources are found on public lands in the region. People build dams and reservoirs to control water. The dams hold water for irrigation and to produce hydroelectricity. As people use resources, they look for ways to protect the environment.

REVIEW

1. **WHAT TO KNOW** How do people in the West use and protect the environment?

2. **VOCABULARY** How does a reservoir help make **hydroelectricity**?

3. **ECONOMICS** How have natural resources affected the West?

4. **CRITICAL THINKING** Why is it important for people to protect the environment?

5. ✎ **WRITE A PERSUASIVE LETTER** Decide whether public lands are a good idea or not. Then, write a letter to persuade someone else to agree with your opinion.

6. ⭐ **GENERALIZE**
   On a separate sheet of paper, copy and complete the graphic organizer below.

Facts

Generalization

People take steps to protect the environment.

Margaret Murie

Biography

Trustworthiness
Respect
Responsibility
Fairness
Caring
Patriotism

"I was destined for the outdoors."

Margaret Murie spent much of her life exploring the West's wilderness areas. She spent most of her life working to protect those untouched places.

Murie was born in Seattle, Washington, but grew up in Fairbanks, Alaska. After graduating from college, she and her husband moved to Wyoming. They built a log cabin below the peaks of the Teton Mountains.

Both Muries were considered leaders to those working for conservation. Partly as a result of their work, the United States government set up the Arctic National Wildlife Refuge in 1960. The government also passed the Wilderness Act. This act protects millions of acres of wilderness in the United States.

Margaret Murie received many awards for her conservation work. These awards include the Presidential Medal of Freedom.

Why Character Counts

How did Murie work to protect what she cared about?

Time

1902			2003
Born			Died

1924 Murie becomes the first woman to graduate from the University of Alaska

1964 Congress passes the Wilderness Act

1998 Murie is awarded the Presidential Medal of Freedom

GO ONLINE For more resources, go to www.harcourtschool.com/ss1

How Should Public Lands Be Used?

For decades, Americans have disagreed about how our public lands should be used. Some people believe that public lands should be used for their natural resources. Others believe that these resources should be protected. Still others argue that public lands should be made private. Here are some different points of view on this subject.

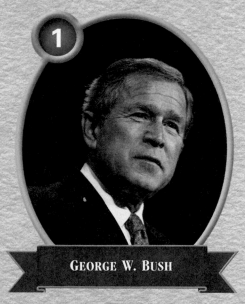

1

GEORGE W. BUSH

George W. Bush is President of the United States. He believes public lands can be used for their resources and be protected.

❝ I believe we can develop our natural resources and protect our environment. ❞

2

NANCI IVIS

Nanci Ivis is an environmentalist in San Francisco, California. She believes that the natural resources on public lands should be protected.

❝ The natural resources on public lands should be protected before they all disappear. ❞

3

GALE NORTON

Gale Norton is the secretary
of the United States Department of the Interior.
She believes public lands should be used for
their natural resources.

66 Our [public lands] improve our
lives by giving us recreation, food,
energy, water, shelter and clothing.
We build houses, hospitals, dams and
bridges from our land's assets. 99

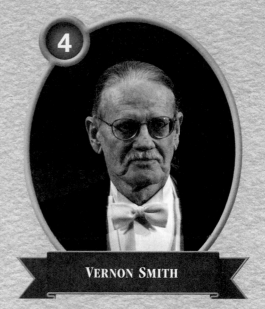

4

VERNON SMITH

Vernon Smith is a professor
at George Mason University in Virginia. He
believes that all public lands should be sold to
individuals.

66 [I support] auctioning off all
public lands over 20 to 40 years. Both
environmental quality and economic
efficiency would be enhanced by private rather than public ownership. 99

It's Your Turn

Compare Points of View Summarize each person's point of
view. Then answer the questions.

1. Who seems to support using the natural resources of
public lands?

2. Who uses conservation to defend their point of view?

3. How is Vernon Smith's point of view different from all the
others?

Make It Relevant What do *you* think? Explain why one argument is more persuasive to you than the other.

1500
The Makah and other Native Americans live along the Pacific coast

Visual Summary

Summarize the Chapter

Generalize Complete this graphic organizer to show that you understand how to make generalizations about the West.

Facts

| The West has the nation's hottest and coldest places. | The West has the nation's driest and wettest places. | The West has the nation's highest and lowest places. |

Generalization

 **Vocabulary**

Choose the correct word from the word bank to complete each sentence.

1. It is too cold for trees to grow above the _____.

2. A _____ can create a mountain when it erupts.

3. An _____ is caused by movement of Earth's crust.

4. _____ went west hoping to find gold.

5. The plants and animals in the environment make up an area's _____.

6. The government controls economic activities on _____.

7. The Rocky Mountains were a _____ to westward travel.

Word Bank

volcano p. 376   forty-niners p. 385

earthquake p. 376   public land p. 391

timberline p. 377   ecosystem p. 393

barrier p. 384

1750   1875   Present

1804
Lewis and Clark
explore the Northwest

1872
Yellowstone National
Park is the world's
first national park

 Time Line

Use the chapter summary time line above to answer these questions.

8. Which happened first, Lewis and Clark explored the Northwest, or Yellowstone became a national park?

9. When did Lewis and Clark begin their expedition?

 Facts and Main Ideas

Answer these questions.

10. Where are most of the West's volcanoes?

11. Why were rivers important to the Native Americans in what is now the West?

12. Why did the Pony Express operate for only a short time?

Write the letter of the best choice.

13. Which physical feature most shapes life in the West?
    A lakes
    B plains
    C deserts
    D mountains

14. What is one way that people are helping protect the environment of the West?
    A by shipping oil
    B by building fish ladders
    C by buying public land
    D by changing ecosystems

 Critical Thinking

15. Explain the meaning of this sentence: The South Pass became a door to the West.

16. Why do you think most settlers in the West traveled there as part of wagon trains?

 **Skills**

Read a Time Zone Map
Use the map on page 381 to answer the questions below.

17. If it is noon in the Mountain time zone, what time is it in the Pacific time zone?

18. In which time zone is Washington, D.C.?

writing

✎ **Write a Narrative** Write a story about a settler moving to the West in the 1800s. In your story, tell why your main character went West, where he or she settled, and what he or she did after arriving.

✎ **Write an Explanation** Imagine that you are writing a news article. Explain one way in which people in the West protect the environment.

STUDY SKILLS

QUESTION-AND-ANSWER RELATIONSHIPS

By knowing that different types of questions need different types of answers, you will know how to write proper responses.

- **Questions with the words *who, what, where, when,* and *how* require you to use details in your answers.**

- **Questions that ask you to look at links between topics require you to state the connections in your answers.**

Questions About Details	Questions About Connections
Question: What states within the West region make up the Mountain states?	Question: How have mountains affected growth in the Mountain states?
Answer: Colorado, Idaho, Montana, Nevada, Utah, and Wyoming	Answer: Mountain areas have limited space for people to build cities. So, the Mountain states have few large cities.
Question: Where is Hawaii located?	Question: How has Hawaii's location affected its population?
Answer:	Answer:

PREVIEW VOCABULARY

satellite p. 403   **consumer** p. 405   **microchip** p. 412

The West Today

▶ A view of downtown Seattle, Washington

Lesson 1

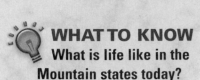

Mountain States

WHAT TO KNOW
What is life like in the Mountain states today?

VOCABULARY

satellite p. 403

Global Positioning System p. 403

consumer p. 405

PEOPLE

Brigham Young

Jeannette Rankin

PLACES

Bozeman

Cheyenne

Salt Lake City

Denver

Las Vegas

Boise

Focus Skill GENERALIZE

You ARE THERE
You and your family are having fun in **Bozeman**, Montana. At the Museum of the Rockies, you explored the history of the Rocky Mountains. You have also learned how to catch trout in a mountain stream and how to ride horses. Today, you're going to go cross-country skiing. It's summer, yet the peaks of the Beartooth Mountains are covered with snow!

Tomorrow, you and your family will drive on part of the Beartooth Scenic Byway on your way to visit Wyoming's capital city, **Cheyenne**.

▶ ABSAROKA-BEARTOOTH WILDERNESS IN MONTANA

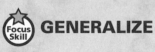

▶ **SALT LAKE CITY** is Utah's largest city and its capital.

Life in the Mountains

The Mountain states cover a large region. These states include Colorado, Idaho, Montana, Nevada, Utah, and Wyoming.

Independence and Challenges

The people in the Mountain states have a history of being independent. In the 1840s, Mormon religious leader **Brigham Young** and his followers looked for a place to worship freely. They settled what is today **Salt Lake City**, Utah. In 1869, the Wyoming Territory became the first place in the United States where women could vote and could hold office. In 1916, **Jeannette Rankin** of Montana became the first woman elected to Congress.

Mountains bring challenges to the people living there. Mountain areas have limited space for people to build cities. So, the Mountain states have few large cities. Mountains also block radio and television signals. However, people now use satellites to send signals over mountains. A **satellite** is an object that orbits Earth. Travel, too, in mountain areas can be dangerous.

A **Global Positioning System**, or GPS, makes mountain travel safer. This system of satellites and computers can show a person or object's exact location. A GPS can help locate people who become lost or stranded.

READING CHECK Ŏ**GENERALIZE**
How do people use technology to help them live among mountains?

Cities and Industries

Denver, Colorado, and **Las Vegas**, Nevada, are the largest cities in the Mountain states. The populations of each of these metropolitan areas is about 2 million people.

The Mile-High City

Denver's nickname is "the Mile-High City" because its elevation is 5,280 feet, or one mile, above sea level. Denver is east of the Rocky Mountains, on the edge of the Great Plains. The flat location has allowed Denver to grow. The city is the economic and transportation center of the region. It is also the capital of Colorado.

Tourism

The same mountains that limit the growth of cities make tourism a leading industry. All of the Mountain states have ski resorts.

National parks, national forests, and state parks cover large areas of the region. Most of Yellowstone National Park is in Wyoming. Humboldt-Toiyabe National Forest spreads over many parts of Nevada, including the shore of Lake Tahoe. Craters of the Moon National Monument and Preserve in Idaho has nearly half a million acres of hardened lava fields. People from around the world visit these places to hike, boat, fish, hunt, snowshoe, and cross-country ski.

▶ **SNOWSKIING** is just one of the many activities that people can enjoy at places such as Steamboat Springs, Colorado.

▶ **NELLIS AIR FORCE BASE** Soldiers load helicopters onto an airplane.

Government

The United States government affects the economy of the Mountain states because it owns large areas of land there. In fact, the government owns two-thirds of Utah's land and four-fifths of Nevada's land. Much of this land is used by the military. In Nevada, Nellis Air Force Base covers about 3 million acres.

Colorado has so many United States government offices that it is nicknamed the Washington of the West. One government center is the North American Aerospace Defense Command, or NORAD. There, the military works to protect the United States and Canada.

High Technology

Several Mountain states also have growing high-tech industries. Some of the high-tech businesses in the region do work for the United States government and the military. Other high-tech businesses make computer products for consumers. A **consumer** is a person who buys a product or a service. For example, you are a consumer when you buy a book or get a haircut. Most high-tech businesses are in the region's cities, which include Denver, Salt Lake City, and **Boise**, Idaho's capital and largest city.

READING CHECK **MAIN IDEA AND DETAILS**
Where are most of the Mountain states' high-tech businesses?

Global Connection

In other regions around the world, people live in mountainous areas. They face some of the same challenges as people living in the Mountain states. The lifestyles of some of those regions are also similar.

The Alps are the tallest mountains on the continent of Europe. Heavy snows sometimes block roads in the Alps. In some areas of the Alps in winter, people use skis, sleds, and snowmobiles to get around. People there also build houses with steep roofs. The snow slides off instead of piling up and crushing their houses!

Tourism, especially skiing, is an important industry in the Alps. Skiers from around the world vacation in these mountains.

READING CHECK **COMPARE AND CONTRAST**
How is life in the Alps like life in the Mountain states?

▶ **STEEP ROOFS keep snow from piling up.**

Summary

The many mountain ranges in the Mountain states shape people's lives and the region's economy. Tourism, government, and high technology are major industries in the region.

REVIEW

1. **WHAT TO KNOW** What is life like in the Mountain states today?

2. **VOCABULARY** How are **satellites** and a **Global Positioning System** related?

3. **GEOGRAPHY** Why do the Mountain states have few large cities?

4. **CRITICAL THINKING** How has Denver Colorado's location helped it to become an economic and transportation center?

5. ✏ **WRITE A PARAGRAPH** Write a short paragraph to describe life in the Mountain states today.

6. **GENERALIZE** On a separate sheet of paper, copy and complete the graphic organizer below.

Facts

| The government owns parks in the region. | The government has many offices there. | The government owns military bases there. |

Generalization

Eppie Archuleta

Biography

Trustworthiness
Respect
Responsibility
Fairness
Caring
Patriotism

"I can [weave] anything."

Eppie Archuleta comes from a family of weavers. Over the last 100 years, her family has included more than 60 weavers. Born in Santa Cruz, Mexico, in 1922, Archuleta learned to weave by age 10. At first, she wove traditional Spanish and Native American designs.

After she grew up in New Mexico, Archuleta and her family moved to Capulin, Colorado, in 1951. There, Archuleta began representing events and stories in her weavings. Archuleta became well known for this style.

Archuleta's weavings hang in museums across the country, including the Smithsonian Institution, in Washington, D.C. In 1985, the National Endowment for the Arts named her a "national treasure." Today, Archuleta shows her respect for her family's tradition of weaving by teaching others her craft.

Why Character Counts

How does Eppie Archuleta show her respect for her family's tradition of weaving?

Time

1922 — Present
Born

1951 Archuleta moves to Colorado

1985 Archuleta receives the National Heritage Fellowship Award

GO ONLINE For more resources, go to www.harcourtschool.com/ss1

Tell Fact from Opinion

Why It Matters To better understand what you hear or read, it is important to be able to tell fact from opinion.

▶ LEARN

Some statements are facts. For example, consider *Denver is the capital of Colorado.* You could prove or check this fact. Other statements are opinions. An **opinion** is what a person feels or believes. For example, consider *Denver is the most beautiful city in the world.* There is no way to prove this statement. Use the information below to help you tell fact from opinion.

Fact:

- Facts often give dates, numbers, or other information.
- See whether the statement is true from your own experience.
- Check trusted reference sources, such as an atlas, an encyclopedia, or another source.

Opinion:

- Opinions often use key words, such as *I feel, I believe, in my opinion,* and *I doubt.*
- Words such as *beautiful, happy, best, worst,* or *greatest* are often part of an opinion.
- Opinions cannot be proved or checked.

▶ **COLORADO STATE CAPITOL BUILDING in Denver**

▶ **DENVER** during the fall season

▶ PRACTICE

Identify each statement below as a fact or an opinion.

1 Boise is the capital of Idaho.

2 The Mountain states have the most beautiful scenery in the world.

3 Most of Yellowstone National Park is in Wyoming.

▶ APPLY

Reread Lesson 1, "Mountain States." Write four statements about the information in the lesson—two that state facts and two that are your own opinions. Trade papers with a classmate. Challenge each other to tell which statements are facts and which are opinions.

Lesson  2

Pacific States

 WHAT TO KNOW
What is life like in the Pacific states today?

VOCABULARY
microchip p. 412
archipelago p. 414
crossroads p. 414
heritage p. 414

PEOPLE
Antonio Villaraigosa
Bill Gates
Queen Liliuokalani
George Ariyoshi

PLACES
San Francisco
Los Angeles
Silicon Valley
Portland
Seattle
Juneau
Prudhoe Bay
Valdez
Honolulu

Focus Skill GENERALIZE

Facts		

Generalization

YOU ARE THERE

"Stay on the trolley," your mother says. "We don't get off until the next stop." On this summer day, you and your family are visiting **San Francisco**, California. You've already explored Chinatown, enjoying its foods and culture. Now you're taking a trolley to Fisherman's Wharf on the waterfront. Along the route, you see the Transamerica Pyramid, the city's tallest skyscraper. As you leave the city tomorrow, you'll stop at the Golden Gate Bridge. Then you'll be on your way to Oregon and Washington.

▶ Hollywood, near Los Angeles, is the movie capital of the world.

▶ Silicon Valley is a major high-tech center.

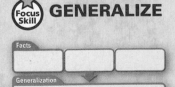
HOLLYWOOD

California

The Pacific states are California, Oregon, Washington, Alaska, and Hawaii. California has the largest population of any state in the nation.

A Diverse Population

Today, more than 35 million people live in California. In fact, about one of every eight Americans lives there.

California's population is one of the most diverse in the world. People from Asia, South America, Mexico, and many other places call California home. Hispanics make up about one-third of the state's population. In 2005, the people of **Los Angeles** elected **Antonio Villaraigosa** (VEE•la•ri•GO•sa) as its first Hispanic mayor since 1872.

A Diverse Economy

California has a diverse economy, too. It is the nation's leading agricultural producer. California grows about half of all the fruits, vegetables, and nuts sold in the United States.

California also leads all other states in manufacturing. The state's top manufacturing industries include aerospace equipment and computers. **Silicon Valley,** south of San Francisco, is a major high-tech center.

Los Angeles is the center of the nation's entertainment industry. Companies there produce music, movies, television programs, and other forms of entertainment.

READING CHECK ⚙ **GENERALIZE**
Why is California's economy diverse?

▶ The Golden Gate Bridge connects San Francisco to northern California.

▶ San Francisco's buildings show many architectural styles.

▶ The Central Valley is California's center of agriculture.

▶ **MICROCHIPS** In Oregon, workers wear special suits to make microchips.

Pacific Northwest

Oregon and Washington are located in the Pacific Northwest. These states share many features.

Living and Working

Most people in Washington and Oregon live and work in metropolitan areas. Most of these areas are in the western parts of the states.

Portland is Oregon's largest city and its business center. Workers there make products for the electronics, food, and wood industries. Nearby, workers manufacture microchips. A **microchip** is a tiny electronic circuit used in equipment such as computers.

Seattle is Washington's largest city and a major port. Several large corporations have their headquarters in the Seattle metropolitan area. Their businesses include insurance, computer, and wood products. One is the world's largest software company, which was cofounded by **Bill Gates**. The Seattle metropolitan area is also a leading producer of passenger planes.

Oregon and Washington are also leading agricultural states. Major crops in both states include flower bulbs, wheat, vegetables, and fruits.

READING CHECK **COMPARE AND CONTRAST**
How are the economies of Oregon and Washington alike?

Alaska

Canada separates Alaska from the 48 other states that are on the North American continent. Alaska is the northernmost state in the nation.

The Largest State

Alaska is the largest state. It makes up one-sixth of all the land in the United States. This rugged land has no large cities and very few roads. In fact, even **Juneau**, the state's capital, is not connected by roads to other cities.

Due to the cold and snow, many Alaskans travel by plane, boat, train, snowmobile, and dogsled. For school, some children take classes on the Internet instead of traveling to a school.

Oil and Fishing

Oil and fishing are Alaska's main industries. Oil flows through an 800-mile pipeline from **Prudhoe Bay** on the Arctic Ocean to the port of **Valdez** on the Gulf of Alaska. Fishers catch salmon, crabs, halibut, and herring.

Native Americans

About one in seven Alaskans is Native American, from groups such as the Aleut, the Inuit, or the Yupik. Many Native Americans follow both old and new ways of life. For example, a person may work as a teacher and practice traditional fishing and hunting methods.

READING CHECK 🅖 **GENERALIZE**
How do Alaskans often travel?

▶ **ALASKANS** Barrow—the northernmost settlement in Alaska—is the home to these Inuit children (left). Juneau (below) is located farther south in the Alaskan Panhandle.

Hawaii

Hawaii is a group of islands, or **archipelago** (ar•kuh•PEH•luh•goh). These volcanic islands are known for their warm climate and their beauty.

The Island State

Hawaii lies near the middle of the Pacific Ocean, between North America and Asia. Because of this location, Hawaii is called the "Crossroads of the Pacific." A **crossroads** is a place that connects people, goods, and ideas.

The first Hawaiians came from other Pacific islands. In the 1700s and 1800s, people from Europe, Asia, and the United States came. Their arrival caused conflicts. **Queen Liliuokalani** (lih•lee•uh•woh•kuh•LAH•nee) was the ruler when the United States took over in 1893.

Today, native Hawaiians make up only a small part of the state's population. In fact, about four of every ten Hawaiians have an Asian background. Former Hawaii governor **George Ariyoshi** was the nation's first Asian American governor. Still, the people of Hawaii continue the islands' **heritage**, or ways of life passed down. Hawaii is the only state with two official languages—English and Hawaiian.

Honolulu, on the island of Oahu, is the state's capital, largest city, and center of industry. Most of the people in Honolulu, and in the rest of the state, work in the tourism industry. People also grow crops and work on the state's military bases.

READING CHECK **MAIN IDEA AND DETAILS**
Why is Hawaii a crossroads?

▶ **WAIKIKI BEACH** is a world-famous beach on Oahu, one of the eight main Hawaiian Islands.

414

Global Connection

Washington and Hawaii are the only states with rain forests. Hawaii's rain forest is tropical, that is, it lies in the tropical zone. Washington's rain forest lies in the temperate zone.

Rain forests are found in several other regions of the world. The world's largest rain forest is located in the Amazon River basin in South America.

Rain forests can provide important resources. People are finding ways to use hundreds of rain-forest plants for medicines. People also cut trees for wood and clear land for farming and ranching. Many people are worried about the clearing of the rain forests. They are working to find a balance between preserving and using the forest land.

READING CHECK **MAIN IDEA AND DETAILS**
How do people use the rain forests?

Products from the Rain Forest

TREE OR PLANT	PRODUCT
Rubber tree	tires, toys
Palm leaves	wicker baskets, furniture
South American tree	chocolate, cocoa butter
Kola tree seed	soft drinks
Palm Hearts	cooking oil
Brazil Nut tree seed	cereals, snack foods
Sapodilla tree	base of chewing gum

TABLE Which products come from seeds?

Summary

The Pacific states represent different cultures. The states of California, Oregon, and Washington have diverse populations and diverse economies. Alaskans combine old and new ways to live in the nation's largest and northernmost state. Hawaiians keep their islands' language and heritage alive.

REVIEW

1. **WHAT TO KNOW** What is life like in the Pacific states today?

2. **VOCABULARY** How are **microchips** important to Oregon's economy?

3. **ECONOMY** What are the main industries in Alaska?

4. **CRITICAL THINKING** What makes the climates of Hawaii and Alaska different?

5. **WRITE A PARAGRAPH** Write a paragraph telling which Pacific state you would most like to visit. Give two reasons for your choice.

6. **GENERALIZE**
   (Focus Skill) On a separate sheet of paper, copy and complete the graphic organizer below.

   Facts

   | California's population is diverse. | Hawaii has many Asian Americans. | Many Alaskans are Native Americans. |

   Generalization

Make a Thoughtful Decision

Why It Matters People make decisions, or choices, every day. Knowing how to make thoughtful decisions can help you reach your goals.

❯ LEARN

Some decisions have lasting consequences. A **consequence** (KAHN•suh•kwens) is what happens because of an action. To make a thoughtful decision, follow these steps.

Step 1 Make a list of choices.

Step 2 Gather the information you will need to make a good decision.

Step 3 Think about the possible consequences of each choice. Decide which choice will have the best results.

Step 4 Put your decision into action.

❯ **RAIN FORESTS** support more than half of all plant and animal species.

▶ **DEFORESTATION** People clear some areas of rain forests to use the wood and the land.

▶ PRACTICE

People are trying to make thoughtful decisions about the world's rain forests. Some people argue that rain forests are home to many of the world's plant and animal species. They support preserving rain forests to protect these species. Others argue that rain forests can provide much-needed wood or land. These people support cutting rain forest trees or clearing land for farming and ranching. Think about the possible consequences for each decision.

1 What arguments do people give for and against using rain forest resources?

2 Explain the consequences of each decision.

3 Which decision do you support? Explain.

▶ APPLY

Make It Relevant Think about a decision you made recently. What were the consequences of your decision? Do you think you made a thoughtful decision? Explain.

Critical Thinking Skills

Visual Summary

All of the Mountain States have ski resorts.

Summarize the Chapter

Focus Skill **Generalize** Complete this graphic organizer to show that you understand how to make generalizations about the West.

Facts

| About 1 in 3 Californians is a Hispanic. | About 1 in 7 Alaskans is a Native American. | About 4 in 10 Hawaiians have an Asian background. |

Generalization

Vocabulary

Identify the term from the word bank that correctly matches each definition.

1. a miniature electronic circuit that is used in computers

2. a group of islands

3. an object that orbits Earth

4. a place that connects people, goods, and ideas

5. a person who buys a product or service

6. a system of satellites and computers that can locate a person or object

Word Bank

satellite p. 403	**microchip** p. 412
Global Positioning	**archipelago** p. 414
System p. 403	**crossroads** p. 414
consumer p. 405	

The federal government uses land in the Mountain states.

Alaska is the largest state in the United States.

TEST PREP

 Facts and Main Ideas

Answer these questions.

7. What kinds of challenges do people in the Mountain states face?

8. Who was Jeannette Rankin?

9. What are two large cities in the Pacific Northwest?

10. What ethnic group makes up one-third of California's popluation?

11. In what ways are Washington and Oregon alike?

Write the letter of the best choice.

12. What city did Brigham Young help settle?
    A Boise
    B Denver
    C Las Vegas
    D Salt Lake City

13. Which state has the largest land area?
    A Alaska
    B California
    C Hawaii
    D Nevada

 Critical Thinking

14. Summarize the role of the United States government in the Mountain states.

15. Describe one way in which Alaska and Hawaii are alike and one way in which they are different.

 Skills

Tell Fact from Opinion
Identify each statement as a fact or an opinion.

16. The mountains of the West bring challenges to the people living there.

17. The steep roofs found in the Alps keep snow from piling up on them.

18. Everyone visits Hawaii for its natural beauty.

writing

✎ **Write a Report** Write a report about the West today. Tell about the people and the economies of the Mountain states and of the Pacific states.

✎ **Write a Description** Write a description of a specific place in the West. Do not name the place you are writing about. Have a classmate read your description and try to guess what place you wrote about.

Go-Together Tic-Tac-Toe

VOCABULARY

What three words or pictures go together? They make a tic-tac-toe row.

	hydroelectricity	crater
timberline		fault
lava		

Silly Suitcase

 Pack for a trip to Hawaii. Which three items do not belong?

Dog Days

Match each dog with its owner.

I Love Cows	Movie ★	Lumber Jack	Snow Shoe

Online Adventures

GO ONLINE

In this online game, you and Eco will fly a plane over the West while you work to solve the final puzzles. Soon you'll have all the clues you need. Which one of the suspects is guilty? Where is the missing American symbol? If you use the clue cards and the lessons you've learned, you can solve the mystery and win the game. Play now at **www.harcourtschool.com/ss1**

Review and Test Prep ✔

💡 THE BIG IDEA

Diversity As the largest of the five regions of the United States, the West is a region of diversity.

Reading Comprehension and Vocabulary

The West

Much of the West is covered with mountains. The highest, lowest, hottest, coldest, wettest, and driest places in the United States all are in the West. Forests, minerals, and fish are among the region's natural resources.

Native Americans of the West used rivers as trading routes. The discovery of a pass opened the region to settlers. Once gold was discovered in the region, thousands of settlers moved to the West, creating boomtowns.

Minerals, forests, waterways, and other natural resources are important to the West's economy. Tourism, government, and high-tech businesses are also major industries in the region.

People in the West are working to protect the region's ecosystems. They have built fish ladders and set aside land in national parks.

The Pacific states have diverse cultures and economies. California leads the nation in population, farm products, and manufacturing. Hawaii and Alaska are not part of the mainland. In Hawaii, there are two languages. Many Alaskans follow old and new traditions.

Read the summary above. Then answer the questions that follow.

1. A boomtown is—
   A a small town.
   B a trading post.
   C a town that grew quickly.
   D a town owned by the government.

2. Which industry is a major industry in the region?
   A coal mining
   B insurance
   C steel
   D tourism

3. An ecosystem is—
   A a human-made lake.
   B a kind of power plant.
   C a community of living things.
   D a piece of land owned by the government.

4. Which state is separated from the 48 mainland states?
   A Alaska
   B California
   C Colorado
   D Utah

Answer these questions.

5. What is the Continental Divide?

6. How do mountains affect the climate of the West?

7. How did Sacagawea help the explorers Lewis and Clark?

8. Why did the United States government take over some of the land in the West?

9. How do national parks protect the environment?

10. Why can California be called a "state of diversity"?

Write the letter of the best choice.

11. Which of these is the highest peak in the United States?
    A Mount Hood
    B Mount McKinley
    C Mount Rainier
    D Mount St. Helens

12. Which Native American group invented a language for trading with other groups on the Columbia River?
    A the Chinook
    B the Makah
    C the Paiute
    D the Yokuts

13. Where is Denver?
    A in the Rocky Mountains
    B on the Great Plains
    C in the Great Basin
    D in Death Valley

14. Which state is an archipelago?
    A Alaska
    B California
    C Hawaii
    D Washington

15. What are two reasons why much of the land in the West cannot be farmed?

16. Why did the Pony Express route begin in St. Joseph, Missouri?

Read a Time Zone Map

Use the map below to answer this question.

17. Imagine that you live in Butte, Montana. You want to call your cousin in Anchorage, Alaska at 8 A.M. Alaska time. What time will it be in Montana when you make the call?

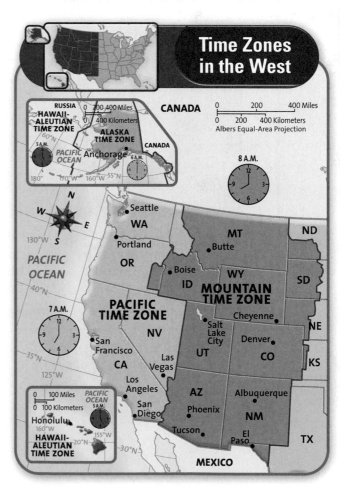

Time Zones in the West

Activities

 Unit Writing Activity

Write a Scene Write a scene for a play about the West.

- Describe the setting.
- Include three characters that come from different parts of the West.
- Have the characters tell about where they live and what they do.

 Unit Project

Make a Bulletin Board Make a bulletin board display about the West.

- Include pictures and drawings of people, places, and events that are important to the West.
- Write short passages about the people, places, and events displayed on your bulletin board.

Read More

- *Harvesting Hope: The Story of Cesar Chavez* by Kathleen Krull. Harcourt.

- *I Am Sacajawea, I Am York* by Claire Rudolf Murphy. Walker and Company.

- *Going to Yellowstone* by Peter and Connie Roop. Farcountry Press.

 GO ONLINE

For more resources, go to
www.harcourtschool.com/ss1

For Your Reference

ATLAS/
ALMANAC

RESEARCH
HANDBOOK

BIOGRAPHICAL
DICTIONARY

GAZETTEER

GLOSSARY

INDEX

For Your Reference

ATLAS/
ALMANAC

RESEARCH
HANDBOOK

BIOGRAPHICAL
DICTIONARY

GAZETTEER

GLOSSARY

INDEX

The World: Political

ARCTIC OCEAN

180° 160°W 140°W 120°W 100°W 80°W 60°W
80°N

Greenland (DENMARK)

ALASKA (U.S.)

60°N

CANADA

NORTH AMERICA

UNITED STATES

40°N

Azores (PORTUGAL)

Midway Islands (U.S.)

Bermuda (U.K.)

ATLANTIC OCEAN

Area of inset

20°N

Tropic of Cancer

MEXICO

CAPE VERDE

HAWAII (U.S.)

PACIFIC OCEAN

VENEZUELA GUYANA
SURINAME

COLOMBIA FRENCH GUIANA (FRANCE)

Equator

ECUADOR

Tokelau (N.Z.)

KIRIBATI

Galápagos Islands (ECUADOR)

BRAZIL

SOUTH AMERICA

SAMOA

American Samoa (U.S.)

French Polynesia (FRANCE)

PERU

Cook Islands (N.Z.)

BOLIVIA

PARAGUAY

20°S

TONGA

Pitcairn (U.K.)

Tropic of Capricorn

Easter Island (CHILE)

CHILE

Niue (N.Z.)

URUGUAY

ARGENTINA

Falkland Islands (U.K.)

40°S

PACIFIC OCEAN

South Georgia (U.K.)

60°S

Antarctic Circle

80°S

180° 160°W 140°W 120°W 100°W 80°W

Central America and the Caribbean

100°W

30°N

N
W   E
S

ATLANTIC OCEAN

Gulf of Mexico

BAHAMAS

Tropic of Cancer

20°N

CUBA

Turks and Caicos (U.K.)

Cayman Islands (U.K.)

HAITI

DOMINICAN REPUBLIC

Puerto Rico (U.S.)

Anguilla (U.K.)
St. Martin (FRANCE AND NETH.)
ANTIGUA AND BARBUDA
Montserrat (U.K.)

BELIZE

JAMAICA

Virgin Islands (U.S. AND U.K.)

Guadeloupe (FRANCE)

ST. KITTS AND NEVIS

DOMINICA

GUATEMALA HONDURAS

Caribbean Sea

Martinique (FRANCE)

ST. LUCIA

EL SALVADOR

NICARAGUA

Aruba (NETH.)

Netherlands Antilles (NETH.)

BARBADOS

ST. VINCENT AND THE GRENADINES

PACIFIC OCEAN

GRENADA

TRINIDAD AND TOBAGO

10°N

Panama Canal

10°N

COSTA RICA

PANAMA

90°W 80°W 70°W 60°W

0   200   400 Miles
0   200   400 Kilometers
Azimuthal Equal-Area Projection

National border

R2

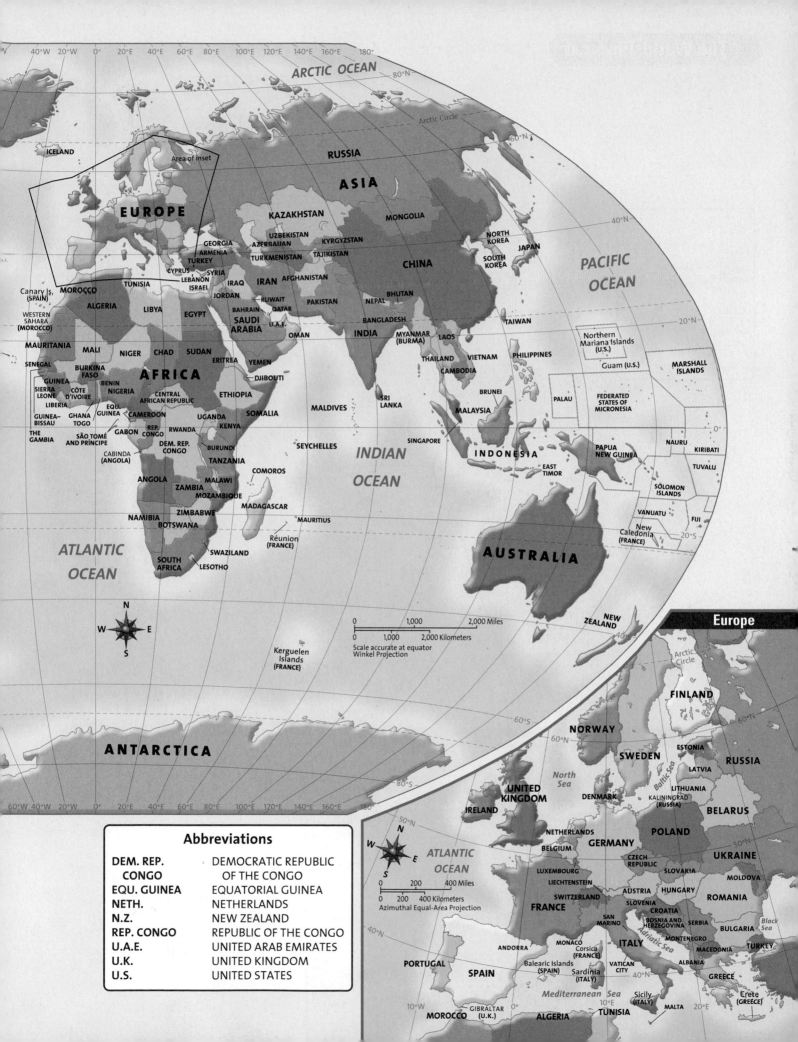

The World: Physical

Legend
- Arid
- Evergreen forest
- Grassland
- Mixed forest
- Mountains
- Tundra
- —— National border
- ▲ Mountain peak

Main Map Labels

ARCTIC OCEAN

Beaufort Sea

Queen Elizabeth Islands

Baffin Island

Denali (Mt. McKinley) 20,320 ft. (6,194 m)

Great Bear Lake

Great Slave Lake

Hudson Bay

NORTH AMERICA

Yukon R.

Mt. Logan 19,550 ft. (5,959 m)

Bering Sea

Aleutian Islands

Gulf of Alaska

Vancouver Island

Columbia R.

ROCKY MOUNTAINS

Mackenzie R.

Missouri R.

Great Lakes

Mississippi R.

Ohio R.

APPALACHIAN MTS.

Newfoundland

Azores

Mt. Whitney 14,495 ft. (4,418 m)

Colorado R.

GREAT PLAINS

Bermuda

ATLANTIC OCEAN

Gulf of California

Rio Grande

Tropic of Cancer

Gulf of Mexico

Bahamas

Hawaiian Islands

PACIFIC OCEAN

Pico de Orizaba 18,855 ft. (5,747 m)

Yucatán Peninsula

Cuba

West Indies

Hispaniola

Caribbean Sea

Equator

Galápagos Islands

Orinoco River

Guiana Highlands

AMAZON BASIN

Amazon R.

ANDES MOUNTAINS

SOUTH AMERICA

Brazilian Highlands

Polynesia

Tropic of Capricorn

Atacama Desert

Gran Chaco

Paraná River

Mt. Aconcagua 22,834 ft. (6,960 m)

Pampa

PACIFIC OCEAN

Patagonia

Falkland Islands

Strait of Magellan

Cape Horn

Tierra del Fuego

Antarctic Circle

Antarctic Peninsula

Ross Sea

Northern Polar Region

Sea of Okhotsk

ASIA

Novaya Zemlya

EUROPE

Baltic Sea

Kamchatka Peninsula

Severnaya Zemlya

Barents Sea

New Siberian Is.

Norwegian Sea

North Sea

British Isles

ARCTIC OCEAN

NORTH POLE

Svalbard

Wrangel Island

Bering Sea

Bering Strait

BROOKS RANGE

Beaufort Sea

NORTH MAGNETIC POLE

Queen Elizabeth Islands

Greenland Sea

Greenland

Iceland

ATLANTIC OCEAN

Baffin Bay

Arctic Circle

PACIFIC OCEAN

NORTH AMERICA

0 400 800 Miles
0 400 800 Kilometers
Azimuthal Equidistant Projection

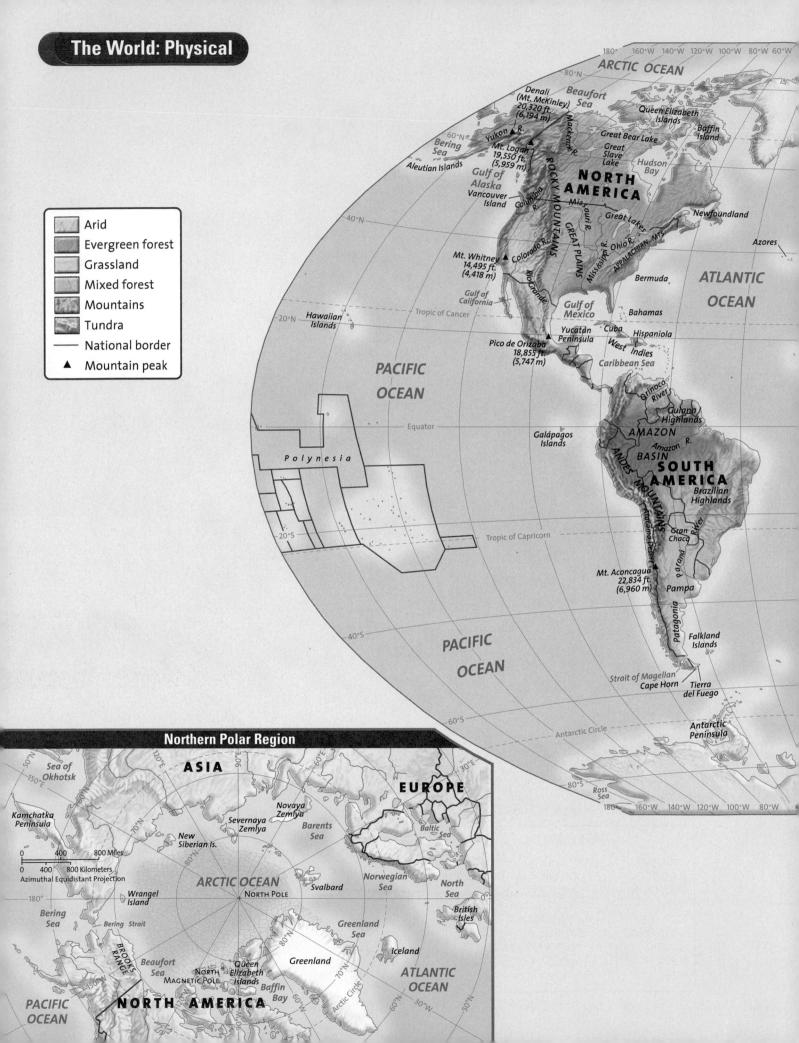

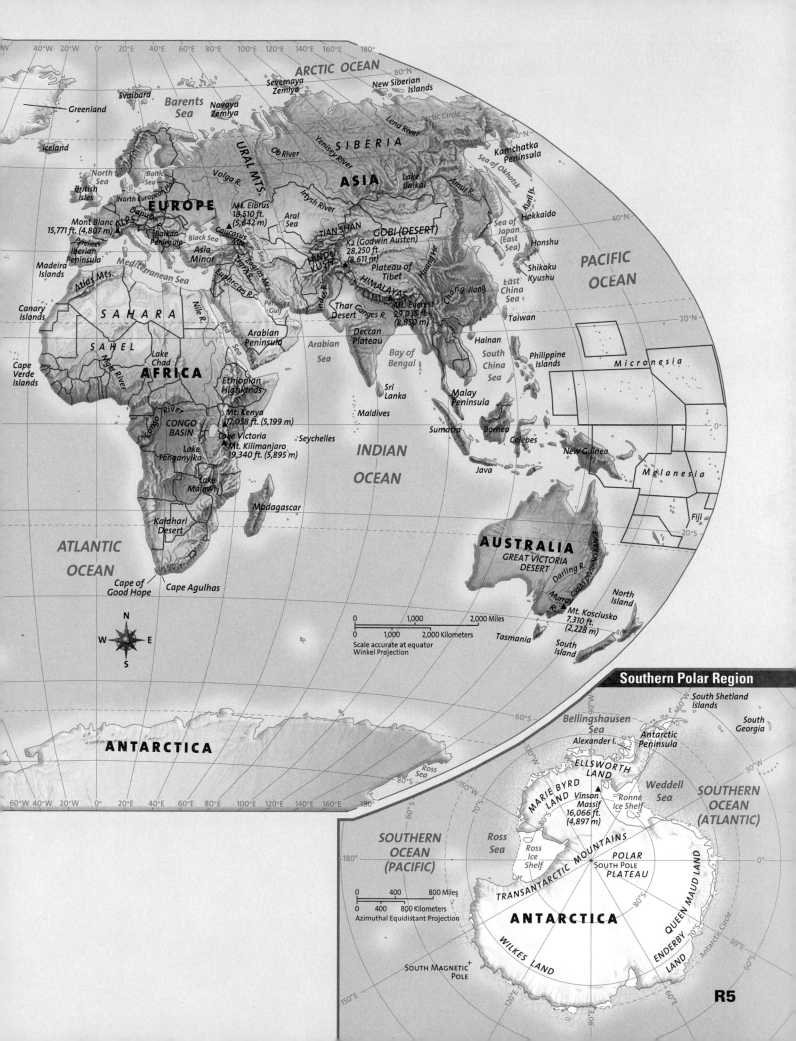

ARCTIC OCEAN

80°N

Greenland

Svalbard

Barents
Sea

Novaya
Zemlya

Severnaya
Zemlya

New Siberian
Islands

Arctic Circle

60°N

Iceland

North
Sea

Baltic
Sea

North European Plain

URAL MTS.

Ob River

Yenisey River

SIBERIA

Lena River

Kamchatka
Peninsula

Sea of
Okhotsk

British
Isles

EUROPE

Mt. Elbrus
18,510 ft.
(5,642 m)

Volga R.

Irtysh River

ASIA

Lake
Baikal

Amur R.

Kuril Is.

Hokkaido

40°N

Mont Blanc
15,771 ft. (4,807 m)

ALPS

Danube R.

Balkan
Peninsula

Black Sea

Caucasus
Mts.

Aral
Sea

TIAN SHAN

GOBI (DESERT)

Sea of
Japan
(East
Sea)

Honshu

Pyrenees

Iberian
Peninsula

Asia
Minor

Caspian Sea

Zagros Mts.

HINDU
KUSH

K2 (Godwin Austen)
28,250 ft.
(8,611 m)

Plateau of
Tibet

Huang He

Chang Jiang

East
China
Sea

Shikoku
Kyushu

PACIFIC
OCEAN

Madeira
Islands

Atlas Mts.

Mediterranean Sea

Tigris R.

Euphrates R.

Persian
Gulf

Indus R.

HIMALAYAS

Mt. Everest
29,035 ft.
(8,850 m)

Taiwan

20°N

Canary
Islands

SAHARA

Nile R.

Red Sea

Arabian
Peninsula

Thar
Desert

Ganges R.

Deccan
Plateau

Bay of
Bengal

Hainan

South
China
Sea

Philippine
Islands

Micronesia

Cape
Verde
Islands

SAHEL

Niger River

Lake
Chad

AFRICA

Arabian
Sea

Sri
Lanka

0°

Ethiopian
Highlands

Mt. Kenya
17,058 ft. (5,199 m)

Congo River

CONGO
BASIN

Lake Victoria

Mt. Kilimanjaro
19,340 ft. (5,895 m)

Seychelles

Maldives

INDIAN
OCEAN

Malay
Peninsula

Sumatra

Borneo

Celebes

New Guinea

Melanesia

Fiji

Lake
Tanganyika

Lake
Malawi

Java

20°S

ATLANTIC
OCEAN

Kalahari
Desert

Madagascar

AUSTRALIA

GREAT VICTORIA
DESERT

Darling R.

GREAT DIVIDING RANGE

Cape of
Good Hope

Cape Agulhas

N
W E
S

0   1,000   2,000 Miles
0 1,000 2,000 Kilometers
Scale accurate at equator
Winkel Projection

Murray
R.

Mt. Kosciusko
7,310 ft.
(2,228 m)

North
Island

Tasmania

South
Island

40°S

ANTARCTICA

Ross
Sea

60°S

80°S

60°W 40°W 20°W 0° 20°E 40°E 60°E 80°E 100°E 120°E 140°E 160°E 180°

40°W 20°W 0° 20°E 40°E 60°E 80°E 100°E 120°E 140°E 160°E 180°

South Shetland
Islands

Bellingshausen
Sea

Alexander I.

Antarctic
Peninsula

South
Georgia

ELLSWORTH
LAND

MARIE BYRD
LAND

Vinson
Massif
16,066 ft.
(4,897 m)

Ronne
Ice Shelf

Weddell
Sea

SOUTHERN
OCEAN
(ATLANTIC)

SOUTHERN
OCEAN
(PACIFIC)

Ross
Sea

Ross
Ice
Shelf

TRANSANTARCTIC MOUNTAINS

POLAR
PLATEAU

SOUTH POLE

QUEEN MAUD LAND

ENDERBY
LAND

0   400   800 Miles
0 400 800 Kilometers
Azimuthal Equidistant Projection

WILKES LAND

ANTARCTICA

SOUTH MAGNETIC
POLE

Antarctic Circle

R5

Western Hemisphere: Political

ARCTIC OCEAN

Beaufort Sea

Bering Strait

Viscount Melville Sound

Baffin Bay

Greenland (DENMARK)

ALASKA (U.S.)

Yukon River

Fairbanks

Anchorage

Whitehorse

Juneau

Gulf of Alaska

Bering Sea

60°N

Mackenzie River

Great Bear Lake

Liard River

Yellowknife

Great Slave Lake

Peace River

CANADA

Lake Athabasca

Davis Strait

Foxe Basin

Arctic Circle

Hudson Strait

Labrador Sea

Edmonton

Saskatchewan R.

Athabasca R.

Lake Winnipeg

Hudson Bay

James Bay

Calgary

Saskatoon

Regina

Winnipeg

Vancouver

UNITED STATES

Thunder Bay

Great Lakes

St. Lawrence River

St. John's

Seattle

Puget Sound

Columbia R.

Snake R.

Missouri R.

Ottawa

Quebec

St. John

Gulf of St. Lawrence

Portland

Boise

Great Salt Lake

Salt Lake City

Chicago

Detroit

Toronto

Albany

Montreal

Boston

Halifax

Reno

Denver

St. Louis

Cleveland

Indianapolis

New York City

Philadelphia

San Francisco

Las Vegas

Colorado R.

Memphis

Richmond

Washington, D.C.

Norfolk

Los Angeles

Phoenix

Atlanta

Raleigh

ATLANTIC OCEAN

San Diego

Tucson

El Paso

Dallas

Charleston

Hermosillo

Rio Grande

Houston

New Orleans

San Antonio

Savannah

Jacksonville

30°N

Chihuahua

Tampa

Orlando

Gulf of California

MEXICO

Monterrey

Gulf of Mexico

Miami

BAHAMAS

Nassau

Tropic of Cancer

Durango

Tampico

Havana

CUBA

HAITI

Port-au-Prince

Santo Domingo

HAWAII (U.S.)

Honolulu

León

Guadalajara

Mexico City

Veracruz

JAMAICA

Kingston

Puerto Rico (U.S.)

DOMINICAN REPUBLIC

Puebla

BELIZE

Acapulco

GUATEMALA

Belmopan

PACIFIC OCEAN

Guatemala City

HONDURAS

Tegucigalpa

San Salvador

EL SALVADOR

Managua

Caribbean Sea

NICARAGUA

San José

Maracaibo

COSTA RICA

Panama City

Caracas

GUYANA

PANAMA

VENEZUELA

Georgetown

SURINAME

Paramaribo

Medellín

Cayenne

Cali

Bogotá

FRENCH GUIANA (FRANCE)

COLOMBIA

Equator

0°

Quito

Galápagos Islands (ECUADOR)

Guayaquil

ECUADOR

Manaus

Rio Negro

Amazon R.

Belém

Fortaleza

Iquitos

Recife

Trujillo

PERU

Tapajós R.

Xingu R.

Tocantins R.

São Francisco R.

Lima

Cuzco

BRAZIL

Salvador

French Polynesia (FRANCE)

Papeete

Lake Titicaca

La Paz

Brasília

Belo Horizonte

Arequipa

BOLIVIA

Goiânia

Rio de Janeiro

Sucre

Campo Grande

Tropic of Capricorn

Antofagasta

PARAGUAY

São Paulo

Paraguay R.

Asunción

Curitiba

Salta

San Miguel de Tucumán

CHILE

Córdoba

Pôrto Alegre

URUGUAY

Valparaíso

Rosario

Paraná R.

30°S

Santiago

Buenos Aires

Montevideo

Concepción

La Plata

Rio de la Plata

Mar del Plata

Valdivia

Bahía Blanca

ARGENTINA

Falkland Islands (U.K.)

South Georgia (U.K.)

Punta Arenas

0 1,000 2,000 Miles

0 1,000 2,000 Kilometers

Miller Cylindrical Projection

— National border
⊛ National capital
• City

N
W   E
S

R6

150°W   120°W   90°W   60°W   30°W

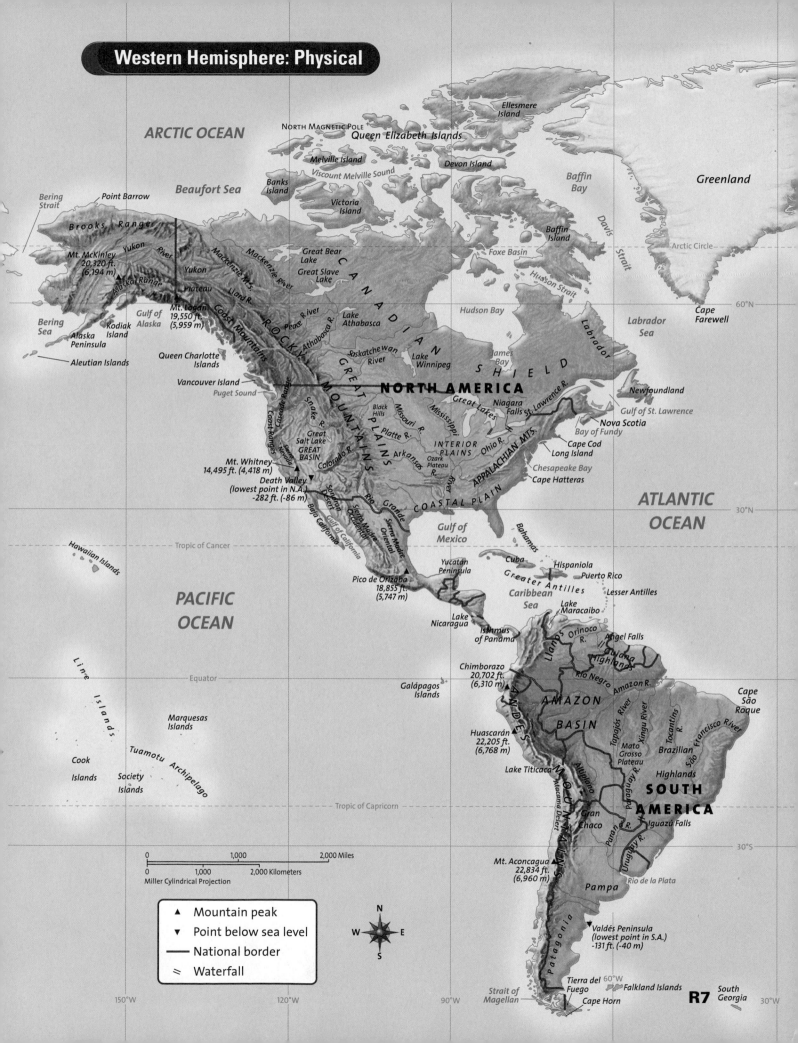

Western Hemisphere: Physical

ARCTIC OCEAN

NORTH MAGNETIC POLE +

Ellesmere Island

Queen Elizabeth Islands

Bering Strait
Point Barrow
Beaufort Sea

Melville Island
Viscount Melville Sound
Banks Island

Devon Island

Baffin Bay

Greenland

Brooks Range
Yukon River

Mt. McKinley
20,320 ft.
(6,194 m)
Alaskan Range

Yukon Plateau

Victoria Island

Baffin Island

Davis Strait

Arctic Circle

60°N

Bering Sea
Alaska Peninsula
Kodiak Island
Gulf of Alaska

Mt. Logan
19,550 ft.
(5,959 m)
Coast Mountains

Mackenzie Mts.
Liard R.
Mackenzie River
Peace River

Great Bear Lake
Great Slave Lake

Lake Athabasca

Foxe Basin

Cape Farewell

Aleutian Islands

Queen Charlotte Islands

ROCKY

CANADIAN

SHIELD

Labrador

Labrador Sea

Vancouver Island
Puget Sound

Cascade Range

Snake R.

GREAT

Saskatchewan River

Lake Winnipeg

Hudson Bay

James Bay

Hudson Strait

Newfoundland

Coast Ranges

Sierra Nevada

Great Salt Lake
GREAT BASIN

MOUNTAINS

PLAINS

Black Hills

Missouri R.

Platte R.

NORTH AMERICA

Great Lakes

Niagara Falls

St. Lawrence R.

Gulf of St. Lawrence

Nova Scotia

Bay of Fundy

Mt. Whitney
14,495 ft. (4,418 m)
Death Valley
(lowest point in N.A.)
-282 ft. (-86 m)

Colorado R.

Sonoran Desert

Arkansas R.

INTERIOR
PLAINS

Ozark Plateau

Ohio R.

Mississippi

APPALACHIAN MTS.

Cape Cod
Long Island

Chesapeake Bay
Cape Hatteras

30°N

ATLANTIC
OCEAN

Rio Grande

Baja California

Sierra Madre Occidental

Sierra Madre Oriental

COASTAL PLAIN

Gulf of Mexico

Bahamas

Tropic of Cancer

Hawaiian Islands

PACIFIC
OCEAN

Gulf of California

Yucatán Peninsula

Cuba

Hispaniola

Greater Antilles

Puerto Rico

Lesser Antilles

Pico de Orizaba
18,855 ft.
(5,747 m)

Lake Nicaragua

Caribbean Sea

Lake Maracaibo

Lime Islands

Isthmus of Panama

Chimborazo
20,702 ft.
(6,310 m)

Llanos

Orinoco R.

Angel Falls

Guiana Highlands

Galápagos Islands

Rio Negro

Amazon R.

Cape São Roque

Equator

Marquesas Islands

AMAZON
BASIN

Tapajós River

Xingu River

Tocantins R.

São Francisco River

Huascarán
22,205 ft.
(6,768 m)

Brazilian

Tuamotu Archipelago

Cook Islands

Society Islands

Lake Titicaca

Altiplano

A
N
D
E
S

Atacama Desert

Mato Grosso Plateau

Paraguay R.

Highlands

SOUTH
AMERICA

Tropic of Capricorn

Gran Chaco

Paraná R.

Iguazú Falls

Uruguay R.

30°S

0   1,000   2,000 Miles
0   1,000   2,000 Kilometers
Miller Cylindrical Projection

Mt. Aconcagua
22,834 ft.
(6,960 m)

Rio de la Plata

Pampa

N
W   E
S

▲ Mountain peak
▼ Point below sea level
— National border
≈ Waterfall

Valdés Peninsula
(lowest point in S.A.)
-131 ft. (-40 m)

Patagonia

60°W

Tierra del Fuego

Falkland Islands

Strait of Magellan

Cape Horn

South Georgia

150°W   120°W   90°W   30°W

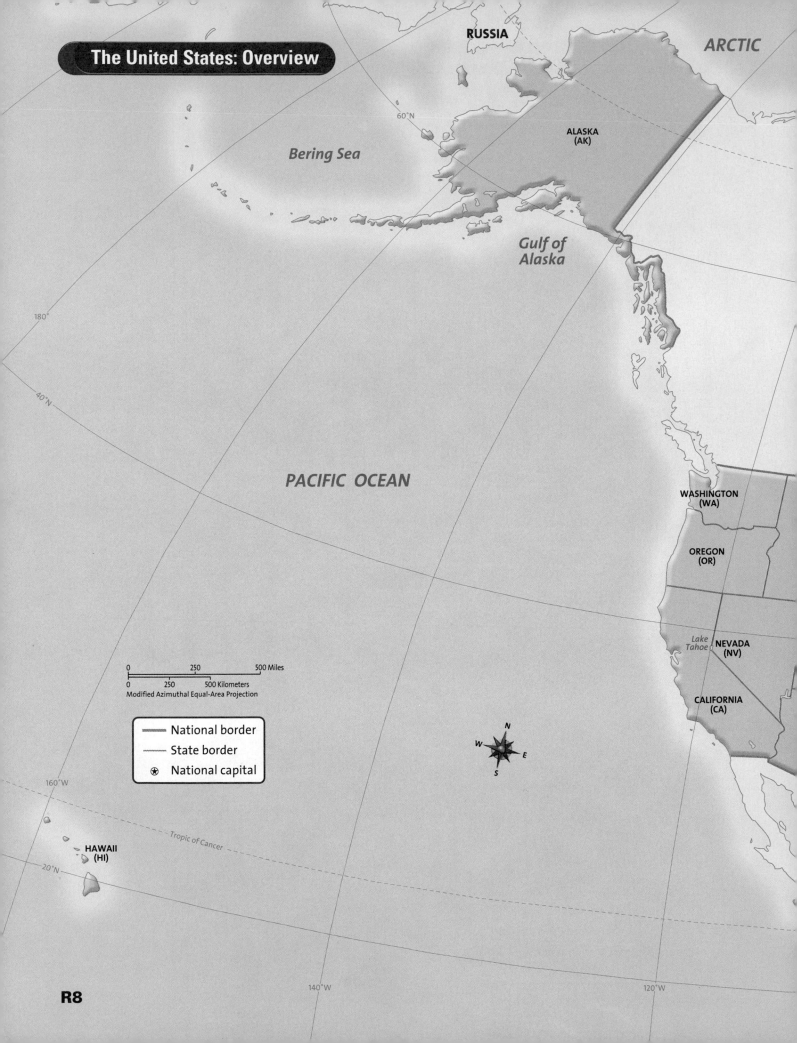

The United States: Overview

RUSSIA

ARCTIC

Bering Sea

60°N

ALASKA
(AK)

Gulf of
Alaska

180°

40°N

PACIFIC OCEAN

WASHINGTON
(WA)

OREGON
(OR)

0   250   500 Miles
0   250   500 Kilometers
Modified Azimuthal Equal-Area Projection

Lake
Tahoe

NEVADA
(NV)

CALIFORNIA
(CA)

National border
State border
⊛ National capital

N
W E
S

160°W

Tropic of Cancer

HAWAII
(HI)

20°N

140°W

120°W

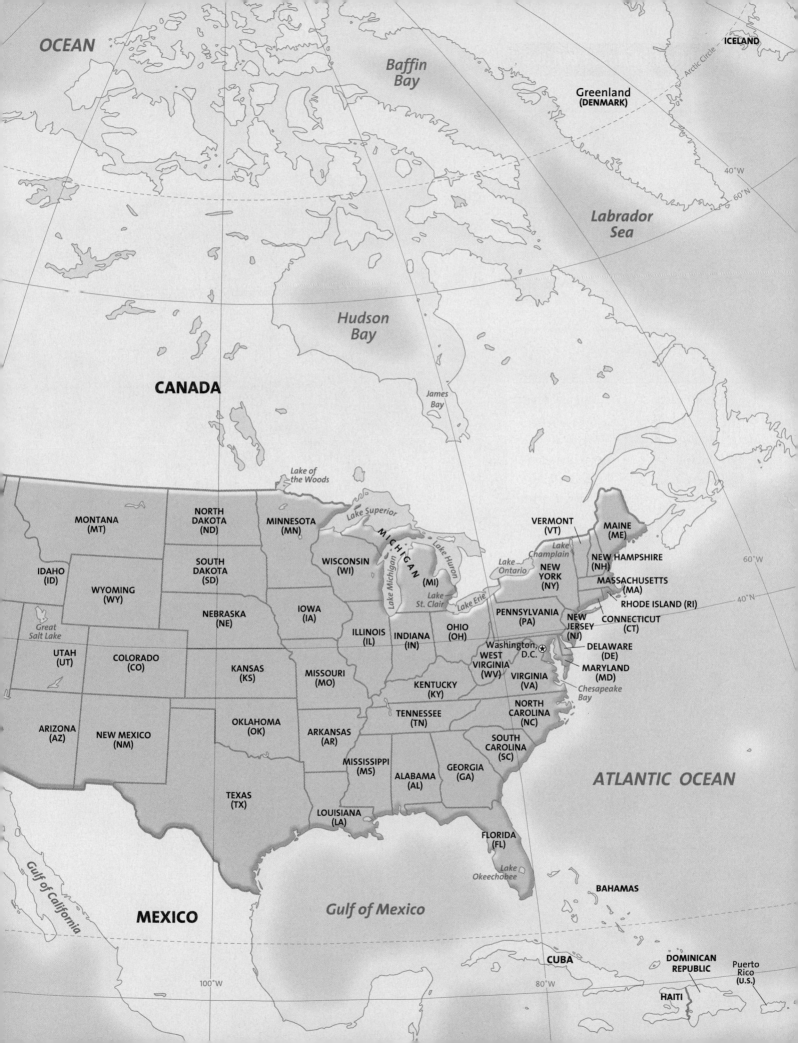

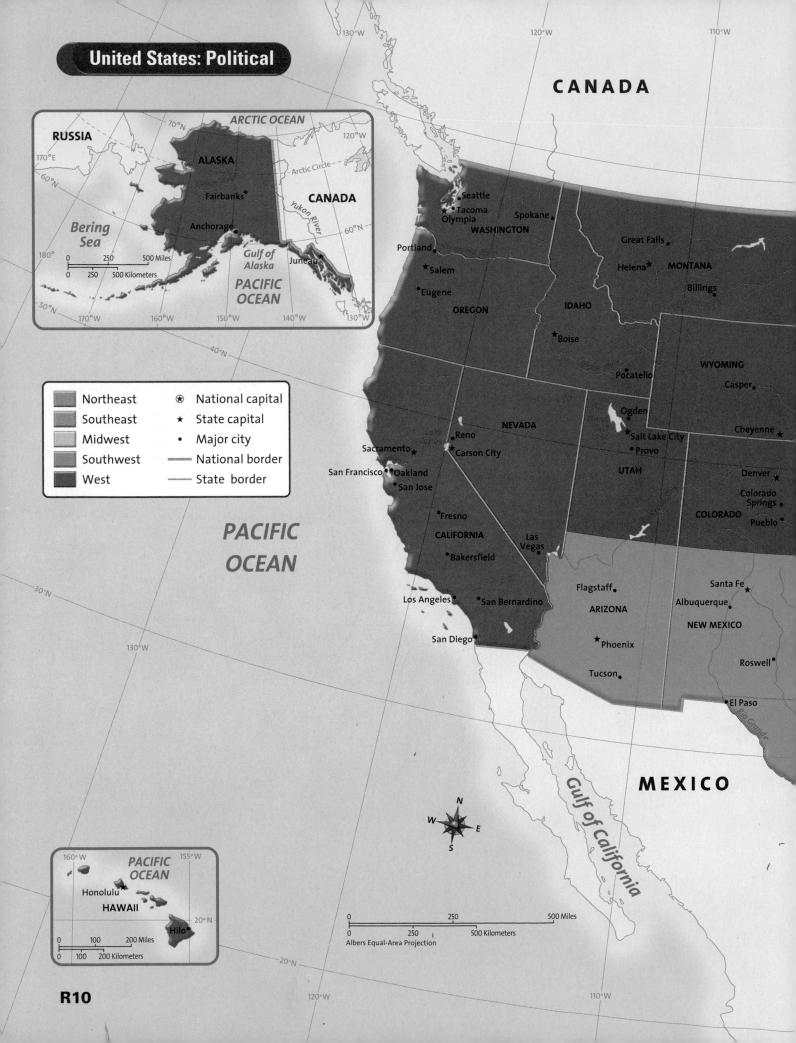

United States: Political

Legend

- Northeast
- Southeast
- Midwest
- Southwest
- West
- ⊛ National capital
- ★ State capital
- • Major city
- National border
- State border

Alaska Inset

RUSSIA

ARCTIC OCEAN

ALASKA

CANADA

Fairbanks

Anchorage

Bering Sea

Gulf of Alaska

Juneau

Yukon River

Arctic Circle

PACIFIC OCEAN

0   250   500 Miles
0   250   500 Kilometers

170°E · 180° · 170°W · 160°W · 150°W · 140°W · 130°W
70°N · 60°N · 50°N

Hawaii Inset

PACIFIC OCEAN

Honolulu

HAWAII

Hilo

160°W · 155°W
20°N

0   100   200 Miles
0   100   200 Kilometers

Main Map

CANADA

WASHINGTON
- Seattle
- Tacoma
- Olympia ★
- Spokane
- Portland
- Salem ★
- Eugene

OREGON

IDAHO
- Boise ★

MONTANA
- Great Falls
- Helena ★
- Billings

WYOMING
- Casper
- Cheyenne ★

NEVADA
- Reno
- Carson City ★
- Las Vegas

UTAH
- Ogden
- Salt Lake City ★
- Provo
- Pocatello

CALIFORNIA
- Sacramento ★
- San Francisco
- Oakland
- San Jose
- Fresno
- Bakersfield
- Los Angeles
- San Bernardino
- San Diego

COLORADO
- Denver
- Colorado Springs
- Pueblo

ARIZONA
- Flagstaff
- Phoenix ★
- Tucson

NEW MEXICO
- Santa Fe ★
- Albuquerque
- Roswell
- El Paso

Rio Grande

MEXICO

Gulf of California

PACIFIC OCEAN

N W E S

0   250   500 Miles
0   250   500 Kilometers
Albers Equal-Area Projection

130°W · 120°W · 110°W
40°N · 30°N · 20°N

R10

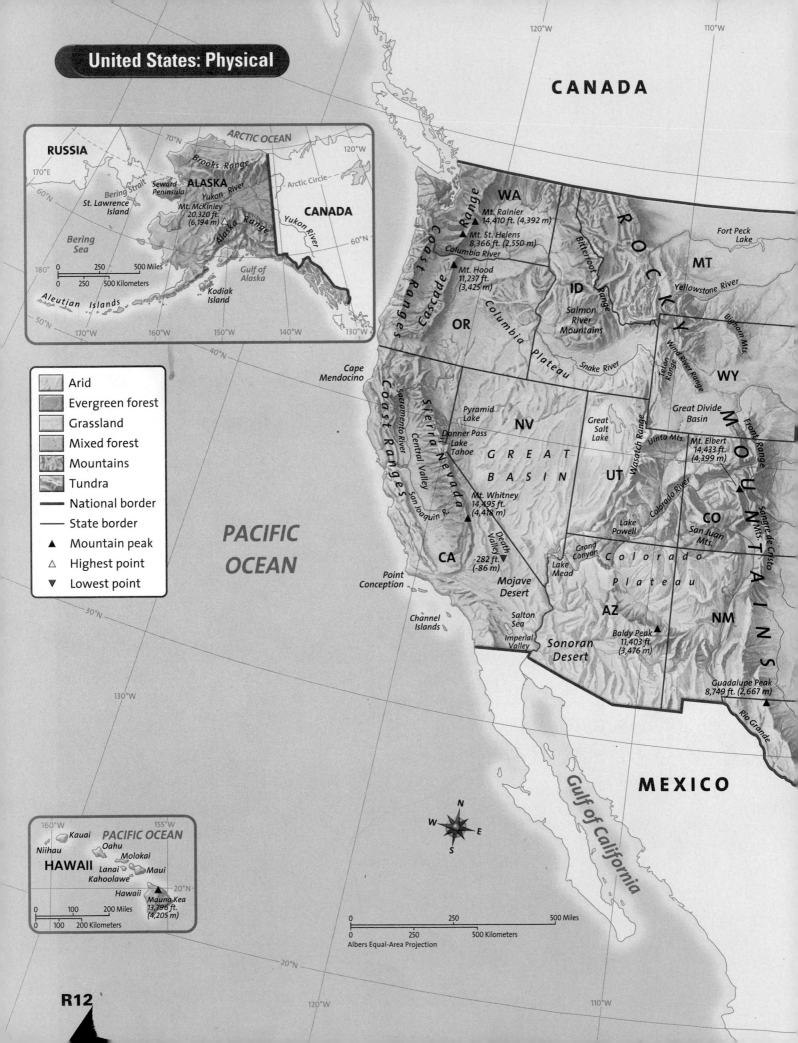

United States: Physical

CANADA

120°W   110°W

RUSSIA

ARCTIC OCEAN

170°E

70°N

Brooks Range

120°W

Arctic Circle

Bering Strait

Seward Peninsula

ALASKA

Yukon River

CANADA

60°N

St. Lawrence Island

Mt. McKinley 20,320 ft. (6,194 m)

Alaska Range

Yukon River

60°N

Bering Sea

180°

0   250   500 Miles

0   250   500 Kilometers

Gulf of Alaska

Kodiak Island

50°N

Aleutian Islands

130°W

40°N

Cape Mendocino

Arid
Evergreen forest
Grassland
Mixed forest
Mountains
Tundra
— National border
— State border
▲ Mountain peak
△ Highest point
▼ Lowest point

Cascade Range

Mt. Rainier 14,410 ft. (4,392 m)
Mt. St. Helens 8,366 ft. (2,550 m)
Columbia River

WA

Mt. Hood 11,237 ft. (3,425 m)

OR

Columbia Plateau

Bitterroot Range

ID

Salmon River Mountains

Snake River

MT

Fort Peck Lake

Yellowstone River

Bighorn Mts.

Teton Range

Wind River Range

WY

Great Divide Basin

Front Range

Mt. Elbert 14,433 ft. (4,399 m)

R
O
C
K
Y

M
O
U
N
T
A
I
N
S

PACIFIC OCEAN

Coast Ranges

Sacramento River

Sierra Nevada

Central Valley

San Joaquin R.

Pyramid Lake

Donner Pass

Lake Tahoe

NV

Great Salt Lake

Wasatch Range

Uinta Mts.

UT

G R E A T
B A S I N

Mt. Whitney 14,495 ft. (4,418 m)

Death Valley

CA

Point Conception

Channel Islands

-282 ft. (-86 m) ▼

Mojave Desert

Salton Sea

Imperial Valley

Lake Powell

Lake Mead

Grand Canyon

Colorado River

Colorado Plateau

Sangre de Cristo Mts.

San Juan Mts.

CO

AZ

Baldy Peak 11,403 ft. (3,476 m)

Sonoran Desert

NM

Guadalupe Peak 8,749 ft. (2,667 m) ▲

Rio Grande

MEXICO

30°N

130°W

20°N

HAWAII

160°W   155°W

PACIFIC OCEAN

Kauai

Niihau

Oahu

Molokai

Lanai   Maui

Kahoolawe

Hawaii

Mauna Kea 13,796 ft. (4,205 m)

20°N

0   100   200 Miles

0   100   200 Kilometers

N
W   E
S

0   250   500 Miles

0   250   500 Kilometers

Albers Equal-Area Projection

Gulf of California

120°W   110°W

CANADA

ME
Mt. Katahdin
5,269 ft.
(1,606 m)
Moosehead Lake
St. Lawrence River
Lake Champlain
VT
White Mts.
Mt. Washington
6,288 ft.
(1,917 m)
NH
Cape Ann
NY
Adirondack Mountains
Green Mts.
Lake Ontario
Niagara Falls
Finger Lakes
Hudson R.
MA
Cape Cod
CT
RI
Connecticut R.
Long Island
NJ
PA
MD
DE
Delaware Bay
Potomac R.
Allegheny Mts.
WV
VA
Cape Charles
Chesapeake Bay
Albemarle Sound
James R.
Roanoke R.
NC
Cape Hatteras
Cape Fear River
Cape Fear
SC
Savannah River
Oconee R.
Ocmulgee R.
Altamaha R.
GA
Stone Mountain
Clark Hill Lake
Okefenokee Swamp
Chattahoochee R.
St. Johns River
Cape Canaveral
FL
Tampa Bay
Lake Okeechobee
Everglades
Cape Sable
Florida Keys
Straits of Florida

ATLANTIC OCEAN

BAHAMAS

CUBA

APPALACHIAN MOUNTAINS
PIEDMONT
COASTAL PLAIN

Lake Superior
Isle Royale
Keweenaw Peninsula
Upper Peninsula
Lake Huron
Lake Michigan
Lower Peninsula
MI
Lake St. Clair
Lake Erie
OH
Ohio River
IN
Wabash River
IL
Illinois River
CENTRAL PLAINS
KY
Cumberland Gap
Lake Barkley
Cumberland R.
Mt. Mitchell
6,684 ft.
(2,037 m)
TN
Tennessee R.
Tombigbee R.
MS
AL
Alabama R.
Mobile Bay
Mississippi Delta

Lake of the Woods
Upper Red Lake
Lower Red Lake
Leech Lake
Mesabi Range
Mille Lacs Lake
MN
WI
Wisconsin River
Lake Winnebago
Mississippi River
ND
Lake Sakakawea
SD
Lake Oahe
Black Hills
Missouri River
IA
NE
Sand Hills
North Platte R.
Platte River
South Platte R.
KS
Smoky Hills
Red Hills
MO
Missouri River
Lake of the Ozarks
Harry S. Truman Reservoir
Ozark Plateau
Mississippi River
OK
Arkansas River
Canadian River
Red River
Ouachita Mountains
Lake Texoma
AR
TX
Llano Estacado
Pecos River
Rio Grande
Edwards Plateau
Colorado River
Brazos River
Sabine River
LA
Toledo Bend Reservoir
Sam Rayburn Reservoir
Lake Maurepas
Lake Pontchartrain
Galveston Bay

Gulf of Mexico

GREAT PLAINS
INTERIOR PLAINS

100°W
90°W
80°W
70°W
50°N
40°N
70°W
30°N
100°W
90°W
80°W

R13

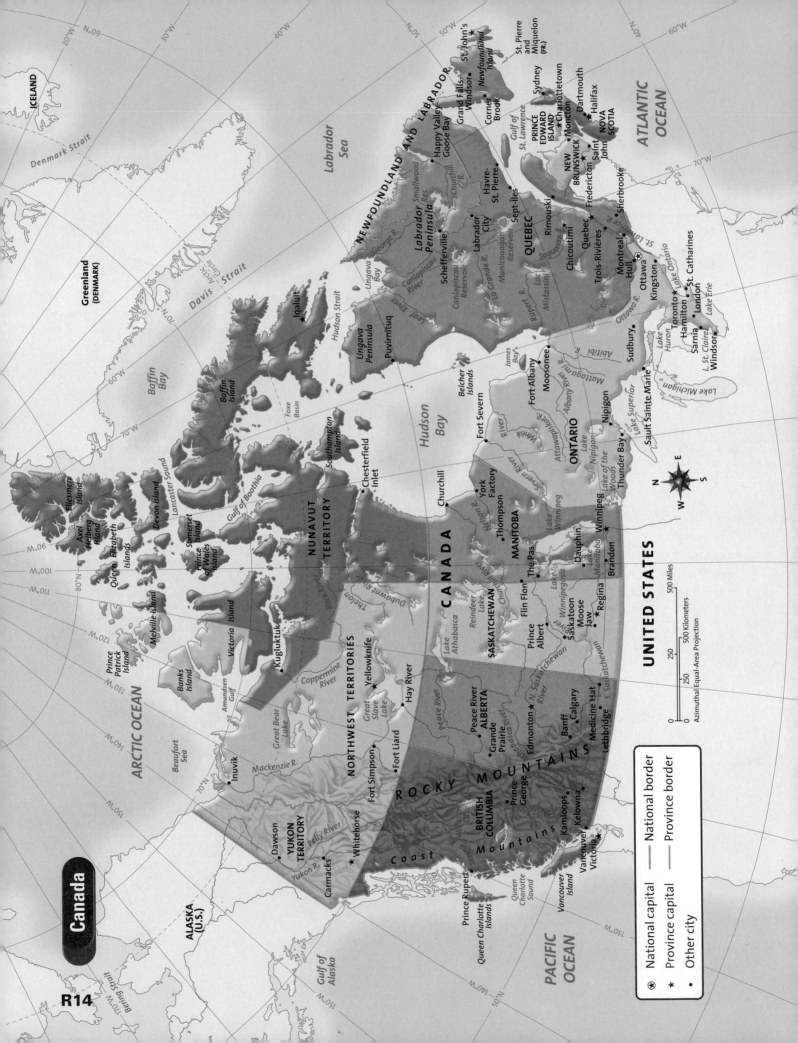

Canada

ICELAND

Denmark Strait

Greenland
(DENMARK)

Labrador
Sea

ATLANTIC
OCEAN

ARCTIC OCEAN

Beaufort
Sea

Baffin
Bay

Davis
Strait

Arctic Circle

Ellesmere
Island

Axel
Heiberg
Island

Queen Elizabeth
Islands

Devon Island

Baffin
Island

Iqaluit

Hudson Strait

Ungava
Bay

Ungava
Peninsula

Puvirnituq

NEWFOUNDLAND AND LABRADOR

St. John's

St. Pierre
and Miquelon (FR.)

Grand Falls-
Windsor

Corner
Brook

Newfoundland
Island

Gulf of
St. Lawrence

Sydney

Charlottetown

PRINCE
EDWARD
ISLAND

Dartmouth

Moncton

Halifax

NOVA
SCOTIA

NEW
BRUNSWICK

Fredericton

Saint
John

Sherbrooke

Happy Valley-
Goose Bay

Churchill

Labrador
Peninsula

Schefferville

Labrador
City

Havre-
St. Pierre

Sept-Îles

Smallwood
Res.

Churchill

La Grande R.

Manicouagan
Reservoir

Canipiscau
Reservoir

Canipiscau
River

George R.

Leaf River

Rupert R.

Lac
Mistassini

QUEBEC

Rimouski

St. Lawrence R.

Chicoutimi

Saguenay

Quebec

Trois-Rivières

Montreal

Hull

Ottawa

Ottawa R.

Kingston

Lake Ontario

Toronto

St. Catharines

London

Hamilton

Sarnia

Windsor

L. St. Claire

Lake Erie

Lake Huron

Lake Michigan

Belcher
Islands

James
Bay

Hudson
Bay

Foxe
Basin

Southampton
Island

Chesterfield
Inlet

Chesterfield

Churchill

York
Factory

Fort Severn

Fort Albany

Moosonee

Abitibi R.

Mattagami R.

Attawapiskat R.

Albany River

Severn River

Winisk R.

ONTARIO

Nipigon

Lake
Nipigon

Sudbury

Sault Sainte Marie

Thunder Bay

Lake Superior

Lake of
the Woods

CANADA

NUNAVUT
TERRITORY

Gulf of Boothia

Lancaster Sound

Somerset
Island

Prince
of Wales
Island

Prince
Patrick
Island

Melville Island

Banks
Island

Victoria
Island

Amundsen
Gulf

Kugluktuk

Coppermine
River

Back River

Thelon River

Dubawnt River

Great Bear
Lake

Great
Slave
Lake

Yellowknife

Hay River

Fort Simpson

Fort Liard

NORTHWEST TERRITORIES

Inuvik

Mackenzie R.

Reindeer
Lake

Lake
Athabasca

Churchill River

Flin Flon

Thompson

The Pas

Lake
Winnipegosis

Lake
Manitoba

Lake
Winnipeg

Winnipeg

Dauphin

Brandon

MANITOBA

SASKATCHEWAN

Prince
Albert

Saskatoon

Moose
Jaw

Regina

S. Saskatchewan

Saskatchewan R.

N. Saskatchewan River

Medicine Hat

Calgary

Banff

Lethbridge

Edmonton

ALBERTA

Grande
Prairie

Peace River

Peace River

Athabasca R.

UNITED STATES

ROCKY   MOUNTAINS

BRITISH
COLUMBIA

Prince
George

Kamloops

Kelowna

Vancouver

Victoria

Vancouver
Island

Queen Charlotte
Islands

Prince Rupert

Queen
Charlotte
Sound

Coast   Mountains

PACIFIC
OCEAN

YUKON
TERRITORY

Whitehorse

Dawson

Carmacks

Yukon R.

Pelly River

ALASKA
(U.S.)

Gulf of
Alaska

Bering Strait

Gulf of
Alaska

Legend

- ⊛ National capital   — National border
- ★ Province capital   — Province border
- • Other city

500 Miles

500 Kilometers

250

250

0

0

Azimuthal Equal-Area Projection

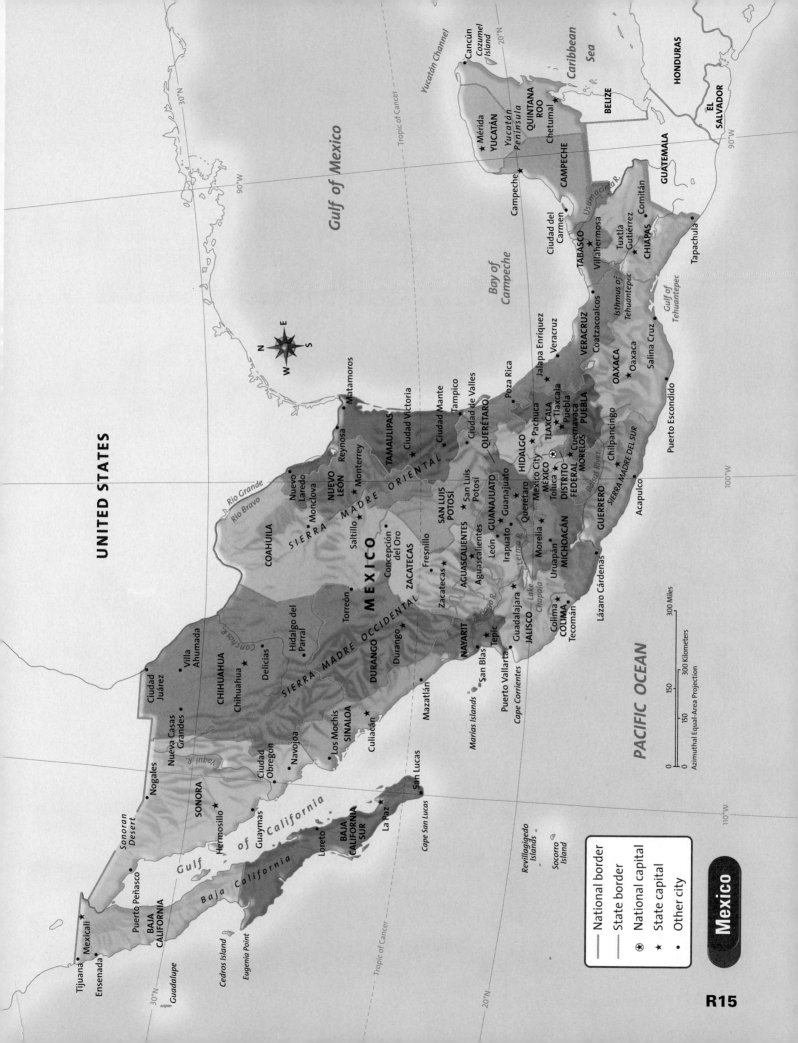

UNITED STATES

Gulf of Mexico

Caribbean Sea

HONDURAS

BELIZE

EL SALVADOR

GUATEMALA

Cancún
Cozumel Island

Mérida ★ YUCATÁN
QUINTANA ROO
Chetumal

Yucatán Peninsula

CAMPECHE
Campeche ★

Ciudad del Carmen

TABASCO
Villahermosa ★

Comitán

CHIAPAS
Tuxtla Gutiérrez ★

Tapachula

Bay of Campeche

Isthmus of Tehuantepec

Gulf of Tehuantepec

Coatzacoalcos

VERACRUZ
Jalapa Enríquez ★
Veracruz

OAXACA
Oaxaca ★

Salina Cruz

Poza Rica

Tampico

Ciudad de Valles

Ciudad Mante

Ciudad Victoria ★

TAMAULIPAS

Matamoros

Reynosa

Monterrey ★
NUEVO LEÓN
Nuevo Laredo
Monclova

Saltillo ★

COAHUILA

S I E R R A   M A D R E   O R I E N T A L

Pachuca ★
HIDALGO
TLAXCALA
Tlaxcala ★
Puebla ★
PUEBLA
MÉXICO
Mexico City ⊛
Toluca ★
DISTRITO FEDERAL
MORELOS
Cuernavaca ★
Chilpancingo ★

Querétaro ★
QUERÉTARO

San Luis Potosí ★
SAN LUIS POTOSÍ

GUANAJUATO
Guanajuato ★
León
Irapuato
Querétaro

AGUASCALIENTES
Aguascalientes ★

Zacatecas ★
ZACATECAS
Fresnillo

Concepción del Oro

M E X I C O

Torreón

Hidalgo del Parral

Delicias
CHIHUAHUA
Chihuahua ★

Ciudad Juárez

Villa Ahumada

Nueva Casas Grandes

Nogales

SONORA
Hermosillo ★

Guaymas

Gulf of California

Loreto

La Paz ★
BAJA CALIFORNIA SUR

Cape San Lucas
San Lucas

Cedros Island

BAJA CALIFORNIA
Mexicali ★
Tijuana
Ensenada

Puerto Peñasco

Sonoran Desert

Conchos R.

SIERRA MADRE OCCIDENTAL

DURANGO
Durango ★

Ciudad Obregón
Navojoa
Los Mochis
Culiacán ★
SINALOA

Mazatlán

Marías Islands

San Blas
Tepic ★
NAYARIT
Puerto Vallarta
Cape Corrientes

JALISCO
Guadalajara ★
Lake Chapala

COLIMA
Colima ★
Tecomán

MICHOACÁN
Morelia ★
Uruapan

Lázaro Cárdenas

GUERRERO
SIERRA MADRE DEL SUR
Acapulco

Puerto Escondido

Balsas River

Lerma R.
Santiago R.

Revillagigedo Islands
Socorro Island

PACIFIC OCEAN

Rio Grande
Rio Bravo

Yaqui R.

Usumacinta R.

Yucatán Channel

Tropic of Cancer

30°N

20°N

90°W

100°W

110°W

30°N

20°N

N
E
S
W

| Mexico |

National border
State border
⊛ National capital
★ State capital
• Other city

0   150   300 Miles
0   150   300 Kilometers
Azimuthal Equal-Area Projection

R15

Almanac

FACTS ABOUT THE UNITED STATES

LAND	SIZE	CLIMATE	POPULATION*	LEADING PRODUCTS AND RESOURCES

Highest Point:
Mt. McKinley,
in Alaska
20,320 feet

Lowest Point:
Death Valley,
in California
282 feet below sea
level

Largest Freshwater Lake:
Lake Superior,
31,800 square miles

Deepest Lake:
Crater Lake,
in Oregon 1,932 feet

Area:
3,615,292
square miles

Geographic Center:
near
Castle Rock,
Butte County,
South Dakota

Highest Recorded Temperature:
134°F at Death Valley,
in California, on July 10,
1913

Lowest Recorded Temperature:
-80°F at Prospect Creek,
Alaska, on January 23,
1971

Rainiest Place:
Mt. Waialeale, in
Hawaii, average yearly
rainfall of 460 inches

Driest Place:
Death Valley, in California, average yearly
rainfall of 2 inches

Total Population:
296,410,404

*the most recent
figure available

Farming:
Beef cattle, chickens, corn,
cotton, eggs, pigs, milk,
soybeans, wheat

Fishing:
Crabs, salmon, shrimp

Manufacturing:
Airplanes, automobiles and
trucks, chemicals, clothing,
computers, electronic
equipment, gasoline,
machinery, medicines,
metal products, paper,
plastics, printed materials,
processed foods

Mining:
Coal, natural gas, oil

Washington, D.C., became the
nation's capital in 1800.

The United States

RUSSIA

ARCTIC OCEAN

ALASKA

Mt. McKinley ▲
20,320 ft.

CANADA

Juneau ★

PACIFIC OCEAN

0 200 400 Miles
0 400 Kilometers

CANADA

Olympia ★

WA

Salem ★

OR

Helena ★

ID

Boise ★

MT

Columbia River

Missouri River

ND

Bismarck ★

SD

Pierre ★

WY

Cheyenne ★

NE

MN

St. Paul ★

WI

Madison ★

Des Moines ★

IA

Lake Superior

Lake Michigan

Lake Huron

MI

Lansing ★

Lake Ontario

Lake Erie

St. Lawrence River

NH

Montpelier ★

VT

Albany ★

NY

ME

Augusta ★

Concord ★

Boston ★

MA

Providence

CT RI

Hartford ★

Sacramento ★

NV

Carson City ★

Great Salt Lake

Salt Lake City ★

UT

Denver ★

CO

Colorado River

Lincoln ★

Platte River

Topeka ★

KS

Arkansas River

MO

Jefferson City ★

IL

Springfield ★

IN

Indianapolis ★

Columbus ★

OH

Harrisburg ★

PA

Charleston ★

WV

Frankfort ★

KY

APPALACHIAN MTS.

Trenton ★

NJ

MD

Dover ★

DE

Annapolis ★

Washington, D.C. ⊛

Richmond ★

VA

Nashville ★

TN

Mt. Mitchell ▲
6,684 ft.

Raleigh ★

NC

Columbia ★

SC

CA

Mt. Whitney ▲
14,495 ft.

Death Valley

Grand Canyon

Santa Fe ★

AZ

Phoenix ★

NM

OK

Oklahoma City ★

Red River

AR

Little Rock ★

Mississippi R.

MS

Jackson ★

AL

Montgomery ★

Atlanta ★

GA

Savannah R.

ATLANTIC OCEAN

PACIFIC OCEAN

TX

Austin ★

LA

Baton Rouge ★

Tallahassee ★

FL

MEXICO

Rio Grande

Snake River

ROCKY MOUNTAINS

Ohio R.

Mt. Waialeale ▲
5,148 ft.

PACIFIC OCEAN

Honolulu ★

HAWAII

0 100 Miles
0 100 Kilometers

160°W 155°W 19°N

Gulf of Mexico

BAHAMAS

CUBA

JAMAICA

0 200 400 Miles
0 200 400 Kilometers
Albers Equal-Area Projection

70°N 60°N 170°W 150°W

40°N 70°W 30°N 90°W 120°W 110°W 80°W 20°N

N E S W

⊛ National capital	─── National border
★ State capital	─── State border
▲ Mountain peak	

The 50 states are divided into 3,092 counties. The courthouse for Kiowa County, Oklahoma, is shown at right.

Each state has its own flag. Shown at right are Hawaii's flag (upper) and Alaska's flag (lower).

Almanac
Facts About the States

State Flag	State	Year of Statehood	Population*	Area (sq. mi.)	Capital	Origin of State Name
	Alabama	1819	4,557,808	50,750	Montgomery	Choctaw, *alba ayamule*, "one who clears land and gathers food from it"
	Alaska	1959	663,661	570,374	Juneau	Aleut, *alayeska*, "great land"
	Arizona	1912	5,939,292	113,642	Phoenix	Papago, *arizonac*, "place of the small spring"
	Arkansas	1836	2,779,154	52,075	Little Rock	Quapaw, "the downstream people"
	California	1850	36,132,147	155,973	Sacramento	Spanish, a fictional island
	Colorado	1876	4,665,177	103,730	Denver	Spanish, "red land" or "red earth"
	Connecticut	1788	3,510,297	4,845	Hartford	Mohican, *quinnitukqut*, "at the long tidal river"
	Delaware	1787	843,524	1,955	Dover	Named for Lord de la Warr
	Florida	1845	17,789,864	54,153	Tallahassee	Spanish, "filled with flowers"
	Georgia	1788	9,072,576	57,919	Atlanta	Named for King George II of England
	Hawaii	1959	1,275,194	6,450	Honolulu	Polynesian, *hawaiki* or *owykee*, "homeland"
	Idaho	1890	1,429,096	82,751	Boise	Invented name with unknown meaning

State Flag	State	Year of Statehood	Population*	Area (sq. mi.)	Capital	Origin of State Name
	Illinois	1818	12,763,371	55,593	Springfield	Algonquin, *iliniwek*, "men" or "warriors"
	Indiana	1816	6,271,973	35,870	Indianapolis	*Indian + a*, "land of the Indians"
	Iowa	1846	2,966,334	55,875	Des Moines	Dakota, *ayuba*, "beautiful land"
	Kansas	1861	2,744,687	81,823	Topeka	Sioux, "land of the south wind people"
	Kentucky	1792	4,173,405	39,732	Frankfort	Iroquoian, *ken-tah-ten*, "land of tomorrow"
	Louisiana	1812	4,523,628	43,566	Baton Rouge	Named for King Louis XIV of France
	Maine	1820	1,321,505	30,865	Augusta	Named after a French province
	Maryland	1788	5,600,388	9,775	Annapolis	Named for Henrietta Maria, Queen Consort of Charles I of England
	Massachusetts	1788	6,398,743	7,838	Boston	Massachusetts tribe of Native Americans, "at the big hill" or "place of the big hill"
	Michigan	1837	10,120,860	56,809	Lansing	Ojibwa, "large lake"
	Minnesota	1858	5,132,799	79,617	St. Paul	Dakota Sioux, "sky-blue water"
	Mississippi	1817	2,921,088	46,914	Jackson	Indian word meaning "great waters" or "father of waters"
	Missouri	1821	5,800,310	68,898	Jefferson City	Named after the Missouri Indian tribe. *Missouri* means "town of the large canoes."

* latest available population figures

Almanac ■ R19

State Flag	State	Year of Statehood	Population*	Area (sq. mi.)	Capital	Origin of State Name
	Montana	1889	935,670	145,566	Helena	Spanish, "mountainous"
	Nebraska	1867	1,758,787	76,878	Lincoln	From an Oto Indian word meaning "flat water"
	Nevada	1864	2,414,807	109,806	Carson City	Spanish, "snowy" or "snowed upon"
	New Hampshire	1788	1,309,940	8,969	Concord	Named for Hampshire County, England
	New Jersey	1787	8,717,925	7,419	Trenton	Named for the Isle of Jersey
	New Mexico	1912	1,928,384	121,365	Santa Fe	Named by Spanish explorers from Mexico
	New York	1788	19,254,630	47,224	Albany	Named after the Duke of York
	North Carolina	1789	8,683,242	48,718	Raleigh	Named after King Charles II of England
	North Dakota	1889	636,677	70,704	Bismarck	Sioux, *dakota*, "friend" or "ally"
	Ohio	1803	11,464,042	40,953	Columbus	Iroquois, *oheo*, "great water"
	Oklahoma	1907	3,547,884	68,679	Oklahoma City	Choctaw, "red people"
	Oregon	1859	3,641,056	96,003	Salem	Unknown; generally accepted that it was taken from the writings of Maj. Robert Rogers, an English army officer
	Pennsylvania	1787	12,429,616	44,820	Harrisburg	*Penn + sylvania*, meaning "Penn's woods"

State Flag	State	Year of Statehood	Population*	Area (sq. mi.)	Capital	Origin of State Name
	Rhode Island	1790	1,076,189	1,045	Providence	From the Greek island of Rhodes
	South Carolina	1788	4,255,083	30,111	Columbia	Named after King Charles II of England
	South Dakota	1889	775,933	75,898	Pierre	Sioux, *dakota*, "friend"or "ally"
	Tennessee	1796	5,962,959	41,220	Nashville	Name of a Cherokee village
	Texas	1845	22,859,968	261,914	Austin	Native American, *tejas*, "friend" or "ally"
	Utah	1896	2,469,585	82,168	Salt Lake City	From the Ute tribe, meaning "people of the mountains"
	Vermont	1791	623,050	9,249	Montpelier	French, *vert*, "green," and *mont*, "mountain"
	Virginia	1788	7,567,465	39,598	Richmond	Named after Queen Elizabeth I of England
	Washington	1889	6,287,759	66,582	Olympia	Named for George Washington
	West Virginia	1863	1,816,856	24,087	Charleston	From the English-named state of Virginia
	Wisconsin	1848	5,536,201	54,314	Madison	Possibly Algonquian, "the place where we live"
	Wyoming	1890	509,294	97,105	Cheyenne	From Delaware Indian word meaning "land of vast plains"
	District of Columbia		550,521	67		Named after Christopher Columbus

* latest available population figures

Almanac
Facts About the Presidents

1 George Washington

1732–1799
Birthplace: *Westmoreland County, VA*
Home State: *VA*
Political Party: *None*
Age at Inauguration: *57*
Served: *1789–1797*
Vice President: *John Adams*

2 John Adams

1735–1826
Birthplace: *Braintree, MA*
Home State: *MA*
Political Party: *Federalist*
Age at Inauguration: *61*
Served: *1797–1801*
Vice President: *Thomas Jefferson*

3 Thomas Jefferson

1743–1826
Birthplace: *Albemarle County, VA*
Home State: *VA*
Political Party: *Democratic-Republican*
Age at Inauguration: *57*
Served: *1801–1809*
Vice Presidents: *Aaron Burr, George Clinton*

4 James Madison

1751–1836
Birthplace: *Port Conway, VA*
Home State: *VA*
Political Party: *Democratic-Republican*
Age at Inauguration: *57*
Served: *1809–1817*
Vice Presidents: *George Clinton, Elbridge Gerry*

5 James Monroe

1758–1831
Birthplace: *Westmoreland County, VA*
Home State: *VA*
Political Party: *Democratic-Republican*
Age at Inauguration: *58*
Served: *1817–1825*
Vice President: *Daniel D. Tompkins*

6 John Quincy Adams

1767–1848
Birthplace: *Braintree, MA*
Home State: *MA*
Political Party: *Democratic-Republican*
Age at Inauguration: *57*
Served: *1825–1829*
Vice President: *John C. Calhoun*

7 Andrew Jackson

1767–1845
Birthplace: *Waxhaw settlement, SC*
Home State: *TN*
Political Party: *Democratic*
Age at Inauguration: *61*
Served: *1829–1837*
Vice Presidents: *John C. Calhoun, Martin Van Buren*

8 Martin Van Buren

1782–1862
Birthplace: *Kinderhook, NY*
Home State: *NY*
Political Party: *Democratic*
Age at Inauguration: *54*
Served: *1837–1841*
Vice President: *Richard M. Johnson*

9 William H. Harrison

1773–1841
Birthplace: *Berkeley, VA*
Home State: *OH*
Political Party: *Whig*
Age at Inauguration: *68*
Served: *1841*
Vice President: *John Tyler*

10 John Tyler

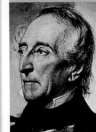

1790–1862
Birthplace: *Greenway, VA*
Home State: *VA*
Political Party: *Whig*
Age at Inauguration: *51*
Served: *1841–1845*
Vice President: *none*

11 James K. Polk

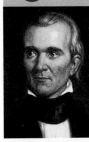

1795–1849
Birthplace: *near Pineville, NC*
Home State: *TN*
Political Party: *Democratic*
Age at Inauguration: *49*
Served: *1845–1849*
Vice President: *George M. Dallas*

12 Zachary Taylor

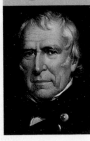

1784–1850
Birthplace: *Orange County, VA*
Home State: *LA*
Political Party: *Whig*
Age at Inauguration: *64*
Served: *1849–1850*
Vice President: *Millard Fillmore*

13 Millard Fillmore

1800–1874
Birthplace: *Locke, NY*
Home State: *NY*
Political Party: *Whig*
Age at Inauguration: *50*
Served: *1850–1853*
Vice President: *none*

14 Franklin Pierce

1804–1869
Birthplace: *Hillsboro, NH*
Home State: *NH*
Political Party: *Democratic*
Age at Inauguration: *48*
Served: *1853–1857*
Vice President: *William R. King*

Home State refers to the state of residence when elected.

15 James Buchanan

1791–1868
Birthplace:
near Mercersburg, PA
Home State: *PA*
Political Party:
Democratic
Age at Inauguration: *65*
Served: *1857–1861*
Vice President:
John C. Breckinridge

16 Abraham Lincoln

1809–1865
Birthplace:
near Hodgenville, KY
Home State: *IL*
Political Party:
Republican
Age at Inauguration: *52*
Served: *1861–1865*
Vice Presidents:
Hannibal Hamlin,
Andrew Johnson

17 Andrew Johnson

1808–1875
Birthplace: *Raleigh, NC*
Home State: *TN*
Political Party:
National Union
Age at Inauguration: *56*
Served: *1865–1869*
Vice President: *none*

18 Ulysses S. Grant

1822–1885
Birthplace:
Point Pleasant, OH
Home State: *IL*
Political Party:
Republican
Age at Inauguration: *46*
Served: *1869–1877*
Vice Presidents:
Schuyler Colfax,
Henry Wilson

19 Rutherford B. Hayes

1822–1893
Birthplace:
near Delaware, OH
Home State: *OH*
Political Party:
Republican
Age at Inauguration: *54*
Served: *1877–1881*
Vice President:
William A. Wheeler

20 James A. Garfield

1831–1881
Birthplace: *Orange, OH*
Home State: *OH*
Political Party:
Republican
Age at Inauguration: *49*
Served: *1881*
Vice President:
Chester A. Arthur

21 Chester A. Arthur

1829–1886
Birthplace: *Fairfield, VT*
Home State: *NY*
Political Party:
Republican
Age at Inauguration: *51*
Served: *1881–1885*
Vice President: *none*

22 Grover Cleveland

1837–1908
Birthplace: *Caldwell, NJ*
Home State: *NY*
Political Party:
Democratic
Age at Inauguration: *47*
Served: *1885–1889*
Vice President:
Thomas A. Hendricks

23 Benjamin Harrison

1833–1901
Birthplace: *North Bend,*
OH
Home State: *IN*
Political Party:
Republican
Age at Inauguration: *55*
Served: *1889–1893*
Vice President:
Levi P. Morton

24 Grover Cleveland

1837–1908
Birthplace: *Caldwell, NJ*
Home State: *NY*
Political Party:
Democratic
Age at Inauguration: *55*
Served: *1893–1897*
Vice President:
Adlai E. Stevenson

25 William McKinley

1843–1901
Birthplace: *Niles, OH*
Home State: *OH*
Political Party:
Republican
Age at Inauguration: *54*
Served: *1897–1901*
Vice Presidents:
Garret A. Hobart,
Theodore Roosevelt

26 Theodore Roosevelt

1858–1919
Birthplace: *New York, NY*
Home State: *NY*
Political Party:
Republican
Age at Inauguration: *42*
Served: *1901–1909*
Vice President:
Charles W. Fairbanks

27 William H. Taft

1857–1930
Birthplace: *Cincinnati, OH*
Home State: *OH*
Political Party:
Republican
Age at Inauguration: *51*
Served: *1909–1913*
Vice President:
James S. Sherman

28 Woodrow Wilson

1856–1924
Birthplace: *Staunton, VA*
Home State: *NJ*
Political Party:
Democratic
Age at Inauguration: *56*
Served: *1913–1921*
Vice President:
Thomas R. Marshall

29 Warren G. Harding

1865–1923
Birthplace:
Blooming Grove, OH
Home State: *OH*
Political Party:
Republican
Age at Inauguration: *55*
Served: *1921–1923*
Vice President:
Calvin Coolidge

30 Calvin Coolidge

1872–1933
Birthplace: *Plymouth Notch, VT*
Home State: *MA*
Political Party: *Republican*
Age at Inauguration: *51*
Served: *1923–1929*
Vice President: *Charles G. Dawes*

31 Herbert Hoover

1874–1964
Birthplace: *West Branch, IA*
Home State: *CA*
Political Party: *Republican*
Age at Inauguration: *54*
Served: *1929–1933*
Vice President: *Charles Curtis*

32 Franklin D. Roosevelt

1882–1945
Birthplace: *Hyde Park, NY*
Home State: *NY*
Political Party: *Democratic*
Age at Inauguration: *51*
Served: *1933–1945*
Vice Presidents: *John N. Garner, Henry A. Wallace, Harry S. Truman*

33 Harry S. Truman

1884–1972
Birthplace: *Lamar, MO*
Home State: *MO*
Political Party: *Democratic*
Age at Inauguration: *60*
Served: *1945–1953*
Vice President: *Alben W. Barkley*

34 Dwight D. Eisenhower

1890–1969
Birthplace: *Denison, TX*
Home State: *NY*
Political Party: *Republican*
Age at Inauguration: *62*
Served: *1953–1961*
Vice President: *Richard M. Nixon*

35 John F. Kennedy

1917–1963
Birthplace: *Brookline, MA*
Home State: *MA*
Political Party: *Democratic*
Age at Inauguration: *43*
Served: *1961–1963*
Vice President: *Lyndon B. Johnson*

36 Lyndon B. Johnson

1908–1973
Birthplace: *near Stonewall, TX*
Home State: *TX*
Political Party: *Democratic*
Age at Inauguration: *55*
Served: *1963–1969*
Vice President: *Hubert H. Humphrey*

37 Richard M. Nixon

1913–1994
Birthplace: *Yorba Linda, CA*
Home State: *NY*
Political Party: *Republican*
Age at Inauguration: *56*
Served: *1969–1974*
Vice Presidents: *Spiro T. Agnew, Gerald R. Ford*

38 Gerald R. Ford

1913–
Birthplace: *Omaha, NE*
Home State: *MI*
Political Party: *Republican*
Age at Inauguration: *61*
Served: *1974–1977*
Vice President: *Nelson A. Rockefeller*

39 Jimmy Carter

1924–
Birthplace: *Plains, GA*
Home State: *GA*
Political Party: *Democratic*
Age at Inauguration: *52*
Served: *1977–1981*
Vice President: *Walter F. Mondale*

40 Ronald W. Reagan

1911–2004
Birthplace: *Tampico, IL*
Home State: *CA*
Political Party: *Republican*
Age at Inauguration: *69*
Served: *1981–1989*
Vice President: *George Bush*

41 George Bush

1924–
Birthplace: *Milton, MA*
Home State: *TX*
Political Party: *Republican*
Age at Inauguration: *64*
Served: *1989–1993*
Vice President: *Dan Quayle*

42 William Clinton

1946–
Birthplace: *Hope, AR*
Home State: *AR*
Political Party: *Democratic*
Age at Inauguration: *46*
Served: *1993–2001*
Vice President: *Albert Gore*

43 George W. Bush

1946–
Birthplace: *New Haven, CT*
Home State: *TX*
Political Party: *Republican*
Age at Inauguration: *54*
Served: *2001–*
Vice President: *Richard Cheney*

Home State refers to the state of residence when elected.

THE PLEDGE OF ALLEGIANCE

I pledge allegiance to the Flag
of the United States of America,
and to the Republic
for which it stands,
one Nation under God, indivisible,
with liberty and justice for all.

The flag is a symbol of the United States of America. The Pledge of Allegiance says that the people of the United States promise to stand up for the flag, their country, and the basic beliefs of freedom and fairness upon which the country was established.

Research Handbook

Before you can write a report or complete a project, you must gather information about your topic. You can find information from many sources, including maps, photos, illustrations, and artifacts. You can also find information in your textbook. Other sources of information are technology resources, print resources, and community resources.

Technology Resources

- Internet
- Computer disk
- Television and radio

Print Resources

- Almanac
- Atlas
- Dictionary
- Encyclopedia
- Nonfiction book
- Periodical
- Thesaurus

Community Resources

- Teacher
- Museum curator
- Community leader
- Older citizen

Technology Resources

The main technology resources you can use for researching information are the Internet and computer disks. Your school or local library may have CD-ROMs or DVDs that contain information about your topic. Other media, such as television and radio, can also be good sources of current information.

Using the Internet

The Internet contains vast amounts of information. By using a computer to go online, you can read letters and documents, see pictures and artworks, listen to music, take a virtual tour of a place, and read about current events.

Information that you find online is always changing. Keep in mind that some websites might contain mistakes or incorrect information. To get accurate information, be sure to visit only trusted websites, such as museum and government sites. Also, try to find two or more websites that give the same facts.

❯ Plan Your Search
- Identify the topic to be researched.
- Make a list of questions that you want to answer about your topic.
- List key words or groups of words that can be used to write or talk about your topic.
- Look for good online resources to find answers to your questions.
- Decide if the information you find is relevant, reliable, and accurate.

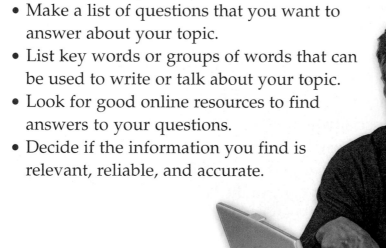

Use a Search Engine

A search engine is an online collection of websites that can be sorted by entering a key word or group of words. There are many different search engines available. You may want to ask a librarian, a teacher, or a parent for suggestions on which search engine to use.

▶ **Search by Subject**   To search by subject, or topic, use a search engine. Choose from the list of key words that you made while planning your search, and enter a key word or group of words in the search engine field on your screen. Then click SEARCH or GO. You will see a list of available websites that have to do with your topic. Click on the site or sites you think will be most helpful. If you do not find enough websites listed, think of other key words or related words, and search again.

▶ **Search by Address**   Each website has its own address, called a Uniform Resource Locator, or URL for short. To get to a website using a URL, simply type the URL in the LOCATION/GO TO box on your screen and hit ENTER or click GO.

▶ **Use Bookmarks**   The bookmark feature is an Internet tool for keeping and organizing URLs. If you find a website that seems especially helpful, you can save the URL so that you can quickly and easily return to it later. Click BOOKMARKS or FAVORITES at the top of your screen, and choose ADD. Your computer makes a copy of the URL and keeps a record of it.

Print Resources

Books in libraries are organized through a system of numbers. These traditional resources have their own title and a number called a call number. The call number tells where in the library the book can be found.

You can locate information in the book by using its table of contents and index. Some reference books, such as encyclopedias, are usually kept in a separate section of a library. Each book there has R or RE—for *reference*—on its spine. Most reference books can only be used in the library. Most libraries also have a special section for periodicals, which include magazines and newspapers.

❯ Almanac

An almanac is a book or electronic resource that contains facts about different subjects. The subjects are listed in alphabetical order in an index, and many number-based facts are shown in tables or charts. New almanacs are published each year, so they have the most current information.

❯ Atlas

An atlas is a book of maps that gives information about places. Different kinds of atlases show different places at different times. Your teacher or librarian can help you find the kind of atlas you need for your research.

❯ Dictionary

A dictionary gives the correct spelling of words and their definitions, or meanings. It also gives the words' pronunciations, or how to say the words aloud. In addition, many dictionaries have lists of foreign words, abbreviations, well-known people, and place names.

> **de•mand**\di-´mand*n* **1:** to ask with authority **2:** the desire or need for a product or service
> **de•pend**\di-´pend*vi* **1:** to be undecided **2:** to rely on for help
> **de•pos•it**\di-´pä-zit*vb* **1:** to put money into a bank account **2:** to place for safekeeping or as a pledge

Dictionary entry

◗ Encyclopedia

An encyclopedia is a book or set of books that gives information about many different topics. The topics are arranged alphabetically. An encyclopedia is a good source to use when beginning your research. In addition to words, electronic encyclopedias often have sound and video clips as well.

◗ Nonfiction Books

A nonfiction book gives facts about real people, places, and things. All nonfiction books in a library are arranged in order and by category according to their call numbers. To find a book's call number, you use a library's card file or computer catalog. You can search for a book in the catalog by subject, author, or title.

◗ Periodicals

A periodical is published each day, each week, or each month. Periodicals are good resources for current information on topics not yet found in books. Many libraries have a guide that lists magazine articles by subject. Two such guides are the *Children's Magazine Guide* and the *Readers' Guide to Periodical Literature*. The entries in guides are usually in alphabetical order by subject, author, or title.

◗ Thesaurus

A thesaurus (thih•SAWR•uhs) gives synonyms, or words that mean the same or nearly the same as another word. A thesaurus also gives antonyms, or words that have the opposite meanings. Using a thesaurus can help you find words that better describe your topic and make your writing more interesting.

Encyclopedia article

Community Resources

People in your community can share oral histories or information about your research topic. You can learn facts, opinions, or points of view by asking these people thoughtful questions. Before you talk to any of them, always ask a teacher or a parent for permission.

Listening to Find Information

It is important to plan ahead whenever you talk with people as part of your research. Planning ahead will help you gather the information you need. Follow these tips as you gather information from people in your community.

▶ Before
- Find out more about the topic you want to discuss.
- Think about the kind of information you still need.
- Consider the best way to gather the information you need.
- List the people you want to talk to.
- Make a list of useful questions you want to ask. Make sure your questions are clear and effective.

▶ During
- Speak clearly and loudly enough when asking questions.
- Listen carefully. Make sure you are getting the information you need, and revise your questions based on what you hear. You may also think of new questions to ask.
- Think about the speaker's perspective, tone of voice, and word choice. Use these clues to evaluate whether the speaker is a good source of information about your topic.
- Be polite. Do not interrupt or argue with the person who is speaking.
- Take notes to help you remember important ideas and details.
- Write down the person's exact words if you think you will want to quote them in your report. If possible, use a tape recorder. Be sure to ask the speaker for permission in advance.

▶ After
- Thank the person you spoke with.
- Follow up by writing a thank-you note.

Writing to Get Information

You can also write to people in your community to gather information. You can write an e-mail or a letter. Keep these ideas in mind as you write:

- Write neatly or use a computer.
- Say who you are and why you are writing. Be clear and specific about what you want to know.
- Carefully check your spelling and punctuation.
- If you are writing a letter, provide a self-addressed, stamped envelope for the person to send you a response.
- Thank the person.

222 Central Avenue
Dover, NJ 07801
October 25, 20- -

Regional Tourism Division
Attn: Ms. Stephanie Nguyen
123 Main Street
Cape May, NJ 08204

Dear Ms. Nguyen:

My name is David Thomas, and I am writing this letter to see if you can send me some information about scenic attractions in southern New Jersey. My family is planning a vacation next month, and we would like to visit some of the attractions in the southern part of the state. Please send a brochure listing the scenic attractions and a highway map. I understand this is a service you provide for those planning vacations in the area. I am excited about visiting your part of the state.

Thank you for your help.

Sincerely,

David Thomas

David Thomas
222 Central Avenue
Dover, NJ 07801

Bureau of Tourism
Attn: Stephanie Nguyen
123 Main Street
Cape May, NJ 08204

Reporting

▶ Written Reports

Your teacher may ask you to write a report about the information you find. Knowing how to write a report will help you make good use of the information. The following tips will help you write your report.

▶ Before Writing

- Choose a main idea or topic.
- Think of questions about your topic. Questions should be clear and focus on specific ideas about your topic.
- Gather information from two or more sources. You may use print resources, technology resources, or community resources. Be sure to look for answers to your questions.
- Take notes that paraphrase or summarize the information.
- Review your notes to be sure you have the information you need. Write down ideas and details about your topic to put in your report.
- Use your notes to make an outline of the information you found. Organize your ideas in a way that is easy to understand.

▶ Citing Sources

An important part of research and writing is citing sources. When you cite a source, you keep a written record of where you got your information. The list of sources will be presented as a bibliography. A bibliography is a list of the books, periodicals, and other sources that you used to find the information in your report.

Outline

Little Rock, Arkansas

I. The History of Little Rock, Arkansas

    A. Little Rock is the state capital of Arkansas.

        1. The site was explored and named by a French trapper in 1722.

        2. Little Rock became the capital of the Arkansas Territory in 1820.

    B. During the Civil War, Little Rock was in the Confederacy.

        1. In 1861, the Confederacy took over a Union arsenal in Little Rock.

        2. In 1863, Little Rock was captured by the Union.

    C. Little Rock became an economic center.

        1. Railroads were built to link industries and natural resources around Little Rock in the 1880s.

        2. In 1969, dams and canals were built to link Little Rock with the Mississippi River.

    D. Important events happened in Little Rock during the Civil Rights movement.

        1. In 1957, nine African American children became students at a previously all-white school.

        2. The school later became a national historic site.

Bibliography

Hernandez, Elizabeth. *Little Rock Through the Years*. San Antonio, Texas: Old Alamo Press, 2004

Wyatt, Adam. *The History of Arkansas*. Philadelphia, Pennsylvania: Scenic River Publishing, 2003

Bibliography Card

Wyatt, Adam. *The History of Arkansas*. Philadelphia, Pennsylvania: Scenic River Publishing, 2003, page 25.

Little Rock became the state capital of the Arkansas territory in 1820.

LITTLE ROCK, ARKANSAS	
Reading Notes	**Class Notes**
• Little Rock was named after a nearby rock formation on the Arkansas River	• Little Rock is in Arkansas, a state in the South
• Little Rock is located in the central part of the state of Arkansas	• After the Civil War, many states in the South were still segregated
• Little Rock expanded economically in the 1940s	• Segregation is the practice of keeping people in separate groups based on their race or culture
• Timber and coal are found in Arkansas	• In 1954, the Supreme Court decided that segregation was unconstitutional
• Farmers from all around Arkansas sell their produce in Little Rock	• In 1957, nine African American students, known as the Little Rock Nine, were sent to Central High School, a previously all-white school
• The University of Arkansas is located in Little Rock	• Today, Central High School is a national historic site

❱ Write a First Draft

- Use your notes and your outline to write a draft of your report. Keep in mind that your purpose is to share information.
- Write in paragraph form. Develop your topic with facts, details, examples, and explanations. Each paragraph should focus on one new idea.
- Get all your ideas down on paper. You can revise your draft and correct errors in the next step.

❱ Revise

- Read over your draft. Does it make sense? Does your report have a beginning, a middle, and an end? Have you answered all your questions?
- Rewrite sentences that are unclear or poorly worded. Move sentences that seem out of place.
- Add details when needed to support your ideas.
- If too many sentences are alike, make some sentences shorter or longer to keep your report interesting.
- Check any quotations to be sure you have shown someone's exact words and that you have noted the source correctly.

❱ Proofread and Edit

- Proofread your report, checking for errors.
- Correct any errors in spelling, capitalization, or punctuation. If you are writing your report on a computer, use the spell-check feature.
- Use a thesaurus to find words that better describe your topic or that make your report more interesting.

❱ Publish

- Make a neat, clean copy of your report.
- Include graphs, tables, maps, or other illustrations to help explain your topic.

Rough draft

Marta Berzina
Social Studies

A History of Little Rock, Arkansas

Little Rock is the capital of the state of Arkansas. The city has a rich history. In 1722, the site where Little Rock is located was explored by a french trapper. He named the area Little Rock after a rock formation that he saw there. About 100 years later, in 1820, Little Rock became the capital of the Arkansas Territory. During the Civil War, Arkansas was one of the states in the Confederacy. In 1861, Confederate troops took over a Union arsenal in Little Rock. The Union captured Little Rock in 1863.

After the Civil War, Little Rock's economy grew. In the 1880s, railroads began to connect the industries in Little Rock with the natural resources around Arkansas. Timber and coal, especially, were important natural resources for Little Rock. Also, farmers from around the state of Arkansas sold their produce in markets in Little Rock. After that in 1969, a network of canals and dams linked Little Rock to the Mississippi River, bringing more trade.

Little Rock is also famous for what happened there during the Civil Rights movement. After the Civil War, Arkansas, like most other states in the South, became segregated. Segregation meant that African Americans and whites were separated. They ate in different restaurants, used different restrooms, and attended different schools. In 1954, the Supreme Court decided that segregation was against the Constitution. The Little Rock Nine were nine African American students from Little Rock who, in 1957, were the first to be sent to a school that before had only allowed white students to attend. Central High School, the school where this took place, is now a national historic site.

Final draft

Marta Berzina
Social Studies

A History of Little Rock, Arkansas

Little Rock is the capital of the state of Arkansas. The city has a rich history. In 1722, the site where Little Rock is located was explored by a French trapper. He named the area Little Rock after a rock formation that he saw there. About 100 years later, in 1820, Little Rock became the capital of the Arkansas Territory.

During the Civil War, Arkansas was one of the states in the Confederacy. In 1861, Confederate troops took over a Union arsenal in Little Rock. The Union captured Little Rock in 1863.

After the Civil War, Little Rock's economy grew. In the 1880s, railroads began to connect the industries in Little Rock with the natural resources around Arkansas. Timber and coal, especially, were important natural resources for Little Rock. Also, farmers from around the state of Arkansas sold their produce in markets in Little Rock. In 1969, a network of canals and dams linked Little Rock to the Mississippi River, bringing more trade to the city.

Little Rock is also famous for what happened there during the Civil Rights movement. After the Civil War, Arkansas, like most other states in the South, became segregated. Segregation meant that African Americans and whites were separated. They ate in different restaurants, used different restrooms, and attended different schools. In 1954, the Supreme Court decided that segregation was unconstitutional. The Little Rock Nine were nine African American students from Little Rock who, in 1957, were the first to be sent to a school that before had only allowed white students to attend. Central High School, the school where this took place, is now a national historic site.

Proofreading marks and their meanings	
Mark	**Meaning**
∧	Insert word.
∧,	Insert comma.
¶	Start a new paragraph.
≡ (cap)	Use capital letter.
ℰ	Delete.
(lc)	Use lowercase letter.

Listening to Find Information

Sometimes in class you may be asked to give an oral presentation. Like a written report, the purpose of an oral presentation is to share information. These tips will help you prepare an oral presentation:

- Follow the steps described in Before Writing on page R33 to gather and organize information.
- Use your notes to plan and organize your presentation. Include an introduction and a conclusion in your report.
- Prepare note cards that you can refer to as you speak.
- Prepare visuals such as illustrations, diagrams, maps, graphs, tables, or other graphics to help listeners better understand your topic.
- Give your audience a controlling idea about your topic. A controlling idea is the main idea that you support with facts and details.
- Practice your presentation.
- Be sure to speak clearly and loudly enough. Keep your listeners interested in your report by using facial expressions and hand movements.

Biographical Dictionary

The Biographical Dictionary lists many of the important people introduced in this book. The page number tells where the main discussion of each person starts. See the Index for other page references.

A

Abbott, Teddy *1860?–1939?* Cowhand in the late 1800s in the United States, who joined his first cattle drive at the age of ten. p. 329

Adams, John *1735–1826* Massachusetts leader who served as a member of Congress and later as the second President of the United States. p. 120

Ailey, Alvin *1931–1989* A New York City dancer who created the Alvin Ailey American Dance Theater which trains dancers and performs worldwide. p. 147

Alcott, Louisa May *1832–1888* The Massachusetts-born author of *Little Women*. p. 139

Anyokah *1500s?* Cherokee girl who helped invent a writing system for the Cherokee. p. 186

Archuleta, Eppie *1922–* A weaver known for her narrative designs. Her weavings hang in museums all across the United States. p. 407

Ariyoshi, George *1926–* A past Hawaii governor, George Ariyoshi was the first Asian American governor in the United States. p. 414

Austin, Stephen F. *1793–1836* An American pioneer who helped lead Texas in its fight for independence from Mexico in 1836. p. 321

B

Banneker, Benjamin *1731–1806* An African American who was chosen by the national government in 1791 to help plan the nation's new capital in Washington, D.C. p. 83

Barton, Clara *1821–1912* A Civil War nurse and founder of the American Red Cross. p. 208

Bates, Katharine Lee *1859–1929* The American poet who wrote "America the Beautiful." p. 115

Bell, Alexander Graham *1847–1922* A scientist and inventor. p. 128

Benton, Thomas Hart *1889–1975* A painter who painted rural scenes inspired by the Great Plains. p. 283

Boone, Daniel *1734–1820* One of the first American pioneers to clear a path through the Appalachian Mountains. p. 187

C

Carson, Benjamin S. *1951–* A doctor known all around the world for helping children with brain injuries. p. 279

Carver, George Washington *1864–1943* An African American scientist who developed new products using peanuts, sweet potatoes, and soy beans. p. 190

Cather, Willa *1873–1947* An American novelist who wrote *O Pioneers!* and several other books about pioneer life on the Great Plains. p. 283

Chavez, Cesar *1927–1993* A Mexican American Civil Rights leader who fought for the rights of migrant workers and others. p. 329

Clark, William *1770–1838* An American explorer who, with Meriwether Lewis, explored the Louisiana Territory and lands west of the Rocky Mountains. p. 384

Clay, Henry *1777–1852* A Congressional member from Kentucky whose Missouri Compromise temporarily solved the slavery issue in 1820. p. 188

Clemens, Samuel *1835–1910* An American writer and steamboat pilot who wrote many books under the pen name Mark Twain. p. 269

Coronado, Francisco Vásquez de (kawr•oh•NAH•doh) *1510?–1554* A Spanish explorer who led an expedition from Mexico City into what is now the southwestern United States. Coronado claimed those lands for Spain. p. 320

Cory, Kate *1861–1958* A prominent artist who lived in Hopi villages and painted pictures of the Hopi Indians and the Grand Canyon. p. 347

Crazy Horse *1842–1877* A Sioux leader whose memorial is being carved into the side of a mountain in South Dakota. p. 283

D

Deganawida (deh•gahn•uh•WIH•duh) *1500s* Legendary Iroquois holy man who called for an end to the fighting among the Iroquois, which led to the formation of the Iroquois League. p. 117

Disney, Walt *1901–1966* An American cartoonist whose famous theme park was opened in 1971 in Orlando, Florida, helping make Orlando one of the top tourism spots in the world. p. 214

E

Edison, Thomas *1847–1931* An American inventor who invented the electric lightbulb; he also built the first power station to supply electricity to New York City. p. 128

Ford, Henry *1863–1947* An American automobile manufacturer who mass-produced cars at a low cost by using assembly lines. p. 267

Franklin, Benjamin *1706–1790* An American leader who helped write the Declaration of Independence and the Constitution. He was also a respected scientist, inventor, and business leader. p. 50

Frost, Robert *1874–1963* A New England poet who wrote about the countryside of Vermont and New Hampshire. p. 139

Fulton, Robert *1765–1815* An American engineer and inventor who, with others, developed the steamboat. p. 265

Gates, Bill *1955–* An American who started a computer software company in 1975 that has become one of the world's largest computer software corporations. p. 412

Geisel, Theodor *1904–1991* A Massachusetts-born writer who started writing fun children's books to encourage reading; he wrote under the pen name "Dr. Seuss." p. 143

Giuliani, Rudolph *1944–* The former mayor of New York City who declared, "We are a city of immigrants." p. 147

Grant, Ulysses S. *1822–1885* 18th U.S. President, and earlier, commander of the Union Army in the Civil War. p. 189

H

Hall, Joyce C. *1891–1982* An American who started a business in 1910 in Kansas City, Missouri, that has become the world's largest greeting card company. p. 285

Hiawatha (hy•uh•WAH•thuh) *1500s* An Onondaga chief who persuaded other Iroquois tribes to form the Iroquois League. p. 117

Homer, Winslow *1836–1910* A New England painter who painted dramatic scenes of Maine's coast. p. 139

Hudson, Henry *1570?–1611* An English explorer who became the first European to sail up what is now called the Hudson River in New York. p. 118

Huerta, Dolores (WAIR•tah, doh•LOH•res) *1930–* A labor leader and organizer who, along with Cesar Chavez, fought for the rights of migrant workers and others. p. 329

Jackson, Andrew *1767–1845* 7th U.S. President. He ordered the removal of many American Indian groups from their lands. p. 120

Jefferson, Thomas *1743–1826* 3rd U.S. President and the main writer of the Declaration of Independence. President Jefferson was also responsible for sending Lewis and Clark on their expedition. p. 120

Jemison, Mae C. *1956–* A former NASA astronaut who was the first African American woman to travel into space. p. 339

Johnson, Lady Bird *1912–* A former First Lady who founded the National Wildflower Research Center in Texas. p. 312

Joliet, Louis (zhohl•YAY) *1645–1700* A French fur trader who, with Jacques Marquette, explored parts of the Great Lakes and the Mississippi River for France. p. 256

Key, Francis Scott *1779–1843* A lawyer who wrote the poem that became known as "The Star-Spangled Banner," the official national anthem. p. 47

King, Dr. Martin Luther, Jr. *1929–1968* An African American Civil Rights leader who worked in nonviolent ways for justice and fairness and the protection of individual rights of African Americans. He won the Nobel Peace Prize in 1964. p. 192

L

La Salle, René-Robert Cavelier, Sieur de (luh•SAL) *1643–1687* A French explorer who found the mouth of the Mississippi River and claimed the whole Mississippi Valley for France. p. 256

Lee, Robert E. *1807–1870* Leader of the Confederate army, who surrendered to Union general Ulysses S. Grant, ending the Civil War. p. 189

Lewis, Meriwether *1774–1809* An American explorer who, with William Clark, explored the Louisiana Territory and lands west of the Rocky Mountains. p. 384

Liliuokalani, Queen *1838–1917* A Hawaiian Queen who was the last ruler of the islands before Hawaii became a United States territory in 1900. p. 414

Lincoln, Abraham *1809–1865* 16th U.S. President; he served during the Civil War and ended slavery. p. 189

Mankiller, Wilma *1945–* The first woman to be chief of the Cherokee people, Wilma was active in the struggle for the rights of Native Americans and women. p. 343

Marquette, Jacques (mar•KET, ZHAHK) *1637–1675* A Catholic priest who, with Louis Joliet, explored North America for France. p. 256

Marshall, Thurgood *1908–1993* NAACP lawyer who argued the school segregation case before the Supreme Court, and was the first African American to serve on the Supreme Court. p. 211

McCoy, Joseph G. *1837–1915* A cattle trader and entrepreneur who opened one of the largest stockyards near the railroad at Abilene, Kansas. p. 266

Monroe, Bill *1911–1996* Known as the Father of Bluegrass. p. 225

Muir, John (MYOOR) *1838–1914* An American naturalist and conservationist who dedicated his life to protecting the environment. p. 37

Murie, Margaret *1902–2003* An American conservationist who dedicated her life to protecting wilderness areas in the United States. p. 395

O'Keeffe, Georgia *1887–1986* An American painter who lived and worked in New Mexico and painted many scenes of the desert. p. 347

Parks, Rosa *1913–2005* A Civil Rights leader who was arrested for refusing to give up her bus seat to a white passenger. p. 193

Phillips, Frank *1873–1950* A barber from Iowa who moved to Oklahoma, where he founded an oil business that became a worldwide company. p. 330

Powell, John Wesley *1834–1902* An American geologist who was one of the first people to explore the Grand Canyon. p. 346

R

Rankin, Jeannette *1880–1973* Born in Montana, she was the first woman elected to Congress. p. 403

Reed, Virginia *1833–1921* Daughter of James Reed, a leader of the Donner party. p. 385

Rockwell, Norman *1894–1978* An American illustrator known for depicting American life in his paintings. p. 139

Roosevelt, Theodore *1858–1919* 26th U.S. President, who worked to protect the nation's natural resources and wilderness areas. p. 394

Ross, John *1790–1866* Cherokee Chief who resisted moving the Cherokee from their lands. p. 322

S

Sable, Jean Baptiste Point du (SAH•bluh, ZHAHN bah•TEEST doo) *1745–1818* A Haitian French trader who founded the settlement that became the city of Chicago, Illinois. p. 256

Sacagawea (sak•uh•juh•WEE•uh) *1786?–1812* A Shoshone woman who acted as a guide for the Lewis and Clark expedition. p. 384

Sequoyah (sih•KWOY•uh) *1770?–1843* A Cherokee leader who created the Cherokee writing system. p. 191

Seuss, Dr. *See* Geisel, Theodor.

T

Tecumseh *1768–1813* Shawnee Chief who attempted to form an Indian confederation to fight for Native American land in the United States. p. 257

V

Velazquez, Nydia M. *1953–* A New Yorker from Puerto Rico who was the first Puerto Rican woman elected to Congress. p. 147

Villaraigosa, Antonio *1953–* The 41st mayor of Los Angeles. He was the first Hispanic mayor to be elected in Los Angeles since 1872. p. 411

W

Walker, Madam C. J. *1867–1919* Born into poverty in rural Louisiana, she was the first African American woman to become a millionaire. p. 268

Washington, George *1732–1799* 1st U.S. President and leader of the American army during the Revolutionary War. p. 50

Wilder, Laura Ingalls *1867–1957* An author who wrote books based on her childhood, growing up on the frontier. p. 287

Winfrey, Oprah *1954–* A popular talk show host whose company in Chicago produces television programs, movies, and magazines. p. 276

Wright, Frank Lloyd *1867–1959* An American architect known for creating what is known as the Prairie Style of architecture. p. 276

Y

Young, Brigham *1801–1877* A Mormon leader who moved his people west to Utah. p. 403

Gazetteer

The Gazetteer is a geographical dictionary that will help you locate places discussed in this book. The page number tells where each place appears on a map.

Adirondack Mountains (a•duh•RAHN•dak) A range of the Appalachian Mountains in northeastern New York. p. 101

Africa One of the world's seven continents. p. 14

Alabama River A river in the southeastern United States. p. 164

Albany The capital of New York. (42°N, 74°W) p. I21

Albuquerque (AL•buh•ker•kee) The largest city in New Mexico. (35°N, 106°W) p. 28

Allegheny Mountains (a•luh•GAY•nee) A range of the Appalachian Mountains in western Pennsylvania. p. 100

Allegheny River A river in the northeastern United States. p. 100

Anchorage (ANG•kuh•rij) The largest city in Alaska. (57°N, 145°W) p. 17

Annapolis The capital of Maryland. (39°N, 76°W) p. I21

Antarctica One of the world's seven continents. p. 14

Appalachian Mountains (a•puh•LAY•chee•uhn) A mountain range in the eastern United States. p. 20

Arctic Ocean One of the world's four oceans. p. 14

Arkansas River A tributary of the Mississippi River. p. 260

Asia One of the world's seven continents. p. 14

Atlanta The capital of the state of Georgia. (34°N, 84°W) p. I21

Atlantic Ocean One of the world's four oceans. p. 14

Augusta The capital of Maine. (44°N, 70°W) p. I21

Austin The capital of Texas. (30°N, 97°W) p. I21

Australia One of the world's seven continents. p. 14

Baltimore The largest city in Maryland. (39°N, 76°W) p. 153

Baton Rouge The capital of Louisiana. (30°N, 91°W) p. I21

Bismarck The capital of North Dakota. (47°N, 101°W) p. I21

Black Hills A group of mountains in western South Dakota and northeastern Wyoming. p. 236

Blue Ridge Mountains A mountain range in the Appalachian Mountains. p. 165

Boise The capital of Idaho. (43°N, 116°W) p. I20

Boston The capital of Massachusetts. (42°N, 71°W) p. I21

Buffalo A city in western New York. (43°N, 79°W) p. 153

Butte A city in southwestern Montana. (46°N, 112°W) p. 381

Canada A country in the northern part of North America. p. 85

Cape Canaveral (kuh•NAV•ruhl) A cape on the Atlantic coast of Florida. (28°N, 80°W) p. 165

Cape Cod A cape on the southeastern coast of Massachusetts. (41°N, 70°W) p. 101

Caribbean (kair•uh•BEE•uhn) A region of hundreds of islands that lie off the east coast of Central America in the Caribbean Sea. p. 87

Carson City The capital of Nevada. (39°N, 120°W) p. I20

Catskill Mountains An Appalachian Mountain range in southeastern New York. p. 101

Central America The southernmost part of the continent of North America. p. 87

Central Plains The eastern part of the Interior Plains. p. 20

Charleston (SC) A port city in South Carolina. (33°N, 80°W) p. 165

Charleston (WV) The capital of West Virginia. (38°N, 81°W) p. I21

Charlotte The largest city in North Carolina. (35°N, 81°W) p. 153

Chesapeake Bay (CHEH•suh•peek) A bay on the Atlantic coast of the United States. Its lower section is in Virginia and its upper section is in Maryland. p. 165

Cheyenne The capital of Wyoming. (41°N, 105°W) p. I20

Chicago A city in Illinois; the third-largest city in the United States. (42°N, 88°W) p. 153

Chihuahuan Desert (chee•WAH•wahn) A desert region that covers parts of Mexico, New Mexico, and Texas; part of the North American Desert. p. 300

Cincinnati (sin•suh•NA•tee) A city in southern Ohio. (39°N, 84°W) p. 153

Cleveland A city in northern Ohio. (41°N, 82°W) p. 28

Coast Ranges The mountain ranges that stretch along the Pacific coast of North America. p. 364

Coastal Plain One of the major plains in the United States, located along the coasts of the Atlantic Ocean and the Gulf of Mexico. p. 20

Colorado Plateau A plateau in the southwestern United States; covers most of northern New Mexico and Arizona. p. 20

Colorado River A river that flows from Colorado to the Gulf of California; part of it forms the border between California and Arizona. p. 20

Columbia The capital of South Carolina. (34°N, 81°W) p. I21

Columbia River A river in the northwestern United States and southwestern Canada. p. 20

Columbus The capital of Ohio. (40°N, 83°W) p. I21

Concord The capital of New Hampshire. (43°N, 71°W) p. I21

Connecticut River The longest river in New England. p. 101

Corn Belt Midwestern United States (Iowa, Illinois, Indiana); a region well suited for raising corn and corn-fed livestock. p. 72

D

Dallas A city in northeastern Texas. (33°N, 97°W) p. 381

Delaware Bay A bay on the coast of the Atlantic Ocean, located between New Jersey and Delaware. p. 101

Delaware River A river in the northeastern United States. p. 101

Denver The capital of Colorado. (40°N, 105°W) p. I20

Des Moines (dih MOYN) The capital of Iowa. (41°N, 94°W) p. I21

Detroit The largest city in Michigan. (42°N, 83°W) p. 153

Dover The capital of Delaware. (39°N, 75°W) p. I21

Durham A city in North Carolina known for its high-tech industry. (36°N, 78°W) p. 165

E

Europe One of the world's seven continents. p. 14

Everglades National Park A large area of wetlands in southern Florida. (25°N, 80°W) p. 165

F

Fargo A city in eastern North Dakota. (47°N, 97°W) p. 236

Florida Keys A chain of islands off the southern tip of the Florida peninsula. p. 165

Frankfort The capital of Kentucky. (25°N, 80°W) p. I21

G

Gila River A river in the southwestern United States. p. 300

Grand Canyon National Park A national park where a canyon in northwestern Arizona was formed by the Colorado River. p. 300

Grand Coulee Dam A dam in central Washington that makes more electricity than any other dam in the United States. (47°N, 119°W) p. 364

Grand Teton National Park A national park where the highest peak of the Teton Range of the Rocky Mountains in Wyoming is located. The peak has an elevation of 13,766 feet. (44°N, 11°W) p. 365

Great Basin National Park A national park in the western United States, including parts of Nevada, Utah, California, Idaho, Wyoming, and Oregon made up of low, dry land. p. 364

Great Dismal Swamp A southern swamp, the northernmost one of many along the Atlantic Ocean's coast that includes the Everglades, Big Cypress, and the Okefenokee in Florida; the Congress and Four Holes Swamps of South Carolina; and some of the Carolina Bays. (36°N, 76°W) p. 165

Great Lakes A chain of five lakes, located in central North America; the largest group of freshwater lakes in the world. p. 20

GAZETTEER

Great Plains The western part of the Interior Plains of the United States. p. 20

Great Smoky Mountains National Park A national park in Tennessee and North Carolina, along the Great Smoky Mountains. (35°N, 83°W) p. 164

Green Mountains An Appalachian Mountain range in the northeastern United States, which extends from Canada through Vermont and Massachusetts. p. 101

Greensboro A city in north-central North Carolina (36°N, 80°W) p. 165

Gulf of Mexico A body of water off the southeastern coast of North America; it is bounded by the United States, Cuba, and Mexico. p. 46

Harrisburg The capital of Pennsylvania. (40°N, 77°W) p. I21

Hartford The capital of Connecticut. (42°N, 73°W) p. I21

Helena (HEH•luh•nuh) The capital of Montana. (46°N, 112°W) p. I20

Hilton Head Island A barrier island off the coast of South Carolina. (32°N, 81°W) p. 165

Honolulu The capital of Hawaii. (21°N, 158°W) p. I20

Hoover Dam A dam on the Colorado River on the Nevada–Arizona state line. (36°N, 114°W) p. 364

Houston The largest city in Texas. (30°N, 95°W) p. 381

Hudson River A river in the northeastern United States. p. 101

Huntsville A city in northern Alabama. (35°N, 87°W) p. 164

Illinois River A river in Illinois. p. 237

Illinois Waterway A waterway that connects Lake Michigan with the Illinois River. p. 237

Indianapolis (in•dee•uh•NA•puh•luhs) The capital of Indiana. (40°N, 86°W) p. I21

Indian Ocean One of the world's four oceans. p. 14

Interior Plains One of the major plains regions of the United States, located between the Appalachian Mountains and the Rocky Mountains; includes the Central Plains and the Great Plains. p. 20

Jackson The capital of Mississippi. (32°N, 90°W) p. I21

Jacksonville A port city in northeastern Florida. (30°N, 82°W) p. 165

James River A river in central Virginia. p. 165

Jefferson City The capital of Missouri. (38°N, 92°W) p. I21

Juneau (JOO•noh) The capital of Alaska. (55°N, 120°W) p. I20

Kansas City The largest city in Missouri, located on the Missouri River on the Kansas–Missouri state line. (39°N, 94°W) p. 236

Lake Champlain (sham•PLAYN) A large lake on the New York–Vermont state line. p. 101

Lake Erie The fourth-largest of the Great Lakes, bordering New York, Pennsylvania, Ohio, Michigan, and Canada. p. 237

Lake Huron The second-largest of the Great Lakes, bordering Michigan and Canada. p. 237

Lake Mead A reservoir on the Colorado River, formed by Hoover Dam. p. 300

Lake Michigan The third-largest of the Great Lakes, bordering Michigan, Indiana, Illinois, and Wisconsin. p. 237

Lake Okeechobee (oh•kuh•CHOH•bee) The largest lake in the southern United States, located in southern Florida along the northern edge of the Everglades. p. 165

Lake Ontario The smallest of the Great Lakes, bordering New York and Ontario. p. 100

Lake Superior The largest of the Great Lakes, bordering Michigan, Wisconsin, Minnesota, and Canada. p. 237

Lansing The capital of Michigan. (43°N, 85°W) p. I21

Las Vegas The largest city in Nevada. (36°N, 115°W) p. 153

Lincoln The capital of Nebraska. (41°N, 97°W) p. I21

Little Rock The capital of Arkansas. (35°N, 92°W) p. I21

Long Island An island located in southeastern New York. p. 101

Los Angeles A city in southwestern California; more than 15 million people live in the Los Angeles metropolitan area; county seat of Los Angeles County. (34°N, 118°W) p. 28

Louisville The largest city in Kentucky. (38°N, 86°W) p. 153

M

Madison The capital of Wisconsin. (43°N, 89°W) p. I21

Mammoth Cave National Park A system of caves in south-central Kentucky; the largest cave system in the world. (37°N, 86°W) p. 164

Memphis The largest city in Tennessee. (35°N, 90°W) p. 28

Mexico A country in southern North America; located between the United States and Central America. p. 86

Miami A city in southern Florida. (26°N, 80°W) p. 28

Midwest One of the five regions of the United States. p. 79

Milwaukee (mil•WAW•kee) The largest city in Wisconsin. (43°N, 88°W) p. 237

Minneapolis (mih•nee•A•puh•luhs) The largest city in Minnesota. (45°N, 93°W) p. 28

Mississippi River A river that flows from Minnesota to the Gulf of Mexico; the longest river in the United States. p. 20

Missouri River A tributary of the Mississippi River; it flows from Montana to St. Louis, Missouri. p. 236

Monongahela River (muh•nahng•guh•HEE•luh) A river that flows through Pennsylvania and West Virginia. p. 100

Montgomery The capital of Alabama. (32°N, 86°W) p. I21

Montpelier The capital of Vermont. (44°N, 72°W) p. I21

Mount Elbert A mountain in Colorado, with an elevation of 14,433 feet (4,399 m). (39°N, 106°W) p. 365

Mount Hood A mountain in Oregon, with an elevation of 11,235 feet (3,424 m). (45°N, 122°W) p. 364

Mount McKinley The highest point in North America, with an elevation of 20,320 feet (6,194 m); located in the Alaska Range. (57°N, 150°W) p. 25

Mount Mitchell The highest point in the eastern United States, with an elevation of 6,684 feet (2,037 m), located in the Appalachian Mountains of North Carolina. (36°N, 82°W) p. 165

Mount Rainier (ruh•NIR) The highest point in the Cascade Range, in Washington, with an elevation of 14,410 feet (4,392 m). (47°N, 122°W) p. 364

Mount Rushmore A mountain in the Black Hills of South Dakota, with an elevation of 5,600 feet (1,707 m). (44°N, 103°W) p. 236

Mount Washington A mountain in the White Mountains, in New Hampshire, with an elevation of 6,288 feet (1,917 m). (44°N, 71°W) p. 101

Mount Whitney The highest point in the continental United States, with an elevation of 14,495 feet (4,418 m); located in the Sierra Nevada, in California. (37°N, 118°W) p. 364

N

Nashville The capital of Tennessee. (36°N, 87°W) p. I21

Natchez A city in southwestern Mississippi, located on the Mississippi River. (31°N, 91°W) p. 219

New Orleans (AWR•lee•uhnz) The largest city in Louisiana. (30°N, 90°W) p. 164

New York City The largest city in the United States. (41°N, 74°W) p. 101

New York State Barge Canal System A system of canals that links the Great Lakes with the Hudson River and the Atlantic Ocean. p. 101

Newark The largest city in New Jersey. (41°N, 74°W) p. 101

Niagara Falls (ny•A•gruh) The large series of waterfalls on the Niagara River. (43°N, 79°W) p. 100

North America One of the world's seven continents. p. 13

GAZETTEER

Northeast One of the five regions of the United States. p. 79

Oahu (oh•AH•hoo) The third-largest of the eight major Hawaiian Islands. p. 364

Ohio River A tributary of the Mississippi River. p. 237

Okefenokee Swamp (oh•kee•fuh•NOH•kee) A swamp that covers part of southeastern Georgia and northern Florida. p. 165

Oklahoma City The capital of Oklahoma. (35°N, 98°W) p. I21

Olympia The capital of Washington. (47°N, 123°W) p. I20

Olympic National Park A national park in Washington that has some of the few rain forest areas in the United States. (48°N, 124°W) p. 364

Omaha The largest city in Nebraska. (41°N, 96°W) p. 381

Orlando A city in central Florida. (28°N, 81°W) p. 165

Ouachita Mountains (WAH•shuh•tah) A mountain range in western Arkansas and southeastern Oklahoma. p. 164

Outer Banks A chain of sand islands and peninsulas along the coast of North Carolina. p. 165

Ozark Plateau (OH•zark) A plateau extending from southeastern Missouri across Arkansas and into Oklahoma. p. 164

Pacific Ocean One of the world's four oceans. p. 14

Painted Desert A desert region in Arizona. p. 300

Pecos River (PAY•kohs) A river that flows through eastern New Mexico and western Texas. p. 300

Philadelphia The largest city in Pennsylvania. (40°N, 75°W) p. 28

Phoenix (FEE•niks) The capital of Arizona. (33°N, 112°W) p. I20

Pierre The capital of South Dakota. (44°N, 100°W) p. I21

Pittsburgh A city in southwestern Pennsylvania. (40°N, 80°W) p. 101

Platte River A river that flows through central Nebraska and is a tributary of the Missouri River. p. 236

Pocono Mountains (POH•kuh•noh) An Appalachian Mountain range in eastern Pennsylvania. p. 101

Portland (OR) The largest city in Oregon. (45°N, 123°W) p. 364

Potomac River (puh•TOH•muhk) A river in the eastern United States. p. 100

Providence (PRAH•vuh•duhns) The capital of Rhode Island. (42°N, 71°W) p. I21

Puget Sound (PYOO•juht) An inlet of the Pacific Ocean in northwestern Washington. p. 364

Raleigh (RAH•lee) The capital of North Carolina. (36°N, 79°W) p. I21

Red River A tributary of the Mississippi River. p. 260

Richmond The capital of Virginia. (38°N, 77°W) p. I21

Rio Grande (REE•oh grand) The river that forms the Texas–Mexico border. p. 260

Rocky Mountains A mountain range that extends through the western United States into Canada. p. 20

S

Sabine River A river that forms part of the Texas–Louisiana border. p. 164

Sacramento (sa•kruh•MEN•toh) A city in the Central Valley; California's state capital. (39°N, 121°W) p. I20

St. Johns River A river in northeastern Florida. p. 165

St. Lawrence River A river that forms part of the border between Canada and the United States. p. 101

St. Louis The second-largest city in Missouri. (38°N, 90°W) p. 28

St. Paul The capital of Minnesota. (45°N, 93°W) p. I21

Salem The capital of Oregon. (45°N, 123°W) p. I20

GAZETTEER

Salt Lake City The capital of Utah. (41°N, 112°W) p. I20

San Diego A city in southern California. (33°N, 118°W) p. 364

San Francisco A city in northern California. (38°N, 124°W) p. 28

Santa Fe (SAN•tah FAY) The capital of New Mexico. (35°N, 106°W) p. I20

Savannah (suh•VA•nuh) The oldest city in Georgia. (32°N, 81°W) p. 165

Seattle (see•AT•uhl) The largest city in Washington. (47°N, 122°W) p. 28

Sonoran Desert (soh•NAWR•uhn) A part of the North American Desert; located in southwestern Arizona. p. 300

South America One of the world's seven continents. p. 14

Southeast One of the five regions of the United States. p. 79

Southwest One of the five regions of the United States. p. 79

Springfield (IL) The capital of Illinois. (40°N, 90°W) p. I21

Susquehanna River (suhs•kwuh•HA•nuh) A river in Pennsylvania. p. 100

Tallahassee The capital of Florida. (30°N, 84°W) p. I21

Tampa A city in west-central Florida. (28°N, 82°W) p. 153

Taos A large town in north-central New Mexico. (36°N, 105°W) p. 353

Tennessee River A tributary of the Ohio River. p. 164

Toledo A city in northern Ohio. (42°N, 84°W) p. 237

Topeka The capital of Kansas. (39°N, 96°W) p. I21

Trenton The capital of New Jersey. (40°N, 74°W) p. I21

Tucson A city in southern Arizona. (32°N, 111°W) p. 381

Tulsa (TUHL•suh) A city in northeastern Oklahoma. (36°N, 96°W) p. 301

United States A country in the Northern and Western Hemispheres that includes 49 states in North America and the state of Hawaii in the Pacific Ocean. p. 12

Valdez (val•DEEZ) A port city in southern Alaska. (61°N, 146°W) p. 364

Virginia Beach A city and ocean resort in Virginia. (37°N, 76°W) p. 165

Wabash River (WAW•bash) A river in Indiana and Illinois that empties into the Ohio River. p. 237

Washington, D.C. The capital of the United States. (39°N, 77°W) p. 79

West One of five regions of the United States. p. 79

White Mountains A mountain range of the Appalachian Mountains in northern New Hampshire. p. 101

Wilmington A city in eastern Delaware. (40°N, 76°W) p. 101

Y

Yellowstone National Park The first national park in the United States, which covers parts of Idaho, Wyoming, and Montana. (45°N, 111°W) p. 365

Yellowstone River A river in the northwestern United States. p. 365

Yosemite National Park A national park located in the Sierra Nevada of eastern California. p. 364

Glossary

The Glossary contains important history and social science words and their definitions, listed in alphabetical order. Each word is respelled as it would be in a dictionary. When you see the mark ' after a syllable, pronounce that syllable with more force. The page number at the end of the definition tells where the word is first used in this book. Guide words at the top of each page help you quickly locate the word you need to find.

add, āce, câre, pälm; end, ēqual; it, īce; odd, ōpen, ôrder; tŏŏk, pōōl; up, bûrn; yōō as *u* in *fuse*; oil; pout; ə as *a* in *above*, e in *sicken*, i in *possible*, o in *melon*, u in *circus*; **ch**eck; ri**ng**; **th**in; **th**is; **zh** as in *vision*

abolish (ə•bä´lish) To end. p. 189

absolute location (ab´sə•loot lō•k´āshən) The exact position of a place on Earth, using lines of latitude and longitude. p. 16

adapt (ə•dapt´) To change in order to make more useful, such as fitting one's way of living into a new environment. p. 255

adobe (ə•dō´bē) A mixture of sandy clay and straw that is dried into bricks. p. 319

aerospace (âr´ō•spās) Having to do with the building and testing of aircraft and equipment for air and space travel. p. 339

aqueduct (a´kwə•dəkt) A large pipe or canal that carries water from one place to another. p. 313

aquifer (a´kwə•fər) A layer of rock, sand, or gravel that absorbs water. p. 313

archipelago (är•kə•pel´•ə•gō) A group of islands scattered over a wide stretch of water. p. 414

architecture (är´kə•tek•cher) A particular style or method of building. p. 276

arid (ar´əd) Dry, or having little rainfall. p. 329

arroyo (ə•roh´yō) A deep, water-carved gully or ditch. p. 312

assembly line (ə•sem´blē līn) A line of workers and machines along which a product moves as it is put together one step at a time. p. 267

ballot (ba´lət) A sheet of paper or some other method used to mark a secret vote. p. 141

barge (bärj) A large, flat-bottomed boat used on rivers and other inland waterways. p. 277

barrier (bar´ē•ər) Something that blocks the way or makes it hard to move from place to place. p. 384

barrier island (bar´ē•ər ī´lənd) A low, narrow island that is near a coast. p. 216

basin (bā´sən) Low, bowl-shaped land with higher ground all around it. p. 22

blizzard (bliz´ərd) A snowstorm driven by strong, freezing winds. p. 112

boomtown (bōōm´toun) A town that grew up quickly, almost overnight. p. 385

border (bôr´dər) A line that shows the end of a place. p. 14

butte (byōōt) A steep, narrow hill or rock with a flat top, like a mesa, but smaller. p. 311

campaign (kam•pān´) A series of actions, such as running advertisements on television, displaying signs, making speeches, and talking with voters, taken with the goal of getting someone elected to office. p. 141

canal (kə•nal´) A waterway dug across land. p. 127

candidate (kan´də•dāt) A person who is running for office in an election. p. 141

canyon (kan´yən) A deep, narrow valley with steep sides. p. 22

cash crop (kash krop) A crop people raise to sell to others rather than to use themselves. p. 188

cause (kôz) An event that makes something else happen. p. 326

century (sen´shə•rē) A period of 100 years. p. 122

checks and balances (cheks and ba´lən•səz) A system that gives each branch of government different powers so that each branch can keep the powers of the others from becoming too great. p. 53

civil rights (si´vəl rīts) The rights of citizens to equal treatment. p. 193

civil war (si´vəl wôr) A war between groups of people in the same country. p. 189

climate (klī´mət) The kind of weather a place has most often, year after year. p. 27

cloudburst (kloud´bûrst) A sudden, heavy rain. p. 312

colonist (kä´lə•nist) A person who lives in a colony. p. 119

colony (kä´lə•nē) A settlement that is ruled by a faraway government. p. 118

commercial (kə•mər´shəl) Relating to business or trade. p. 330

commonwealth (käm´ən•welth) A territory that governs itself. p. 87

communication (kə•myoo•nə•kā´shən) The sending and receiving of information. p. 74

commute (kə•myoot´) To travel back and forth between work and home. p. 148

compromise (käm´•prə•mīz) An agreement in which each side in a conflict gives up some of what it wants. p. 331

Confederacy (kən•fe´də•rə•sē) The Confederate States of America, a new country that was formed by Southern states that seceded from the Union after Abraham Lincoln was elected President in 1860. p. 189

confederation (kən•fe•də•rā´shən) A loosely united group of governments working together. p. 117

conflict (kän´flikt) A disagreement between two or more people or groups. p. 330

consequence (kän´sə•kwens) What happens because of an action. p. 416

conservation (kän•sər•vā´shən) The protection and wise use of natural resources. p. 36

constitution (kän•stə•too´shən) A plan of government. p. 51

consumer (kən•soo´mər) A person who buys a product or service. p. 405

continent (kän´tə•nənt) One of the seven largest land areas on Earth. p. 13

Continental Divide (kän•tə•nen´təl də•vīd´) An imaginary line that runs north and south along the highest points of the Rocky Mountains. Rivers flow west or east from this line. p. 375

cooperate (kō•o´pə•rāt) To work together. p. 331

coral (kôr´əl) A stony material formed in tropical waters by the skeletons of tiny sea animals. p. 216

county (koun´tē) A section of a state. p. 80

county seat (koun´tē sēt) A town or city where the main government offices of the county are located. p. 80

crater (krāt´ər) An opening in Earth's surface created when a volcano erupts and begins to throw out lava. p. 376

crossroads (kros´rōdz) Any place that connects people, goods, and ideas. p. 414

GLOSSARY

crude oil (krōōd oil) Petroleum pumped from the ground. p. 341

culture (kul´chər) The way of life of a group of people. p. 43

D

decade (de´kād) A period of ten years. p. 122

declaration (de•klə•rā´shən) An official statement. p. 120

demand (di•mand´) A need or a desire for a good or service by people willing to pay for it. p. 60

democracy (di•mä´krə•sē) A form of government in which the people rule by making decisions themselves or by electing people to make decisions for them. p. 51

double-bar graph (də•bəl•bär graf) A kind of bar graph that compares two sets of numbers. p. 200

dredge (drej) To dig out the bottom and sides of a waterway to make it deeper and wider. p. 341

drought (drout) A long time with little or no rain. p. 249

E

earthquake (ûrth´kwāk) A sudden shaking of the ground caused by the movement and cracking of rock deep inside Earth. p. 376

economy (i•kä´nə•mē) The way people in a place or region use resources to meet their needs. p. 58

ecosystem (e´kō•sis•təm) The relationship between living things and their nonliving environment, and their working together as a unit. p. 393

effect (i•fekt´ *or* ē•fekt´) What happens as a result of something else happening. p. 326

elevation (e•lə•vā´shən) The height of the land above sea level. p. 24

endangered (in•dān´jərd) Being threatened with extinction. p. 224

entrepreneur (än•trə•prə•nûr´) A person who sets up a new business. p. 266

environment (en•vī´ərn•mənt) Surroundings in which people, plants, and animals live. p. 36

equator (i•kwā´tər) An imaginary line that divides Earth into the Northern Hemisphere and the Southern Hemisphere. p. 13

ethnic group (eth´nik grōōp) A group of people from the same country, of the same race, or with a shared culture. p. 73

evaporation (i•va•pə•rā´shən) The process of the sun's heat turning water into a gas form. p. 350

executive branch (ig•ze´kyə•tiv branch) A branch of government whose main job is to see that laws passed by the legislative branch are carried out. p. 52

export (ek´spôrt) A product shipped from one country to be sold in another; to sell goods to people in another country. p. 197

extinct (ik•stingkt´) No longer in existence, which is what a living thing becomes when all of its kind have died out. p. 224

F

fact (fakt) A statement that can be checked and proved to be true. p. 316

factors of production (fak´tərz uv prə•duk´shən) The human, natural, and capital resources that a business needs to produce goods or services. p. 59

fall line (fôl līn) A place where a river drops from higher to lower land. p. 178

fault A crack in Earth's surface. p. 376

fertilizer (fûr´təl•ī•zər) Materials added to the soil to make it more productive to help crops grow. p. 180

fiction (fik´shen) Made-up writing. p. 316

flatboat (flat´bōt) A large boat with a flat bottom and square ends. p. 264

flowchart (flō´chärt) A drawing that shows the steps in a process. p. 252

food processing (fōōd pro´ses•ing) The cooking, canning, drying, freezing, and packaging of foods for market. p. 209

forty-niner (fôr•tē•nī´nər) A person who went to California in 1849 to search for gold. p. 385

free market (frē mär´kət) An economy in which people can start almost any kind of business and run it however they choose. p. 59

freight (frāt) Goods that are transported. p. 277

frontier (frən•tir´) Land beyond the settled part of a country. p. 257

G

glacier (glā´shər) A huge, slow-moving mass of ice. p. 111

Global Positioning System (glō´bəl pə•zi´shən•ing sis´təm) A navigation system of satellites and computers that can figure out the exact latitude and longitude of a device, or receiver, on Earth. p. 403

government (guv´ərn•mənt) A system of leaders and laws for making decisions for a community, state, or nation. p. 50

governor (guv´ər•nər) The head of the executive branch of state government. p. 208

groundwater (ground´wô•tər) Water that sinks beneath Earth's surface when it rains or snows. p. 34

growing season (grō´ing sē´zən) The period of time when the weather is warm enough for crops to grow. p. 179

gulf (gəlf) A part of an ocean or sea extending into the land. p. 15

H

habitat (ha´bə•tat) A region where a plant or animal naturally grows or lives. p. 223

harbor (här´bər) A protected area of water where ships can dock safely. p. 111

hemisphere (he´mə•sfir) A half of Earth. p. 13

heritage (her´ə•tij) A way of life, a set of customs, or a belief that has come from previous generations and continues today. p. 414

high-tech (hī•tek) Shortened form of the words *high technology*; having to do with inventing, building, or using computers and other kinds of electronic equipment. p. 209

historical map (hi•stôr´ik•əl map) A map that shows information about a place during a certain time in history. p. 260

hub (həb) A center of activity. p. 277

humidity (hyōō•mi´də•tē) The amount of moisture in the air. p. 28

hurricane (hûr´ə•kān) A huge tropical storm with heavy rains and winds of more than 73 miles per hour. p. 179

hydroelectricity (hī•drō•i•lek•tri´sə•tē) Electricity produced by using waterpower. p. 392

GLOSSARY

I

immigrate (i´mi•grāt) To enter a country to live there. p. 44

import (im´pôrt) A good, or product, that is brought into one country from another to be sold; to bring in goods from another country to sell. p. 196

independence (in•də•pen´dəns) Freedom. p. 120

industrial economy (in•dus´trē•əl i•kä´nə•mē) An economy in which factories and machines manufacture most goods. p. 268

Industrial Revolution (in•dəs´trē•əl re•və•lōō´shən) A period in which new sources of power were used to replace machines powered by hand, allowing people to make more goods faster. p. 128

industry (in´dus•trē) All the businesses that make one kind of product or provide one kind of service. p. 34

interdependence (in•tər•di•pen´dəns) The depending on one another for resources and products. p. 71

international trade (in•tər•na´shən•əl trād) Trade with other countries. p. 196

irrigation (ir•ə•gā´shən) The use of canals, ditches, or pipes to carry water to dry places. p. 314

J

judicial branch (ōō•di´shəl branch) A branch of the government whose main job is to see that laws are carried out fairly. p. 53

justice (jəs´təs) The quality of being fair. p. 192

L

land grant (land grant) A gift of land given by the government. p. 322

landform (land´fôrm) One of the shapes that makes up Earth's surface, such as mountains, hills, valleys, or plains. p. 18

lava (lä´və) Hot, melted rock that comes from a volcano. p. 376

legislative branch (le´jəs•lā•tiv branch) The lawmaking branch of government. In the federal government it is called Congress. p. 52

line graph (līn graf) A graph that uses a line to show changes over time. p. 30

lines of latitude (līnz əv la´tə•tōōd) A set of lines that run east and west drawn on maps and globes. They are measured in degrees north and south from the equator. p. 16

lines of longitude (līnz əv län´jə•tōōd) A set of lines that runs north and south, from the North Pole to the South Pole, drawn on maps and globes. They are measured in degrees east and west from the prime meridian. p. 16

M

mainland (mān´land) The continent or the part of a continent nearest to an island. p. 216

majority rule (mə•jôr´ə•tē rōōl) A way of deciding something in which whoever or whatever gets the most votes wins. p. 54

manufacturing (man•yə•fak´chə•ring) The making of goods from raw materials by hand or by machinery. p. 61

map scale (map skāl) The part of a map that compares a distance on the map to a distance in the real world. p. 218

GLOSSARY

mass production (mas prə•duk´shən) A way of manufacturing in which many items that are identical can be made quickly and cheaply. p. 267

meatpacking (mēt pak´ing) The preparing of meat for market. p. 285

megalopolis (me•gə•lä´pə•ləs) A huge urban region formed when two or more metropolitan areas grow together. p. 130

mesa (mā´suh) A hill or small plateau with a flat top and steep sides. p. 311

metropolitan area (me•trə•pä´lə•tən âr´ē•ə) A large city together with nearby cities and suburbs. p. 130

microchip (mī´krō•chip) A tiny electronic circuit used in equipment such as computers. p. 412

migrant worker (mī´grənt wur´kər) A worker who moves from place to place, doing different jobs. p. 329

migration (mī•grā´shən) The movement of people from one place to another. p. 265

mineral (min´rəl) A natural substance found in rocks. p. 35

mission (mish´ən) A religious settlement. p. 320

modify (mäd´ə•fī) To change. p. 74

mouth (mouth) The place where a river empties into a larger body of water. p. 21

municipal (myōō•ni´sə•pəl) Having to do with a city. p. 80

N

natural resource (nach´ə•rəl rē´sôrs) Something found in nature, such as water, soil, or minerals, that people can use to meet their needs. p. 32

natural vegetation (nach´ə•rəl ve•jə•tā´shən) The plant life that grows naturally in an area. p. 72

navigable (na´vi•gə•bəl) Deep and wide enough for ships to use. p. 127

nomad (nō´mad) A person who has no permanent home and moves from place to place. p. 319

nonrenewable (non•ri•nōō´ə•bel) Something that cannot be made again by nature or by people. p. 35

O

observatory (əb•zerv´•ə•tôr•ē) A place where people use instruments, such as telescopes, for observation of objects and events in space. p. 348

opinion (ə•pin´yən) A statement that tells what the person who makes it thinks or believes. p. 408

opportunity cost (ä•pər•tōō´nə•tē kost) The thing that is given up to get something else. p. 64

ordinance (ôr´dən•əns) A law or set of laws. p. 256

ore (ôr) Rock that contains enough of one or more kinds of minerals to be mined. p. 250

P

patriotism (pā´trē•ə•ti•zəm) Love of country. p. 43

peninsula (pə•nin´sə•lə) Land that has water almost all around it. p. 177

piedmont (pēd´mänt) An area of high land at or near the foot of a mountain. p. 178

GLOSSARY

pioneer (pī•ə•nir´) A person who first settles a new place. p. 258

plantation (plan•tā´shən) A huge farm where tobacco, cotton, rice, sugarcane, or indigo were the main crops grown. p. 186

plateau (pla•tō´) An area of high, flat land. p. 20

pollution (pə•lōō´shən) Anything that makes a natural resource dirty or unsafe to use. p. 149

population (pä•pyə•lā´shən) The total number of people who live in a place. p. 45

population density (pä•pyə•lā´shən den´sə•tē) The number of people who live in an area of a certain size. p. 152

port (pôrt) A trading center where ships are loaded and unloaded. p. 119

prairie (prâr´ē) An area of flat or rolling land covered mostly with wildflowers and grasses. p. 247

precipitation (pri•si•pə•tā´shən) Water that falls to Earth's surface as rain, sleet, hail, or snow. p. 27

prime meridian (prīm mə•rid´ē•ən) An imaginary line that is often used to divide Earth into the Western Hemisphere and the Eastern Hemisphere. p. 13

profit (prä´fət) In a business, money left over after all costs have been paid. p. 60

province (pro´vəns) A political region similar to a state. p. 85

public land (pub´lik land) Land that is owned by the government. p. 391

pueblo (pwe´blō) An adobe village. p. 319

pulp (pulp) A soft mixture of ground-up wood chips and chemicals that is used to make paper. p. 209

Q

quarry (kwôr´ē) A large, open pit cut into the ground, from which stone is mined. p. 113

R

rain forest (rān fôr´əst) A wet area, usually warm, where tall trees, vines, and other plants grow close together. p. 88

rain shadow (rān sha´dō) The drier side of a mountain. p. 312

raw material (rô mə•tir´ē•əl) A resource in its natural state, such as a mineral, that can be used to manufacture a product. p. 196

reclaim (ri•klām´) To return something, such as land, to its natural condition. p. 222

reef (rēf) A ridge of rocks, sand, or coral near the surface of the sea. p. 216

refinery (ri•fī´nər•ē) A factory that turns crude oil into useful products, such as gasoline and other fuels. p. 341

region (rē´jən) An area with at least one feature that makes it different from other areas. p. 71

relative location (re´lə•tiv lō•kā´shən) Where a place is in relation to one or more other places on Earth. p. 14

relief (ri•lēf´) The differences in the heights of land shown in maps. p. 24

renewable (ri•nōō´ə•bəl) Something that can be made again by nature or people. p. 33

republic (ri•pub´lik) A form of government in which people select their leaders. p. 51

reservation (re•zər•vā´shən) Land set aside by the government for use by Native Americans. p. 340

GLOSSARY

reservoir (reʹzə•vwär) A lake made by people to collect and store water. p. 313

resolve (ri•zälvʹ) To settle a conflict. p. 332

resort (ri•zôrtʹ) A place where people go to relax and have fun. p. 214

revolution (rev•ə•loͻʹshən) A major, sudden change in government or in people's lives. p. 121

rural (rooͬʹəl) Like, in, or of the country. p. 45

S

satellite (saʹtəl•īt) A human-made object that orbits Earth. p. 403

sea level (sē levʹəl) The level of the surface of the ocean. p. 19

secede (si•sēdʹ) To leave. p. 189

self-sufficient (self sə•fishʹənt) Able to do everything for oneself, with no help from other people. p. 258

service industry (sərʹvəs inʹdəs•trē) Businesses that do things for people instead of making things. p. 61

skyscraper (skīʹskrā•pər) A very tall steel-framed building. p. 147

slavery (slāʹvər•ē) The practice of making one person the property of another person. p. 186

sod (sod) A layer of soil held together by the roots of grasses. p. 258

source (sôrs) The place where a river begins. p. 21

specialize (speʹshə•līz) To work at one kind of job and learn to do it well. p. 140

state legislature (stāt leʹjəs•lā•chər) The legislative branch of state government. p. 208

steamboat (stēmʹbōt) A boat powered by a steam engine that turns a large paddle wheel. p. 265

stockyard (stäkʹyärd) A place with pens and sheds where cattle are kept before being shipped. p. 266

suburb (subʹərb) A town or small city near a large city. p. 45

Sun Belt (sun belt) A wide area of the southern part of the United States that has a mild climate all year. p. 213

supply (sə•plīʹ) The available amount of a product or a service that is offered for sale. p. 60

survey (sər•vāʹ) To measure, especially land. p. 256

T

technology (tek•näʹlə•jē) The use of knowledge or tools to make or do something. p. 74

telegraph (teʹlə•graf) A machine that uses electricity to send messages over wires. p. 386

temperature (temʹpər•chər) The measurement of hot and cold. p. 27

territory (terʹə•tôr•ē) An area owned and governed by a country. p. 85

textile mill (tekʹstīl mil) A factory in which fibers such as cotton and wool are woven into textiles, or cloth. p. 128

timberline (timʹbər•līn) On a mountain, the elevation above which the temperatures are too low for trees to grow. p. 377

time line (tīm līn) A chart that records specific events over a period of time. p. 122

time zone (tīm zōn) A region in which people use the same time. p. 380

tornado (tôr•nā´dō) A funnel-shaped, spinning windstorm, sometimes called a cyclone or twister. p. 249

tourism (toor´iz•əm) The business of serving visitors. p. 214

township (toun´ship) A square section of land in the Northwest Territory measuring 6 miles (about 10 km) on each side; each township was divided into 36 smaller squares of land to be sold to settlers. p. 256

trade-off (trād´ ôf) Giving up one thing to get something else. p. 64

tradition (trə•dish´ən) A custom, a way of life, or an idea that has been handed down from the past. p. 221

transcontinental railroad (trans•kon•tə•nen´təl rāl´rōd) A railroad that crosses the North American continent, linking the Atlantic and Pacific coasts. p. 386

treaty (trē´tē) An agreement between groups or countries. p. 81

tributary (trib´yə•ter•ē) A river or stream that flows into a larger river. p. 21

tropics (trop´iks) Earth's warmest regions, between the Tropic of Cancer and the Tropic of Capricorn. p. 88

tundra (tun´drə) A flat, treeless plain that stays frozen most of the year. p. 89

Union (yoon´yən) The United States of America. p. 189

urban (ûr´bən) Like, in, or of a city. p. 45

urban growth (ûr´bən grōth) The growth of cities. p. 129

urban sprawl (ûr´bən sprôl) The outward spread of urban areas. p. 148

urbanization (ûr•bə•nə•zā´shən) The growth of the proportion of people living in cities compared with that of people in rural areas. p. 285

volcano (vol•kā´nō) An opening in Earth's surface out of which hot gases, ash, and lava may pour. p. 376

volunteer (vä•lən•tir´) A person who offers to do something without pay. p. 141

wagon train (wa´gən trān) A group of wagons, each pulled by horses or oxen. p. 385

waterway (wô´tər•wā) A body of water that boats can use. p. 127

wetland (wet´land) Low-lying land where the water level is always near or above the surface of the land. p. 177

wildlife refuge (wīld´līf re´fyooj) An area of land set aside to protect animals and other living things. p. 216

xeriscape (zir´ə•skāp) A landscaping method that conserves water. p. 349

Index

Page references for illustrations are set in italic type. An italic *m* indicates a map. Page references set in boldface type indicate the pages on which vocabulary terms are defined.

INDEX

INDEX

INDEX

INDEX

INDEX

INDEX

INDEX

...on to reprint copyrighted mate-
...acknowledgment is made to the
...ources:

...s for Young Readers, A Division of
...Young Readers Group, A Member of
...n Group (USA) Inc., 345 Hudson Street,
New York, NY 10014: From *Tanya's Reunion* by Valerie Flournoy, illustrated by Jerry Pinkney. Text copyright © 1995 by Valerie Flournoy; illustrations copyright © 1995 by Jerry Pinkney.

Harcourt, Inc.: From *A River Ran Wild* by Lynne Cherry. Copyright © 1992 by Lynne Cherry. Cover illustration by Yuyi Morales from *Harvesting Hope: The Story of Cesar Chavez* by Kathleen Krull. Illustration copyright © 2003 by Yuyi Morales.

HarperCollins Publishers: Cover illustration by Joy Fisher Hein from *Miss Lady Bird's Wildflowers* by Kathi Appelt. Illustration copyright © 2005 by Joy Fisher Hein. Cover illustration from *Under the Wild Western Sky* by Jim Arnosky. Copyright © 2005 by Jim Arnosky. Cover illustration from *A New England Scrapbook: A Journey Through Poetry, Prose, and Pictures* by Loretta Krupinski. Copyright © 1994 by Loretta Krupinski. From *On the Banks of Plum Creek* by Laura Ingalls Wilder, illustrated by Garth Williams. Text copyright 1937 by Laura Ingalls Wilder; text copyright renewed 1965 by Roger Lea MacBride. Illustrations copyright 1953 by Garth Williams; illustrations copyright renewed 1981 by Garth Williams.

Holiday House, Inc.: Cover illustration by Bill Farnsworth from *Bad River Boys: A Meeting of the Lakota Sioux with Lewis and Clark* by Virginia Driving Hawk Sneve. Illustration copyright © 2005 by Bill Farnsworth.

Henry Holt and Company, LLC: Cover illustration by Bryan Collier from *Rosa* by Nikki Giovanni. Illustration copyright © 2005 by Bryan Collier. *Cactus Hotel* by Brenda Z. Guiberson, illustrated by Megan Lloyd. Text copyright © 1991 by Brenda Z. Guiberson; illustrations copyright © 1991 by Megan Lloyd. Cover illustration by Wade Zahares from *Liberty Rising: The Story of the Statue of Liberty* by Pegi Deitz Shea. Illustration copyright © 2005 by Wade Zahares.

Houghton Mifflin Company: Cover illustration by Rodica Prato from *Journeys in Time: A New Atlas of American History* by Elspeth Leacock and Susan Buckley. Illustration copyright © 2001 by Rodica Prato. Cover illustration by David A. Johnson from *On Sand Island* by Jacqueline Briggs Martin. Illustration © 2003 by David A. Johnson.

Little, Brown and Company (Inc.): Cover illustration by Chris Gall from *America the Beautiful* by Katharine Lee Bates. Illustration copyright © 2004 by Chris Gall.

The Madison Press Limited: Cover illustration by Laurie McGaw from *Journey to Ellis Island: How My Father Came to America* by Carol Bierman. Cover design © 1998 by The Madison Press Limited. A Hyperion/Madison Press Book.

Margaret K. McElderry Books, an imprint of Simon & Schuster Children's Publishing Division: From *America is. . .* by Louise Borden, illustrated by Stacey Schuett. Text copyright © 2002 by Louise Borden; illustrations copyright © 2002 by Stacey Schuett.

National Geographic Society: Cover illustration from *Quilt of States: Piecing Together America* by Adrienne Yorinks and 50 Librarians from Across the Nation. Illustration copyright © 2005 by Adrienne Yorinks; cover copyright © 2005 by National Geographic Society.

Random House Children's Books, a division of Random House, Inc.: From *I Can Read with My Eyes Shut!* by Dr. Seuss. TM and copyright © 1978 by Dr. Seuss Enterprises, L. P.

Walker & Company: Cover illustration by Higgins Bond from *I Am Sacajawea, I Am York: Our Journey West with Lewis and Clark* by Claire Rudolf Murphy. Illustration copyright © 2005 by Higgins Bond.

Yosemite Association: From *Two Bear Cubs: A Miwok Legend from California's Yosemite Valley*, retold by Robert D. San Souci, illustrated by Daniel San Souci. Text copyright © 1997 by Robert D. San Souci; illustrations copyright © 1997 by Daniel San Souci.

PHOTO CREDITS FOR GRADE 4 SOCIAL STUDIES

Placement key: (t) top; (b) bottom; (l) left; (r) right; (c) center; (bg) background; (fg) foreground; (i) inset.

COVER AND ENDSHEET

Front Cover: Getty Images. Back Cover: Getty Images. Front End Sheets: Getty Images. Title Page: Getty Images. Back End Sheets: Getty Images.

Frontmatter: iv (bg) David Muench/Corbis; iv (r) Creatas/age fotostock; iv (l) Ron Dahlquist/Getty Images; v (l) Mark Richards/PhotoEdit; v (c) Joseph Sohm/PictureQuest; vi (bg) Andrew Gordon/Panoramic Images; vi (c) Bill Ross/Corbis; vi (r) McConnell & McNamara; x (c) Richard Day/Panoramic Images; x (l) Rick Miller/Corbis; x (bg) The Granger Collection, New York; xi (c) Ralf-Finn Hestoft/Corbis; xii (l) Bettmann/Corbis; xii (br) The Granger Collection, New York; xii (tr) Tom Brakefield/Superstock; xiv (l) Bryan Mullennix/Getty images; xiv (r) The Granger; Collection, New York; xv (l) Andre Jenny/Alamy Images; xv (r) Cosmo Condina/Mira; xv (c) Marc Muench/Corbis; I14 (t) Dennis MacDonald/PhotoEdit; I14 (b) Randy Wells/Getty Images; I15 (t) age fotostock/Superstock; I15 (b) M.L. Sinibaldi/Corbis; I15 (c) Steven Widoff/Alamy Images.

UNIT 1

1 Kim Heacox/Getty Images; 7 Alamy Images; 10 (c) Joel W. Rogers/Corbis; 10 (r) Marc Muench/Getty Images; 10-11 John M. Roberts/Corbis; 15 Unicorn Stock Photos; 18 (bl) David Muench/Corbis; 18 (t) Greg Probst/Getty/Images; 18 (br) Ron Spomer/Visuals Unlimited; 19 (l) David Muench/Corbis; 19 (r) Getty Images; 21 (tl) Andre Jenny/Alamy Images; 21 (tr) Corbis; 21 (b) Getty Images; 21 (c) NASA/GSFC / Photo Researchers; 22 Hugh Sitton/Getty Images 23 Toyohiro Yamada/Getty Images; 24 Gary Crabbe/Alamy Images; 25 Frank Staub/Index Stock Imagery; 25 Frank Staub/Index Stock Imagery; 26 (r) Ron Dahlquist/Getty Images; 26 (l) Stephen Wilkes/Getty Images; 26-27 (bg) Getty Images; 27 (r) AP Images; 27 (l) Jonathan Nourok/PhotoEdit; 29 AP Images; 30 Alan Kearney/Getty Images; 32 Ric Ergenbright; 34

Stuart Westmorland/Corbis; 35 Inc., Design Pics/Index Stock Imagery; 36 Creatas; 37 Corbis; 40-41 Kelly-Mooney Photography/Corbis; 42 Creatas/age fotostock; 43 Lester Lefkowitz/Corbis; 44 (l) Bridgeman Art Library; 44 (r) Getty Images; 44 (cr) John Wang/Getty Images; 44 (cl) The Granger Collection, New York; 45 The Granger Collection, New York; 48 (c) Bridgeman Art Library; 48 (l) Pentagram Design, Inc., San Francisco; 49 (tr) Alamy Images; 49 (b) Alan Schein/Zefa/Corbis; 49 (tl) Lester Lefkowitz/Corbis; 49 (tr) Pete Saloutos/Corbis; 50 (b) The Granger Collection, New York; 51 (t) Joseph Sohm; Chromosohm, Inc./Corbis; 53 (tc) Craig Aurness/Corbis; 53 (tl) Wendell Metzen/Index Stock Imagery; 53 (bg) Joseph Sohm/PictureQuest; 54 AP Images; 55 David J. Phillip/AP Images; 56 Craig Aurness/Corbis; 56-57 (bg) Jason Hawkes/Corbis; 57 (bl) Annie Griffiths Belt/Corbis; 57 (br) Corbis; 57 (tc) Michael Ventura Photography; 57 (tl) Peter Gridley/Getty Images; 57 (tr) PNC/agefotostock; 58 (b) Gayle Harper/In-Sight Photography, Inc.; 58 (t) Getty Images; 59 Robert Maass/Corbis; 60 (l) Ben Weddle/AGStock USA; 60 (r) Mary Kate Denny/PhotoEdit; 61 (l) Gibson Stock Photography; 61 (r) LWA-Dann Tardif/Corbis; 63 Getty Images; 64 (l) Bill Aron/PhotoEdit; 64 (r) Jonathan Nourok/PhotoEdit; 65 David Young-Wolff/PhotoEdit; 68 (r) Alamy Images; 68 (l) David Jay Zimmerman/Corbis . 68-69 K. Yamashita/PanStock/Panoramic Images; 71 (tl) AP Images; 71 (bl) Corbis; 71 (tr) David Muench/Corbis; 71 (br) Gene Ahrens/SuperStock; 71 (c) Altrendol Travel/Getty Images; 73 David R. Frazier Photolibrary/Alamy Images; 74 (r) Getty Images; 74 (c) Hot Ideas/Index Stock Imagery; 75 (r) David Young-Wolff/PhotoEdit; 75 (l) Eric Long/Smithsonian Institution; 75 (c) William Whitehurst/Corbis; 76 (c) Catherine Karnow/Corbis; 76 (l) Ed Kashi/IPN/Kashi Photo Archive; 76 (r) Renee Lynn/Photo Researchers; 78 age fotostock/Superstock; 82 (inset) Dwayne Newton/Photo Edit; 82 Mark Richards/PhotoEdit; 84-85 K. Yamashita/PanStock/Panoramic Images/NGSImages.com; 86 Randy Faris/Corbis; 87 Tony Arruza/Corbis; 88 (inset) Stuart Westmorland/Getty Images; 88 Michael DeYoung/Corbis; 89 Bryan & Cherry Alexander Photography.

UNIT 2

96-97 Alan Schein Photography/Corbis; 100 Lee Snider/Corbis; 101 (t) Ric Ergenbright; 101 (b) Jose Fuste Raga/Corbis; 103 AP Images; 108-109 Gerald Brimacombe; 110 Ron Schramm/Panoramic Images; 112 Richard Paisley Photography; 113 Alamy Images; 114 Jonathan Blair/Corbis; 116 (t) Werner Foreman / Topham / The Image Works; 118 Houserstock; 119 Richard Pasley; 121 Superstock; 122 David Gallery/SuperStock; 123 (l) Granger Collection, New York; 123 (r) H. Armstrong Roberts/Robertstock; 125 (c) Lester Lefkowitz/Corbis; 125 (t) The Smithsonian Institution; 125 (b) Atwater Kent Museum of Philadelphia/Bridgeman Art Library; 128 Bettmann/Corbis; 129 Corbis; 130 (b) James Leynse/Corbis; 130 (inset) Reuters/Corbis; 132 (l) Corbis; 132 (r) Library of Congress; 133 The Granger Collection, New York; 136 (l) GettyImages; 136 (r) Lucidio Studio, Inc./Corbis; 136-137 (c) Alan Schein Photography/Corbis; 138